THE STRUCTURE OF THE CORPORATION

A LEGAL ANALYSIS

THE STRUCTURE OF THE CORPORATION

A LEGAL ANALYSIS

MELVIN ARON EISENBERG

Koret Professor of Law at School of Law,
University of California, Berkeley

Washington, D.C.

Originally published by Little, Brown and Company
Reprinted 2006 by Beard Books, Washington, D.C.

ISBN 13: 978-1-58798-288-9
ISBN 10: 1-58798-288-9

Printed in the United States of America

To the Memory of
Max Eisenberg

Preface

This book is based on a series of four articles – The Legal Roles of Shareholders and Management in Modern Corporate Decisionmaking, 57 Calif. L. Rev. 1 (1969); Access to the Corporate Proxy Machinery, 83 Harv. L. Rev. 1489 (1970); Megasubsidiaries: The Effect of Corporate Structure on Corporate Control, 84 Harv. L. Rev. 1577 (1971); and Legal Models of Management Structure in the Modern Corporation: Officers, Directors, and Accountants, 63 Calif. L. Rev. 375 (1975). The book is not, however, intended to be a collection of the articles: in writing the book, the material in the articles was extensively restructured, revised, and updated.

In preparing the articles and the book I have received much valuable help from a number of people. These include my corporate-law colleagues at the School of Law of the University of California at Berkeley – Richard Buxbaum, Jesse Choper, and Richard Jennings; various editors of the California and Harvard Law Reviews – particularly Phillip J. Bakes, Douglas W. Beck, David E. Gordon, and Bruce Maximov; my secretary of many years, Pat Brudney, and my present secretary, Mary Hardy; and several research assistants, particularly Robert E. Mittendorff and David Utevsky. To all of these people, many thanks. I also thank the Guggenheim Foundation, which awarded me a Guggenheim Fellowship in 1971 to support the underlying research, and the Law School's Committee on International Legal Studies, in its capacity as administrator of a Ford Foundation grant, which provided support for studying certain comparative-law aspects of the subject.

A note on citations: In September 1975 the California Legislature adopted a revised California Corporations Code, to be effective on January 1, 1977. It was not practicable to amend all of the

California citations in the book to reflect this change, but the revised Code is cited where it differs from the present Code in substance.

Melvin Aron Eisenberg

Berkeley, California
March 30, 1976

Summary of Contents

Table of Contents

PART III MANAGEMENT STRUCTURE, 137

11 Officers and Directors, 139

12 The Flow of Information to the Board and the Role of the Accountant, 186

PART V STRUCTURAL CHANGES: CONTRACTIONS AND DIVISIONS, 253

PART VI VOTING AND APPRAISAL RIGHTS IN PARENT-SUBSIDIARY COMPLEXES, 275

The Structure of the Corporation

A LEGAL ANALYSIS

1

Introduction

THE RECEIVED LEGAL MODEL OF THE CORPORATION

Corporate law is constitutional law; that is, its dominant function is to regulate the manner in which the corporate institution is constituted, to define the relative rights and duties of those participating in the institution, and to delimit the powers of the institution vis-à-vis the external world.[1] However, the general principles governing the legal structure of the corporation have never been well articulated. There does exist a more or less standardized model of formal corporate decisionmaking – which may be called the received legal model – whose outlines are well known. Under this model, the board of directors manages the corporation's business and makes business policy; the officers act as agents of the board and execute its decisions; and the shareholders elect the board and decide on "major corporate actions," or "fundamental," "extraordinary," or "organic" changes:

> The standard operating procedure for corporations, frequently referred to as the corporate norm, might be described as pyramidal in form. At the base are the shareholders whose vote is required to elect the board of directors and to pass on other major corporate actions. . . . The next level is represented by the directors who constitute the policy making body of the corporation, and select the officers, annually as a rule. The keystone of corporate procedure is the provision common to most corporation laws that "the business of a corporation shall be

1. Cf. 1 J. Davis, Corporations 10-11 (1905); R. Eells, The Government of Corporations 31-122 (1962); F. Mechem, Outlines of the Law of Agency 2 (4th ed. P. Mechem 1952); Brewster, The Corporation and Economic Federalism, in The Corporation in Modern Society 72-76 (E. Mason ed. 1959).

> managed by its board of directors." Finally, at the top of the pyramid are the officers who have some discretion but in general are deemed to execute policies formulated by the board.[2]

Perhaps the most striking aspect of the received legal model is the distinctive position of management. Simple business organizations are managed either by the owners or by persons who are legally agents of the owners. Under the received legal model of the corporation, however, the officers are agents not of the shareholders but of the board, while the board itself is conceived of not as an agent of the shareholders but as an independent institution. For example, while the authority of an agent can normally be terminated by his principal at any time,[3] directors are normally removable by shareholders only for good cause shown.[4] Similarly,

2. W. Cary, Corporations – Cases and Materials 150 (4th ed. 1969). Similarly, Ballantine: "The board of directors is the supreme and original authority in matters of regular business management. . . . The authority of the directors is restricted to the management of the regular business affairs of the corporation, unless more extensive power is expressly conferred. Their authority does not extend to fundamental changes in the character or organization of the corporation . . . unless by express provision, for such matters do not relate to ordinary business. . . . Extraordinary and unusual changes in corporate organization, not relating to the ordinary business, must be authorized by . . . the shareholders." H. Ballantine, Corporations 119-120, 643 (rev. ed. 1946). And Lattin: "The management of the modern corporation is almost exclusively in the hands of the board of directors. Unusual powers such as those of amending the corporate charter, the sale of all or a large part of the corporate assets, merger and consolidation, and dissolution belong to the shareholders." N. Lattin, Corporations 239 (2d ed. 1971). See also, e.g., 1 G. Hornstein, Corporation Law and Practice 446-447 (1959).

3. Restatement (Second) of Agency §118 (1958).

4. See, e.g., Toledo Traction, Light & Power Co. v. Smith, 205 F. 643, 645-646 (N.D. Ohio 1913); Manice v. Powell, 201 N.Y. 194, 94 N.E. 634 (1911). This rule does not prevail in England; indeed, a leading English commentator found it to be "strange," and pointed out that if the board is staggered "one who has acquired a majority of the stock may have to wait, not merely until the next annual meeting but perhaps for several years before he can gain control of the board." Gower, Some Contrasts Between British and American Corporation Law, 69 Harv. L. Rev. 1369, 1389 (1956). Two years after that comment was made, a Florida court held that a sole shareholder could not remove directors during their term without cause. Frank v. Anthony, 107 So. 2d 136 (Fla. Dist. Ct. App. 1958); cf. Yoran, Shareholders v. Directors, 7 Israel L. Rev. 517 (1972).

The rule is one of common law; some statutes permit shareholders to remove directors without cause. See, e.g., Cal. Corp. Code §810 (West 1955); Ohio Rev. Code Ann. §1701.58(C) (Page 1964); Pa. Stat Ann. tit. 15, §1405(A) (Supp. 1974); ABA Model Bus. Corp. Act §39 (1969 rev.). Also, directors can usually be removed without cause if the certificate or by-laws so provided at the time they took office. See, e.g., Matter of Stylemaster Dept. Store, Inc., 7 Misc. 2d 207, 154 N.Y.S.2d 58 (Sup. Ct. 1956); Singer v. State Laundry Co., 189 Misc. 150, 70 N.Y.S.2d 550 (Sup. Ct.), affd. mem., 273 App. Div. 755, 75 N.Y.S.2d 514 (App. Div. 1947).

while an agent must normally follow his principal's instructions,[5] shareholders have no legal power to give binding instructions to the board on matters within its powers.[6] Any study of corporate structure must therefore consider two very different interfaces: that between the shareholders and the managerial organs taken together, and that between the managerial organs themselves.

Although the received legal model provides a starting point for such a study, it does not do much more than that. Whether viewed as a descriptive or a normative device,[7] the model proves inadequate. Viewing the model descriptively, it states that the board manages the corporate business and sets business policy. As a practical matter, however, the board typically does neither. Again, the model states that major corporate actions or fundamental changes are shareholder matters. As a legal matter, however, while the traditional corporate statutes typically do require shareholder approval of transactions which may be referred to as the *classical* fundamental changes – merger, sale of substantially all assets, certificate amendment, and dissolution – they fail to explicitly require shareholder approval for a number of other actions which may be referred to as the *modern* fundamental changes – business combinations other than mergers, corporate contractions, and corporate divisions. Furthermore, even the treatment of the classical fundamental changes diverges significantly from that suggested by the received legal model. The rules for mergers[8] – which are also generally applicable to the sale of

5. Restatement (Second) of Agency §385(1) (1958).

6. Cf. Charlestown Boot & Shoe Co. v. Dunsmore, 60 N.H. 85 (1880); Manice v. Powell, 201 N.Y. 194, 94 N.E. 634 (1911); Automatic Self-Cleansing Filter Syndicate Co. v. Cuninghame, L.R. [1906] 2 Ch. 34, 94 L.T.R. 651; R. Stevens, Handbook on the Law of Private Corporations 650-651 (2d ed. 1949); Aicken, Division of Power Between Directors and General Meeting as a Matter of Law, and as a Matter of Fact or Policy, 5 Melb. U.L. Rev. 448 (1967) (reviewing the English cases).

7. The term "normative" is ambiguous, since "norm" has both a prescriptive and a descriptive sense. In this book, the term is used in its prescriptive sense.

8. See, e.g., Cal. Corp. Code §§4100, 4103, 4107, 4108 (West 1955 & Supp. 1974); Del. Code Ann. tit. 8, §§251(a)-(c) (1974); Ill. Ann. Stats. ch. 32, §§157.61, 157.63, 157.64 (Smith-Hurd 1954 & Supp. 1974); N.J. Stat. Ann. §§14A:10-1, 14A:10-3 (Supp. 1974); N.Y. Bus. Corp. Law §§902, 903 (McKinney 1963 & Supp. 1974); Ohio Rev. Code Ann. §1701.78 (Page Supp. 1974); Pa. Stat. Ann. tit. 15, §1902 (Supp. 1974); ABA Model Bus. Corp. Act §§71, 73 (1969 rev.).

Under some provisions it may be arguable that "the statutory requirement of a vote by the board of directors [is] a purely administrative or ministerial device preliminary to a shareholder vote," and therefore not an absolute requirement. Manne, Some

substantially all assets,[9] certificate amendment,[10] and voluntary dissolution[11] – are illustrative. Although the received model assigns mergers to the shareholders, the statutes provide that a merger normally must be approved by the board as well. Moreover, the statutes usually require a merger agreement to be adopted by the board prior to its consideration by the shareholders, and limit the shareholders' power to approval or disapproval of the package which the board formulates. The statutes could have dispensed with a legal requirement of board approval entirely (although the board would retain informal power

---

Theoretical Aspects of Share Voting, 64 Colum. L. Rev. 1427, 1437 n. 28 (1964); cf. Ward, The Legal Effect of Merger and Asset Sale Agreements Before Shareholder Approval, 18 W. Res. L. Rev. 780, 788-790 (1967). There appears to be no case on the question, but the language of most statutes makes the argument doubtful (as Professor Manne recognizes, see Manne, supra, at 1437), and the SEC has expressly ruled that board approval cannot be dispensed with. See Clusserath, The Amended Stockholder Proposal Rule: A Decade Later, 40 Notre Dame Law. 13, 25-26, 47 (1964).

Methodologically, in this and subsequent chapters, when dealing with statutory provisions I will not attempt to canvass the statutes of the fifty-odd corporate jurisdictions, but instead will focus on the provisions of the California, Delaware, Illinois, New Jersey, New York, Ohio, and Pennsylvania statutes, and the ABA's Model Business Corporation Act. The seven states are the dominant corporate jurisdictions, accounting for approximately 40 percent of all new corporations and three-quarters of all corporations listed on the New York Stock Exchange, see Corporation Service Company, The Red Book Digest of Delaware Corporate Procedures i (1968); Dun & Bradstreet, New Business Incorporations by States, Dec. 1974; W. Hurst, The Legitimacy of the Business Corporation in the Law of the United States 1780-1970, at 150 (1970); Conard, An Overview of the Laws of Corporations, 71 Mich. L. Rev. 621, 633 n. 63 (1973); Eisenberg, The Legal Roles of Shareholders and Management in Modern Corporate Decisionmaking, 57 Calif. L. Rev. 1, 61 n. 184 (1969). Together with the Model Act, these statutes represent a fair spread of corporate philosophy, and frequently serve as a basis for statutory revision in other states.

9. See, e.g. Cal. Corp. Code § § 3901-03 (West 1955); Del. Code Ann. tit. 8, § 271 (1974); Ill. Ann. Stat. ch. 32, § 157.72 (Smith-Hurd 1954); N.J. Stat. Ann. § 14A:10-11 (Supp. 1974); N.Y. Bus. Corp. Law § 909 (McKinney Supp. 1974); Ohio Rev. Code Ann. § 1701.76 (Page 1964); Pa. Stat. Ann. tit. 15, § 1311(B) (Supp. 1974); ABA Model Bus. Corp. Act § 79 (1969 rev.).

10. See, e.g., Cal. Corp. Code § 3632 (West Supp. 1974); Del. Code Ann. tit. 8, § 242 (1974); Ill. Ann. Stat. ch. 32, § 157.53 (Smith-Hurd Supp. 1974); N.J. Stat. Ann. § 14A:11-1(1)(b) (Supp. 1974); N.Y. Bus. Corp. Law § 803(a) (McKinney Supp. 1974); Ohio Rev. Code Ann. § 1701.71 (Page 1964); Pa. Stat. Ann. tit. 15, § § 1802, 1803, 1805 (1967 & Supp. 1974); ABA Model Bus. Corp. Act § 59 (1969 rev.).

11. See, e.g., Cal. Corp. Code § 4600 (West 1955); Del. Code Ann. tit. 8, § 275 (1974); Ill. Ann. Stat. ch. 32, § § 157.75, 157.76 (Smith-Hurd 1954); N.J. Stat. Ann. § 14A:12-4 (1969); N.Y. Bus. Corp. Law § 1001 (McKinney 1963); Ohio Rev. Code Ann. § 1701.86 (Page 1964); Pa. Stat. Ann. tit. 15, § 2102 (1967); ABA Model Bus. Corp. Act § 84 (1969 rev.).

to initiate and recommend), as is evidenced by the fact that some statutes do just that in connection with dissolution or certificate amendment, or both.[12] The statutes could have required board approval and yet permitted shareholder initiation, as is evidenced by the fact that a few statutes do just that in connection with sales of substantially all assets.[13] The statutes could have required fundamental changes to be initiated and approved by the board in general outline, and yet permitted shareholders to formulate or reformulate details, as is evidenced by the fact that many statutes do just that in connection with the sale of substantially all assets.[14] By providing instead that for the most part shareholders have no power of initiation, no power to formulate details, and only concurrent power of approval over the classical fundamental changes, the traditional statutes have given the board not only a formal voice but a major and decisive legal role in such transactions.

Viewing the received legal model as a normative rather than a descriptive device merely shifts the problems. To begin with, the model attempts to embrace all corporations, although it has come to be recognized that the corporate form is utilized by two types of business associations which may have little in common except their form: closely held corporations, owned by a relatively small number of closely associated persons, and publicly held corporations, owned by a relatively large number of persons who usually have no relationship transcending the nexus of common ownership.[15] Next, the model is insufficiently articulated to provide useful guidance on the difficult issues which relate to the allocation of powers between shareholders and management – issues such as What constitutes a fundamental change?, What is the appropriate

12. See, e.g., Cal. Corp. Code §4600 (West 1955) (dissolution); N.Y. Bus. Corp. Law §§803(a), 1001 (McKinney 1963 & Supp. 1974) (certificate amendment and dissolution); Pa. Stat. Ann. tit. 15, §§1802, 1805 (1967 & Supp. 1974) (certificate amendment).

13. See, e.g., Cal. Corp. Code §§3901-02, 4100-08 (West 1955 & Supp. 1974); Ohio Rev. Code Ann. §1701.76 (Page 1964).

14. See, e.g., the Illinois, New Jersey, New York, Pennsylvania, and Model Act provisions cited in note 9 supra.

15. Publicly held corporations can themselves be divided, for certain purposes, according to whether they have a relatively large or relatively small number of shareholders. See, e.g., Vagts, Reforming the "Modern" Corporation: Perspectives From the German, 80 Harv. L. Rev. 23, 31-32 (1966). However, with limited exceptions this distinction is unnecessary for purposes of the issues addressed in this book.

scope of appraisal rights?, Who should have access to the corporate proxy machinery?, and What rules should govern the allocation of power among corporate organs in the context of a holding-company complex? Finally, the validity of the principle that the board, as opposed to the officers, should manage the business and make business policy is far from clear; and in this area, too, the model is insufficiently articulated, since it gives no guidance on the difficult issues relating to the domination of the board by the officers, and the role of the accountant in the corporate structure.

A major purpose of this book is to develop new and more highly articulated models of corporate structure which will address these and comparable issues. The elements of these models will include the allocation of power between shareholders and management (Part I); the allocation of access to the corporate proxy machinery (Part II); the internal structure of the managerial organs and the role of the accountant (Part III); the treatment of major structural changes – particularly combinations (Part IV), and contractions and divisions (Part V); and the allocation of power in a holding-company structure (Part VI). In the course of developing these models I shall reexamine both the existing rules governing corporate structure and some of the factual premises which have underlain discussion of corporate structure during the last thirty or forty years. Throughout the discussion, consideration will be given both to the extent to which elements of the normative models can be implemented by the courts under present law, and the extent to which statutory revision is necessary or desirable.

I

The Legal Role of the Body of Shareholders

2

Voting Rights in Closely Held Corporations

A NORMATIVE MODEL

One way to approach the question of what decisions should be allocated to shareholders in closely held corporations is through a comparison with partnership, the major alternative form of business association involving a small number of closely associated owners. Partnership law takes a posture toward decision-making which is essentially suppletory.[1] The relevant sections of the Uniform Partnership Act impliedly validate whatever agreements the owners may make between themselves, and provide rules to govern only those situations which the owners have failed to cover – rules which appear to be based largely on the owners' probable expectations. Such a posture also seems appropriate for the closely held corporation. Since the number of shareholders in such a corporation is, by hypothesis, relatively small, the law may normally assume that agreements between the shareholders are likely to be bargained out – to be real agreements, and not merely contracts of adhesion. Since such enterprises are seldom giant in size, the only principle of social policy that would seem applicable to their internal organization is the promotion of business efficiency, an objective best served by enabling the owners to arrange the organization as they choose[2] and by providing rules – based

1. Cf. H. Hart & A. Sacks, The Legal Process: Basic Problems in the Making and Application of Law 35-36 (tent. ed. 1958).

2. Cf. Kessler, The Statutory Requirement of a Board of Directors: A Corporate Anachronism, 27 U. Chi. L. Rev. 696, 721-722 (1960).

The extent to which shareholders can by agreement vary the rules laid down by the traditional statutes as to internal corporate organization has been the subject of many cases and much literature. See, e.g., Jackson v. Hooper, 76 N.J. Eq. 592, 75 A. 568

on the owners' probable expectations – to govern decisionmaking where such arrangements have not been made.[3]

What are those expectations? Here again the partnership model provides a starting point. Four major aspects of that model are relevant.

(1) Absent contrary agreement, no person can become a member of a partnership without the consent of all the partners.[4]

(2) Absent contrary agreement, all partners have equal rights in the management and conduct of the partnership business.[5]

(3) Absent contrary agreement, differences among the partners "as to ordinary matters connected with the partnership business" are determined by a majority of the partners, but differences as to matters outside the scope of the partnership business, mat-

---

(Ct. Err. & App. 1910); Benintendi v. Kenton Hotel, 294 N.Y. 112, 60 N.E.2d 829 (1945); Clark v. Dodge, 269 N.Y. 410, 199 N.E. 641 (1936); F. H. O'Neal, 1 Close Corporations: Law and Practice 222-332 (1958). Although the law's original response was to prohibit such variation, the desirability of permitting shareholders in privately held corporations to make their own rules is now almost universally recognized by the commentators and is coming to be recognized by the courts and the legislatures. See Arditi v. Dubitzky, 354 F.2d 483 (2d Cir. 1965); Galler v. Galler, 32 Ill. 2d 16, 203 N.E.2d 577 (1964); Peck v. Horst, 175 Kan. 479, 264 P.2d 888 (1953), on rehearing, 176 Kan. 581, 272 P.2d 1061 (1954); Leventhal v. Atlantic Fin. Corp., 316 Mass. 194, 55 N.E.2d 20 (1944); Del. Code Ann. tit. 8, §§341-356 (1974); N.Y. Bus. Corp. Law §620 (McKinney's 1963, as amended, Supp. 1974).

Of course it is also important that persons who come in contact with corporations be dealt with fairly, and this objective may interact with questions of internal organization, but generally speaking the two problems are separable. For example, under partnership law the partners can arrange internal decisionmaking as they choose, but regardless of their internal arrangements any partner has apparent authority to bind the partnership on a matter in the ordinary course of business unless the third party has knowledge that the particular partner has no authority in fact. See Uniform Partnership Act §§9(1), 18(h) [hereinafter cited as U.P.A.]. Similarly, it is arguable that limited liability should be restricted to cases where not all owners have a right to participate in management decisions, but the question under what circumstances an owner-manager should be permitted to limit his liability is separable from the question whether persons who use the corporate form should be permitted to set up their own decisionmaking mechanisms.

3. Like partners, shareholders in privately held corporations often fail to deal with many important questions when they organize their corporation. Cf. Dykstra, Molding the Utah Corporation: Survey and Commentary, 7 Utah L. Rev. 1 (1960); Hayes, Iowa Incorporation Practices – A Study (pts. 1-5), 39 Iowa L. Rev. 409, 608; 40 Iowa L. Rev. 157, 459, 588 (1954-1955); Hayes, Iowa Incorporation Practices Reexamined – Pt. 1, 22 Drake L. Rev. 1 (1972); Hetherington, Special Characteristics, Problems and Needs of the Close Corporation, 1969 U. Ill. L. Forum 1, 15-19; O'Neal, Close Corporation Legislation: A Survey and Evaluation, 1972 Duke L.J. 867, 889.

4. See U.P.A. §18(g). This Act has been adopted in most jurisdictions. See J. Crane & A. Bromberg, Partnership 13, 15-16 (1968).

5. U.P.A. §18(e).

ters which would be in conflict with the partnership agreement, or matters "which would make it impossible to carry on the ordinary business of the partnership," require unanimous consent.[6]

(4) Partnerships are normally created for a limited term (usually a relatively short term),[7] and dissolution is easy.[8]

Putting the first and fourth aspects aside for a moment (since they do not ostensibly relate to decisionmaking), the basic elements of the partnership model might be adapted to closely held corporations by providing that, absent contrary agreement, all shareholders have the right to participate in management; differences of opinion on "ordinary matters connected with the . . .

6. U.P.A. § 18(h) provides that "[A]ny difference arising as to ordinary matters connected with the partnership business may be decided by a majority of the partners; but no act in contravention of any agreement between the partners may be done rightfully without the consent of all the partners." The dichotomy set up by this section is obviously incomplete: a decision which does not relate to "ordinary matters" may yet not be explicitly covered by the partnership agreement. However, U.P.A. § 9(3)(c) provides that "[o]ne or more but less than all the partners have no authority to [d]o any . . . act which would make it impossible to carry on the ordinary business of a partnership," and the received learning is that, as stated in the text, matters "outside the scope of the partnership business" require unanimous approval, whether or not explicitly covered by the agreement. See J. Crane & A. Bromberg, supra note 4, at 304 ("Normally, the majority of the members of a partnership have the power to decide matters within the scope of the business, but they do not have the power to override the minority in the doing of an act which is outside the scope of the business they have agreed to carry on or which is in violation of a provision of the articles."); id. at 381-382 ("[T]he democratic principle of majority rule . . . extends only to ordinary matters connected with the partnership business, and not to matters which are extraordinary . . . or in violation of the partnership agreement; for these, unanimity is required."); N. Lindley, Law of Partnership 355-356 (E. Scamell ed. 1962) ("It has been over and over again decided that no majority, however large, can lawfully engage the partnership in matters outside the partnership business against the will of even one dissentient partner."). See also Arado v. Keitel, 353 Mo. 223, 229, 182 S.W.2d 176, 179 (1944); J. Crane & C. Magruder, Cases on the Law of Partnership 298-299 n. 31 (2d ed. 1959). This formulation can be bottomed on several theories, including fair expectations; the natural implications of § 9(3)(c), cf. Fortugno v. Hudson Manure Co., 51 N.J. Super. 482, 498-499, 144 A.2d 207, 215-216 (1958); and the idea that important actions not explicitly permitted by the partnership agreement are implicitly prohibited, cf. Kentucky Distilleries & Warehouse Co. v. Louisville Pub. Warehouse Co., 19 F.2d 866, 867-868 (6th Cir. 1927).

7. Cf. J. Crane & A. Bromberg, supra note 4, at 1-2 n. 1.

8. If the partnership is not for a specified term, any partner may cause dissolution at any time. U.P.A. § 31(1)(b). If the partnership is for a specified term, dissolution occurs at the end of the term, U.P.A. § 31(1)(a), or on the death of any partner, U.P.A. § 31(4), and may be caused by any partner even during the term, although in that case the dissolving partner will have acted wrongfully and will be liable to the remaining partners in damages. U.P.A. § § 31(2), 38(2)(a)(II). These causes of dissolution are not exclusive; for additional causes, see U.P.A. § § 31(1)(c), (d), (3), (5), (6).

business" are to be determined by majority vote; and decisions on matters outside the scope of the business require unanimous consent. Such a model would certainly conform to the fair expectations of shareholders in many closely held corporations, who regard themselves as partners and incorporate only to achieve tax savings, limit their liability, or the like, not because of a desire to avoid the partnership model of decisionmaking.[9] Indeed, shareholders in such corporations will often draw up elaborate agreements substituting partnership incidents – such as easy dissolution, restrictions on the free transferability of shares, and full participation by all shareholders in management – for normal corporate incidents,[10] and must be bullied by their attorney into practicing the most elementary corporate courtesies, such as shareholder and director meetings. Nevertheless, such a model would not be suited to privately held corporations as a class, because it is based on the assumption that all owners are managers; and it will frequently happen even in closely held corporations that by accident or design there are some shareholders who do not wish to be active in the management of the business. For example, shareholdings may have devolved upon widows or children, or the corporation may be owned by one or more families but managed by only a few family members or even by professional managers, or the corporation may have been organized by a group of individuals some of whom regard themselves as investors rather than managers. Where ownership and management are identical, whether power over a particular type of decision is allocated to owners or managers is likely to be of limited consequence, except perhaps for purposes of determining what constitutes a majority. Where ownership and management are not identical, however, such an allocation will often be of critical importance. Therefore, unless different rules are formulated for the two situations, which might involve problems of administrability, the allocation of decisionmaking power should be tailored with the latter case in mind.

What, then, are the expectations of the parties in such a case? This question might be reformulated as follows: Suppose a rela-

9. See, e.g., Kessler, supra note 2, at 717-718.

10. Id. Following this idea, under the new Maryland close corporations law, Md. Ann. Code art. 23, §§100-111 (1973), where a corporation elects to be a "close corporation" its shares become transferable only if all the shareholders consent or a shareholders' agreement so provides, §101(a); dissolution is easy, §§101(b), 109(a); and mergers and sales of substantially all assets require unanimous approval. §110.

tively small number of individuals organize a business and agree with each other that several persons (including some but not all of the owners) will manage the business on a year-to-year contract, it being understood that the remaining owners have full-time interests outside this business. What matters would the owners expect to decide by themselves, and what matters would they expect the managers to decide? In answering this question the following factors seem particularly relevant:

– The extent to which the matter requires skills of a specifically business nature, as opposed to financially oriented enterprise-evaluation or investment skills. The greater the need for specific business skills, the more likely that the owners would expect the matter to be decided by the managers, since the managers would normally have such skills while the nonmanaging owners would not. On the other hand, the greater the need for investment skills, the more likely the owners would expect to make the decisions themselves, since they would normally have such skills (or have advisors who did), while the possession of such skills by the managers would be relatively fortuitous.

– The economic significance of the matter, in terms of relative magnitude, relative risk, timespan of effect, and cost of reversal. The greater the economic significance, the more likely that the owners would expect to decide it themselves.

– The frequency with which the type of matter arises. The greater the frequency, the more likely that the owners would expect the managers to make it, partly because such decisions tend to become routine, and partly because of the inefficiency for both the enterprise and the owners in their individual capacities if frequent meetings of all the owners are required.

– The speed with which the type of matter must be decided. The greater the need for speed, the more likely that the owners would expect the managers to make the decision, since the managers are on the spot and can act quickly, while a meeting of the owners would inevitably involve delay.

Taking these factors into account, a normative model of decisionmaking power in the close corporation can be constructed by placing the kinds of decisions which arise in a business enterprise into four general categories: business decisions in, and out, of the ordinary course; decisions involving a substantial change in the structure of the enterprise; and decisions relating to the control structure of the entity in which the enterprise is enveloped.

1. Business decisions in the ordinary course. The first category consists of decisions made in the ordinary course of business. Examples include decisions on hiring and firing, on the selection of suppliers, and on the price to be paid for materials. Characteristically, such decisions require specialized business skills, are not individually of great economic significance, affect a relatively short timespan, occur in profusion, and must be made very quickly. Requiring shareholder approval for such decisions would obviously be impossible. Where not all shareholders are managers, the enterprise could not function. Even permitting shareholders to participate in such decisions on an ad hoc basis, as and when they chose to do so, might not reflect the expectations of the parties: some shareholders may have agreed to participate in the enterprise on the assumption that such decisions would be made by management without shareholder interference.[11]

2. Business decisions out of the ordinary course. The second category consists of decisions which are not in the ordinary course of business but are nevertheless within the general framework of the business as it exists when the decision arises. Examples include decisions to substantially expand plant capacity, to enter into a contract for the sale of a significant portion of a firm's output, or to recognize a union. Unlike decisions in the ordinary course, such decisions characteristically involve fairly high stakes, affect a relatively long timespan, occur with a low degree of frequency (although, taken as a class, with some regularity), and need not be made on the spot (although time is normally a significant consideration). Like decisions in the ordinary course, however, such decisions characteristically require business rather than investment skills, and shareholder approval should therefore not be required. It is less clear whether shareholders should be permitted to make such decisions on an ad hoc basis. Their expectation in this case might very well be that while management can make such decisions without their approval, a majority of the shareholders could

11. Cf. Charlestown Boot & Shoe Co. v. Dunsmore, 60 N.H. 85 (1880); Manice v. Powell, 201 N.Y. 194, 94 N.E. 634 (1911); Automatic Self-Cleansing Filter Syndicate Co. v. Cuninghame, L.R. [1906] 2 Ch. 34, 94 L.T.R. 651; R. Stevens, Handbook on the Law of Private Corporations 650-651 (2d ed. 1949); Aicken, Division of Power Between Directors and General Meeting as a Matter of Law, and as a Matter of Fact or Policy, 5 Melb. U.L. Rev. 448 (1967) (reviewing the English cases).

either veto such an action (if the rights of third parties are not prejudiced) or direct that it be taken.[12]

3. Decisions involving a substantial change in the structure of the business enterprise. The third category consists of decisions which, although economic in character, are not made within the general framework or structure of the business enterprise as it then exists, but make a substantial change in that structure. Examples include a complete liquidation, a sale of substantially all assets, or a combination with another enterprise which significantly realigns ownership interests and significantly increases total size. Such decisions normally require what would usually be thought of as investment rather than purely business skills. For example, the skills involved in formulating a decision to merge with Corporation *B* or to liquidate Corporation *B* are similar to the skills involved in formulating a decision to invest in Corporation *B*, and are quite different from the skills needed to formulate an advertising campaign, conduct employee relations, or make steel. Management may or may not have the investment skills needed to make the former type of decision.[13] Shareholders in the closely held corporation (or, what is functionally the same thing, those upon whom they rely for investment advice) may very well have such

12. The principal area in which corporate law has recognized a distinction between business decisions in and out of the ordinary or usual course has been in connection with the authority of officers to bind the corporation in the absence of express board authorization. See Lee v. Jenkins Bros., 268 F.2d 357, 365 (2d Cir.), cert. denied, 361 U.S. 913 (1959); Note, Inherent Power as a Basis of a Corporate Officer's Authority to Contract, 57 Colum. L. Rev. 868 (1957); cf. U.P.A. § 9(3)(e). On the issue of shareholder decisionmaking power, the little case-law that exists does not appear to recognize the distinction, suggesting instead that shareholders cannot make decisions as to any business matter, whether in or out of the ordinary course, see authorities cited in note 11, supra. However, rule 14a-8 of the SEC's Proxy Rules requires the inclusion of a shareholder proposal in the corporate proxy statement if, among other things, it concerns a "proper subject for action by security holders" under the laws of the issuer's domicile, and does not consist "of a recommendation or request that the management take action with respect to a matter relating to the conduct of the *ordinary business operations* of the issuer." Rule 14a-8(c)(1), (5), 17 C.F.R. § 240.14a-8(c)(1), (5) (1974) (emphasis added). The precise meaning of "ordinary business operations" as used in this rule is disputable, see Crown Cork & Seal Co., SEC Minute (Feb. 28, 1964), in W. Cary, Corporations – Cases and Materials 327 (4th ed. 1969), but the phrase seems to reflect the distinction drawn in the text between matters in and out of the ordinary course.

13. See Smith, The Goldberg Dilemma: Directorships, Wall St. J., Feb. 7, 1973, at 14, col. 4.

skills even though they are unequipped to make ordinary or extraordinary business decisions. Decisions involving a substantial change in the structure of the business are suitable for shareholders in other respects as well. Characteristically, they occur infrequently – in some cases no more than once in the life of an enterprise; they mature slowly; they are irreversible for most practical purposes; and they are of the greatest economic significance.

4. Decisions relating to the control apparatus of the entity in which the business enterprise is enveloped. The fourth category consists of decisions relating to the control apparatus of the entity in which the business enterprise is enveloped. Examples would include changes in the ground rules of control (e.g., cumulative or straight voting, number of directors, information flow to shareholders), and election and removal of directors. It seems clear that shareholders in a closely held corporation would expect that such decisions would be made by them, not by their managers.

To summarize, in closely held corporations (or at least those in which ownership and management are not identical), absent contrary agreement, business decisions in the ordinary course should be for management; business decisions which are out of the ordinary course but do not make a substantial change in the structure of the business enterprise should normally be for management, but subject to shareholder intervention; and decisions involving a substantial change in the structure of the business enterprise, or relating to the control apparatus of the entity in which it is enveloped – two categories which can be subsumed under the heading "structural decisions" – should be for shareholders. In later chapters these general principles will be fleshed out by applying them to specific cases. For now it should be observed that this model does not differ from the received legal model so much in principle as in its degree of articulation, and in its emphasis on whether a matter is structural rather than whether it is "major," "fundamental," or "extraordinary."

Two further questions must now be dealt with. First, given that structural decisions are shareholder matters, what degree of approval should be required? If structural decisions are equated with the kinds of decisions which partnership law categorizes as "outside the scope of the partnership business," the partnership model would require unanimity. But this may not be desirable in the closely held corporation. Since partnerships tend to be for a relatively short term and are easily dissolved, the timespan of a single partner's veto is limited. However, since corporations are normally perpetual and not easy to dissolve,[14] it would seem unwise to permit any shareholder, no matter how small his interest, to veto a structural change.[15] The statutes have frequently required two-thirds approval for many of the structural changes they cover.[16] This solution seems to be appropriate, provided that some type of relief is available to the dissenting minority.[17]

The second question is whether management's approval should be required for structural changes, as is often the case under present statutes. It is difficult to see why it should be. It has been suggested that such a requirement protects against "impetuous, ill-considered, and uncoordinated" actions.[18] This seems excessively paternalistic in the context of the closely held corporation. A stronger argument is that such a requirement protects minority shareholders against oppression, on the theory that management will act as disinterested fiduciaries, while majority shareholders may act out of purely selfish motives. But the attribution of disinterestedness to management in the case of structural changes is highly unrealistic, as will be shown below.[19] Granted that the majority may act unfairly in making structural changes, it is preferable to protect the minority in other ways; in particular, by recognizing that when corporate decisions are made by shareholders, the majority may stand in a fiduciary relationship to the minority, and that structural changes in which benefits do not flow equally to all shareholders, or in which majority shareholders are on both sides of a bargain, are therefore subject to judicial review for fairness.[20]

14. Unless the parties otherwise agree, voluntary dissolution of a corporation normally requires a majority or two-thirds vote, see citations in chapter 1, note 11 supra, and shareholders' agreements to vary the usual dissolution rules have met with mixed results. See Note, Statutory Assistance for Closely-Held Corporations, 71 Harv. L. Rev. 1498, 1502 (1958). In contrast, any partner can dissolve a partnership at any time, and certain events, such as the death of a partner, automatically cause dissolution. See note 8 supra. Futhermore, generally speaking the liquidation of a partnership is less likely to result in tax liability than the liquidation of a corporation. See C. Rohrlich, Organizing Corporate and Other Business Enterprises 256-265 (4th ed. 1967).

15. Cf. McNulty, Corporations and the Intertemporal Conflict of Laws, 55 Calif. L. Rev. 12, 28-29 (1967).

16. See citations in chapter 1, notes 8-11 supra.

17. See chapter 7 infra.

18. Dyer v. SEC, 289 F.2d 242, 245 (8th Cir. 1961).

19. See chapter 4 infra.

20. Cf. Jones v. Ahmanson, 1 Cal. 3d 98, 460 P.2d 464, 81 Cal. Rptr. 592 (1969).

3

Voting Rights in Publicly Held Corporations

THREE SCHOOLS OF THOUGHT

In formulating a normative model of decisionmaking in the closely held corporation, no consideration of public policy appeared applicable except the protection of fair expectations. Is this also true in the case of publicly held corporations? Many think not. In wide areas of our economy a relatively small number of giant publicly held corporations have become so large, both in absolute size and in relation to their competitors, that they have freed themselves of servitude to the market and have become able to authoritatively determine, within broad limits, matters of such fundamental importance as the rate and direction of capital investment and technological innovation, and even price levels and degree of product differentiation.[1] Such economic power is not only significant in itself, but carries in its train a significant amount of power to control the social order. Some of those who are concerned with this state of affairs have advocated reform programs which include changes in the shareholders' role. Broadly speaking, these proposals fall into three schools.

1. See, e.g., A. A. Berle, The 20th Century Capitalist Revolution 9-60 (Harvest ed. 1954); J. Blair, Economic Concentration – Structure, Behavior and Public Policy 3-24 (1972); Berle, Modern Functions of the Corporate System, 62 Colum. L. Rev. 433, 439-442 (1962); Chayes, The Modern Corporation and the Rule of Law, in The Corporation in Modern Society 25 (E. Mason ed. 1959); Kaysen, The Corporation: How Much Power? What Scope?, in E. Mason, supra, at 85; Mason, Introduction, in E. Mason, supra, at 1; Schwartz, Institutional Size and Individual Liberty; Authoritarian Aspects of Business, 55 Nw. U.L. Rev. 4 (1960).

§3.1. "Shareholder Democracy"

One school consists of those who, sensitive to the dangers of concentrating great power in private hands, advocate the "republicanization" or "democratization"[2] of the corporation through (among other things) increased shareholder power. It has been said that this school "assumes what must be challenged — that the rest of society need not worry about corporations so long as the 'owners' are running them."[3] This criticism seems apt, although if power to determine vital aspects of national economic life has become concentrated in the hands of a few enterprises, it might seem better to disperse decisionmaking within those enterprises. Also, however unhealthy may be a de facto self-perpetuating oligarchy, it is only the shareholders' role that prevents something which seems even worse, that is, a de jure self-perpetuating oligarchy. Nevertheless, it remains true that if giant enterprise conflicts with national economic and social goals, it is unlikely that this conflict will be resolved by increasing shareholder power, since it seems fair to assume that most shareholders are at least as interested in profits as is management.

§3.2. Client-group Participation

Indeed, two other schools of thought appear to assume that shareholder power makes conflicts between giant enterprise and national goals more rather than less likely. But after starting with that shared premise, the two schools then diverge in their prescriptions. One school advocates giving a formal role in corporate decisionmaking to client-groups of the corporation, such as em-

2. See Latham, The Body Politic of the Corporation, in E. Mason, supra note 1, at 218; Latham, Anthropomorphic Corporations, Elites, and Monopoly Power, 1957 Am. Econ. Rev. 303; Latham, The Commonwealth of The Corporation, 55 Nw. U.L. Rev. 25 (1960); cf. F. Emerson & F. Latcham, Shareholder Democracy (1954).

3. Manning, Corporate Power and Individual Freedom: Some General Analysis and Particular Reservations, 55 Nw. U.L. Rev. 38, 42 (1960); cf. Chayes, supra note 1, at 40.

ployees, suppliers, and customers (including distributors, dealers, and consumers), at the expense of, or even to the exclusion of, the shareholders themselves. Professor Chayes says:

> Of all those standing in relation to the large corporation, the shareholder is least subject to its power. . . . Shareholder democracy, so-called, is misconceived because the shareholders are not the governed of the corporation whose consent must be sought. . . . Their interests are protected if financial information is made available, fraud and overreaching are prevented, and a market is maintained in which their shares may be sold. A priori, there is no reason for them to have any voice, direct or representational, in . . . prices, wages, and investment. They are no more affected than non-shareholder neighbors by these decisions. . . .
>
> A concept of the corporation which draws the boundary of "membership" thus narrowly [i.e., restricts it to shareholders] is seriously inadequate . . . because the line between those who are "inside" and those who are "outside" the corporation is the line between those whom we recognize as entitled to a regularized share in its processes of decision and those who are not.
>
> A more spacious conception of "membership," and one closer to the facts of corporate life, would include all those having a relation of sufficient intimacy with the corporation or subject to its power in a sufficiently specialized way. Their rightful share in decisions on the exercise of corporate power would be exercised through an institutional arrangement appropriately designed to represent the interests of a constituency of members having a significant common relation to the corporation and its power.
>
> It is not always easy to identify such constituencies nor is it always clear what institutional forms are appropriate for recognizing their interests.[4]

This kind of approach, however, tends to gloss over the fact that many client-groups already have some sort of institutionalized relationship with the corporation which involves modes other than voting, and that these alternative modes may be preferable to voting in any given case. In dealing with the interests of a given client-group it is therefore critical to separate two questions: (1) Is it desirable to augment by law the client-group's power vis-à-vis the corporation; (2) If so, should such power be augmented by increasing the client-group's power of negotiation (as under the

4. Chayes, supra note 1, at 40-41; cf. R. Eells, The Government of Corporations 79-85, 206 (1962); Dion, Property and Authority in Business Enterprise, 38 U. Det. L.J. 600 (1961); Manning, The Shareholder's Appraisal Remedy: An Essay for Frank Coker, 72 Yale L.J. 223, 239 (1962).

National Labor Relations Act); by conferring upon it new substantive rights which can then be enforced, if necessary, through litigation or litigation-like processes (as under the Automobile Dealers' Day-In-Court Act or certain of the antitrust laws);[5] or by giving it direct voting participation in corporate decisions? Those who wish to augment the power of client-groups frequently fail to make clear whether they are merely suggesting that the traditional kinds of institutional relationships be strengthened or extended, or are advocating that the relationships between client-group and corporation move beyond the traditional modes. The latter approach is usually implicit, surfacing both in phrases such as "a regularized share in [the corporation's] processes of decision," and in the general tone of such proposals, which usually indicates that the author contemplates some radically new institutional relationship. The failure to be explicit, however, is frequently critical to the argument, because, like euthanasia or eugenics, the idea of direct participation by client-groups is susceptible of meaningful discussion only at the level of execution. Consider, for example, the difficulties presented at that level in the case of suppliers and customers:

(1) Suppliers and customers do not have the skills required to make corporate decisions – at least, not *qua* suppliers and customers. The skills needed to be a leather merchant are not necessarily those needed to decide the business or structural problems faced by shoe manufacturers, nor are such skills acquired with the purchase of one or more pairs of shoes.

(2) Lurking in the background of such proposals is the idea that all suppliers and customers are small. Of course, if that were true, giant corporations would be neither suppliers nor customers. Since they are both, the question must be answered, are *all* customers and purchasers to have a voice in corporate affairs, or only small ones? If the latter is the case, the proposal seems romantic to a fault. But if the former is the case, does that not mean that GM will have a vote in Greyhound, by virtue of being a supplier, and in U.S. Steel, by virtue of being a customer? If so, a disease worse than the cure is hard to imagine, since instead of limiting the power of giant corporations, this proposal would extend it even further and thoroughly cartelize American business in the process.

5. See Clayton Act, §§4-5, 15 U.S.C. §§15-16 (1970); Automobile Dealers Day in Court Act, 15 U.S.C. §§1221-1225 (1970). See generally S. Macauley, Law and The Balance of Power (1966).

(3) There appears to be no feasible way to allocate votes among the members of such groups. To treat every supplier equally seems absurd; to allocate votes by dollar volume simply points up the cartelization problem.

(4) The interests of suppliers and customers in large part conflict with those of the corporation. The primary objective, although not necessarily the sole objective, of a business corporation must be to turn a profit. If a corporation takes in less than it pays out, it must soon be liquidated. If it merely attains equilibrium it will not long survive, because without profits or the prospect of profits neither internal nor external funds will be available when, as will inevitably occur, new funds are needed to adapt the corporation's business to changes in technology or the structure of the market. But suppliers and customers do not share this primary objective. Perhaps they recognize some vague long-range interest in assuring that the enterprise with which they deal survives, but this will seldom affect their short-range here-and-now calculations. If suppliers and customers are nevertheless to be given a voice in corporate decisionmaking, will it really be necessary to take a vote? How long does it take to figure out how growers will vote on a canner's merger into an agri-business corporation? Is it not perfectly clear that a supplier would apply one test to determine every vote he is called upon to cast: that is, whether the decision will result in larger or smaller purchases from him at higher or lower prices; and that customers will apply a comparable test? Is there any possibility that this is desirable? Must it not be concluded that

> A scheme of representation of these interests [in the corporation] would be a travesty on democratic procedures. It would result in business political gangsterism that would destroy the efficiency of business management. It would inject, into circles requiring the most intimate confidence, individuals whose reliability was uncertain and whose motives and ambitions . . . would be injurious to the true welfare of [those] who have an interest in the success of the business.[6]

Turning to labor, we see many of the same problems, although perhaps in less severe degree. There is the lack of skill: working in a shoe factory or being head of a machinist's union does not equip one to deal with decisions on either materials or

6. Ruml, Corporate Management as a Locus of Power, 29 Chi.-Kent L. Rev. 228, 242-243 (1951).

mergers. There is the implicit questionable[7] assumption that labor is invariably weak and the corporation invariably strong. There is the conflict of interest: although employees may have the survival of the enterprise somewhat more in mind than customers and suppliers, their short-run interests will often severely conflict with the long-run interests of the enterprise, as in the case of technological advance.

Labor can, however, be differentiated from suppliers and customers in at least one important way: there is readily at hand a feasible principle for allocating labor's votes – one per employee. Indeed, in Germany labor has been given a formal role in corporate decisionmaking. German corporate law parcels out the functions performed by our board of directors between the managing board, which is an executive organ, and the supervisory board, which elects the managing board and has an overseeing and broad policymaking function.[8] Under the so-called codetermination principle, German labor law provides for labor representation on the supervisory board of most large corporations and also on the board of managers of large coal-, iron-, and steel-producing corporations.[9]

Clearly, then, labor participation in corporate decisionmaking is mechanically feasible. But granted its feasibility, is it desirable in the American context? Again it must be borne in mind that labor's objectives can be (and have been) pursued and obtained through other modes, built on an adversary model, which may better reflect the underlying relationship than would voting, and that American labor itself may prefer those alternative modes,[10] precisely because they are better suited to our own cultural and social realities.

7. Cf. Winter, Collective Bargaining and Competition: The Application of Antitrust Standards to Union Activity, 73 Yale L.J. 14 (1963).

8. See §11.1(B), infra.

9. Steefel & Von Falkenhausen, The New German Stock Corporation Law, 52 Cornell L. Rev. 518, 537-539 (1967); Vagts, Reforming the "Modern" Corporation: Perspectives from the German, 80 Harv. L. Rev. 23, 64-78 (1966). See generally W. Blumenthal, Codetermination in the German Steel Industry (1956); H. Spiro, The Politics of German Codetermination (1958); Comment, Codetermination in West Germany, 51 Ore. L. Rev. 214 (1971); Giving Employees a Say in Firms' Management Seen Gaining in Europe, Wall St. J., Feb. 23, 1973, at 1, col. 6. Several European countries have recently adopted variants of the German system. See pp. 177-178, infra.

10. See Blumberg, The Constituencies of the Corporation: New Directions for Employees, 28 Bus. Law., March 1973, at 177, 181 (special issue); cf. E. Stein, Harmonization of European Company Law 123-124, 146 (1971); Marty-Lavauzelle, Labor Law Developments in France, 27 Bus. Law. 857 (1972); Tunks, Book Review, 47 Wash. L.

> . . . America has a long tradition of collective bargaining fostered by law which has admitted the unions to a voice in questions of policy and administration. Management must talk and bargain with union representatives about topics on which in Germany codetermination has the most effect. . . . In this way the unions have a voice in making decisions without the operational responsibilities that inhere in the German approach. This already highly developed institution could hardly exist side-by-side with codetermination. Most American commentators find a system in which management and labor bargain as representatives of conflicting interests less likely to produce pressures and conflicts within individual roles and see a major reconstruction of the labor relations structure on the German model as undesirable.
>
> It should also be remembered that years of collective bargaining emphasis here have produced a union leadership very different from that of Germany. . . . It is doubtful that the collaboration involved in codetermination would run as smoothly in many American unions as it has in Germany. In short, codetermination is a complex institution. Its adoption involves a great deal more than having some labor representatives sitting on corporation boards of directors. It would involve a substantial rearrangement of our industrial relations picture, even assuming that it were considered desirable to enhance labor's power in this fashion.[11]

Considering the number and desirability of alternative modes of client-group participation, the fervor with which the voting mode is pressed recalls the observation of William F. Whyte that Americans are preoccupied with democratic models of organization, and that efforts to force this model on institutions in which a central administration has the legal power and customarily sanctioned responsibility to make ultimate decisions are bound to lead to conflict and frustration.[12]

§3.3. Managerialism

The first school of thought would achieve ends of social policy by increasing shareholder power, the second by reducing shareholder power and co-opting other constituencies into the cor-

Rev. 201, 205 n. 3 (1971). There have been occasional exceptions in relatively atypical cases. See, e.g., Blumberg, supra, at 181-182; Strike Hardens Attitudes at Modern, N.Y. Times, Feb. 5, 1974, at 28, col. 1.

11. Vagts, supra note 9, at 76-78. Accord: W. Blumenthal, supra note 9, at 114.

12. Whyte, Building Better Organizational Models, in Essays in Industrial Relations Theory 109-110, 112 (G. Somers ed. 1969).

porate structure. The third school, sometimes known as the managerialists, would achieve ends of social policy by increasing management power, on the theory that while shareholders are interested only in profits, and client-groups only in their own welfare, management is in a position to balance the claims of all groups dependent on the corporation, including not only client-groups and shareholders, but the general public; in a position, that is, to run the corporation in the public interest.[13]

But the managerialists seem to greatly exaggerate the inclination and ability of management to serve as instruments of national policy. As Kaysen has observed:

> It is not sufficient for the business leaders to announce that they are thinking hard and wrestling earnestly with their wide responsibilities. . . . Some of the more sophisticated accounts of the revolutionary transformation of business identify business as a "profession" in the honorific sense, and imply that professional standards can be relied on as a sufficient social control over the exercise of business power, as society does rely on them to control the exercise of the considerable powers of doctors and lawyers. This is a ramifying problem which we cannot here explore; it is sufficient to remark that there is, at least as yet, neither visible mechanism of uniform training to inculcate, nor visible organization to maintain and enforce, such standards; and, further, that even if business decisions in the business sphere could be "professionalized" and subject to the control of a guild apparatus, it seems less easy to expect that the same would be true of the exercise of business power in the social and political spheres.[14]

Vide: automobile safety, billboards, cigarettes, pollution, strip mining, television, and thalidomide.

Actually, the premises of managerialist theory, even if granted, do not necessarily require a redistribution of corporation decisionmaking power. While the managerialists, like those who favor formal client-group participation, tend to shy away from details at the level of execution, most appear to be primarily concerned with insulating from shareholder attack management decisions which favor the claims of client-groups at the expense of

13. See, e.g., A. A. Berle, The 20th Century Capitalist Revolution 61-115, 164-188 (Harvest ed. 1954); cf. Manning, Corporate Power and Individual Freedom, supra note 3, at 41. For a critical statement of this view, see Mason, The Apologetics of "Managerialism," 31 J. Bus. 1 (1958).

14. Kaysen, The Corporation: How Much Power? What Scope?, supra note 1, at 104.

higher profits.[15] Since most situations in which management must choose between higher profits and the claims of a given client-group involve business decisions in which shareholders have no formal voice in any event, managerialist theory might in most cases be reconciled with the shareholders' role in decisionmaking by confining its application to the scope of judicial review when decisions running in favor of a client-group are brought under fire.

At least one branch of managerialist theory, however, has explicitly advanced beyond reconstruction of fiduciary ideology to redistribution of decisionmaking power. The views of this branch have been most forecefully articulated by Bayless Manning in a well-known book review of J. A. Livingston's *The American Stockholder.*[16] Manning begins with the proposition that we have today "a virtually omnipotent management and an impotent shareholdership." He continues:

> For the last generation, the prevailing school of thought among corporate reformers, writers and legislators has been that the key to ensuring managerial responsibility lies in the shareholder's power to vote. . . .
>
> Managements are almost never reprimanded or displaced by the shareholder electorate; shareholders remain stubbornly uninterested in exerting control. Management recommendations on mergers, option plans or other corporate matters are virtually never rejected by the shareholders. . . .
>
> [I]n the fever of the "democratic" proxy contest, the corporate patient is approaching the period of crisis. The modern proxy contest has become a grotesque travesty of an orderly machinery for corporation decision-making.[17]

While many commentators have drawn from similar conclusions the lesson that more effective regulation of proxy machinery may be needed,[18] Manning raises the question whether the machinery should not be entirely scrapped:

15. Actually, the managerialists seem to overestimate the extent to which traditional fiduciary ideology prohibits management from exercising a decent regard for the legitimate interests of those with whom the corporation deals. See Scott v. Stanton Heights Corp., 388 Pa. 628, 131 A.2d 113 (1957); cf. Hayek, The Corporation in a Democratic Society, in Management and Corporations 1985, at 99-100 (M. Anshen & G. Bach eds. 1960); Katz, Responsibility and the Modern Corporation, 3 J. Law & Econ. 75, 78-79 (1960).

16. Manning, Book Review, 67 Yale L.J. 1477 (1958).

17. Id. at 1485-1488.

18. See, e.g., Bayne, Caplin, Emerson & Latcham, Proxy Regulation and the Rule-Making Process: The 1954 Amendments, 40 Va. L. Rev. 387 (1954); Caplin, Share-

> . . . [T]he myth of shareholder democracy . . . [creates] an impression in the public mind . . . that a degree of shareholder supervision exists which in fact does not. It is quite arguable that the net effect of the corporate Jacksonians has been to impede their ultimate objective of responsible corporate management. The forms and mechanisms of shareholder democracy divert attention from the real problems of holding business managements to a desirable standard of responsibility. . . .
>
> Altogether, the tenets of Corporate Democracy have served us little. . . . [L]ooking to the shareholder franchise for management supervision, we have been trying to design remedies for a make-believe world rather than a real one.[19]

What troubles Manning, in other words, is that management is really responsible to no one, and in creating an appearance that management is responsible to the shareholders, the legal system is selling quack medicine, thereby diverting the patient, society, from seeking AMA advice.

The problem is that Manning never states exactly what ails the patient, other than a lack of managerial responsibility. In a companion article Manning wrote that "[w]ithout an infinitive, 'Power' is a bell without a clapper,"[20] – meaning that it does not get us very far to talk about corporate power in general; rather we must ask what it is the corporation has power to do, and what, if anything, is wrong with that. But the same may be said about responsibility. It is hard to evaluate a suggestion that the present system has not kept managers responsible unless we are told exactly what it is management should be responsible for. Running the corporation to generate maximum profits? Running the corporation in the interest of specific client-groups? Running the corporation explicitly "in the public interest"? Some blend of these?

But whatever the illness, Manning suggests a cure – a voteless model of the corporation:

> Assume a large modern corporation similar to its typical commercial counterpart in all respects but two. First, the model abandons the *a priori* legal conclusion that the shareholders "own the corporation" and substitutes the more restricted conception that the only thing they

---

holder Nominations of Directors: A Program for Fair Corporate Suffrage, 39 Va. L. Rev. 141 (1953); cf. Caplin, Proxies, Annual Meetings and Corporate Democracy: The Lawyer's Role, 37 Va. L. Rev. 653 (1951).

19. Manning, supra note 16, at 1489.

20. Manning, Corporate Power and Individual Freedom, supra note 3, at 45.

> "own" is their shares of stock. Second, the shareholder in this model corporation has no voting rights. His position would be quite similar to that of a voting trust certificate-holder with all economic rights in the deposited stock but no power to elect or replace the trustees by vote.[21]

Pursuing his central theme of management responsibility, Manning asks: "In such a corporate world, how would one go about ensuring the desired degree of management responsibility while permitting corporate officers the necessary discretion to run the business?"[22] He finds his answer in a fourfold scheme, involving full and periodic disclosure to shareholders and perhaps also to a judicial or other public agency; supervision of management in corporate matters affecting its own personal interest by some governmental or nongovernmental machinery; available avenues to the shareholders (presumably, a well-functioning market) for pulling out; and continuation or even extension of the business judgment rule[23] to ensure that management has the broadest discretion in business matters.

Now since, generally speaking, shareholders in publicly held corporations are not presently entitled to vote on business decisions in any event, the sole thrust of a voteless model is to deal shareholders out of a formal role in the election of directors and other structural decisions. This is pretty severe. In context, it is also a bit peculiar; having begun by rejecting the shareholder vote on the ground that it does not insure management responsibility, Manning ends with a system in which management is responsible for absolutely nothing and to absolutely no one. (The proposal to supervise self-dealing affects management responsibility only tangentially, and in any event judicial supervision of self-dealing is part of the present corporate system.) Indeed, Manning himself pretty quickly backs off from the suggestion that he is really offering the model as a prescriptive device:

> The model is not to be taken literally of course. Legally votable stock is in fact votable, and the vote can, in some circumstances, make a difference. . . .

21. Manning, supra note 16, at 1490. See also A. A. Berle, Power Without Property 104-107 (Harvest ed. 1959); P. Drucker, The New Society 333-343 (1950); Chayes, supra note 1, at 40-41; Rutledge, Significant Trends in Modern Incorporation Statutes, 22 Wash. U.L.Q. 305, 329-330 (1937).

22. Manning, supra note 16, at 1490.

23. Id. at 1490-1491.

> . . . [S]omeone has to select directors, and there would be no advantage in permitting them overtly to choose their own successors. Further, . . . improvement of disclosure requirements has been largely linked to shareholder voting. . . . Similarly, at least until a better solution can be found, the proxy fight will be difficult to dispense with, however much it may have gotten out of focus. . . .[24]

In light of this, why build the model at all? First, for the reason any corporate model is built — to test present law and proposals for law reform. But further, Manning suggests, "the model is useful because in the case of the large, publicly held modern corporation, it approximates reality."[25]

Does it? Although the voteless model of the corporation is ultimately based on broad-gauged notions of social policy, it proceeds more immediately from two factual premises: The first is that shareholders in publicly held corporations have no interest in or expectation of participating in the election of directors and other structural decisions (bearing in mind that this is about all they can vote on today). The second is that the managers of such corporations, if left to their own devices, would generally make structural decisions on the basis of considerations other than their own self-interest (bearing in mind that direct ongoing supervision of self-interested structural transactions by governmental machinery does not seem practicable[26]). The two premises are not unrelated. Before confronting the former, it will be useful to examine the latter.

24. Id. at 1493-1494.
25. Id. at 1492.
26. See Chapter 4 infra, text at notes 17-20; Chapter 11 infra, text at notes 105-106 and note 106.

4

Voting Rights in Publicly Held Corporations

THE CONFLICT-OF-INTEREST PROBLEM

The premise that management will normally run corporate affairs without regard to its own self-interest is probably accurate as to business decisions. Most such decisions do not give rise to a conflict of interest for management.[1] When they do (as in the case of self-dealing), the conflict is usually easy to discern. Furthermore, where a conflict arises out of a business decision there is frequently a market which can be used as a standard to measure the decision's fairness.

Unlike business decisions, however, structural decisions almost invariably give rise to management conflicts-of-interest; conflicts which are, moreover, uniquely difficult either to discern or review. Such conflicts stem from the fact that while a shareholder's objective is that the corporation maximize its per-share earnings[2] (consistent, perhaps, with the doing of economic and

1. This is not to say that a conflict of interest in such decisions is unknown. See, e.g., Jennings, Trading in Corporate Control, 44 Calif. L. Rev. 1, 14-15 (1956).

2. See R. A. Gordon, Business Leadership in the Large Corporation 315-316 (Calif. ed. 1961); Donaldson, Financial Goals: Management vs. Stockholders, Harv. Bus. Rev., May-June 1963, at 116, 121; Hayek, The Corporation in a Democratic Society, in Management and Corporations 1985, at 99, 111-112 (M. Anshen & G. Bach, eds. 1960).

Of course, corporate earnings per share do not go directly into the shareholder's pocketbook, and it might therefore be more accurate to say that the shareholder's primary interest is dividend maximization and market-price appreciation, in a mix depending on the shareholder's financial circumstances. However, "[W]hile factors making for improvement in market price are many and their effects are rather obscure, it will be generally agreed that the most central quantitative ratio by which anticipated change is measured is earnings per share .... The same is true for dividends since most dividend-paying companies tend to adjust payments according to some standard relationship to

social justice to client-groups), the maximization of per-share earnings is not the sole, and often not even the primary, objective of a manager.[3] To begin with, insofar as monetary rewards are concerned direct compensation is commonly much more significant to managers than gains in their shareholder capacities, and direct compensation is usually not tied to earnings.[4] More important, however, the desire for financial gain is only one, and perhaps the weakest, of the motives which shape a manager's conduct,[5] and many of the nonfinancial motives which drive the manager bear heavily on structural changes. For example, among the most important nonfinancial motives are the desires for personal power and prestige.[6] These desires may lead management to engage in acquisition for its own sake, rather than for the purpose of maximizing per-share earnings. In *Business Leadership in the Large Corporation* the economist R. A. Gordon described this phenomenon as follows:

> One of the most important of the non-financial incentives offered by the large corporation is the opportunity to satisfy the urge for personal power. . . . [The executive's] power is a product of position rather than of personal wealth. Power in this case means authority over subordinates, control of the disposal of vast resources, and great influence over persons and affairs outside the firm. The corporation is the vehicle through which power comes to be held and exercised. . . .
>
> Power thus secured increases with the size of the firm. Here lies an important explanation of the tendency of many large firms to become larger, even if sometimes the profitability of such expansion is open to serious question. The working of the power urge in this respect is reinforced by the tendency of businessmen to identify themselves

---

earnings." Donaldson, supra at 121. Furthermore, the factors other than earnings per share which affect market price are often not under the corporation's control. For example, if Corporations *A* and *B* have the same earnings per share, and *A* is in a glamour business, the market price of *A's* stock will be higher, but what constitutes a glamour business at any one point in time is determined by traders' tastes, which are relatively unpredictable.

3. R. A. Gordon, supra note 2, at 312.

4. Cf. id, at x, 313, 334.

5. See J. Baker, Executive Compensation Practices of Retail Companies 1928-1937, 1-2 (Harvard University Graduate School of Business Administration Business Research Study No. 23, 1939); C. Barnard, The Functions of the Executive 142-145 (1938); cf. Papandreou, Some Basic Problems in the Theory of the Firm, in 2 A Survey of Contemporary Economics 183, 205-213 (B. F. Hayley ed. 1961).

6. J. Baker, supra note 5, at 2; C. Barnard, supra note 5, at 145-156; R. A. Gordon, supra note 2, at 305-307.

with their enterprises. Expansion is desired for the enhancement of personal power and also because of the satisfaction of being associated with a powerful organization. . . .

The large corporation can also offer prestige, over and above that which results from the executive's receipt of a large salary and bonus. Power itself brings prestige, as does the mere fact of heading a large and successful firm. As in the case of personal power, prestige is to some extent linked with the size of the firm, and too strong a desire for it may lead to overexpansion.[7]

A second important set of nonfinancial managerial motives is the desire for security and the tendency to identify ego and enterprise.

When executives talk of "the company," they refer not to some mental abstraction but to a tangible, organic group. It is a group to which a man can become personally attached, and corporation executives are increasingly accustomed to think of themselves and to introduce themselves as company men. Their lives center more and more in their corporations, even their social life: friends are friends from the company. The corporation meets their money needs, provides legal advice, medical service, loans when necessary, finances advanced education and travel throughout the country or over the world; it usually takes note of the birth of children and may even help the children get jobs. It looks after the aged and the widowed and frequently stands the expense of burials; its representatives regularly attend funerals. And it increasingly provides . . . a sense of being an integral and valuable part of a common effort.[8]

Just as desire for power and prestige may lead management to undertake acquisitions, so identification with the enterprise and the desire for security may lead management to oppose corporate contractions, liquidations, or merger into an acquiring corporation, even where such an action would be desirable on economic grounds. "[C]orporate managements seldom consider liquidation an alternative to unprofitable operations. The chief executive who has been long with his company rebels against the idea of 'his' firm's passing out of existence."[9]

7. R. A. Gordon, supra note 2, at 305-307.

8. H. Maurer, Great Enterprise 150-151 (1955). See also J. Baker, supra note 5, at 2; R. A. Gordon, supra note 2, at 308-309, 310-311.

9. R. A. Gordon, supra note 2, at 308-310. See also H. Simon, Administrative Behavior 117-118 (2d ed. 1957); Papandreou, supra note 5, at 188; cf. Hess Shake-Up: 'Less Than Meets Eye,' N. Y. Times, Aug. 7, 1972, at 39, col. 5.

In many proposed structural changes, financial motives serve to reinforce the nonfinancial. For example, liquidation, contraction, or merger into an acquiring corporation may very well result in loss of the manager's job,[10] while expansion through acquisition may enhance the manager's responsibility and therefore his salary. Conversely, management may support a structural change which runs counter to its nonfinancial interest, if it is provided with sufficient side payments in the way of employment contracts and the like. One commentator has gone so far as to say:

> When we find [management] recommending [such] a change it is generally safe to assume that some side payment is occurring. . . . The most obvious kind of side payment to managers is a position within the new structure either paying a salary or making them privy to valuable market information. This arrangement, easily established with mergers, can look like normal business expediency, since the argument can always be made that the old management provides continuity and a link with past experience of the corporation.[11]

In short, management is likely to be deeply self-interested in structural decisions, often on a financial level, and almost invariably on a nonfinancial level. The latter is, if anything, the more dangerous, partly because nonfinancial motivations are likely to be more intense, and partly because in the case of decisions which relate to the very structure of the firm, management is likely to view the shareholders as outsiders, selfishly interested only in

10. Thus Graham and Dodd comment: "It is a trite but true remark that the determining factor in keeping an unprofitable business running is often the natural desire of the management to hold on to their jobs. Unfortunately, poor-caliber management is more anxious to hang on than high-caliber management, since the latter can usually find other and perhaps better employment elsewhere." B. Graham & D. Dodd, Security Analysis 608 (3d ed. 1951).

11. Manne, Mergers and the Market for Corporate Control, 73 J. Pol. Econ. 110, 118 (1965); see, e.g., Ed Reddig is Abrasive, Profane and Ruthless, But He Gets Results, Wall St. J., Oct. 12, 1971, at 1, col. 1; Some Officials Scored for Personal Bargaining When Companies Join, Wall St. J., Aug. 28, 1968, at 1, col. 6; Three Top Sheraton Officials to Benefit in Event of Merger, Wall St. J., Jan. 31, 1968, at 28, col. 4. The Wall Street Journal article on Ed Reddig, chairman of White Consolidated Industries, reports that: "On more than one occasion, Mr. Reddig has been accused of making overly generous deals with top management of some of the companies he has wanted to acquire. Mr. Reddig denies outright 'buys,' but he readily concedes that he's not opposed to extending such things as five-year 'consulting contracts' to key members of management. 'It's just part of the cost of the acquisition,' he says." The practice is sometimes referred to as the Golden Handshake.

profits, while it, management, is motivated by a greater good, the good of the firm.[12] Thus, far from perceiving its own conflict of interest, management is likely to perceive its position as morally neutral or even morally admirable. All experience teaches us the acute danger of such a fusion of self-interest and self-satisfaction.

How can these dangers be dealt with? Judicial review of conflicts of interest stemming from nonfinancial motives is virtually impossible. Indeed, even where a structural change involves management in a financial conflict of interest, as where jobs or salary levels are involved, the courts have been reluctant to apply the usual conflict-of-interest rules. For example, in *Smith v. Good Music Station, Incorporated,*[13] RKO offered to purchase all of the stock of GMS from its owners, Rogers, Smith, and Underwood, and to employ Rogers and his wife as consultants for five years at $15,000 per year. The price for the stock and the employment offer were both deemed insufficient, and the offer fell through. RKO then offered to purchase all of GMS's assets at a higher price than it had offered for the stock, and also raised its employment offer to the Rogers. Meanwhile, another party made an offer for the stock which apparently was higher than RKO's, but which was conditioned on reaching an agreement on compensation for Rogers and the station manager. Despite the fact that the new offer was higher, GMS's board, including Rogers, authorized the sale to RKO. Smith attacked the transaction on various grounds, including lack of a disinterested quorum of directors. The court refused to apply the traditional self-interest rules on the theory that the conflict of interest was "remote." In effect, if not literally, the court appeared to have put the burden on Smith to show unfairness, rather than on Rogers to show fairness. Such a burden would normally be all but impossible to shoulder in the case of a structural change, because of the complexity of such transactions, and the fact that there is normally no market against which the transaction can be measured.[14]

12. See R. A. Gordon, supra note 2, at 308-311: "The executive not infrequently tends to look upon the stockholders as outsiders, whose complaints and demands for dividends are necessary evils, which must be reconciled with what is considered best from the point of view of the business itself as a continuing institution having an existence apart from that of its owners." Id. at 309; cf. J. Burnham, The Managerial Revolution 88-92, 192-193 (Midland ed. 1960); Baumhart, How Ethical Are Businessmen? Harv. Bus. Rev., July-Aug. 1961, at 6, 10.

13. 36 Del. Ch. 262, 129 A.2d 242 (Ch. 1957).

If judicial review on the complaint of dissatisfied shareholders is generally not feasible, what alternatives are available to deal with the problem of managerial self-interest in structural changes? One alternative is to require disclosure of all material facts in connection with proposed structural changes, as under the SEC's proxy rules. Even a naked requirement of disclosure is efficacious: many men will not do publicly what they would do privately.[15] But disclosure without more has a disembodied quality, particularly if it is an after-the-fact, keeping-everyone-informed kind of disclosure.[16] Therefore, if disclosure is to be relied upon as a primary tool it should be action-oriented disclosure, disclosure required in connection with an approval to be sought. And this seems true even if the approval will be granted more or less pro forma, simply because men have a different attitude when they must seek approval, even a pro forma approval, than when their only obligation is to let others know what they have already done or are thinking of doing.

A second alternative, easily meshed with disclosure, is to require that decisions relating to structural changes be approved by a government agency. Such an approach, which has been partially adopted by California,[17] has much to recommend it, but it has

14. Cf. Muschel v. Western Union Corp., 310 A.2d 904 (Del. Ch. 1973); Northwest Industries, Inc. v. B. F. Goodrich Co., 301 F. Supp. 706 (D. Ill. 1969).

15. Cf. Cary, Corporate Standards and Legal Rules, 50 Calif. L. Rev. 408 (1962); von Mehren & McCarroll, The Proxy Rules: A Case Study in the Administrative Process, 29 Law & Contemp. Prob. 728, 739 n. 33 (1964).

16. Cf. Schlick v. Penn-Dixie Cement Corp., 507 F.2d 374 (2d Cir. 1974), cert. denied, 421 U.S. 976 (1975); Laurenzano v. Einbender, 448 F.2d 1 (2d Cir. 1971).

17. See Cal. Corp. Code §§25017, 25120-25122, 25140(a), (c), 25103 (West Supp. 1974). See also Dahlquist, Regulation and Liability under the California Corporate Securities Act (pts. 1-2), 33 Calif. L. Rev. 343, 349-353 (1945), 34 Calif. L. Rev. 344, 350-362 (1946); Jennings, The Role of the States in Corporate Regulation and Investor Protection, 23 Law & Contemp. Prob. 193, 213-218 (1958); Orschel, Administrative Protection for Shareholders in California Recapitalizations, 4 Stan. L. Rev. 215 (1952); Note, Protection for Shareholder Interests in Recapitalizations of Publicly Held Corporations, 58 Colum. L. Rev. 1030, 1048-1055 (1953). In theory, but apparently not in practice, other state blue-sky laws also extend some degree of administrative regulation to certain structural changes. See Cowett, Reorganizations, Consolidations, Mergers and Related Corporate Events Under the Blue-Sky Laws, 13 Bus. Law. 418, 760 (1958); Note, supra, at 1048 n. 122. See also R. Jennings & H. Marsh, Securities Regulation – Cases and Materials 585-586 (3d ed. 1972); L. Loss & E. Cowett, Blue Sky Law 36 n. 99 (1958).

There is also a scattered amount of administrative regulation of structural changes, with the object of protecting shareholders, in the regulated industries. See Note, supra, at 1055-1064.

two basic limitations as a general solution. First, although the California experience tends to establish the workability of such regulation, and its compatibility with the corporate institution,[18] the solution is nevertheless commonly perceived as inefficient and not institutionally compatible,[19] and it is therefore unlikely to be adopted on a widespread basis unless a crisis situation develops. Indeed, California itself recently retrenched by exempting from such regulation securities listed on stock exchanges which impose designated listing and delisting criteria.[20] Second, administrative regulation tends to take a reviewing rather than an initiating cast. Therefore, while such regulation can deal with structural changes that are proposed but not advisable, it normally cannot deal with structural changes that are advisable but not proposed.

A third alternative, which meets the two problems posed by administrative regulation and can be easily meshed with such regulation and with disclosure, is to put structural matters directly into the shareholders' province. This alternative, however, brings us to another premise of the voteless model – that shareholders in publicly held corporations have no interest in participating in corporate affairs at any level, so that such an approach would be of only theoretical import. As Manning puts it:

> It is clear beyond question that shareholders as a lot have little or no real concern with . . . the "fundamental" transactions. . . . It is commonplace to observe that the modern shareholder is a kind of investor and does not think of himself as or act like an "owner." He hires his capital out to the managers and they run it for him; how they do it is their business, not his, and he always votes "yes" on the proxy.[21]

Certainly this premise is a widely shared one.[22] But to what extent is it true?

18. See Jennings, supra note 17, at 214, 225-226; Orschel, supra note 17; Note, supra note 17, at 1051-1052, 1064-1065 (1958).

19. Cf. L. Loss & E. Cowett, supra note 17, at 327-329.

20. See Cal. Corp. Code §25100(o) (West Supp. 1974).

21. Manning, The Shareholder's Appraisal Remedy: An Essay for Frank Coker, 72 Yale L.J. 223, 261 (1962).

22. See, e.g., Mason, Introduction, in The Corporation in Modern Society 2 (E. Mason ed. 1959) ("The equity owner is joining the bond holder as a functionless rentier").

5

Voting Rights in Publicly Held Corporations

THE EXPECTATIONS OF SHAREHOLDERS

In the absence of any hard evidence concerning the expectations of shareholders in publicly held corporations, the following assumption will be made: The extent to which a shareholder in such a corporation is interested in and expects to participate in structural decisions is intimately related to the size of his shareholding. In discussing shareholder expectations from this perspective, most commentators have taken either AT&T or GM as their model, and on the basis of that model, have argued that shareholders today have no such interest or expectation.[1] But in terms of number of record shareholders, at least, these corporations are not very typical. AT&T has over 2.9 million shareholders, and GM almost 1.3 million.[2] In contrast, no other corporation has more than 725,000 shareholders, only 20 or so others have more than 200,000, and the 500th largest industrial has less than 3600.[3]

Of course, the ultimate question as to the typicality of AT&T and GM is not how many other corporations have a like number of shareholders, but how many have a pattern of stock distribution such that the shareholders probably would not expect to participate even in structural decisions. Unfortunately, there is very little

1. See, e.g., Chayes, The Modern Corporation and the Rule of Law, in The Corporation in Modern Society 25 (E. Mason ed. 1959); Dion, Property and Authority in Business Enterprise, 38 U. Det. L.J. 600, 611 (1961); Hornstein, Corporate Control and Private Property Rules, 92 U. Pa. L. Rev. 1, 3 (1943).

2. New York Stock Exchange, 1974 Fact Book 35. Throughout this chapter figures are rounded unless otherwise indicated.

3. Id. at 35; The Fortune Directory of the 500 Largest Industrial Corporations, Fortune, May 1974, at 231, 250; 1 Moody's Industrial Manual 258 (1974).

direct information on this subject. However, a variety of data (most of it collected for other purposes) can be stitched together to provide at least the outline of a pattern. I shall begin with data on the overall corporate population, and then turn to data limited to the very largest corporations.

§5.1. The Overall Corporation Population

Both direct evidence[4] and experience indicate that there is at least a rough correlation between the manner in which a corporation's stock is distributed among its shareholders – that is, whether shareholdings are relatively concentrated, on the one hand, or distributed atomistically, on the other – and the corporation's total number of shareholders. Therefore, one method of exploring the extent of concentration or dispersion of shareholdings is to explore the distribution of corporations by number of shareholders. While the data on that distribution lacks precision, a series of approximations can be made which at least indicates relative orders of magnitude.

1. Total number of corporations. Based on Internal Revenue Service statistics on corporations filing tax returns, the total number of active corporations in this country as of 1969-1970 was approximately 1.74 million.[5] The current figure is probably comparable. Only a very few of these 1.74 million corporations are publicly held: the New York Stock Exchange estimates that approximately 40,000 corporations have their shares quoted over the counter, and according to the SEC, another 3400 or so are listed on national or regional exchanges.[6] On the basis of a sampling of over-the-counter corporations made by the SEC in connection with its *Special Study of Securities Markets,* it appears reasonable to assume that approximately 20 percent, or 8000, of the 40,000

4. See text at note 23, infra.

5. Internal Revenue Service, Statistics of Income – 1969, Corporation Income Tax Returns 1, 3 (Table A) (1973).

6. New York Stock Exchange, 1974 Fact Book, at 34; Interview with Agnes W. Creedon, Special Assistant to the Director, Office of Registrations and Reports, Securities Exchange Commission, March 24, 1975. According to the NASD, estimates for the total number of OTC-traded securities range from 30,000 to 50,000. Letter to the author from Paul F. Luther, Director, Market Statistics Dept., NASD, Feb. 12, 1975.

over-the-counter corporations had less than 100 shareholders.[7] Conversely, since most corporations with 100 or more shareholders would have their shares quoted at least occasionally, the remaining 32,000 over-the-counter corporations, together with the 3400 listed corporations, probably account for most of the corporations with 100 or more shareholders. Thus the number of corporations with 100 or more shareholders can be estimated at approximately 35,000, and the number of corporations with less than 100 shareholders can be estimated at approximately 1.7 million.

2. Corporations with 1 to 10 and 11 to 99 shareholders. Undoubtedly the great bulk of these 1.7 million corporations with less than 100 shareholders had relatively few shareholders. Just how many had just how few cannot be definitely determined. We know that a minimum of 257,000 corporations, about one-seventh of the total, had ten or less shareholders, because that many corporations elected special tax treatment under Subchapter S of the Internal Revenue Code,[8] and a corporation cannot qualify for such treatment if it had more than ten shareholders. (We also know that of those 257,000 corporations, 75,000 had one shareholder, 84,000 had two, 46,000 had three, 28,000 had four, 10,000 had five, 5000 had six, 3000 had seven, 3000 had eight, 2000 had nine, and 2000 had ten.[9]) Furthermore, an analysis by Professor Alfred Conard of a sample of Michigan franchise tax returns indicates that the ratio between corporations with 1 to 10 and 11 to 100 shareholders was approximately 23:1.[10] Applying this ratio to the 1.7 million corporations with less than 100 shareholders yields an estimate of approximately 1.63 million corporations with ten or less shareholders, and 70,000 with 11 to 99.

7. See SEC, Report of the Special Study of Securities Markets, H.R. Doc. No. 95, 88th Cong., 1st Sess., pt. 3, at 19-20 & Chart IX-a (1963) (hereinafter cited as Special Study). To conduct its survey, the SEC analyzed record shareholdings in 20 percent of the corporations in whose securities the broker-dealer community had shown interest during the last three months of 1961; listed and foreign issuers were then excluded from the sample. Id. at 18-19.

8. Internal Revenue Service, Statistics of Income – 1970, Business Income Tax Returns 158 (1973).

9. Id. at 166.

10. Conard, The Corporate Census: A Preliminary Exploration, 62 Calif. L. Rev. 440, 457-458 (1975).

3. Corporations with 100 to 299 shareholders. The New York Stock Exchange estimates that approximately 11,000 corporations have 300 or more shareholders and $1 million or more in assets.[11] By subtracting this figure from the estimated 35,000 total number of corporations with 100 or more shareholders (and assuming a relatively close correlation between assets and shareholders), it can be estimated that there are approximately 24,000 corporations with 100 to 299 shareholders.

4. Corporations with 300 to 499 shareholders. About 8500 corporations are either listed on a national securities exchange or registered under section 12(g) of the 1934 Act.[12] It seems likely that almost all of these corporations have 500 or more shareholders, and conversely that most corporations with 500 or more shareholders fall into this category.[13] By subtracting this figure from the 11,000 corporations with 300 or more shareholders, it can be estimated that approximately 2500 corporations have 300 to 499 shareholders.

5. Corporations with 500 to 1499, 1500 to 2999, and over 3000 shareholders. Of the 8500 corporations with 500 or more shareholders, about 3400 have listed their stock on a national securities exchange.[14] Of those 3400, the common stock of approximately 1225 corporations is traded on the American Stock Exchange and the common stock of about 1550 corporations is listed on the New York Stock Exchange.[15] For original listing the American Stock Exchange normally requires at least 1200 public shareholders (but most have at least 1500 shareholders),[16] and the

11. New York Stock Exchange, 1974 Fact Book 34; Letter to the author from Dorothy Geraghty, Research Associate, New York Stock Exchange, Jan. 22, 1974.

12. Letter to the author from Agnes W. Creedon, Special Assistant to the Director, Office of Registrations and Reports, Securities Exchange Commission, Feb. 6, 1975; Interview with Agnes W. Creedon, March 24, 1975. Of these 8500 corporations, approximately 3400 are listed and approximately 5100 are registered under § 12(g) of the 1934 Act. Another 2100 corporations are subject to reporting requirements under § 15(d) of the 1933 Act. Ibid.

13. See Securities Exchange Act of 1934, § 12(g), 15 U.S.C. § 78l (1970).

14. Interview with Agnes W. Creedon, supra note 12.

15. Letter to the author from Robert A. Coplin, Vice President, Information Services Division, American Stock Exchange, Feb. 27, 1975; Letter to the author from Dorothy Geraghty, Research Associate, New York Stock Exchange, March 3, 1975. Forty-nine common stocks are traded on the American Stock Exchange on an unlisted basis, but almost all of these stocks meet that Exchange's requirements for original listing.

16. 2 CCH, American Stock Exchange Guide ¶ 10,001. Other minimum criteria include 800 round-lot shareholders; net tangible assets of at least $4 million; net income

New York Stock Exchange normally requires at least 2000 round-lot holders.[17] Because of the many advantages which accrue from listing on these exchanges, such as increased marketability of stock and increased ease of establishing market value for acquisitions, new and secondary issues, shareholder borrowing, estate taxes, and the like, a corporation which can list on one of these exchanges will normally do so.[18] Furthermore, because of the greater prestige of a New York Stock Exchange listing, a corporation which can list its stock on that exchange will usually do so. Assuming that a corporation which meets the number-of-public shareholders criteria will usually meet the other listing requirements as well, and that most corporations with 2000 or more round-lot holders will have at least another 1000 or so odd-lot holders, it therefore appears likely that most of the 1550 corporations with common stock listed on the New York Stock Exchange have 3000 or more shareholders, and that most of the 1225 corporations with common stock admitted to trading on the American Stock Exchange have 1500 to 2999 shareholders. It can be estimated that approximately 125 corporations listed on the American Stock Exchange would be eligible to list on the New York Stock Exchange;[19] that another 100 or so corporations meet the number-of-shareholder criteria for New York Stock Exchange listing, but either do not meet the other criteria or are not listed at all; that approximately 600 to 700 corporations eligible to list on the American Stock Exchange have not done so;[20] and that most of the remaining listed and registered corporations have 500 to 1499 shareholders. On this basis, approximately 1800 American corporations have 3000 or more shareholders; approximately 1700 have 1500 to 2999 shareholders; and the balance of the 8500 listed and registered corporations, approximately 5000, have 500 to 1499 shareholders.

---

in its last fiscal year of $750,000; income of at least $400,000 after taxes and all charges; 400,000 publicly held shares; and a price per share of at least five dollars for a reasonable time prior to filing of the listing application.

17. New York Stock Exchange, Company Manual, at B-3. Other minimum criteria include net tangible assets of $16 million; pre-federal tax profits of $2.5 million in the latest fiscal year and $2 million in each of two preceding years; one million shares outstanding; and one million shares publicly held.

18. See American Stock Exchange, Listing on the American Stock Exchange (1974); New York Stock Exchange, A Listing on the New York Stock Exchange (1961).

19. See American Stock Exchange, supra note 18, at 29.

20. Letter to the author from Robert A. Coplin, Vice President, Information Services Division, American Stock Exchange, Feb. 7, 1975.

6. Corporations with more than 10,000 shareholders. Based on an analysis of companies in the *Fortune* lists of the largest industrial, banking, life insurance, retailing, and transportation companies, Professor Conard reports that as of 1970 the number of corporations with more than 10,000 shareholders was 572.[21] Since the *Fortune* lists failed to include certain types of corporations (such as broadcasters and construction and service companies),[22] this figure can probably be rounded up to 600, leaving approximately 1200 corporations with 3000 to 10,000 shareholders.

7. Summary. The resulting approximations are summed up in table 5-1.

Table 5-1

Number of Shareholders	*Approximate Number of Corporations*
1-10	1,630,000
11-99	70,000
100-499	26,500*
500-1499	5,000
1500-2999	1,700
3000-10,000	1,200
Over 10,000	600

*This figure combines corporations with 100-299 shareholders (24,000) and corporations with 300-499 shareholders (2,500).

All of the data reviewed so far relates only to the distribution of corporation by number of shareholders, not to intracorporate distribution of shareholdings. However, there is information on record which allows the former kind of data to be converted into the latter. In connection with its *Special Study,* the SEC made a survey to determine the correlation between distribution of shareholdings and number of shareholders in an extensive sample of over-the-counter corporations. In about half or more of the corporations in each category of sampled corporations with less than 1000 shareholders (these categories were 1 to 24, 25 to 99, 100 to

21. Conard, supra note 10, at 458.
22. See Editor's Desk, Fortune, May 1971, at 131.

199, 200 to 299, 300 to 499, 500 to 749, and 750 to 999), the ten largest record shareholders held 50 percent or more of the stock. In more than half of the sampled corporations with 1000 to 1999 shareholders, the ten largest record shareholders held at least 40 percent of the stock. In about half or more of the sampled corporations with 2000 to 2999 and 3000 to 4999 shareholders, the ten largest record shareholders held at least 30 percent of the stock. In almost 30 percent of the sampled corporations with 5000 or more shareholders, the ten largest record shareholders held over 30 percent of the stock. In about 40 percent of corporations with 5000 or more shareholders the ten largest record shareholders held almost 20 percent of the stock.[23] In short, assuming that a shareholder with a significant holding will much more likely than not have both a legitimate interest in and a reasonable expectation of participation in structural changes, in most publicly held corporations — or at least, in all but the very largest — the distribution of stock is such that a majority of the shareholders probably have such an interest and expectation.

§5.2. The Fallacy of the Average Shareholder: Concentration of Shareholdings in the Very Largest Corporations

How much different is the situation in the case of the very largest corporations? Not too much. Of course, the holdings of many if not most of the shareholders in such corporations are likely to be negligible in terms of relative size, and it may perhaps be assumed that the interests and expectations of such shareholders are correspondingly negligible. Indeed, much of the thinking about the modern corporation is based on the assumption that

23. Special Study, pt. 3, supra note 7, at 30.

Of course, some record shareholdings may represent a large number of small individual shareholdings held in the name of one broker, but New York Stock Exchange calculations as of 1965 showed that the total amount of publicly held stock held in the name of brokers and dealers was only 7.5 percent by number of shares and 7.1 percent by market value — and some of this was probably owned by the brokers and dealers themselves. See New York Stock Exchange, Methodology and Sample Design of 1965 Census of Shareowners, Tables III, IV (1965). A great deal of stock is held by nominees for bank trust funds, but in such cases the bank is likely to have either voting rights or influence over the way stock is voted. See §5.6, infra.

the average shareholder – "shareholders taken as a lot," to use Manning's phrase – has no interest in any kind of corporate decision. But this assumption, even if true, is virtually meaningless, since it is based on the fallacious premise that the expectations and interests of "the average shareholder" are of great economic or legal significance. This premise is fallacious because corporate economics and corporate law are not bottomed on the democratic principle of one-man-one-vote, but on the proprietary principle of one-share-one-vote: what counts is not shareholders, but shareholdings. An inquiry into the expectations of "the average shareholder" will therefore have only sociological relevance, unless there is a true People's Capitalism, in which shareholders and shareholdings correlate closely. But the opposite is the case: the ownership of stock even in very large corporations is so highly concentrated that the shareholdings of "the average shareholder" are unimportant, if not entirely negligible.

The most comprehensive demonstration of this phenomenon is the TNEC analysis of the distribution of shareholdings, as of 1937, in the 200 largest corporations and in 1710 corporations with securities listed on a national securities exchange. In the case of the 200 largest corporations, the analysis showed that 3 percent of record holdings accounted for half the aggregate common stock outstanding, and 10 percent of record holdings accounted for 75 percent of the aggregate common stock outstanding.[24] In the case of the 1710 listed corporations, the analysis showed that 3 percent of the common shareholdings accounted for half the value of common shares outstanding, 4 percent of the holdings accounted for 65 percent of the value, and 8 percent of the holdings accounted for 75 percent of the value, while at the other end of the scale 70 percent of the holdings accounted for only 8 percent of the value.[25] Although no analysis of equivalent scope has been performed since that time,[26] the more recent data indicates that the

24. Temporary National Economic Committee, The Distribution of Ownership in the 200 Largest Financial Corporations 40 (TNEC Monograph No. 29, 1940). Since record holdings would tend to be fewer than beneficial holdings, concentration based on beneficial holdings would also tend to be less. However, an analysis of the beneficial holdings in ten of the two hundred corporations showed concentrations "not much different" from the unadjusted distribution. Id. at 53.

25. Temporary National Economic Committee, Survey of Shareholdings in 1,710 Corporations with Securities Listed on a National Stock Exchange 51, 241 (Table 96) (TNEC Monograph No. 30, 1941).

26. Cf. E. Cox, Trends in the Distribution of Stock Ownership 35-36 (1963).

kind of concentration found by the TNEC still prevails. Thus a survey of common shareholdings in 2932 publicly held corporations conducted under the auspices of the Brookings Institution and the New York Stock Exchange showed that as of 1951, 2.1 percent of such shareholdings accounted for over half of the total value, while two-thirds of the holdings accounted for only 13 percent of the value.[27] In 1963 Edwin Cox reported that in a sample of unidentified companies for which he had gathered data, 5 percent of the shareholdings accounted for 60 percent of the stock and 20 percent of the holdings accounted for 77 percent of the stock.[28] And the SEC's *Special Study,* discussed in the previous section, although coming at the matter somewhat differently, indicates a comparable degree of concentration.

§5.3. Concentration of Shareholdings, cont'd. The Very Largest of the Very Largest

Finally, there is substantial data showing the presence of a significant degree of concentration of shareholdings even where one would least expect it — among the very largest of the very largest. Much of the work concerning these corporations, starting with Berle & Means[30] has been aimed at showing that most such corporations were management- rather than shareholder-controlled. Whether or not that is the case,[31] the data also shows that in many if not most of these corporations a substantial percentage of the stock is held by a relatively small number of shareholders.

27. L. Kimmel, Share Ownership in the United States 43 (1952).

28. E. Cox, supra note 26, at 85-88. The corporations were unidentified because most had requested anonymity.

29. See also R. Soldovsky, Institutional Holdings of Common Stock, 1900-2000, at 219 (Table 46) (1971).

30. A. Berle & G. Means, The Modern Corporation and Private Property (1932).

31. Berle & Means used the distribution of a corporation's stock ownership — and more particularly, the size of its largest outstanding block of stock — as a virtually absolute index to whether a corporation was management- or shareholder-controlled. This technique has been criticized on the ground that examination of the pattern of stock distribution is not an adequate substitute for a factual inquiry to determine the locus of control. See Beed, The Separation of Ownership From Control, 1 J. Econ. Studies 29 (1966); de Vroey, The Measurement of the Separation of Ownership and Control in Large Corporations — A Critical Review (unpublished thesis presented at the Institut d' Economie of the Universite Catholique de Louvain).

For example, the SEC's *Special Study* found that in almost 30 percent of the sampled corporations with 5000 or more shareholders, the ten largest record holders held over 30 percent of the stock. In 1972 a House subcommittee issued a questionnaire designed to determine the holdings of the 30 largest shareholders in the 500 largest industrials, the 50 largest commercial banks, the 50 largest retailers, the 50 largest transportation companies, the 50 largest utilities, and the 24 largest stock life insurance companies. Eighty-nine of these corporations provided full responses.[32] As the following table shows, in 26 of these corporations the 30 largest shareholders (other than Cede & Co., the nominee for the New York Stock Exchange's Depository Trust[33]) owned 40 percent or more of the stock; in 43 they owned 30 percent or more; and in 76 they owned 20 percent or more. If the 20 utilities are eliminated, the 30 largest shareholders (other than Cede) owned 40 percent or more of the stock in just over a third of the remaining 69 corporations, and 30 percent or more of the stock in well over half.[34]

Other investigators, coming at the matter from a different perspective, have generated data which shows that a significant number of the very largest corporations have at least one very large – 10 percent or more – block of stock outstanding. For example, in a study of the 500 largest nonfinancial corporations as of 1963, measured by size of assets, Robert Larner found that an individual, a family, or a group of business associates held at least 10 percent of the stock in approximately 25 percent of the cases.[35] Furthermore, eliminating utilities (which were over-

32. Subcommittee on Intergovernmental Relations, and Budgeting Management, and Expenditures, of the Senate Committee on Government Operations, 93d Cong., 1st Sess., Disclosure of Corporate Ownership 6, 17 (Comm. Print 1973).

33. See id. at 6, 21, 341-343.

34. Id. at 26-28 (Table 5).

35. R. Larner, Management Control and the Large Corporation 9-11, 17 (Table 3) (1970).

Larner's book is an expansion of an earlier article, Ownership and Control in the 200 Largest Nonfinancial Corporations, 1929 and 1963, 56 Am. Econ. Rev. 777 (1966). (The article was confined to the 200 largest nonfinancials because its principal purpose was to examine the trends since the publication of Berle & Means.) Since Berle & Means were primarily interested in determining the extent of management control, where Corporation A was controlled by Corporation B they inquired into the distribution of stockholdings in Corporation B to determine the "ultimate" – as opposed to the "immediate" – type of control of A. Larner followed this technique in both his article and his book. For purposes of determining the interests and expectations of share-

Table 5-2

Holdings of the 30 largest shareholders in 89 corporations

Corporation	*Percent of stock held by 30 largest stock-holders other than Cede & Co.*
Industrials	
Mobil Oil	26.7
Atlantic Richfield	24
Continental Oil	26.4
Ashland Oil	15.6
Ford Motor	34.1
General Electric	19.5
Chrysler	29.1
Westinghouse	21.4
RCA	24.0
Union Carbide	23.5
Kraftco	24.6
Greyhound	11.9
Litton Industries	37.1
Caterpillar Tractor	28.7
Monsanto	28.8
Dow Chemical	25.0
R. J. Reynolds	27.6
United Aircraft	40.1
Xerox	27.6
Bendix	32.5
Textron	34.4
United Brands	49.0
CPC International	23.2
Warner-Lambert	25.9
Raytheon	37.1
Transportation Companies	
United Airlines	43.4
American Airlines	41.7
Pan American World Airways	34.2
Northwest Airlines	48.2
Braniff Airways	40.8

Table 5-2 (Continued)

Corporation	Percent of stock held by 30 largest stock-holders other than Cede & Co.
Transportation Companies	
Western Air Lines	64.0
Pacific Southwest Airlines	35.5
North Central Airlines	15.5
Frontier Airlines	55.5
Penn Central	23.5
Norfolk & Western	37.0
Burlington & Northern	36.0
Chesapeake & Ohio	19.7
Southern	40.2
Missouri Pacific	72.2
Chicago-Rock Island & Pacific	92.0
Chicago, Milwaukee, St. Paul & Pacific	35.9
St. Louis-San Francisco	48.2
Reading	70.6
Kansas City Southern	35.4
Rio Grande Industries	46.5
Soo Line	65.3
Gulf, Mobile & Ohio	52.0
Seaboard Coast Line	35.7
Seatrain Lines	84.1
Spector Industries	56.9
Utilities	
AT&T	6.8
American Electric Power	20.0
General Telephone & Electric	14.3
Texas Eastern Transmission	26.9
Virginia Electric & Power	29.9
Pennzoil United	40.9
Texas Utilities	24.5
American Natural Gas	23.9
Niagara Mohawk Power	10.0
Northeast Utilities	11.1
Transcontinental Gas Pipeline	22.8

Table 5-2 (Continued)

Corporation	Percent of stock held by 30 largest stock-holders other than Cede & Co.
Utilities	
Continental Telephone	27.0
Allegheny Power System	22.0
Baltimore Gas & Electric	20.2
Pennsylvania Power & Light	14.8
Potomac Electric Power	8.7
Long Island Lighting	21.8
Pacific Power & Light	10.0
Western Union	36.1
Cleveland Electric Illuminating	20.8
Retailing Companies	
Safeway Stores	28.2
Gamble-Skogmo	49.7
Grand Union	31.6
R. H. Macy	42.1
Interstate Stores	44.9
Cook United	51.4
Pueblo International	76.9
Melville Shoe	40.7
Commercial Banks	
First National City	20.9
Chemical New York	21.6
Bankers Trust – New York	27.2
First Bank System	38.8
Republic National of Dallas	35.8
Girard Co.	29.1
First National Bank in Dallas	34.4
Citizens & Southern National	42.5
Shawmut Association	15.0
Life Insurance	
Travelers	22.2

represented by virtue of the asset test[36] and which are of limited interest from the perspective of corporate law because their freedom of action is severely hedged by regulation and economics), Larner found that a single individual, a family, or a group of business associates held 10 percent or more of the stock in one-third of the industrials and the transportation companies.[37] Two studies of the *Fortune* 500 largest industrials produced similar results. An analysis of the 1967 *Fortune* 500 by Robert Sheehan found 30 percent in which an individual or the members of a single family held 10 percent or more of the outstanding stock.[38] An analysis by John Palmer of 488 firms in the 1965 *Fortune* 500 and the 425 of these firms which were still in existence in 1969 found that in one-third of each sample there was a 10-percent-or-more block outstanding.[39]

The finding that one-third of the very largest industrials have at least a single 10 percent block outstanding is striking enough. In fact, however, the proportion is almost unquestionably larger. The *Fortune* 500 does not include all of the 500 largest industrials, but only those which publish certified financial statements.[40] In 1966 *Fortune* estimated that approximately 20 privately owned corporations would have been included in the *Fortune* 500 if they had published such statements,[41] and since most of these corporations almost certainly had 10-percent-or-more blocks outstanding, their inclusion would have raised the relevant percentages. Moreover, Sheehan, at least, restricted his count to 10-percent-blocks held by an individual or a single family. Finally, Larner,[42] and probably

holders, however, the data concerning "immediate control" is of greater relevance. For example, in the case just described B is a shareholder in A regardless of how B is itself controlled. In any event, there was no significant difference between the immediate and ultimate control of the industrials in Larner's population.

36. Id. at 10.

37. Id. at 17 (Table 3).

38. Sheehan, Proprietors in The World of Big Business, Fortune, June 15, 1968, at 178.

39. Palmer, Separation of Ownership From Control in Large US Industrial Corporations, 12 Q. Rev. Econ. & Bus. 55 (1972). Twelve firms were excluded from the 1965 population because of insufficient information.

40. See Sheehan, There's Plenty of Privacy Left in Private Enterprise, Fortune, July 15, 1966, at 224.

41. Id. at 224.

42. See R. Larner, supra note 35, at 116-117, 133 n. 10.

Sheehan and Palmer, obtained data on stockholdings in the industrials principally from the corporate proxy materials. The proxy rules, however, only require disclosure of shareholdings by holders whose record or beneficial holding exceeds 10 percent of the outstanding voting stock; directorial nominees; or the associates of a nominee if the nominee and his associates own more than 10 percent of any class.[43] Therefore, the proxy materials may fail to disclose a just-under-10-percent block which is not held by a directorial nominee, or an over-10-percent block which is held in the name of two or more nominees by a bank trust department or other nonbeneficial holder. In fact, after Larner had published an earlier article which concerned only the 200 largest nonfinancials, a congressional staff report found that although Larner had not included Federated Department Stores, Illinois Central, American Smelting & Refining, Burlington Industries, or Kennecott among corporations with at least one significant (i.e., 10-percent-or-more) shareholding, First National Bank of Chicago held 10.2 percent of Federated, Continental Illinois held 9.5 percent of Illinois Central, and Morgan Guaranty Trust held 15.5 percent of American Smelting, 14.5 percent of Burlington, and 17.5 percent of Kennecott.[44]

What accounts for the very high concentration of shareholdings in even the very largest corporations? First, that portion of the stock of such corporations which is held by individuals is highly concentrated among a relatively small number of top wealthholders. Second, a very large portion of the stock in such corporations is not held by individuals at all, but by financial institutions. Typically, the total number of institutions holding stock in a given corporation is small, and most of the holdings are concentrated among a small number of that small number. Let us consider these factors in turn.

43. Proxy Rules Schedule 14A, Items 5(d), 6(a)(4), (5), 17 C.F.R. 240.14a-101, Items 5(d), 6(a)(4) (1974). An associate is defined to include a corporation of which the director is the beneficial owner of 10 percent of any class of equity securities, a trust or estate in which he has a substantial interest or of which he is a trustee, and certain of his close relatives.

44. 1 Staff of House Comm. on Banking and Currency, Subcomm. on Domestic Finance, 90th Cong., 2d Sess., Commercial Banks and Their Trust Activities: Emerging Influence on the American Economy 13-15 (1968). See also R. Larner, supra note 35, at 23-24. In several other corporations excluded by Larner, two or three banks held interests which together aggregated 10 percent, and in a number of other cases at least one bank held an interest of 5-10 percent.

§5.4. Concentration of Shareholdings Among Individuals

Although most estimates of distribution of shareholdings among individuals concern the distribution of all stock, rather than just stock in publicly held corporations, and not all of the estimates may be completely reliable, the data that does exist indicates a very high degree of concentration among a relatively small number of top wealthholders. For example, in *Effects of Taxation – Investments by Individuals,* Butters, Thompson, and Bollinger estimated that as of 1949 the marketable stock held by individuals was owned by approximately 4.5 million spending units.[45] Of these, 50,000 to 100,000, or 1 to 2 percent of the units, owned approximately 65 percent of the stock by value, another 950,000 units owned approximately 30 percent of the stock, and the remaining 3.5 million units owned approximately 5 percent.[46] A 1962 survey for the Federal Reserve System by Projector and Weiss estimated that as of 1962, 41 percent of publicly held stock owned by individuals (by value) was held by spending units whose total wealth was 500,000 dollars or more; 65 percent was held by spending units whose total wealth was more than 250,000 dollars, and only 11 percent was held by units whose total wealth was less than 50,000 dollars.[47] A later analysis based on the same data, prepared in connection with the SEC's *Institutional Investor Study,* reported that of all corporate securities owned by individuals, 40.5 percent was owned by individuals with total assets over $1 million, 53 percent was owned by individuals with total assets over $500,000, 71 percent was owned by individuals with total assets over $250,000, only 11 percent was owned by individuals with total assets less than $60,000, and only 3.6 percent was owned by individuals with total assets less than $30,000.[48] Similarly, an analysis by Blume, Crockett, & Friend,

45. Defined as stock open to investment by the public, that is, listed on an exchange or readily sold over the counter. J. Butters, L. Thompson, & L. Bollinger, Effects of Taxation – Investments by Individuals 373, 402, 499 (1953).

46. See id. at 373-389. For a comparable analysis, see Staff of Senate Committee on Banking and Currency, 84th Cong., 2d Sess., Factors Affecting the Stock Market 90 (1955).

47. D. Projector & G. Weiss, Survey of Financial Characteristics of Consumers 136 (1966).

48. Institutional Investors and Corporate Stock – A Background Study 406

based on 1971 income-tax returns and census data, concluded that slightly over half of all corporate stock is held by family units whose income is in the first percentile, two-thirds is held by family units whose income is in the top 5 percent, and three-quarters by family units whose income is in the top 10 percent.[49]

§5.5. Institutional Shareholdings

The second factor accounting for the great degree of concentration in the ownership of the stock of even the very largest corporations is the great (and increasing) proportion of such stock held by a relatively small number of bank trust departments, mutual funds, insurance companies, and other financial institutions. The percentage of outstanding stock held by such institutions has been undergoing a steady and significant increase over a long period of time, due to both the institutions' own growth and an increase in the percentage of their assets which is invested in common stock.[50] Furthermore, such investors tend to prefer the stock of large, listed corporations,[51] so that their holdings are concentrated in the stock of the very largest corporations. Consequently, as of 1973, institutional shareholders held an estimated 45 percent (by value) of all the stock listed on the New York Stock Exchange,[52] and by 1980 institutional holdings of such stock will probably be up to 52 percent.[53]

Most of these shareholdings, moreover, are held by a relatively small percentage of all institutions: the SEC's *Institutional*

(Table V-6) (M. Goldsmith ed. 1973); SEC, 1 Institutional Investor Study Report, H.R. Doc. No. 92-64, 92d Cong., 1st Sess. 95 (Table III-16(B)) (1971) (hereinafter cited as Institutional Investor Study).

49. Blume, Crockett, & Friend, Stockownership in the United States: Characteristics and Trends, Surv. Current Bus., Nov. 1974, at 16, 27. See also Smith & Franklin, The Concentration of Personal Wealth, 1922-1969, Am. Econ. Rev., May 1974, at 162, 166 (Table 1).

50. See 1 Institutional Investor Study, supra note 48, at 67-68, 96-112; R. Soldovsky, Institutional Holdings of Common Stock 1900-2000, at 19-22, 36-39, 63-67 (1971); New York Stock Exchange, Institutional Shareownership 8, 13-14 (1964); 1 L. Loss, Securities Regulation 17 n. 56 (2d ed. 1961, Supp. 1962 at 1).

51. 5 Institutional Investor Study, supra note 48, at 1331-1333.

52. New York Stock Exchange, 1974 Fact Book 52.

53. Compare Freund & Minor, Institutional Activity on NYSE: 1975 and 1980 at 2 (NYSE Perspectives on Planning No. 10 (1972)), with New York Stock Exchange, 1974 Fact Book 52.

Investor Study reported in 1971 that the 50 largest bank trust departments accounted for 72 percent of the common stock managed by all bank trust departments; the 71 investment advisers managing the largest investment-company complexes accounted for 64 percent of all common stock managed by all investment advisers; the 26 largest life insurance companies accounted for 82 percent of all common stock held by such companies; and the 25 largest property-and-liability insurance companies accounted for 71 percent of all common stock held by such insurers.[54]

The net result is that a relatively small number of institutional investors hold, in the aggregate, a very substantial proportion of the stock of many or most of the country's very largest corporations. For example, the *Institutional Investor Study* found that 213 selected institutions[55] held:

– 50 percent or more of the common stock of Xerox, Gulf Oil, Ford, Merck, Houston Lighting & Power, Middle South Utilities, Ampex, Trane, and National Airlines.

– 40 to 50 percent of the common stock of IBM, Eastman Kodak, Sears, Avon, Polaroid, Goodyear, International Paper, TRW, Celanese, National Steel, Upjohn, TWA, Tampa Electric, Lone Star Cement, Beckman Instruments, U.S. Freight, Northrop, and Hanes.

– 30 to 40 percent of the common stock of Standard Oil of New Jersey, Texaco, GE, 3-M, Mobil, Standard Oil of California, Proctor & Gamble, Standard Oil of Indiana, IT&T, American Home Products, International Nickel of Canada, J.C. Penney, Westinghouse, Owens-Corning, Chrysler, May Department Stores, Litton Industries, Schering, Kimberly-Clark, Hilton, Foremost-McKesson, Zayre, Metromedia, and General Portland Cement.

– 20 to 30 percent of the common stock of GM, DuPont, GT&E, RCA, Phillips Petroleum, Pacific Gas & Electric, Woolworth, Singer, Teledyne, Beatrice Foods, American Metal Climax, Standard Brands, Kaiser Aluminum, St. Regis Paper, Bendix, Continental Telephone,

54. 5 Institutional Investor Study, supra note 48, at 1309.

55. 3 Institutional Investor Study, supra note 48, at 1308-1309, 1364-1373 (Table IX-13). The 213 financial institutions consisted of the 50 largest bank trust departments; 71 investment-advisers managing the portfolios of the largest registered investment-company complexes; the 26 largest life insurance companies; the 25 largest property-and-liability insurance company groups; and 41 self-administered portfolios belonging to the largest corporate-employee-benefit plans, educational endowments, and foundations. It should be emphasized that the data does not show all institutional holdings in the portfolio corporations, but only the holdings of the 213 institutional investors in the sample; the bank trust departments in the sample accounted for 69.5 percent of the total assets managed by all bank trust departments, and the figures for the other institutions in the sample were similar.

Long Island Lighting, Freeport Sulphur, Del Monte, Hart Schaffner & Marx, Emery Air Freight, Fluor, Arizona Public Service, Fuqua, Grand Union, Hammermill Paper, National Can, and Revere Copper & Brass.[56]

Similarly, an earlier congressional staff study[57] of the holdings of 49 selected bank trust departments (which included many but not all of the 49 largest departments)[58] found 176 cases in which one bank held 5 percent or more of the common stock of one or more of the 500 largest industrials, 20 cases in which one bank held 5 percent or more of the common stock of one or more of the 50 largest merchandisers, and 23 cases in which one bank held 5 percent or more of the common stock of one or more of the 50 largest transportation companies.[59] Some examples:

– First National Bank of Chicago held 15 percent of National Tea; 13 percent of Walgreen; 10 percent of Whirlpool; 9 percent of HFC, Scott Foresman, and Zenith; 8 percent of Container Corporation, Wrigley, and Hart, Schaffner & Marx; 7 percent of Jewel Companies and U.S. Banknote; and 6 percent of Bobbie Brooks, Dayco, Holt Rinehart, Hoover, Lucky Stores, Stokely Van Camp, and Sunbeam.

– Morgan Guaranty held 18 percent of Kenecott and Cutler Hammer; 17 percent of Carrier; 16 percent of American Smelting and Simplicity Pattern; 15 percent of Burlington and Hudson Pulp & Paper; 14 percent of Cheesebrough Ponds; 12 percent of Scovill, Tiffany, and Vanity Fair Mills; 11 percent of Endicott Johnson and Harcourt-Brace World; 10 percent of Dow Jones, U.S. Plywood-Champion Paper, W.T. Grant, and Xerox; 9 percent of American Metal Climax, Consolidated Freightways, and Jonathan Logan; 8 percent of American Airlines, Celanese, Revere Copper & Brass, United Airlines, and Time, Inc.; 7 percent of Kaiser Aluminum, Olin Mathieson, Pennsylvania R.R., Pepsico, St. Joseph Lead, and TWA; 6 percent of John Wiley, Long Island Lighting, Panhandle Eastern Pipeline, Phelps Dodge, and Polaroid; and 5 percent of Alcan Aluminum.

– First National City Bank held 23 percent of Doubleday; 15 percent of Blue Diamond Coal; 9 percent of Corning Glass Works and Prentice Hall; 8 percent of Foote, Cone & Belding and Harcourt-Brace World; 7 percent of Phillips Petroleum; 6 percent of Consolidated Cigar and Upjohn; and 5 percent of Xerox.

56. About 10 to 20 portfolio corporations in the relevant categories are omitted from the lists in the text, since only the better-known corporations have been included.

57. 1 Staff of Subcomm. on Domestic Finance, House Comm. on Banking & Currency, 90th Cong., 2d Sess., Commercial Banks and Their Trust Activities: Emerging Influence on the American Economy (1968).

58. Id. at 78, 89-90, 91.

59. Id. at 91.

– Chase Manhattan Bank held 20 percent of Hammond; 14 percent of Universal Oil Products; 11 percent of Northwest Airlines and Varian Associates; 10 percent of Air Products, Cummins Engine, Richardson-Merrel, and Pacific Intermountain Express; 9 percent of Bausch & Lomb, Boeing, Sunbeam, Addressograph-Multigraph, Moore & McCormack, Consolidated Freightways, and Texas Instruments; 8 percent of TWA, Harris Intertype, Wyandotte Chemicals, and Ryder System; 7 percent of Diebold, Pan Am, Western Airlines, Safeway Stores, and Miehle-Goss-Dexter; 6 percent of CBS, Hercules, United Aircraft, National Steel, Eastern Air Lines, Pennsylvania R.R., Reynolds Metals, Armstrong Rubber, G.D. Searle, and Panhandle Eastern Pipeline; and 5 percent of Jonathan Logan, Aetna Life, Allegheny-Ludlum, Commercial Solvents, J.C. Penney, and Sperry Rand.[60]

§5.6. The Role of Institutional Investors as Shareholders

The appropriate relation between institutional shareholders and their portfolio corporations has prompted considerable debate. Managers and their allies seek to constrain the discretion of such shareholders; shareholder democrats seek to expand it. One issue in the debate has been whether, considering their power and

60. See id., charts facing 608, 700, 706, 716.

Bank trust departments hold common stock in three types of account: private trust (including estate) accounts; employee-benefit (normally, pension) accounts; and agency (custodial) accounts. Reporting banks had total trust assets of $253.3 billion, of which 49.8 percent was held for private trusts, 28.8 percent was held in employee-benefit accounts, and 21.4 percent was held in agency accounts. The Institutional Investor Study reported that about 80 percent of the common stock held by bank trust departments was held in the first two types of account. 2 Institutional Investor Study, supra note 48, at 420-421, 430 (Table V-5). Banks had some form of voting authority in 97 percent of the large private trust accounts, 92 percent of the large employee-benefit accounts, 47 percent of the large personal agency accounts, and 36 percent of the large institutional and corporate agency accounts, in a surveyed sample. 2 id. at 438 (Table V-13). In the large-trust category, the banks had sole voting authority over portfolio stock in 37 percent of the cases, consulted on voting in 41 percent of the cases, and voted absent instruction in 17 percent of the cases. In the large-employee-benefit category, the bank had sole voting authority in 81 percent of the cases, consulted in 2 percent, and voted absent instruction in 7 percent. In the large-personal-agency category, the banks had sole voting authority in 12 percent of the cases, consulted in 3 percent, and voted absent instruction in 22 percent. In the large-institutional-and-corporate-agency category, the banks had sole voting authority in 15 percent, consulted in 8 percent, and voted absent instruction in 10 percent.

Even where a bank does not have a sole, shared, or contingent right to vote portfolio stock, as in many agency accounts, it probably has a voice in voting, since one major reason for setting up such accounts is to get the bank's investment advice. See id. at 421.

sophistication, institutional investors owe an obligation to their fellow shareholders to oversee corporate managers and to effect management changes when necessary.[61] Generally speaking, the institutional investors have taken the position that their primary obligation lies to their own beneficiaries, not to their fellow shareholders in portfolio companies; that they have neither the time nor the skills to exercise an oversight function; and that a company whose management should be changed is normally an unsound investment, so that an investor which does not like incumbent management should switch out of the investment as quickly as possible, rather than stay in and try to accomplish a change.[62] Some of these arguments appear overstated. There are undoubtedly many cases in which a corporation's assets outshine its management and an institution's position is too large to be liquidated except at a substantial loss, so that it would do better to try to change management than to sell the stock.[63] It seems likely that there have been additional, unstated, reasons for the institutions' promanagement position, including obedience to the mores of the financial community,[64] a desire to stay on good terms with management in order to promote a free flow of inside information,[65] and in the case of certain institutions, particularly banks, a desire to obtain or retain business in their noninvestor capacities. Nevertheless, the position that the primary duty of a financial institution is to protect the interests of its own benefici-

61. See, e.g., D. Baum & N. Stiles, The Silent Partners 149 and passim (1965); SEC, Public Policy Implications of Investment Company Growth, H. R. Rep. No. 2274, 87th Cong., 2d Sess. 27, 307-311 (1966); Wharton School of Finance and Commerce, A Study of Mutual Funds, H.R. Rep. No. 2274, 87th Cong., 2d Sess. 24-27, 399-428 (1962) (hereinafter cited as Wharton Study); Symposium, Mutual Funds as Investors of Large Pools of Money, 115 U. Pa. L. Rev. 669, 673-682 (1967).

62. See, e.g., Wharton Study, supra note 61, at 418-419; Brown, The Institutional Investor as Shareholder, in Duke Conference on Securities Regulation 207, 210-212, 217-219, 223-224; Buek, Trust Companies and Banks as Institutional Investors, in Duke Conference of Securities Regulation 147, 156 (R. Mundheim ed. 1964); Symposium, supra note 61, at 675-682. Another argument is that selling shares itself constitutes a sanction against management. Cf. Manne, Current Views on the "Modern Corporation," 38 U. Det. L.J. 559, 572 n. 35 (1961).

63. Cf. Wharton Study, supra note 61, at 26-27; Louis, The Mutual Funds Have The Votes, Fortune, May 1967, at 205.

64. Cf. Brown, supra note 62, at 217 ("positive action [against management] . . . is never pleasant. . . ."); Manning, Book Review, 67 Yale L.J. 1477, 1486 (1968).

65. See Wharton Study, supra note 61, at 418-419; Herman & Safanda, Proxy Voting by Commercial Bank Trust Departments, 90 Bank. L.J. 91, 103-105 (1973).

aries, and that such institutions are in any event not equipped to oversee management, seems essentially sound.[66]

However, voting on structural changes in portfolio corporations involves much different considerations. Although the staffs of financial institutions may not have the time or the skills to oversee business decisions, structural decisions occur only infrequently and tend to involve precisely the kind of financial analysis at which such staffs are expert.[67] Similarly, a decision to reject a proposed structural change in a portfolio corporation is perfectly consistent with confidence in the way the corporation's business is being managed. Indeed, the proposed change may be rejected just because the portfolio corporation is sounder as it stands than it would be if the proposed structural change were made. Finally, although an institutional investor may have no obligation to its fellow shareholders to retain a bad investment, it does have a clear obligation to its own beneficiaries to make sound decisions in connection with the investments it holds. Therefore, unless an institutional investor is prepared to sell every time a structural change is proposed, it is under a fiduciary obligation to use its best judgment in voting on the matter. And this merely reinforces what should be its own self-interest, that is, to maximize its investment performance.

It is therefore to be expected that institutional investors would give serious study to proposals for structural changes, and the available data indicates that this expectation is borne out to a significant extent in practice. For example, the *Wharton Study* of mutual funds found that proxies raising more-than-routine issues, or issues involving policy questions, tended to get careful scrutiny:

> Particularly among the very large companies, fairly elaborate routines have been sometimes developed whereby proxy requests are automatically turned over to industry specialists, who initially examine each proxy statement. Where the agenda involves issues calling for more careful consideration, the industry specialist usually prepares a memorandum on the issues, along with his recommendations, which are then taken up by an officer or committee of officers. This is roughly the

66. See Wharton Study, supra note 61, at 26.

67. See Brown, supra note 62, at 214-215; Louis, supra note 63, at 150; Enstam & Kamen, Control and The Institutional Investor, 23 Bus. Law. 289, 300 (1968); cf. Mundheim, The British Experience: Institutions as Shareholders, The Institutional Investor, January 1968, at 36.

procedure followed by MIT, Investors Diversified Services, Keystone Custodian Funds, and National Securities & Research Corp.

A more common procedure is one in which proxy solicitations are referred to an officer delegated to handle them, who refers them where deemed necessary to the research staff of the company. Solicitations received by Dividend Shares, e.g., are scrutinized by [the officer in charge of portfolio administration] before being approved for execution. In cases where further study appears indicated, the appropriate industry specialist of the investment adviser is requested to investigate and report his findings. Where basic policy questions are involved, the matter is discussed with the investment committee of the company. . . .

Open-end companies have shown a greater willingness to oppose portfolio company managements on matters affecting the voting, preemption, and income rights of shareholders. . . . The Wellington Fund has voted regularly against proposals to eliminate preemptive rights of shareholders. . . . MIT, National Securities Series, and others, have voted on several different occasions against changes in the voting rights of common stockholders, reduced preemptive rights, increases in common stock issues, the issuance of convertible bonds or preference shares, and similar matters.[68]

Similarly, the SEC's *Institutional Investor Study* reported that most banks have established procedures for distinguishing between routine and nonroutine matters. The *Study* also found that during the period January 1, 1967-September 30, 1969, 215 surveyed institutions recorded 584 votes against management proposals (including 351 by bank trust departments), and 262 abstentions (including 183 by bank trust departments).[69] These numbers provide only a crude index of the influence of institutional investors in their shareholder capacities. The very fact that institutions are ready to cast negative votes in appropriate cases undoubtedly helps shape managerial proposals. Furthermore, in many cases a management proposal may be killed by institutional shareholders before it even comes to a vote. For example, the *Wharton Study* reported that prospective mergers of portfolio companies are frequently discussed between the companies and

68. Wharton Study, supra note 61, at 418-420.

69. 5 Institutional Investor Study, supra note 48, at 2752-2755. See also Morgan Guaranty Trust Company, Report of the Trust and Investment Division 13 (1972) (Morgan Guaranty voted against management proposals, or in favor of shareholder proposals opposed by management, fourteen times in 1970 and eight times in 1971). For earlier, more random data, see Louis, supra note 63, at 207; Duke Conference on Securities Regulation, supra note 62, at 225.

the larger mutual funds. One such fund reported that "[i]n cases where [we are] a large holder (and this is the usual case) companies almost invariably submit merger proposals for informal consideration prior to the formal making of the proposal."[70] The *Institutional Investor Study* surveyed the participation of 215 institutional investors in connection with acquisitions involving 109 specified corporations during the period January 1, 1968-September 30, 1969, and reported that 26 of the institutions had expressed their views to portfolio corporations one or more times in connection with such acquisitions, and that in 28 instances the participation had an impact.[71] And a poll of 300 listed companies conducted in 1970 for the American Stock Exchange showed that 46 percent receive "suggestions" from institutional shareholders on such matters as mergers, acquisitions, and financings, and that of those corporations which are more-than-15-percent owned by institutions, 63 percent received such suggestions.[72]

The tendency of institutional investors to exercise an independent judgment on structural changes seems likely to increase with the passage of time.[73] Mutual funds have on several occasions gone so far as to vote for insurgent directorial nominees.[74] The decisions in *SEC v. Texas Gulf Sulphur Company,*[75] *Mitchell v. Texas Gulf Sulphur Company,*[76] and the proceedings growing out of the use by Merrill Lynch and others of inside information re-

70. Wharton Study, supra note 61, at 426.

71. 5 Institutional Investor Study, supra note 48, at 2755-2762, 2769 (Table XV-48(2)).

72. Welles, Are the Big Banks Too Big?, Instl. Investor, Dec. 1973, at 73, 175, 181. See also SEC, Public Policy Implications of Investment Company Growth, supra note 61, at 309-310.

73. Cf. Investor Responsibility Research Center, Inc., How Institutions Voted on Shareholder Resolutions – 1974; Ford Fund Shifts Proxy Practices, N.Y. Times, May 20, 1972, at 39, col. 4; Two Big Funds Decide To Split Proxy Votes on Activist Proposals, Wall St. J., May 2, 1972, at 6, col. 2; Dreyfus Leverage's Holders Support GM on 4 Proxy Proposals, Wall St. J., May 21, 1971, at 3, col. 4; Yale Will Take Activist Role as Investor, N.Y. Times, April 14, 1972, at 1, col. 1; Fund Backs Move Seeking GM Data, Wall St. J., May 1, 1971, at 68, col. 1; First Pennsylvania Backs 1 of 3 Proposals by GM Citizens' Group, Wall St. J., April 14, 1971, at 4, col. 4; Abacus Fund to Oppose Merger of Security, Royal National Banks, Wall St. J., Feb. 19, 1970, at 13, col. 2.

74. See SEC, Public Policy Implications of Investment Company Growth, supra note 61, at 309; Louis, supra note 63, at 150.

75. 401 F.2d 883 (2d Cir. 1968), cert. denied sub. nom. Coates v. SEC, 394 U.S. 976 (1969).

76. 466 F.2d 90 (10th Cir.), cert. denied, 404 U.S. 1004 (1971).

lating to Douglas Aviation,[77] are likely to eat away the amount of inside information flowing from management to institutional investors, thereby eroding one economic basis for a predisposition to support management. Finally, as institutional investors soak up ever larger amounts of stock, they come under increasing pressure to maximize performance by cultivating their existing investments rather than switching into new ones, because of the difficulty in liquidating enormous dollar holdings and the fact that alternative investments of equal attraction may not be readily available.[78]

Some concern has been expressed over whether the concentration of shareholdings in institutional hands is consonant with sound public policy.[79] Certainly these shareholdings pose serious problems, since the managers of financial institutions are often subject to severe conflict-of-interest problems resulting from their ties to portfolio corporations through other capacities, as in the case of commercial banks, which are lenders and pension-fund trustees as well as shareholders.[80] But given a choice between highly concentrated institutional shareholdings and highly dispersed individual shareholdings, the former seems preferable, because that alternative at least gives some hope of a check — a

77. Financial Industrial Fund, Inc. v. McDonnell Douglas Corp., [1970-71 Transfer Binder] CCH Fed. Sec. L. Rep. ¶93,004 (D. Colo. 1971), revd. on other grounds, 474 F.2d 514 (10th Cir.), cert. denied, 414 U.S. 874 (1973); Shapiro v. Merill, Lynch, Pierce, Fenner & Smith, Inc., 495 F.2d 228 (2d Cir. 1974); Investors Management Co., [1970-71 Transfer Binder] CCH Fed. Sec. L. Rep. ¶78,163 (SEC 1971); Merill, Lynch, Pierce, Fenner & Smith, Inc., [1967-69 Transfer Binder] CCH Fed. Sec. L. Rep. ¶77,629 (SEC 1968).

78. See Sobieski, In Support of Cumulative Voting, 15 Bus. Law. 316, 321 (1960); Rockefeller, Address before the Special Conference for Financial Executives of the American Management Association, quoted in D. Baum & N. Stiles, supra note 61, at 80; Big-block Buyers May Speak Up, Bus. Week. Nov. 26, 1966, at 139, 140; Yen of Big Investors to Buy Growth Stocks Alarms Some Analysts, Wall St. J., March 2, 1974, at 1, col. 6. According to the Wall Street Journal article, "So many shares of International Business Machines, Eastman Kodak, Procter & Gamble, Minnesota Mining & Manufacturing, Merck, Avon Products and Xerox, to mention but a few, are in the hands of institutions that it has been estimated it would take 10 to 15 years for these institutions to sell some of their holdings."

79. See, e.g., Huge Sums Managed By Bank Trust Units Stir up Controversy, Wall St. J., Jan. 7, 1975, at 1, col. 6.

80. See id; Bialkin, Eisenberg, Paul, O'Boyle, & Loomis, Conflicts of Interest and the Regulation of Securities, 28 Bus. Law. 545, 546-558 (1973) (remarks of Professor Eisenberg); Herman & Safanda, Commercial Bank Trust Departments and the "Wall," 14 B.C. Ind. & Comm. L. Rev. 21 (1972); Herman & Safanda, Proxy Voting by Commercial Bank Trust Departments, supra note 65; Lybecker, Regulation of Bank Trust Department Activities, 82 Yale L.J. 977 (1973).

countervailing force – to management, while the latter alternative does not.[81] As the SEC stated in its *Investment Trusts Report:*

> Investment companies may serve the useful role of representatives of the great number of inarticulate and ineffective individual investors in industrial corporations in which investment companies are also interested. Throughout the course of the existence of such industrial corporations, various problems are presented to their stockholders which require a degree of knowledge of financial and management practices not possessed by the average stockholder. Investment companies by virtue of their research facilities and specialized personnel are not only in a position to adequately appraise these situations but also have the financial means to make their support or opposition effective. These investment companies can perform the function of sophisticated investors, disassociated from the management of their portfolio companies. They can appraise the activities of the management critically and expertly, and in that manner not only serve their own interests but the interest of the other public stockholders.[82]

The conflict-of-interest problem is a real one, but it can be operated on by techniques which have not yet been deployed. Probably the ideal solution would be to prohibit the joinder of trust business and commercial banking entirely,[83] in the same way that the Glass-Steagall Act already prohibits the joinder of investment and commercial banking.[84] If that is politically or economically unfeasible, the banks should at least be required to spin off their trust activities to a trust subsidiary, as some banks have indeed already done.[85] It could then be made unlawful for any

81. Cf. Solomon, Institutional Investors: Stock Market Impact and Corporate Control, 42 Geo. Wash. L. Rev. 761, 781-786 (1974).

82. SEC, 5 Investment Trusts and Investment Companies, H.R. Doc. No. 246, 77th Cong., 1st Sess. 371 (1941).

83. See Bialkin, Eisenberg, Paul, O'Boyle, & Loomis, supra note 80, at 555-556 (remarks of Professor Eisenberg).

84. Banking Act of 1933, §§20, 21, 32, 48 Stat. 188, 189, 194 (1933), 12 U.S.C. §§78, 377, 378 (1970).

85. See Bialkin, Eisenberg, Paul, O'Boyle, & Loomis, supra note 80, at 556, n. 46 (remarks of Professor Eisenberg).

It has been argued that "[b]anks which are outside major money centers, and which therefore have smaller capital bases, would not be capable of spinning off sufficient assets to allow new trust companies to survive. Estate planning in many sections of the United States places great importance on the availability of a corporate trustee whose services would be lost if such trust companies failed." Lybecker, Regulation of Bank Trust Department Investment Activities, 82 Yale L.J. 977, 1002 n. 131 (1973). See also Report of the President's Commission on Financial Structure and Regulation [Hunt

bank executive or employee not in the subsidiary's full-time employ to attempt to influence its investment or voting decisions, and for any person in the subsidiary's employ to discuss any proposed or completed investment or voting decision with nonsubsidiary bank personnel, except insofar as disclosure of such decisions is made to the public at large.

Commission] 104 (1971); Griswold, Divorcement of Trust Functions From Commercial Banks, 63 Trust Companies 293 (1936). As to a requirement of complete divestiture, the argument at most indicates that an exception should be made for banks whose trust assets fall below some designated minimum; since trust assets are highly concentrated, such an exception might very well be tolerable. Moreover, this argument is completely inapplicable to a requirement that trust business be done through a separate subsidiary, since a subsidiary could share capital facilities with its parent.

6

Voting Rights in Publicly Held Corporations

A NORMATIVE MODEL

§6.1. The Significance of the Data

The managerialist model of the corporation is one in which the shareholder's voting right appears to lack meaning, because shareholdings are atomistically dispersed and "the average shareholder" therefore owns only a microscopic amount of stock. Examination of the data, however, shows that this model is empirically unfounded. About 43,000 corporations in this country can be considered publicly held. Roughly speaking, probably 8000 of these corporations have less than 100 shareholders, 26,500 have 100 to 499 shareholders, 5000 have 500 to 1499 shareholders, 1700 have 1500 to 2999 shareholders, and only 1800 have more than 3000 shareholders. In each of these strata, shareholdings are very heavily concentrated. In probably half or more of the corporations with less than 1000 shareholders, the ten largest record holders hold 50 percent or more of the stock. In probably half or more of the corporations with 1000 to 2999 shareholders, the ten largest record shareholders hold 30 to 40 percent of the stock. Even in the 1800 or so corporations with 3000 or more shareholders, only a small fraction of the stock is owned by unsophisticated investors with small investments. Almost half of the stock in these corporations is in the hands of highly sophisticated institutional investors, whose holdings are large enough to justify the time required to analyze proposed structural changes, and who are or can be made interested in passing upon such changes. Most of the balance is held by wealthy individual shareholders with very substantial shareholdings, who may be assumed to be either financially sophisticated themselves or guided by professionals in their investment decisions. In fact, even in the 500 largest industrials, 30 to 40 percent of the stock of any given corporation is probably held by a very small number of shareholders, and in at least one-third of the 500 largest industrials, 10 percent or more of the stock is in the hands of a single individual, a family, or a group of business associates. In short the "average shareholder," who holds center stage in the theories of so many commentators, is only an extra in the real corporate world. The shareholdings of the average shareholder are negligible, and if all the shareholdings of all the average shareholders are aggregated the result is still negligible, because the ownership of stock is very highly concentrated. Most of the stock in any given publicly held corporation is in the hands of a relatively small number of sophisticated holders who know how to interpret financial data and can be expected to have a strong interest in structural changes.[1]

1. Even the case that shareholders with very small holdings do not regard voting as an important process is yet to be proved. Many such shareholders seem to regularly sign and return their proxies. This suggests, at least, that they regard voting as a meaningful process. It is only natural for a small shareholder to support management proposals in the absence of a contest, since it would be an inefficient allocation of such a shareholder's time to review every management proposal. Cf. R. A. Gordon, Business Leadership in the Large Corporation 305-307 (Calif. ed. 1961); Manne, Current Views on the "Modern Corporation," 38 U. Det. L.J. 539, 577, n. 54. Where, however, the presence of a contest concerning a structural change alerts the small shareholder to the presence of a problem, it is far from clear that he will support management by reflex. Within recent years a number of proposals for structural change in large corporations have failed of passage, have been withdrawn because of shareholder opposition, or have passed by only narrow margins. See, e.g., LTV Holders Reject Plan to Restructure Via Stock Changes, Wall St. J., June 18, 1974, at 14, col. 3; Charter Change Loses at General Fireproofing Co., Wall St. J., Dec. 4, 1972, at 8, col. 2; National General, Penn Life Merger Is Off, But Clouds Now Hang Over Both Companies, Wall St. J., Sept. 11, 1972, at 28, col. 1; Rank Withdraws Watney Mann Bid, N.Y. Times, June 9, 1972, at 49, col. 2; Allied Control Holders Defeat Tie With Gould, Sept. 24, 1971, at 6, col. 2; Royal National, Blaming Proxy Crossfire, Calls Off Merger With Security National, Wall St. J., Oct. 28, 1970, at 12, col. 2; AVC Corp.'s Holders Refuse to Authorize New Preferred Stock, Wall St. J., May 5, 1970, at 16, col. 2; Allis and Signal End Merger Plan, N.Y. Times, January 17, 1968, at 61, col. 2; Alpha Portland Surrenders In Its Pursuit of Proxies, Wall Street J., May 2, 1968, at 6, col. 4; Cook Electric Drops Merger Plan, Cites Opposition by Lab for Electronics Group, Wall Street J., January 26, 1968, at 12, col. 1; Gearhart-Owen Meeting Adjourned Due to Low Number of Proxies, Wall St. J., May 27, 1968, at 7, col. 2; General Public Utilities Drops Consideration of Payout Policy Shift, Wall Street J., April 2, 1968, at 11, col. 1; Missing Proxies Upsetting Annual Meetings At Unusual Rate; Brokers Logjam Blamed, Wall Street J., May 8, 1968, at 8, col. 2; Plan for Southwestern Life, American General Merger Is Called Off, Wall Street J., July 24, 1968, at 5, col. 3; Republic Investors Merger Spurned by Shareholders, Wall Street J., July 16, 1968, at 20,

§6.2. The Value of an Inconsequential Vote

The discussion so far has concerned two aspects of shareholders' voting rights in publicly held corporations: the degree to which that right reflects the interests and expectations of such shareholders, and the value of that right as a potential check on managerial self-interest and improvidence in structural decisions. A third aspect is yet to be considered: the degree to which the voting right provides a potential check on managerial inefficiency. Although this aspect of the voting right occasionally finds direct expression, as where incumbent directors are ousted by a proxy fight, its most important expression is manifested indirectly, through the institution of takeover bids.

Assuming that there is a relationship between efficiency of corporate management and the price of the corporation's stock,[2] then the stock of a corporation which is inefficiently managed will tend to be underpriced in relation to its potential value. When the differential is sufficiently large an outsider may attempt to acquire sufficient shares to obtain control, with the ultimate objective of installing efficient management and thereby causing the acquired stock to appreciate to its full potential value.[3] Takeovers based on such considerations tend to benefit the public as a whole, by increasing the likelihood that economic resources will be used in the most efficient manner; shareholders of the target corporation, since the outsider will usually pay a premium over market price to acquire the shares; and shareholders as a class, since the very possibility of a takeover may be expected to stimulate management efficiency. The entire takeover concept, however, is predicated on the shareholder's voting right, because unless the outsider can

---

col. 4; Transamerica Offer to Buy Management Assistance is Canceled, Wall Street J., August 9, 1967, at 4, col. 2.

Of course, the small shareholder cannot determine an outcome with his vote, and he knows it; but the individual citizen also cannot normally determine an election, and knows it, and yet casts his vote and regards it as important that he does so. Speculation concerning the psychology of shareholder voting has far outraced the data.

2. See Manne, Cash Tender Offers for Shares – A Reply to Chairman Cohen, 1967 Duke L.J. 231, 236; Manne, Mergers and the Market for Corporate Control, 73 J. Pol. Econ. 110, 112 & n. 10 (1965).

3. See Manne, Mergers and the Market for Corporate Control, supra note 2, at

obtain voting control he cannot oust inefficient incumbent management, and therefore has no incentive to acquire shares in the first place.

The desirability of facilitating takeovers prompted by considerations of efficiency indicates that the shareholder's voting right may be significant even if shares are atomistically dispersed, since a third party can reaggregate dispersed votes into a control block. Perhaps more important as a practical matter, the desirability of facilitating such takeovers indicates the importance of maximizing the efficacy of the voting right by statutorily insuring either that directors are removable without cause, or that structural changes can be accomplished without board approval, or both. For example, assume that in a given corporation neither of these conditions is met, and the board is classified into several staggered terms. In that case an outsider may be unable to gain immediate control of the corporation even if he acquires a majority of its stock. Under such circumstances no outsider is likely to attempt a takeover, since ordinarily no one would invest heavily in an inefficiently managed company if he must lock in his investment for a substantial period of time before installing new management.[4]

Similarly, stock combinations sometimes provide an alternative route to the conventional cash takeover, and may be more desirable both from the shareholders' and the outsider's perspective.[5] However, this route may not be feasible where the board's approval is required to effect a combination and the board cannot be removed from office during its term. In such cases, even if management chooses not to block the combination entirely it has power to hold the combination hostage so as to extort, through

113; Manne, Cash Tender Offers, supra note 2, at 236; Manne, Some Theoretical Aspects of Share Voting, 64 Colum. L. Rev. 1427, 1430-1431 (1964).

4. See, e.g., Tankersley v. Albright, 374 F. Supp. 538 (N.D. Ill. 1974); Elgin Natl. Industries v. Chemtron Corp., 299 F. Supp. 367 (D. Del. 1969); Instrument Systems Is Asking Its Holders to Make It Even Harder to Oust Directors, Wall St. J., Feb. 24, 1975, at 9, col. 1; cf. Gower, Some Contrasts Between British and American Corporation Law, 69 Harv. L. Rev. 1369, 1389 (1958); Yoran, Restraints on Incumbent Directors in Intracorporate Battles for Control, 7 U. Rich. L. Rev. 431, 440-445 (1973).

5. See Manne, Mergers and the Market for Corporate Control, supra note 2, at 117-119; Manne, Some Theoretical Aspects of Share Voting, supra note 3, at 1432-1434, 1437-1439.

unduly favorable employment contracts and the like, some portion of the premium which would otherwise go to the shareholders.[6]

§6.3. A Normative Model

In light of the need for a check on managerial self-interest and inefficiency, and the manner in which shareholdings in publicly held corporations are actually distributed, the rules governing the allocation of decisionmaking power between shareholders and management should not differ substantially from those governing closely held corporations in which management and ownership are not identical. In two important ways, however, the models diverge. First, in the publicly held corporation all business decisions should be solely for management, whether in or out of the ordinary course, because as the number of shareholders grows larger and the business grows more complex, the shareholders are more likely to expect management to make all such decisions, and it grows increasingly difficult to distinguish between what is in and what is out of the ordinary course.[7] Second, in the publicly held corporation true shareholder agreement is all but impossible. "[S]tockholders . . . [in such corporations] do not know of the provisions of the articles of incorporation, and, generally, if they did, they would not realize what the consequences of such provisions might be until it is too late."[8] Therefore, statutory decisionmaking rules, although based in whole or in part on shareholder expectations, should not be made subject to variation by private action; that is, should be mandatory rather than suppletory.

6. Cf. Manne, Mergers and the Market for Corporate Control, supra note 2, at 118; Manne, Some Theoretical Aspects of Share Voting, supra note 3, at 1437-1438.

7. Cf. Garrett, Attitudes on Corporate Democracy – A Critical Analysis, 51 Nw. U.L. Rev. 310, at 310-311 (1956).

8. Harris, The Model Business Corporation Act – Invitation to Irresponsibility?, 50 Nw. U.L. Rev. 1, 9 (1955).

7

The Place of the Appraisal Right in a Normative Model of the Corporation

§7.1. The Assault on Appraisal Rights

So far the discussion has been concerned solely with voting rights. There is, however, a second formal right accorded to a shareholder who dissents from certain fundamental or structural changes: the right to require the corporation to buy his shares at their "value," "fair value," "fair market value," or the like, as determined through appraisal proceedings.[1] If the corporate form is viewed through the prism of any other form of business organization, this right may seem very unusual. Moreover, no such right is reflected in the received legal model of the corporation. Does the appraisal right then have a place in a normative model? Within the last few years, the view seems to have been growing that it does not. Few states have expanded the right; many have cut it back.[2] In large part, the assault on the appraisal right has found its intellectual justification in an extensive critique by Manning[3] which is a counterpart to his critique of the voting right. An examination of his position therefore provides a starting point for

1. See, e.g., Cal. Corp. Code §4300 (West Supp. 1974) ("fair market value"); Del. Code Ann. tit. 8, §262 (1974) ("value"); ABA Model Bus. Corp. Act §81 (1969 rev.) ("fair value").

2. See, e.g., text at notes 29-30, infra.

3. Manning, The Shareholder's Appraisal Remedy: An Essay For Frank Coker, 72 Yale L.J. 223 (1962). See also Folk, De Facto Mergers in Delaware: Hariton v. Arco Electronics, Inc., 49 Va. L. Rev. 1261 (1963); McDonough, The Appraisal Remedy for Dissenting Shareholders in Iowa and the De Facto Merger Doctrine: Rath v. Rath Packing Company, 16 Drake L. Rev. 22 (1966).

analysis of whether the appraisal right does indeed have a place in a normative model, and if so, what that place should be.

The thrust of Manning's critique is twofold: that the appraisal right ill-serves both the shareholder who asserts it, and the corporation against which it is asserted.[4] On the shareholder side, Manning notes that the procedure for asserting the right is highly technical, drawn-out, and expensive; that if the corporation's stock is publicly traded the courts will not go beyond an inquiry into market price (a proposition which the cases do not fully support),[5] while if it is not publicly traded the amount of the award is unpredictable; and that when the award is finally made it will be taxable, while the transaction dissented from may very well have been tax-free to the shareholder. Generally speaking, these points are accurate, although some of them are equally applicable to many other legal rights which must be asserted through litigation. However, they are hardly dispositive, because they indicate not that the right is unsound, but merely that its usefulness, like that of all legal rights, may be limited by the boundaries of reality and legislative drafting.

When, however, Manning turns to the effect of the appraisal right on the corporation, he does conjure up problems intended to bring the very soundness of the right into question. First, he argues that the assertion of appraisal rights may wipe out the enterprise.

> Even a relatively modest number of shareholders claiming the appraisal remedy may constitute a severe economic threat to the corporate enterprise. . . . If some shareholders go the appraisal road, a sudden and largely unpredictable drain is imposed upon the corporation's cash position. This demand for a cash pay-out to shareholders often comes at a time when the enterprise is in need of every liquid dollar it can put its hands on.

4. Manning actually begins his critique with another point – that the presence of the appraisal remedy has often influenced the courts to cut down the availability, or even preclude the granting, of other types of relief, particularly injunctive relief based on unfairness. The true extent of this tendency is very difficult to determine, see Vorenberg, Exclusiveness of the Dissenting Stockholder's Appraisal Right, 77 Harv. L. Rev. 1189 (1964), but in any event the problem is legislatively remediable. Cf. Lattin, A Reappraisal of Appraisal Statutes, 38 Mich. L. Rev. 1165 (1940).

5. See In re Kaufman, Alsberg & Co., 30 Misc. 2d 1025, 1030-1031, 220 N.Y.S.2d 151, 158 (Sup. Ct. 1961), affd. per curiam, 15 App. Div. 2d 468, 222 N.Y.S.2d 305 (1961). See also In re Olivetti Underwood Co., 246 A.2d 800 (Del. Ch. 1968).

> Some kind of corporate surgery is going on: the enterprise is much more apt to be in need of a blood transfusion than a leeching. . . . [T]he period following the closing will likely be a period of intense activity as a general reshuffling takes place in the administrative, productive, and distributional arrangements of the combined enterprise. The management hopes that in time these steps will prove economic; but in the short run many of them will require a cash in-put.[6]

The gravity of the "threat to the corporate enterprise" seems highly exaggerated. No evidence is adduced that corporations involved in mergers are apt to be "in need of a blood transfusion." My own observation has been that most mergers involve two perfectly healthy enterprises. Of course, even in that case there may be a short-run need for a cash input, but it is seldom material. Furthermore, in considering the appraisal right from the shareholder's point of view, Manning stresses that the procedure by which the right must be asserted is a long and weary one. If that is so, then by the time a dissenter is actually paid off the short-run period of adjustment will be far behind.

Next, Manning argues that the payments made to dissenters may lead creditors to start a run on the corporation's treasury.

> This may be a time, too, when uneasy trade creditors, suppliers, or banks may decide that they would be happier to have cash in their pockets rather than a claim against the still untried combined enterprise. The creditor of Corporation A suddenly finds an unknown horde of creditors of Corporation B standing equally beside him, and, typically, he knows little or nothing about the amount of liquidity of the assets that Corporation B has brought to the marriage. The creditors of Corporation B feel the same apprehension about Corporation A. Both are inclined to get a little itchy for cash. When, at precisely the wrong psychological moment, the corporation ladles out a dollop of dollars to its shareholders under the appraisal statutes, the reaction of creditors may be one of consternation and the run begins.[7]

Again, no evidence is adduced, and again my own observation has been that while the "trade creditors, suppliers, [and] banks" are indeed at the door following a merger, they are soliciting, not pounding. Their object is not to get out, but to get in – at best, to garner all the business of the reconstituted enterprise, at worst, to

6. Manning, The Shareholder's Appraisal Remedy, supra note 3, at 234.
7. Id. at 234.

retain the business they had. Furthermore, the time when payment must actually be made to dissenting shareholders will, as Manning's earlier point emphasizes, lie in the dim, distant future.

Finally, Manning argues that the uncertainty as to how many shareholders will dissent may itself raise serious problems.

> Even though the Company may be economically very strong, it may not be able to go ahead with the merger at all if the aggregated claim of dissenting shareholders under the appraisal statutes comes to a high figure. This means that for purposes of planning its course of action, and deciding whether to go ahead with the merger, the management needs to know as soon as possible what the total cash demand is likely to be. And here is the rub. The answer obviously depends upon the claim procedure prescribed in the appraisal statute. But under the procedures of many of the statutes, claimants are not required to file their claims until some time after the merger. The situation is both circular and dangerous.[8]

In practice, however, this potential uncertainty hardly ever turns out to be a real problem, because if the situation is threatening, the lawyers will insert in the relevant agreement a provision allowing one or both sides to back off prior to the closing if too many shareholders dissent.[9]

8. Id. at 235.

9. Manning states that these provisions "[Do] not fully solve the problem. They introduce an extraneous element of contingency into the transaction. They impose a severe bargaining disadvantage where only one of the participating companies thinks that it has a substantial number of potential dissenters: the shareholders and management of the unanimous company are not apt to be happy at seeing *their* cash siphoned off to shareholders of the other corporation immediately after the merger. Under some of the corporation statutes there are legitimate questions about the legal authority of the directors to move even under these contractual provisions.

"The availability of the kick-out tends to poison the whole atmosphere of the negotiation and to expose other terms of the transaction to continuous redickering. . . .

"It is not easy to ask the shareholders to approve an 'iffy' merger. It is not necessarily politic to explain all the implications of the kick-out clause in the proxy statement – and it may be dangerous to explain too little. The situation is prickly all around." Manning, The Shareholder's Appraisal Remedy, supra note 3, at 237-238.

Again, these problems are exaggerated. Such provisions seldom pose "a severe bargaining disadvantage," because normally agreements are negotiated on the premise that mass dissent will not take place. Such provisions are common, and there is no evidence that they "poison the whole atmosphere of the negotiation" or "expose other terms of the transaction to continuous redickering." Nor is there any evidence that corporations have the slightest hesitation in either asking or getting shareholders to approve agreements containing such a provision. Finally, the likelihood that such provisions are invalid is minimal. They appear to be permissible even in the absence of

Following this criticism of the way in which the appraisal right operates, Manning turns to a critical analysis of the types of transactions that give rise to the appraisal right in the first place — "triggering transactions," as he aptly calls them. For purposes of this analysis, Manning sets forth a number of transactions grouped into several lists and asks why some of them are triggering transactions while others are not. Thus the first list includes, among other things, a "Presidential heart attack" and "large scale disarmament."[10] Manning notes that the usual answer given to the question why events like these are not triggering transactions is that they are not brought about by the will of the majority. But, he says, this explanation is unsatisfactory, "for it leaves open the question: Why are we interested in protecting the investor against internal risks only?"[11]

Now it will be noted that this last question, "Why are we interested in protecting the investor against internal risks only," subtly but radically rephrases the original question, Why are we interested in protecting the investor only against transactions brought about by the will of the majority?, since a risk may be internal and yet not brought about by majority shareholders. Having shifted the issue in this way, Manning then develops a second list, consisting of just such internal but nonshareholder-created events — for example, "a demand by the relevant union for higher wages, accompanied by strike threat" and "a refusal by important suppliers to continue to supply the company."[12] Observing that the events on this second list do not trigger appraisal

---

statutory authority. See Hoit v. American Bantam Car Co., 69 F. Supp. 731, 734 (W.D. Pa. 1947); Zobel v. American Locomotive Co., 182 Misc. 323, 327-328, 44 N.Y.S.2d 33, 37 (Sup. Ct. 1943); Fuld, Some Practical Aspects of a Merger, 60 Harv. L. Rev. 1092, 1094-1099 (1947); cf. In re McKinney, 306 N.Y. 207, 117 N.E.2d 256 (1954). Furthermore, modern statutes commonly include provisions which give the board either absolute power to abandon a merger, see Cal. Corp. Code §4112 (West 1955), or power to abandon a merger if so authorized by the merger plan, see, e.g., Del. Code Ann. tit. 8, §251(d) (1974); Ill. Ann. Stat. ch. 32, §157.61(e) (Smith-Hurd Supp. 1974); N.Y. Bus. Corp. Law §903(b) (McKinney Supp. 1974); Ohio Rev. Code Ann. §1701.78(C)(2) (Page Supp. 1974); Pa. Stat. Ann. tit. 15, §1902(C) (Supp. 1974); ABA Model Bus. Corp. Act §73 (1969 rev.). See generally Note, Withdrawal of Fundamental Changes Before a Vote, an Unrecognized Compliment to Abandonment — A Proposed Change in Ohio's Abandonment Statute, 32 U. Cin. L. Rev. 380 (1963).

10. Manning, The Shareholder's Appraisal Remedy, supra note 3, at 241.

11. Id. at 242.

12. Id.

rights, Manning then draws three conclusions, which build upon each other: (1) The statutes "do not make the differentiation [between triggering and nontriggering transactions] in economic categories, but in lawyer's categories"; (2) It is "apparent that we are not dealing with an economic problem . . . [since] the economic risk to the shareholder does not turn on the question of who was responsible for the event giving rise to the risks"; (3) To "limit statutory concern to shareholders' and directors' acts is wholly arbitrary."[13]

The third conclusion, of course, poses the ultimate issue. The second is wrong on its face, since the fact that the appraisal right is not triggered by all economic risks in no way shows that the right is not intended to deal with an economic problem. What of the first conclusion – that the statutory differentiations between triggering and nontriggering transactions do not correspond to economic categories?

To support this assertion Manning develops an argument based on the theory that the crucial triggering transaction (at least from the point of view of understanding appraisal) is the merger, and that the reasons for giving appraisal rights in the case of merger are grounded in ideology and constitutional principles rather than economics:

> To the nineteenth-century mind . . . a corporate merger . . . involved a species of corporate assassination. . . . A three-dimensional thing, created by the sovereign legislature, had passed away. . . . But something else happened, too. The shareholders of Corporation A somehow became shareholders of Corporation B and no longer shareholders of Corporation A. The mere statement of such a preposterous proposition did violence to fundamental principles. How *could* a man who owned a horse suddenly find that he owned a cow? Furthermore, or perhaps this is but another statement of the same point, even if this transaction could somehow be brought off, surely it could not constitutionally be done without the owner's consent. . . .
>
> . . . When commercial pressures forced the enactment of the general merger statutes, the function of the appraisal statutes was clear. They met a conceptual and ideological problem – how to preserve the constitutionality of the merger statutes. The appraisal provisions were calculated to solve a purely conceptual need – to provide something for the shareholder who was about to undergo a *legal* trauma. . . .[14]

13. Id.
14. Id. at 246-247.

This thesis is open to question on several grounds:

First, Manning's argument that appraisal rights have a constitutional genesis is at best a minority view. Manning mistakenly asserts that the first appraisal statute was enacted by Pennsylvania in 1861 in response to an 1858 decision of the Pennsylvania Supreme Court[15] which suggested that an appraisal right was required to preserve the constitutionality of a merger statute.[16] However, Ohio had enacted rudimentary appraisal statutes even before 1858,[17] while some post-1858 merger and consolidation legislation omitted any provision for appraisal rights.[18] Most commentators hold the opinion that the legislatures conferred appraisal rights on dissenting shareholders as a matter of fairness, not as a matter of constitutional compulsion.[19] Ballantine seems to have gone about as far as one may fairly go on the basis of existing evidence when he said that "It is not easy to ascertain whether this remedy . . . is intended for the benefit and protection of the minority or for the benefit of the majority to remove any doubt about the constitutionality of fundamental changes without unanimous consent."[20]

Manning's argument that appraisal rights depend on the legal rather than the economic significance of transactions is also open to considerable doubt. Typically, the statutes provide appraisal rights for two types of corporate action: mergers, and sales of substantially all assets. Both of these actions tend to be structual in nature and highly significant economically: in fact, a sale of substantially all assets is solely an economic transaction, working no change at all on the legal entity. Of course, the appraisal statutes

15. Lauman v. Lebanon Valley R.R., 30 Pa. 42 (1858).

16. Manning, The Shareholder's Appraisal Remedy, supra note 3, at 246-247 n. 38.

17. Act of March 3, 1851, § 1, 49 Ohio Laws 94 (1851); Act of May 1, 1852, § § 21, 43, 48, 50 Ohio Laws 279-280, 287, 288 (1852); Act of April 10, 1856, § 10, 53 Ohio Laws 145-146 (1856).

18. See, e.g., Act of March 28, 1872, [1871-1872] Ill. Laws 487; Ch. 413, § 17, [1873] N.J. Acts 98.

19. See, e.g., Levy, Rights of Dissenting Shareholders to Appraisal and Payment, 15 Cornell L.Q. 420-421 (1930); Weiner, Payment of Dissenting Stockholders, 27 Colum. L. Rev. 547 (1927); cf. Chicago Corp. v. Munds, 20 Del. Ch. 142, 149, 172 A. 452, 455 (Ch. 1934). A constitutional origin does seem possible in Pennsylvania, cf. Lauman v. Lebanon Valley R.R., 30 Pa. 42 (1858).

20. Ballantine, Questions of Policy in Drafting a Modern Corporation Law, 19 Calif. L. Rev. 465, 482 (1931).

do not deal with all types of economically significant structural changes. To a large extent, however, the gaps in coverage may be due to the failure of the contemporary legislatures to keep up with modern corporate developments, rather than to gaps in the statutes as they were originally enacted. For example, if the statutes when enacted failed to deal with business combinations effected through an acquisition of stock, that may have been because at early common law the power of one corporation to hold stock in another was quite doubtful,[21] so that such acquisitions were uncommon. If the statutes when enacted failed to deal with corporate separations (that is, the transfer by a corporation of one of several businesses), that may have been because in the early days of corporate law most corporations were, by law or custom, single-purpose,[22] so that a corporate separation was an anomaly. Undoubtedly, modern legislatures have been remiss in their handling of corporate problems; but a distinction must be drawn between the corporate statutes as they look to us today, and the statutes as they looked to those who enacted them.

Finally, and most important, if we look at the statutes as a whole, rather than focusing solely on one aspect of the merger provisions, Manning's thesis – that the appraisal right is based on ideological and constitutional principles, not on economics – falls apart. If the thesis is correct, it should follow that: (1) A merger would not trigger appraisal rights for the shareholders of the surviving corporation, since the legal entity of the survivor need not be affected by a merger, and the only necessary effect of a merger on such shareholders is therefore an economic one; (2) An amendment of the certificate of incorporation should normally trigger appraisal rights, since it involves a change in the entity; (3) Dissolution should trigger appraisal rights, for the same reason; (4) A sale of all assets should not trigger appraisal rights, since it does not affect the entity, and its only effect on the shareholders of the seller is an economic one. The hard facts, however, are that in each case just the contrary is true. Under the statutes, a sale of substantially all assets usually triggers appraisal rights,[23] a merger

21. See chapter 17, note 7.

22. E. Latty & G. Frampton, Basic Business Associations – Cases, Text and Problems 312 (1963); A. A. Berle, Economic Power in A Free Society, in The Corporation Take-Over 86, 88 (A. Hacker ed. 1965).

23. See, e.g., Ill. Ann. Stat. ch. 32, § 157.73 (Smith-Hurd Supp. 1974); N.J. Stat. Ann. § 14A:11-1(1)(b) (Supp. 1974); N.Y. Bus. Corp. Law § 910(a)(1)(B) (McKinney

normally triggers appraisal rights even for the survivor's shareholders,[24] certificate amendment usually does not trigger appraisal rights,[25] and neither does dissolution.[26]

But even though Manning's specific criticisms are not well founded, we are still left with the larger question he raises: is the appraisal right desirable? In answering this question, it is once again necessary to separate closely and publicly held corporations.

§7.2. The Place of Appraisal Rights in Closely Held Corporations

To understand the real utility — and perhaps the real origin — of the appraisal right, we must return once more to the partnership form. It will be recalled that absent contrary agreement, decisions on matters outside the scope of the partnership business can be made only by unanimous consent, new partners cannot be admitted without unanimous consent, and partnerships

---

Supp. 1974); Ohio Rev. Code Ann. §1701.76 (Page 1964); Pa. Stat. Ann. tit. 15, §1311(D) (Supp. 1974); ABA Model Bus. Corp. Act §80(b) (1969 rev.).

24. See, e.g., Cal. Corp. Code §4123 (West 1955); Del. Code Ann. tit. 8, §262 (1974); Ill. Ann. Stat. ch. 32, §157.70 (Smith-Hurd Supp. 1974); Ohio Rev. Code Ann. §1701.84(B) (Page Supp. 1973); Pa. Stat. Ann. tit. 15, §1908(A) (Supp. 1974); ABA Model Bus. Corp. Act §80(a) (1969 rev.). Some of the merger statutes now explicitly incorporate a significance test, by providing that the survivor's shareholders do not have appraisal rights if less than a given percentage of the survivor's stock is issued in the merger and no change is made in the survivor's certificate. See section 14.2, infra. The New York statute provides that the survivor's shareholders do not have appraisal rights unless the merger involves a certificate amendment that would independently give rise to appraisal rights. See N.Y. Bus. Corp. Law §910(a)(i)(A)(2) (McKinney Supp. 1974); note 25, infra.

25. In New York, a certificate amendment gives rise to appraisal rights if it adversely affects the shareholder's interest by altering or abolishing a preference or a preemptive right; by creating, altering, or abolishing a redemption or sinking-fund provision; or by excluding or limiting a voting right. N.Y. Bus. Corp. Law. §806(b)(6) (McKinney Supp. 1974). In Ohio a certificate amendment gives rise to appraisal rights if it changes the terms of preferred stock in such a way as to substantially prejudice the holders of such stock, or to discharge, adjust, or eliminate rights to accrued undeclared dividends. Ohio Rev. Code Ann. §1701.74(A), (B) (Page Supp. 1973). In Pennsylvania a certificate amendment gives rise to appraisal rights if it eliminates cumulative voting. Pa. Stat. Ann. tit. 15, §1810 (Supp. 1974). Even in these cases, certificate amendment does not *in itself* give rise to appraisal rights. Instead, appraisal rights are triggered only by those amendments which in the legislature's judgment may have a material adverse impact.

26. Of course, a sale of substantially all assets in the course of dissolution may give rise to appraisal rights. See, e.g., N.Y. Bus. Corp. Law §1005(a)(3)(A) (McKinney 1963); ABA Model Business Corporation Act §80(b) (1969 rev.).

are normally short-lived and easy to dissolve. These various partnership incidents, although apparently disparate, are actually complementary. The veto power of each partner in matters outside the scope of the partnership business seriously restricts his copartners' freedom of action to make changes in the business that seem to them desirable and even necessary to meet changing conditions. This restriction might be intolerable except for the fact that each partner has agreed to the identity of his fellow veto-bearers, and that the timespan of such a veto is ordinarily short, since the remaining partners can either dissolve the partnership or await the end of its term and then reconstitute the enterprise along the desired lines.

But neither of the conditions making a veto tolerable in the partnership is normally present in the corporation: absent contrary agreement, the identity of fellow shareholders is not within a shareholder's control, and the duration of the enterprise is normally perpetual. Given those elements it is predictable that corporate law would permit a majority, or at least a high majority, to make structural changes even over the objection of minority shareholders. But just as a veto power might be intolerable in a corporation, so might be an unrestricted power in the majority to make structural changes, unless some method was provided whereby minority shareholders would not be locked into the restructured enterprise over their objections. The minority, in other words, should have the right to say to the majority, "We recognize your right to restructure the enterprise, provided you are willing to buy us out at a fair price if we object, so that we are not forced to participate in an enterprise other than the one contemplated at the outset of our mutual association." Seen from this perspective, the appraisal right is a mechanism admirably suited to reconcile, in the corporate context, the need to give the majority the right to make drastic changes in the enterprise to meet new conditions as they arise, with the need to protect the minority against being involuntarily dragged along into a drastically restructured enterprise in which it has no confidence.

This rationale does not explain all the legislative variations in appraisal rights, but it explains a good many. It explains, for example, why events not precipitated by majority shareholders – whether external, such as large-scale disarmament, or internal, such as a strike – do not trigger appraisal rights. It explains why the shareholders of the survivor in a merger usually have appraisal rights: a merger normally involves a restructuring of the survivor's enterprise even where it does not involve a restructuring of the entity. It explains why a sale of substantially all assets usually triggers appraisal rights: the transaction invariably involves a complete restructuring of the nature of the seller's business (unless it is in the ordinary course of business, in which case it would not ordinarily trigger appraisal rights[27]). Finally, it explains why dissolution does not trigger appraisal rights: in a dissolution everybody is getting out, and the minority shareholder does not need the protection of a mechanism which is designed to protect him against being locked into a restructured enterprise.

At least as concerns the closely held corporation, then, the appraisal right falls naturally into place to complete a normative model of decisionmaking.[28] But it should be noted that appraisal rights and voting rights need not always go together. For example, the appraisal right might appropriately be reserved for cases involving a relatively drastic restructuring of a continuing enterprise, while the voting right is appropriate in some cases where the restructuring is less than drastic or the enterprise does not continue. Some cases where only one of the two rights seem appropriate will be explored below in Part IV.

§7.3. The Place of Appraisal Rights in Publicly Held Corporations

A shareholder in a closely held corporation ordinarily cannot withdraw from the enterprise in response to a structural change unless he has an appraisal right: there will normally be no market for his shares. In contrast, a shareholder in a publicly held corporation normally can withdraw by selling his shares on the market. The need of such shareholders for an appraisal right is therefore certainly less compelling. Furthermore, the expectations of many

27. See, e.g., Ill. Ann. Stats. ch. 32, §157.73 (Smith-Hurd Supp. 1974); N.J. Stat. Ann. §14A:11-1(b) (Supp. 1974); N.Y. Bus. Corp. Law §§909, 910(a)(1)(B) (McKinney Supp. 1974); Ohio Rev. Code Ann. §1701.76 (Page 1964); Pa. Stat. Ann. tit. 15, §1311(D)(1) (Supp. 1974); ABA Model Bus. Corp. Act §80(b) (1969 rev.).

28. Cf. Folk, De Facto Mergers in Delaware, 49 Va. L. Rev. 1261, 1295 (1963); 51 Iowa L. Rev. 1096, 1101 (1966).

shareholders in publicly held corporations undoubtedly revolve around the market rather than the enterprise. Is the appraisal right therefore unnecessary in the case of publicly held corporations?

There is, initially, a definitional problem; but for purposes of cutting off appraisal rights, a publicly held corporation might be defined as one whose stock is traded on a market which provides a ready means for dissatisfied shareholders to dispose of their stock at a fair price. Such a market, in turn, might perhaps be deemed to exist in the case of stock listed on the New York or American Stock Exchanges, or held by some minimum number of shareholders, say 1000 to 2000. This kind of approach was taken by the 1967 Delaware statute, which cut off appraisal rights in the case of stock held of record by 2000 shareholders or listed on a "national securities exchange,"[29] and since then a number of other statutes, including New Jersey, Pennsylvania, and the Model Act, have adopted comparable approaches.[30]

A second hurdle is not so easily leaped. While it is true that many shareholders in publicly-held corporations are market-oriented, it has already been seen that many others are likely to own an amount of stock sufficient to orient their expectations around the long-term prospects of the enterprise rather than around a market which tends to fluctuate severely over any given short-run period. It may be questioned whether such shareholders should be remitted to the market to find relief from structural

29. 56 Del. Laws 222 (1967), Del. Code Ann. tit. 8, §262(k)(1974).

30. N.J. Stat. Ann. §14A:11-1 (Supp. 1974); Pa. Stat. Ann. tit. 15, §1515(L) (Supp. 1974); Model Act §80 (1969 rev.). See also, e.g., Mich. Comp. Laws. Ann. §450.1762 (1973); Va. Code Ann. §13.1-75 (1973). The reference in many of these statutes to a "national" securities exchange is highly ambiguous, since a number of exchanges – such as the Midwest, PBW, and Boston – are sometimes referred to as "national" because they are registered under the Securities Exchange Act of 1934, and sometimes as "regional" because unlike the New York and American Exchanges they are not economically national. See Securities Exchange Act §§5, 6, 15 U.S.C. §78(e), (f) (1970); SEC, 33d Annual Report 55, 57 (1968). If the statutes were intended to include such exchanges they achieve an unfortunate result, because these exchanges may provide a relatively thin market which is incapable of absorbing a significant amount of stock at a fair price. Yet a booklet by a member of the Delaware Corporate Law Revision Committee and a member of its legal staff stated that "The term 'national securities exchange' means a stock exchange which is registered under the Securities Exchange Act of 1934." S. Arsht & W. Stapleton, Analysis of the New Delaware Corporation Law 340 (1967). In contrast, the Pennsylvania statute, for example, applies only to shares listed on the New York or American Stock Exchanges. Pa. Stat. Ann. tit. 15, §1515(L) (Supp. 1974). See also Utah Code Ann. §16-10-75 (1973).

changes to which they object, unless the market to which they are remitted is not only continuous and deep, but is likely to reflect fairly the value of the enterprise. It seems clear, however, that the stock markets as presently constituted do not serve that function. As the Delaware Chancery court itself has pointed out:

> When it is said that the appraisal which the market puts upon the value of the stock of an active corporation as evidenced by its daily quotations, is an accurate, fair reflection of its intrinsic value, no more than a moment's reflection is needed to refute it. There are too many accidental circumstances entering into the making of market prices to admit them as sure and exclusive reflectors of fair value. The experience of recent years is enough to convince the most casual observer that the market in its appraisal of values must have been woefully wrong in its estimates at one time or another within the interval of a space of time so brief that fundamental conditions could not possibly have become so altered as to affect true worth. Markets are known to gyrate in a single day. The numerous causes that contribute to their nervous leaps from dejected melancholy to exhilarated enthusiasm and then back again from joy to grief, need not be reviewed. . . . Even when conditions are normal and no economic forces are at work unduly to exalt or depress the financial hopes of man, market quotations are not safe to accept as unerring expressions of value.[31]

That was written in 1934, but things have not changed much, in this regard, since then. To give a random illustration, Table 7-1 shows the highs and lows for the first ten common stocks, alphabetically, on the New York Stock Exchange, in 1974. Another example, also random — the first ten common stocks for the first eight months of 1968 — is given in Table 7.2.

When fluctuations like these occur within a twelve-month or even eight-month period, it seems arbitrary, to say the least, to remit an enterprise-oriented shareholder to the market for relief.[32]

Furthermore, even assuming that a market fairly reflects the value of stock in its normal operation, remitting a dissenting shareholder to the market will fail to adequately protect him where (1) his block is so large that the mere act of selling the block will depress the market — and it has already been seen that large blocks

31. Chicago Corp. v. Munds, 20 Del. Ch. 143, 150-151, 172 A. 452, 455 (Ch. 1934).

32. The same criticism is applicable to statutes or decisions under which the appraised value of a dissenter's stock is based solely on market price.

Table 7-1*

Corporation	*High*	*Low*
Abbt Lb	61-1/4	30-1/2
ACF In	61-1/4	28-3/4
Acme Clev	14-5/8	7
Adm Dg	5-5/8	1-3/8
Adm E	13-1/4	7-3/8
Ad Mill	5-1/4	1-3/4
Addres	11-3/4	3
Adv Inv.	11-7/8	6-1/2
Aetna Lf.	31	15-1/8
Aquirre Co.	9-1/8	4-3/8

*N.Y. Times, Jan. 5, 1974, §3, at 50, col. 3.

Table 7-2*

Corporation	*High*	*Low*
Abacus	17-3/4	15-1/2
Abbott Lab	66-7/8	41-7/8
Abex Co.	42-1/8	28
ACF Ind.	68-3/8	39-1/2
Acme Mkt.	44	36
Adam Ex.	18-7/8	16
Ad Millis	30-5/8	18-3/4
Address	91-1/2	52
Admiral	25-1/8	16-1/2
Aeroquip	77	47-1/4

*N.Y. Times, Sept. 4, 1968, at 60, col. 2.

are common even in stocks listed on the New York Stock Exchange; (2) the very effect of the structural change is to depress the market price of the stock because the change is an ill-considered one; or (3) so many shareholders want to opt out that the market is flooded with sell orders.[33]

33. The newly revised California Corporations Code addresses two of these problems by providing that in the case of stock which is not listed on a stock exchange

A final problem with eliminating appraisal rights in publicly held corporations is that in such corporations the appraisal right not only serves the function of permitting shareholders to withdraw under certain circumstances at a fair price, but also serves as a check on management. Granted that a certain proportion of shareholders in publicly held corporations will vote in favor of any management proposal, no matter how ill-conceived, and granted that management is not necessarily either highly skilled or disinterested in the making of structural changes, it may be appropriate to structure the decisionmaking process in publicly held corporations so that something more than a majority — or even a two-thirds majority — is needed to carry a structural decision. As Professor Folk has pointed out:

> [I] t is important to maintain some internal or external control to offset the power of the directors, unless one assumes that directors, especially when backed by a shareholder majority, should have unrestrained discretion. Appraisal rights . . . have, in the past, served as a countervailing power to force the insiders to tailor their plans to minimize the number of dissenters by getting the best deal possible. A high vote requirement (including a class vote) plays the same sort of role. When either weapon is removed, the insiders lack the real self-interest to fashion a plan acceptable to a sufficient number of shareholders.[34]

It has already been seen that the appraisal right presents many difficulties from the shareholder's perspective: it is always technical; it may be expensive; it is uncertain in result; in the case of a publicly held corporation, is unlikely to produce a better result than could have been obtained on the market; and the ultimate award is taxable. It is, in short, a remedy of desperation. Generally speaking, no shareholder in a publicly held corporation will invoke the appraisal right unless he feels that the structural change from which he dissents is shockingly improvident and that the fair value of his shares before the change will far exceed the value of his shares thereafter.[35] But may not the existence of just

---

approved by the Commissioner of Corporations, or included on the list of OTC margin stocks issued by the Federal Reserve System, appraisal rights will be given if, but only if, the holders of 5 percent or more of the outstanding shares dissent and file demands for payment. Ch. 682, §1300(b)(1) [1975-76 Reg. Sess.] Calif. Leg. Serv. 1854.

34. Folk, De Facto Mergers in Delaware, supra note 3, at 1293.

35. See Appraisal Quest Brings Sorrows, N.Y. Times, Sept. 2, 1971, at 48, col. 2. Manning states that: "[T]here is a . . . species of professional shareholder-at-large

such a right – a switch which will be pulled only in case of emergency – be desirable in connection with transactions of the utmost gravity, in which self-interest and lack of financial skills may seriously obscure management's vision? While it would not be irrational to eliminate appraisal rights as to shares which are traded under conditions which are likely to insure the existence of a continuous and relatively deep market, it therefore seems more advisable to retain the appraisal right even in such cases, partly to protect the fair expectations of those shareholders whose legitimate expectations center on the enterprise rather than on the market, and partly to serve as a check on self-interested and unwise structural changes.

[who] . . . sees in the appraisal statutes a jimmy that will open windows. The professional shareholder can use the appraisal statute to give mechanical advantage to his relatively small share holdings. He can abuse the procedural process under the appraisal statute to the cost and disruption of the enterprise. He can also, especially where management is concerned about the company's cash position or is anxious that the number of dissenters not grow great enough to trigger a kick-out clause in a merger agreement, use his marginal swing position in an attempt to make a side deal for himself in exchange for not dissenting. His tactic will usually be to vote 'no' to the transaction, wait until the last minute for filing his claim, and hope that circumstances will give him stick-up power." Manning, The Shareholder's Appraisal Remedy, supra note 3, at 238.

Once more this seems exaggerated. How likely is it that a "side deal" will be made? Why should the corporation give this fellow any premium of any kind? This is not like the so-called strike suit where the shareholder has information relating to individual managers which management is anxious to conceal, and where a side deal using corporate funds for personal objectives is not wholly unlikely. Of course, the scoundrel-shareholder has some leverage, in that if he dissents the corporation will incur expenses; but the scoundrel-shareholder will incur comparable expenses, and will be less able to afford them. Furthermore, he takes a risk that he will end up with an award that may be less valuable than what he would have gotten had he not dissented, see In re Olivetti Underwood Corp., 246 A.2d 800 (Del. Ch. 1968), and taxable in the bargain.

In any event, there are ways to dispose of the bathwater while retaining the baby. For example, the court can be given discretion to levy all the expenses of the proceedings against the shareholder if he has turned down an offer by the corporation and in its judgment his action in doing so was "arbitrary or vexatious or not in good faith." ABA Model Bus. Corp. Act §80 (1969 rev.). See generally Note, Appraisal of Corporate Dissenters' Shares: Apportioning the Proceeding's Financial Burdens, 60 Yale L.J. 337 (1951).

8
The Uses of a Normative Model

Once a model of corporate decisionmaking has been constructed, it can be put to several kinds of use. One such use is obvious – assistance in determining legislative policy. Applications in that area will be taken up in many of the succeeding chapters. The purpose of this chapter is to consider application of the model by the courts.

Such an application may occur in at least three ways. First, the question may arise whether the body of shareholders can properly consider a given matter at all. For example, a dispute may turn on what matters a shareholder's meeting can properly be called to consider,[1] or what matters a shareholder may properly insert in the corporate proxy statement.[2] Absent direct precedent, the court in such cases must of necessity employ a decisionmaking model, implicit or explicit.

Second, where a statute explicitly requires shareholder approval for a given type of transaction, the court can sometimes employ a model to aid in determining the statute's applicability. For example, the corporate statutes commonly require shareholder approval for the sale of "substantially all" assets, but do not define that term. Whether, in a close case, the term is given a more or less expansive construction may turn in part on the court's notion of the appropriate roles of shareholders and directors.

1. See, e.g., Auer v. Dressel, 306 N.Y. 427, 118 N.E.2d 590 (1974).

2. See, e.g., Medical Committee for Human Rights v. SEC, 432 F.2d 659 (D.C. Cir. 1970), judgment vacated and dismissed as moot, 404 U.S. 403 (1972).

A third judicial application may occur in cases where the corporate statute does not explicitly cover a given type of transaction, and the question arises whether the transaction nevertheless requires shareholder approval, or gives rise to appraisal rights. This type of question involves complex and thorny issues, but two principles seem clear. The first is that American corporate statutes, as Gower has said of the English Companies and Companies Clauses Acts, are "in no sense a code of company law. . . . Behind [the statutes] is the general body of law and equity applying to all companies irrespective of their nature, and it is there that most of the fundamental principles will be found."[3]

The second principle, a corollary of the first, is that the legal powers of shareholders are not confined to those powers explicitly conferred upon the shareholders by the statute, certificate, or bylaws. For example, the New York court, in *Auer v. Dressel,* and the Delaware Chancellor, in *Campbell v. Loews, Inc.* have both held that the body of shareholders has the "inherent" power to remove a director for cause, even where such a power was not conferred on that body by statute, certificate, or bylaw (and in *Auer,* notwithstanding a certificate provision which vested the board with such a power).[4] It has also been held that the body of shareholders has inherent power to fill newly created directorships between annual meetings, notwithstanding the absence of a statutory, certificate, or bylaw provision to that effect,[5] and indeed even in the face of a bylaw or statute providing that the board of directors has power to fill such positions.[6] Similarly, it appears settled that the body of shareholders has the inherent power to

3. L. Gower, The Principles of Modern Company Law 8 (2d ed. 1957); cf. Friedman, SEC Regulation of Corporate Proxies, 63 Harv. L. Rev. 796, 804 (1950); Note, Stockholder Participation in Corporate Affairs, 37 Va. L. Rev. 595, 606-607 (1951). See also 1 G. Hornstein, Corporation Law and Practice iv (1959).

4. Campbell v. Loew's, Inc., 36 Del. Ch. 563, 134 A.2d 852 (Ch. 1957); Auer v. Dressel, 306 N.Y. 427, 118 N.E.2d 590 (1954). See also In re Burkin, 1 N.Y.2d 570, 572, 136 N.E.2d 862, 864 (1956); H. Ballantine, Corporations 434 (rev. ed. 1946).

5. See Gold Bluff Mining & Lumber Corp. v. Whitlock, 75 Conn. 669, 55 A. 175 (1903); Burr v. Burr Corp., 291 A.2d 409 (Del. Ch. 1972); Campbell v. Loew's, Inc., 36 Del. Ch. 563, 134 A.2d 852 (Ch. 1957); Automatic Steel Products, Inc. v. Johnston, 31 Del. Ch. 469, 64 A.2d 416 (Sup. Ct. 1949); Moon v. Moon Motor Car Co., 17 Del. Ch. 176, 151 A. 298 (Ch. 1930); In re A. A. Griffing Iron Co., 63 N.J.L. 168, 41 A. 931 (Sup. Ct. 1898), affd. per curiam, 63 N.J.L. 357, 46 A. 1097 (Ct. Err. & App. 1899).

6. See Automatic Steel Products, Inc. v. Johnston, 31 Del. Ch. 469, 64 A.2d 416 (1949); Campbell v. Loew's, Inc., 36 Del. Ch. 563, 571, 134 A.2d 852, 857 (Ch. 1957); cf. Burr v. Burr. Corp., 291 A.2d 409 (Del. Ch. 1972).

appoint an independent auditor, or to require the corporation to issue certain types of reports, such as postmeeting reports, although the statute, certificate, and bylaws are silent on the point.[7]

Beyond these two principles, however, it is unclear precisely what legal principles govern the distribution of power between shareholders and directors in the absence of a specific statutory provision. It is sometimes assumed that the board can exercise all corporate power unless the statute explicitly provides otherwise. Insofar as structural changes are concerned, this assumption is unsound as a matter of policy. It is also unsound as a matter of law.

At common law, a corporation was not required to have a board. All corporate powers were vested in the shareholders, acting by a majority, except insofar as they were explicitly delegated to management. Thus, Morawetz, in an early (1886) treatise on corporate law, stated:

> The rule was laid down by Chief Justice Bigelow . . . ". . . that the majority of the stockholders can regulate and control the lawful exercise of the powers conferred on a corporation by its charter." It is implied that the majority shall have supreme authority to direct the policy of the corporation in attaining its chartered purpose, and shall have the power to appoint the usual managing agents, to whom the immediate control and direction of the company's business is delegated.[8]

Where (as was of course usually the case) the corporation did have a board, the common law rule was that the board had exclusive power to manage the regular business of the corporation, but that the power to determine important or fundamental changes remained with the shareholders. Morawetz again:

> . . . [T]he exclusive powers of the board of directors extend only to the management of the regular business of the corporation. Even an express provision that the powers of the corporation shall be exercised

7. SEC v. Transamerica Corp., 163 F.2d 511 (3d Cir. 1947), cert. denied, 332 U.S. 847 (1948); cf. Clusserath, The Amended Stockholder Proposal Rule: A Decade Later, 40 Notre Dame Law. 13, 45-46 (1964).

8. 1 V. Morawetz, Treatise on the Law of Private Corporations 447-448 (2d ed. 1886). See also Union Pacific Ry. v. Chicago. M. & St. P. Ry., 163 U.S. 564, 596 (1896); 5 W. Fletcher, Cyclopedia of Private Corporations §2097 (rev. vol. M. Wolf ed. 1967); Warren, Voluntary Transfers of Corporate Undertakings, 30 Harv. L. Rev. 335, at 335-336 (1917).

> by its board of directors does not deprive the majority of the power of directing the general policy of the corporation, and of deciding upon the propriety of important changes in the company's business.
>
> ... The general authority of the directors of a corporation extends merely to the supervision and management of the company's ordinary or regular business. A board of directors has no implied authority to make a material and permanent alteration of the business or constitution of a corporation, even though the alteration be within the company's chartered powers. Such an alteration can be effected only by authority of the shareholders at a general meeting.[9]

The corporate statutes were enacted in the context of this common-law pattern, and generally served to perpetuate it. While some statutes confer upon the board all corporate powers except those specifically granted to shareholders,[10] typically the statutes provide only that "the business" or "the business and affairs" of a corporation shall be managed by the board.[11] Read in the context of the common-law background, such statutes were not intended to derogate from the shareholders' power to make decisions on fundamental matters.[12] For example, *Commercial National Bank v. Weinhard*[13] arose under the National Banking Act, which provided that the affairs of a national bank were to be managed by its

9. 1 V. Morawetz, supra note 8, at 479. See also A. A. Berle & G. Means, The Modern Corporation and Private Property 132 (1932); cf. Kessler, The Statutory Requirement of a Board of Directors: A Corporate Anachronism, 27 U. Chi. L. Rev. 696, 706 (1960).

10. See Cal. Corp. Code § 800 (West Supp. 1974); Pa. Stat. Ann. tit. 15, § 1302 (1967, as amended, Supp. 1974); cf. Ohio Rev. Code Ann. § 1701.59 (Page Supp. 1974).

11. See Del. Code Ann. tit. 8, § 141(a) (1974); Ill. Ann. Stat. ch. 32, § 157.33 (Smith-Hurd Supp. 1974); N.J. Rev. Stat, § 14A:6-1 (Supp. 1974); 1 N.Y. Bus. Corp. Law § 701 (McKinney 1963).

12. See H. Ballantine, supra note 4, at 119-120; 2 W. Fletcher, supra note 8, at § 540 (rev. vol. M. Wolf & E. Comiskey eds. 1969); 1 G. Hornstein, supra note 3, at 446-447; N. Lattin, The Law of Corporations 239 (2d ed. 1971). Indeed, this may be true even under provisions which apparently confer *all* corporate powers on the board:

"Moreover, a general provision in the charter of a corporation or a general corporation law, that 'all the corporate powers shall be vested in and exercised by a board of directors, and such officers and agents as said board shall appoint,' refers merely to the ordinary business transactions of the corporation, and does not extend to other acts which are not ordinarily within the powers of the directors, but are done or authorized by the stockholders only – as the reconstruction of and fundamental changes in the corporate body, increase of the capital stock, etc." 2 W. Fletcher, supra, at 583.

See H. Ballantine, supra, at 520; cf. Automatic Steel Products, Inc. v. Johnston, 31 Del. Ch. 469, 64 A.2d 416 (Sup. Ct. 1949); Bruch v. National Guar. Credit Corp., 13 Del. Ch. 180, 185-190, 116 A. 738, 740-743 (Ch. 1922).

13. 192 U.S. 243 (1904).

board, and that if a bank's capital stock became impaired, it "shall, within three months after receiving notice thereof from the Comptroller of the Currency, pay the deficiency . . . by assessment upon the shareholders. . . ." Following receipt of such a notice, the bank's board made an assessment on the shareholders. The Supreme Court held that the assessment was beyond the board's powers.

> . . . [T]he directors are given authority to transact the usual and ordinary business of national banks. Obviously, the power conferred may be exercised in all usual transactions . . . without consultation with the stockholders. In the present case the question to be dealt with is vital to the continuance of the life of the association. . . . The shareholders by their contracts of subscription have agreed to pay in the amount of capital stock subscribed and to discharge the additional liability imposed by the statute. They have not contracted to meet assessments at the will of the directors to perpetuate the business of a possibly losing concern. It would be going far beyond the usual powers conferred upon directors to permit them to thus control the corporation. Corporate powers conferred upon a board of directors usually refer to the ordinary business transactions of the corporation.[14]

Similarly, in *Hodge v. Cuba Company*[15] the directors of Cuba Company formulated a plan under which debenture holders could exchange their existing debentures for new debentures and other consideration. The indenture under which the new debentures were to be issued provided that during a 12-year period Cuba would not, over the objection of stated proportions of debenture holders, sell the stock of Compania Cubana, a subsidiary whose stock constituted Cuba's only substantial asset, or of Consolidated Railroads, a subsidiary of Compania; create a mortgage on the assets of either subsidiary; or recapitalize or reorganize either subsidiary. Cuba shareholders sued to enjoin consummation of the plan on the ground, *inter alia,* that it was beyond the powers of the board. The court granted injunctive relief:

> While the power of directors to agree on the terms of payment of the Company's debt and to arrange for security cannot be doubted, yet when they plan so to exercise the power as to change substantially the capital structure of the Company and to control in important re-

14. Id. at 248-249.
15. 142 N.J. Eq. 340, 60 A.2d 88 (Ch. 1948).

> spects the discretion of their successors and of the stockholders for a long period, they should seek the approval of the stockholders before committing the Company.[16]

Again, in *Aiple v. Twin City Barge & Towing Co.,*[17] the management of Twin City, a Minnesota corporation, had sought to amend its certificate of incorporation to authorize additional shares of common stock, for the purpose of increasing its equity capital. Under the Minnesota statute a certificate amendment normally had to be approved by the holders of two-thirds of a corporation's stock. Aiple, the owner of more than one-third of Twin City's outstanding stock, blocked the proposed amendment. Management then adopted an alternative plan, under which Twin City organized a new subsidiary to which it transferred the assets of a Twin City division and cash in exchange for 4000 of the subsidiary's 50,000 authorized shares. It was apparently contemplated that the subsidiary would thereafter sell a portion of its remaining 46,000 shares, thereby indirectly increasing Twin City's capital.[18] Before these shares could be sold, however, Aiple moved to set the transaction aside. Management contended, *inter alia,* that its actions were expressly authorized by provisions of the Minnesota statute which empowered a corporation to acquire shares and to convey or otherwise dispose of real and personal property. The court rejected this contention on the ground that "these general powers refer to the ordinary business transactions of the corporation and do not extend to a reconstruction of the corporate body itself."[19]

16. Id. at 348, 60 A.2d at 93.

17. 274 Minn. 38, 143 N.W.2d 374 (1966).

18. The subsidiary also assumed the liabilities attributable to the division.

19. 274 Minn. at 44, 143 N.W.2d at 378. Similarly, in Ostlind v. Ostlind Valve Co., 178 Ore. 161, 191, 165 P.2d 779, 791 (1946), the court stated:

"There is a distinction between the powers of the corporation itself and the powers of the board of directors, and an act may be within the powers of the former and not of the latter. . . . The powers of the directors are not unlimited but extend only to the ordinary or regular business of the corporation."

See also Railway Co. v. Allerton, 85 U.S. 233 (1873); Baker's Appeal, 109 Pa. 461, 472 (1885); Moore v. Los Lugos Gold Mines, 172 Wash. 570, 588, 21 P.2d 253, 260 (1933); cf. Sherman & Ellis, Inc. v. Indiana Mut. Cas. Co., 41 F.2d 588 (7th Cir. 1930); Kennerson v. Burbank Amusement Co., 120 Cal. App. 2d 157, 260 P.2d 823 (1953); Eisenberg v. Central Zone Property Corp., 306 N.Y. 58, 115 N.E.2d 652 (1963). But see Hutchinson v. Green, 91 Mo. 367, 1 S.W. 853 (1886); Beveridge v. New York Elevated R.R., 112 N.Y. 1, 22-23, 19 N.E. 489, 494-495 (1889); cf. Tankersley v.

A common application of the principle that fundamental changes are shareholder matters is the rule that the board's power to issue authorized stock may not be used for the purpose of maintaining or reallocating corporate control, even if the board believes that its actions will serve the corporation's best interests.[20] Thus in *Howard Smith Ltd. v. Ampol Petroleum Ltd.*,[21] a judgment of the Privy Council, Ampol Petroleum and Bulkships Ltd. had acquired 55 percent of the stock of R. W. Miller Ltd., under a $2.27 per share tender offer. Miller's board then issued additional stock to Howard Smith for the purpose of reducing the Ampol-Bulkships holdings to less than 50 percent, thereby keeping alive Smith's rival (but later) tender offer of $2.50 per share. Although the board had power to issue stock, and the directors "were not motivated by any purpose of personal gain or advantage, or by any desire to retain their position on the board," the issuance was nevertheless improper:

> The constitution of a limited company normally provides for directors, with powers of management and shareholders, with defined voting powers having power to appoint the directors, and to take, in general meeting, by majority vote, decisions on matters not reserved for management. Just as it is established that directors, within their management powers, may take decisions against the wishes of the majority of shareholders . . . so it must be unconstitutional for directors to use their fiduciary powers over the shares in the company purely for the purpose of destroying an existing majority, or creating a new majority which did not previously exist. To do so is to interfere with that element of the company's constitution which is separate from and set against their powers.[22]

Albright, 374 F. Supp. 538 (N.D. Ill. 1974); Gimbel v. Signal Cos., 316 A.2d 599 (Del. Ch.), affd. per curiam, 316 A.2d 619 (Del. 1974); Adams v. Clearance Corp., 35 Del. Ch. 459, 121 A.2d 302 (1956).

20. See, e.g., Kullgren v. Navy Gas & Supply Co., 110 Colo. 454, 135 P.2d 1007 (1943); Condec Corp. v. Lunkenheimer Co., 43 Del. Ch. 353, 230 A.2d 769 (Ch. 1967); Rowland v. Times Publishing Co., 160 Fla. 465, 35 So. 2d 399 (1948); Biltmore Motor Corp. v. Rogue, 291 So.2d 114 (Fla. D.C.A.), cert. denied, 291 So.2d 114 (1974); Trask v. Chase, 107 Me. 137, 77 A. 698 (1910); Andersen v. Albert & J.M. Andersen Mfg. Co., 325 Mass. 343, 90 N.E.2d 541 (1950); Katzowitz v. Sidler, 24 N.Y.2d 512, 249 N.E.2d 359 (1969); Browning v. C & C Plywood Corp., 258 Ore. 574, 434 P.2d 339 (1967); Glenn v. Kitanning Brewing Co., 259 Pa. 510, 103 A. 340 (1918).

21. [1974] 3 Aust. L.R. 448.

22. Id. at 457.

See also Bamford v. Bamford, [1970] Ch. 212 (1968), affd., [1970] Ch. 228 (1969); Hogg v. Cramphorn Ltd., [1967] Ch. 254 (1963); Piercy v. S. Mills & Co.,

While most applications of the principle that a transaction may constitute a fundamental change, even though not covered by the statute, go to whether shareholder approval is required, there is also some authority – most notably, the leading case of *Jones v. Ahmanson*[23] – for the proposition that in appropriate cases the court may provide the equivalent of an appraisal right. *Jones v. Ahmanson* was a class action brought by a minority shareholder in

---

[1920] Ch. 77 (1919); Punt v. Symons & Co., [1903] 2 Ch. 506 (1903); L. Gower, The Principles of Modern Company Law 524-525 (3d ed. K. Wedderburn, O. Weaver, & A. Park 1969); Wedderburn, Shareholders' Control of Directors' Powers: A Judicial Innovation?, 30 Mod. L. Rev. 77, 79 (1967).

In the Savoy affair, in England, a corporation had defended against a takeover threat by vesting control over one of its major properties in the trustees of a staff benevolent fund, thereby putting it out of a bidder's power to effectively determine the use of that property if he obtained control of Savoy. The Board of Trade appointed E. Milner Holland, a prominent corporate lawyer, to report whether the board's action was proper. He concluded it was not, despite the directors' belief that the transaction was in the best interests of the corporation and its shareholders, because the purpose for which the board acted was not a proper board purpose: "The powers conferred on the directors were contained in articles the opening words of which were 'The business of the Company shall be managed by the Board' and I therefore construe them as having been given for the purpose of managing the business of the Company. . . . The . . . scheme however was designed to retain the hotel business at the Berkeley, but to withdraw from the stockholders any power, by any means direct or indirect, to control the business thus retained. . . . The exercise of the directors' powers was therefore used in order to render irrevocable for all time the policy view of the present Board. In my opinion, such a use of directors powers . . . however proper the motive behind it, is not a purpose for which those powers were conferred on the Board. . . ." The Savoy Hotel Limited and The Berkeley Hotel Limited, Investigation Under Section 165(b) of the Companies Act, 1948, Report of Mr. E. Milner Holland, Q.C., at 27 (Her Majesty's Stationery Office 1954). See also Gower, Corporate Control: The Battle for the Berkeley, 68 Harv. L. Rev. 1176 (1955).

In a comparable situation, it has been held that the power of the body of shareholders to consummate a merger is intended for business purposes, and may not be used for the purpose of effecting a freeze-out. Bryan v. Block & Blevins Co., 490 F.2d 563 (5th Cir.), cert. denied, 419 U.S. 844 (1974); Albright v. Bergendahl, CCH Fed. Sec. L. Rep. ¶94,997 (D. Utah 1974); cf. Levine v. Biddle Sawyer Corp., 383 F. Supp. 618 (S.D.N.Y. 1974). But see Grimes v. Donaldson, Lufkin & Jeanerette, Inc., CCH Fed. Sec. L. Rep. ¶94,722 (N.D. Fla. 1974); cf. Teschner v. Chicago Title & Trust Co., 322 N.E.2d 54 (Ill. 1974); Rubel v. Rubel Corp., 25 Misc. 2d 388, 206 N.Y.S.2d 396 (1960).

Cf. Coalition to Advocate Public Utility Responsibility, Inc. v. Engels, 364 F. Supp. 1202 (D. Minn. 1973); Walsh v. State ex rel. Cook, 199 Ala. 123, 74 So. 45 (1917); Schnell v. Chris-Craft Industries, Inc., 285 A.2d 437 (Del. 1971); Condec v. Lunkenheimer Corp., 43 Del. Ch. 353, 230 A.2d 769 (Ch. 1967); Penn-Texas Corp. v. Niles-Bement-Pond Co., 34 N.J. Super. 373, 112 A.2d 302 (Ch. 1955). But cf. Northwest Industries, Inc. v. B. F. Goodrich Co., 301 F. Supp. 706 (N.D. Ill. 1969).

23. Jones v. Ahmanson, 1 Cal. 3d 93, 460 P.2d 464, 81 Cal. Rptr. 592 (1969).

a California savings and loan Association. The complaint alleged that in 1956 the Association had been converted from a mutual to a stock corporation, and approximately 85 percent of its stock had been owned by a small group of shareholders. In 1959, the members of this group organized a new Delaware corporation, United, and exchanged their stock in the Association for stock in United. The minority shareholders in the Association were not afforded an opportunity to make the same exchange. Subsequently, there were two public offerings of United stock, and a widespread market developed for that stock. No comparable market developed for stock in the Association, which was traded even more thinly after the formation of United than before. As a result, the market price of United stock was considerably higher than the proportionate market price of stock in the Association, although the latter constituted the major asset of the former. Plaintiff claimed that in creating United, without giving the minority a chance to go along, the members of the majority group had breached a fiduciary duty to minority shareholders by using control of the Association for their own advantage and to the detriment of minority shareholders. The California Supreme Court, in an opinion by Chief Justice Traynor, overruled a demurrer to the complaint.

The best-known portion of Traynor's opinion is addressed to the fiduciary-obligation issue. Briefly, Traynor held that "where control of the corporation is material," controlling shareholders were governed by a "comprehensive rule of good faith and inherent fairness to the minority."[24] Based on the allegations of the complaint, the defendants had breached that duty by using their control to obtain a special advantage, without regard to the resulting detriment to the minority, without a compelling business purpose, and despite the fact that alternatives were available which would have benefited all shareholders proportionately.[25] More interesting for present purposes is a lesser-known portion of the opinion, dealing with remedies, in which Traynor held that the

24. 1 Cal. 3d at 112, 460 P.2d at 474.

25. 1 Cal. 3d at 113, 460 P.2d at 474-476. Traynor added that at the trial the defendants could present evidence showing "good faith or compelling business purpose that would render their action fair under the circumstances." 1 Cal. 3d at 114, 460 P.2d at 476.

formation of United constituted a fundamental change in the Association, and that the plaintiff was therefore entitled, at a minimum, to the equivalent of an appraisal right:

> From the perspective of the minority stockholders of the Association, the transfer of control under these circumstances to another corporation and the resulting impact on their position as minority stockholders accomplished a fundamental corporate change as to them. Control of a closely held savings and loan association, the major portion of whose earnings had been retained over a long period while its stockholders remained stable, became an asset of a publicly held holding company. The position of the minority shareholder was drastically changed thereby. His practical ability to influence corporate decision-making was diminished substantially when control was transferred to a publicly held corporation that was in turn controlled by the owners of more than 750,000 shares. The future business goals of the Association could reasonably be expected to reflect the needs and interest of the holding company rather than the aims of the Association stockholders thereafter. In short, the enterprise into which the minority stockholders were now locked was not that in which they had invested. . . .
>
> Appraisal rights protect the dissenting minority shareholder against being forced to either remain an investor in an enterprise fundamentally different than that in which he invested or sacrifice his investment by sale of his shares at less than a fair value. . . . Plaintiff here was entitled to no less. . . .
>
> If, after the trial of the cause, plaintiff has established facts in conformity with the allegations of the complaint and stipulation, then upon tender of her Association stock to defendants she will be entitled to receive . . . the appraised value of her shares on the date of the exchange [of majority stock in the Association for stock in United] . . . .[26]

Subsequent chapters will consider how the normative models developed in Part I bear on the interpretation of traditional corporate statutes, on the treatment of fundamental or structural changes not explicitly governed by those statutes, and on directions for statutory revision.

26. 1 Cal. 3d at 116-118, 460 P.2d at 477-478, 81 Cal. Rptr. at 605-06; cf. American Seating Co. v. Bullard, 290 F. 896 (6th Cir. 1923); Marks v. Autocar Co., 153 F. Supp. 768 (E.D.Pa. 1954); Lauman v. Lebanon Valley R.R., 30 Pa. 42, 46-47 (1858).

In the alternative, plaintiff was held entitled to the present value of the United stock she would have received had she been allowed to participate in the original exchange.

II

Access to the Corporate Proxy Machinery

9

Access to the Corporate Proxy Machinery in Connection with the Election of Directors

§9.1. Introduction

Notwithstanding the concentration of shareholdings in publicly held corporations, in many if not most such corporations de facto control resides with management rather than with shareholders. What accounts for this phenomenon? In large part it is undoubtedly due to economic realities. For example, if management is performing at a level between good and excellent, it may make no sense to replace it or to disagree with its recommendations. Even where management's performance is less than good, no better alternative may be available. And of course management itself may hold or represent a large block of stock.

But management control may sometimes result not from economic realities, but from legal rules, or at least from supposed legal rules. In particular, it is generally assumed that the legal rules governing the proxy system help insure management control by giving management, in the person of the board, virtually exclusive and practically unlimited access to the corporate proxy machinery.

If this assumption is correct, it would be of utmost significance. It is well known that proxy voting has become the dominant mode of shareholder decisionmaking in publicly held corporations. There are a number of reasons for this. Shareholders in such corporations are often geographically dispersed, so that a given shareholder may not live near the site of the meeting. Shareholders often have some principal business other than investing, so that a given shareholding may not represent a substantial proportion of a shareholder's total wealth.[1] And whether a shareholder supports or opposes the matters scheduled for action at a meeting, he may not wish to speak on the issues. Physical attendance at a shareholders' meeting is normally an uneconomical use of a shareholder's time when he can vote by proxy.[2]

A natural outgrowth of the preference for proxy voting is proxy solicitation – the process of systematically contacting shareholders and urging them to execute and return proxy cards which authorize named proxies to cast the shareholder's votes, either in a manner designated in the proxy card or according to the proxies' discretion. If a substantial proportion of the corporation's stock is controlled by a few persons, or if the total number of shareholders is relatively small, a solicitation can, absent legal regulation, be relatively casual – a few dozen phone calls or letters may suffice. If not, a more elaborate solicitation is required. This would normally include a widespread mailing of written materials to shareholders, and follow-up letters and phone calls to those who do not respond. In many cases, professional proxy solicitors may be hired to do the follow-up, adding significantly to total expense.[3] Finally, solicitations in respect of certain securities are subject to the SEC's Proxy Rules[4] and therefore entail the additional expense of preparation or screening by counsel.

Persons who solicit proxies may pay these expenses out of their own pockets. However, they prefer to shift the financial burden of a solicitation to the corporation itself by using corporate funds to pay for printing, lawyers, professional proxy solicitors, and other expenses, and by using corporate personnel and facilities to make mailings, phone calls, and personal contacts – in short, by using the complex of people, money, and facilities known as the

1. See F. Emerson & F. Latcham, Shareholder Democracy 14-15 (1954).

2. See id. at 15; cf. Manne, Some Theoretical Aspects of Share Voting, 64 Colum. L. Rev. 1427, 1439-1441 (1964).

Following conventional usage, the term "proxy" will be used to refer to: (a) a person appointed by a shareholder to appear at a meeting and cast the shareholder's vote, and (b) the form (usually a printed card) in which such an appointment is embodied.

3. See generally E. Aranow & H. Einhorn, Proxy Contests for Corporate Control 260-266 (2d ed. 1968); L. Whetten, The Rise of Professional Proxy Solicitors (1961); Elias, The Role of Professional Proxy Solicitors, Mergers & Acquisitions, Fall 1966, at 79; The Old Touch, The New Yorker, March 27, 1954, at 24.

4. SEC Reg. 14A, 17 C.F.R. § 240.14a (1974).

corporate proxy machinery. The questions then arise: Who can make use of the corporate proxy machinery? Under what circumstances can such use be made?

Given the dominance of proxy voting, if the common assumption that the law gives the board virtually exclusive access to this machinery is correct, obviously the law itself would contribute substantially toward entrenching management control of publicly held corporations. Examination of the authorities, however, reveals that this assumption has little or no direct support. State corporation statutes are for the most part silent on questions of proxy regulation in general, and access in particular. At common law a shareholder could not vote by proxy unless the corporation's certificate or bylaws expressly so provided.[5] This rule was early changed by the corporate statutes,[6] and today every state permits proxy voting even in the absence of certificate or bylaw provision.[7] But the purpose of the relevant statutory provisions was merely to empower proxy voting, not to regulate its mechanics, and while the proxy system grew in significance and complexity, the corporate statutes failed to grow with it. By and large, state corporate statutes do not even recognize the existence of proxy solicitation, let alone regulate it.[8]

Parts of the gap left by the state statutes have been filled by other sources. Case law has addressed itself in a general and somewhat unsatisfactory way to certain problems of management

5. Axe, Corporate Proxies, 41 Mich. L. Rev. 38, 38-46 (1942).

6. Id. at 46-48.

7. See 2, 5 L. Loss, Securities Regulation 857-858 n. 1, 2829-2830 (2d ed. 1961, Supp. 1969) [hereinafter cited as Loss].

8. See 2 id. at 866; cf. N. Lattin, R. Jennings & R. Buxbaum, Corporations: Cases and Materials 454 (4th ed. 1968); Stifel, Shareholder Proxy Fight Expenses, 8 Clev.-Mar. L. Rev. 339 (1959). For a discussion of solicitation abuses under state law, see Note, The SEC Proxy Rules and Shareholder Participation in Management, 53 Harv. L. Rev. 1165 (1940). There are limited exceptions, the most prominent of which is §604 of the recently revised California Corporations Code, ch. 682, Calif. Leg. Serv. [1975-76 Reg. Sess.] 1838, which regulates the form of proxy along the lines of the Proxy Rules.

Under the 1964 amendments to the Securities Exchange Act, securities issued by an insurance company may be exempt from registration under the Act if, among other things, "[s]uch insurance company is subject to [proxy] regulation by its domiciliary State . . . and such regulation conforms to that prescribed by the National Association of Insurance Commissioners." Securities Exchange Act of 1934, §12(g)(2)(G)(ii), 15 U.S.C. §78*l*(g)(2)(G)(ii) (1964). In order to permit domiciled insurance companies to qualify for exemption, most states now regulate the solicitation of proxies by such companies, either by statute or by statutorily authorized rules issued by the commissioner of insurance. See 5 Loss 2752-2753 (Supp. 1968).

access,[9] and also to problems arising out of misleading statements in proxy solicitation materials,[10] but it is extremely sparse on problems of shareholder access.[11] In contrast to the case law, the Proxy Rules issued by the SEC under section 14 of the Securities Exchange Act of 1934[12] fill large parts of the gap in a highly elaborate way. Indeed, the presence of these rules and the central administrative mechanism for enforcing them may account in part for the inaction of state legislatures in this area. But even the Proxy Rules leave substantial lacunae. They do not extend to all proxy solicitations, but only those in respect of certain securities – generally speaking, securities which are either listed on a national securities exchange, or are equity securities issued by a corporation with assets of more than one million dollars and held by 500 or more shareholders.[13] Furthermore, the Proxy Rules reflect the original philosophy of the securities legislation, which was to require disclosure of relevant information and to prohibit the use of false information, rather than to control the internal government of corporations.[14] Accordingly, the Proxy Rules deal elaborately with the information that must accompany a proxy solicitation, but only tangentially with access to the corporate proxy machinery.

In the absence of direct authority, questions of access to the corporate proxy machinery must be decided by the application of

9. See text at notes 25-40 infra.

10. E.g., American Hardware Corp. v. Savage Arms Corp., 37 Del. Ch. 59, 65-66, 136 A.2d 690, 693-694 (1957); Kerbs v. California Eastern Airways, Inc., 33 Del. Ch. 395, 94 A.2d 217 (1953); Dal-Tran Service Co. v. Fifth Avenue Coach Lines, Inc., 14 App. Div. 2d 349, 353-355, 220 N.Y.S.2d 549, 554-556 (1961); In re R. Hoe & Co., 14 Misc. 2d 500, 137 N.Y.S.2d 142 (Sup. Ct. 1954), affd. mem., 285 App. Div. 927, 139 N.Y.S.2d 883, affd. mem., 309 N.Y. 719, 128 N.E.2d 420 (1955); Wyatt v. Armstrong, 186 Misc. 216, 59 N.Y.S.2d 502 (Sup. Ct. 1945).

11. See §§9.3, 10.2, infra.

12. 15 U.S.C. §78n(a) (1970).

13. See Securities Exchange Act of 1934, §§12(a), (g), 15 U.S.C. §§78*l*(a), (g) (1970).

The Proxy Rules are also generally applicable to securities of registered investment companies and registered holding companies and their subsidiaries. Investment Company Act, Rule 20a-1(a), 17 C.F.R. §270.20a-1(a) (1974); Public Utility Holding Company Act, Rules 60-61, 17 C.F.R. §§250.60-61 (1974). Banks, while usually not governed by the SEC's Proxy Rules, are subject to similar rules promulgated by the Federal Reserve Board, the Federal Deposit Insurance Corporation, and the Comptroller of the Currency. See 5 Loss 2982-2984 (Supp. 1969).

14. Cf. 1, 4 Loss 121-131, 2269-2275 (2d ed. 1961, Supp. 1969).

general corporate principles, elaborated in light of those considerations of policy and practicability relevant to the particular question. The purpose of this chapter and the next is to reconsider the direct authorities, and to identify, elaborate, and apply the relevant general principles, with a view toward delineating the legal rules by which such questions should be governed. Two general propositions will underlie much of the discussion, and should therefore be stated briefly at the outset. First, the corporate proxy machinery is just that — *corporate* proxy machinery, constructed of corporate assets, and fueled with corporate funds. Therefore, it cannot be appropriated to personal ends; if set in motion at all, it must be operated in a neutral manner. Second, the proxy system has developed to the point where it not merely leads up to but supplants the shareholders' meeting for most substantive purposes and, in some respects, for formal purposes as well.[15] "[R]ealistically the solicitation of proxies is today the stockholders' meeting."[16] Typically a shareholder in a publicly held corporation will effectively cast his vote at some point during the solicitation process rather than at the meeting and therefore, insofar as his decision is based upon persuasion, the persuasion will occur during the solicitation process rather than at the meeting. This shift in the locus of shareholder decisionmaking informs all aspects of shareholder decisionmaking: beginning with the proxy card, which is normally in the form of a ballot;[17] proceeding through Proxy Rule 14a-4, which prohibits, except in very limited cases, the distribution of proxy cards which give the proxy holder unfettered discretionary authority to vote at the meeting;[18] and ending at a meeting room which is normally too small to seat more than a tiny fraction of the corporation's shareholders.[19] Because of this shift

15. H. Ballantine, Corporations 411 (rev. ed. 1946); Bernstein & Fischer, The Regulation of the Solicitation of Proxies: Some Reflections on Corporate Democracy, 7 U. Chi. L. Rev. 226, 227 (1940); Caplin, Shareholder Nominations of Directors: A Program for Fair Corporate Suffrage, 39 Va. L. Rev. 141, 159 (1953); Hearings on H.R. 1493, H.R. 1821, and H.R. 2019 [Proxy Rules] Before the House Comm. on Interstate and Foreign Commerce, 78th Cong., 1st Sess. 174, 225, 230 (1943); cf. Washington State Labor Council v. Federated American Ins. Co., 78 Wash. 263, 474 P.2d 98 (1970).

16. Bernstein & Fisher, supra note 14, at 227.

17. See Proxy Rule 14a-4(a), (b), 17 C.F.R. §§240.14a-4(a), (b) (1974).

18. See Proxy Rule 14a-4(b)(1), (c)-(e), 17 C.F.R. §§240.14a-4(b)(1), (c)-(e) (1974).

19. Cf. Hanna Mining Co. Zips Through its Meeting in Under 8 Minutes, Wall St.

in locus, at least some of the principles and rules developed to govern the process known as shareholders' meetings must now be applied to the process known as proxy solicitation.

§9.2. Management Access

It might seem surprising that the incumbent board should have any access at all to the corporate proxy machinery in connection with the election of directors. A directorship is after all a position of value: it normally pays a fee; it confers upon the holder a share in the control of a business enterprise; it may shore up a lucrative employment position (in the case of an inside director) or provide a preferential track to business dealing with the corporation (in the case of an outside director); it can be a learning experience; and it carries prestige in the managerial peer group.[20] Thus, to permit incumbent directors to use the corporate proxy machinery to help gain a new term of office might appear to be a blatant appropriation of corporate assets to personal ends. So Professor Brudney has observed that "[s]trict fiduciary standards would categorically preclude insiders from spending corporate funds to perpetuate their power. . . ."[21]

Nor is the only problem that of fiduciary standards. Corporate organs can act only within their authority; but what authority does the board have to use the corporate proxy machinery in connection with the election of the board? Certainly this is not a specific board function. On the contrary, under the corporate statutes the power to elect the board is vested in the shareholders.[22]

J., April 9, 1970, at 14, col. 2.

Delaware has dropped the necessity of a meeting entirely. See Del. Code Ann. tit. 8, §228 (1975); Fuqua's Shareholders Endorse Plan to Drop its Annual Meeting, Wall St. J., April 18, 1972, at 24, col. 2; Greyhound Is Seeking Acquisition Approval Without a Meeting, Wall St. J., Jan. 30, 1970, at 3, col. 4.

20. See The Director Looks at his Job 146-147 (C. Brown & E. Smith eds. 1957); M. Mace, Directors: Myth and Reality 104-106 (1971); 1 G. Washington & V. Rothschild, Compensating the Corporate Executive 255-260 (3d ed. 1962).

21. Brudney, Fiduciary Ideology in Transactions Affecting Corporate Control, 65 Mich. L. Rev. 259, 283 (1966); cf. Braude v. Havenner, 38 Cal. App. 2d 526, 532, 113 Cal. Rptr. 386, 389 (1974).

22. See, e.g., Cal. Corp. Code §§2200-01 (West 1955); Del. Code Ann. tit. 8, §211(b) (1974); Ill. Ann. Stat. ch. 32, §157.34 (Smith-Hurd Supp. 1974); N.J. Stat. Ann. §14A:6-3 (1969); N.Y. Bus. Corp. Law §703(a) (McKinney 1963); Ohio Rev.

While the statutes normally give the board a broad residual power to manage the business of the corporation,[23] recommendations by the board that the shareholders reelect its members hardly seem to fall within the scope of that provision, particularly considering that the election of the board is assigned specifically to the shareholders.[24]

Consistent with these principles, the courts have regularly said that the board cannot use the corporate proxy machinery for the purpose of perpetuating itself in office.[25] Of course the board can use that machinery to call a shareholders' meeting, to produce a quorum, and presumably to prepare and distribute any materials required by law.[26] Such a use neither violates strict fiduciary standards nor exceeds the board's authority. The board, however, will normally wish to do more. At a minimum, it will want to designate its members as candidates in the corporate proxy materials. The incremental expenditures involved in this practice are minimal, and when the election is uncontested it probably presents no serious problem. If the election is contested, however, the members of the board will want to use the corporate proxy machinery to wage an active campaign on their own behalf. To the question whether this is permissible in the face of the rule that the board cannot use the corporate proxy machinery to perpetuate itself in office, the courts have answered, "yes," provided that (1) the con-

---

Code Ann. §1701.39 (Page 1964); Pa. Stat. Ann. tit. 15, §1401 (Supp. 1974); ABA Model Bus. Corp. Act §36 (1969 rev.). Over a dozen states also permit voting rights to be accorded to bondholders. See 1 American Bar Foundation, Model Business Corporation Act Annotated 655-656 (2d ed. 1971, & 1973 Supp. at 151). For present purposes, bondholders who have such rights may be treated like the holders of equity securities.

23. See, e.g., Del. Code Ann. tit. 8, §141(a) (Supp. 1975); Ill. Ann. Stat. ch. 32, §157.33 (Smith-Hurd Supp. 1974); N.J. Stat. Ann. §14A:6-1 (Supp. 1974); N.Y. Bus. Corp. Law §701 (McKinney Supp. 1974).

24. Some statutes provide that the board shall exercise "all corporate powers." E.g., Calif. Corp. Code §800 (West Supp. 1974). However, the voting of a corporation's own shares is not a corporate power.

25. Braude v. Havenner, 38 Cal. App. 2d 526, 532, 113 Cal. Rptr. 386, 389 (1974); Hall v. Trans-Lux Daylight Picture Screen Corp., 20 Del. Ch. 78, 84, 171 A. 226, 228 (1934); Streett v. Laclede-Christy Co., 409 S.W.2d 691, 698-699 (Mo. 1966); Rosenfeld v. Fairchild Engine & Airplane Corp., 309 N.Y. 168, 173-174, 128 N.E.2d 291, 293 (1955) (Froessel, J.).

26. See Hall v. Trans-Lux Daylight Picture Screen Corp., 20 Del. Ch. 78, 82-83, 171 A. 226, 228 (1934); Rosenfeld v. Fairchild Engine & Airplane Corp., 309 N.Y. 168, 128 N.E.2d 291 (1955); Lawyers' Advertising Co. v. Consolidated Ry. Lighting & Refrigerating Co., 187 N.Y. 395, 80 N.E. 199 (1907); E. Aranow & H. Einhorn, supra note 3, at 548-549, 557; cf. Standard Gas & Electric Co., 24 S.E.C. 337, 340-341 (1946).

test involves an issue of policy rather than merely one of personnel, (2) the expenses involved are for the purpose of informing the shareholders concerning the policy issue, and (3) the expenses are reasonable.[27]

Superficially, use of this test enables the courts to stay within a rationale that the board can use the corporate proxy machinery when, but only when, it is acting within its authority and not violating normal fiduciary standards. Surely, the argument runs, the board has authority to make recommendations to the shareholders on issues of corporate policy, and surely making such recommendations does not violate the board's fiduciary duty.

But despite its surface appeal, this test is fundamentally defective. In terms of authority, the rationale underlying the test loses sight of the statutory principle that a director serves only a limited term of office.[28] This principle insures that the shareholders have the right to redetermine corporate policy periodically, if they wish to do so, by electing new directors who favor policy changes. An incumbent board, of course, has authority to implement its policies during its term of office, and this is normally so even though the effects of its action will persist beyond its term. But when an incumbent board seeks to use the corporate proxy machinery to speak to a policy issue in the context of an election campaign, it must necessarily be addressing itself to policy the corporation should follow *after* expiration of the board's term of office; that is, to policy which the incumbent board has no authority to implement. In this, if the statutory principle of a limited term of office is to be respected, its members must be regarded not as officeholders but as officeseekers.[29]

In terms of fiduciary duties also, the rationale underlying the policy-information-reasonability test loses sight of the crucial fact that toward the expiration of his term an incumbent director

27. See, e.g., Hall v. Trans-Lux Daylight Picture Screen Corp., 20 Del. Ch. 78, 80-83, 171 A. 226, 227-228 (1934); Streett v. Laclede-Christy Co., 409 S.W.2d 691, 698-699 (Mo. 1966); Rosenfeld v. Fairchild Engine & Airplane Corp., 309 N.Y. 168, 172-174, 128 N.E.2d 291, 292-293 (1955).

28. See, e.g., N.J. Stat. Ann. § § 14A:6-3 to :6-4 (1969); N.Y. Bus. Corp. Law § § 703-704 (McKinney 1963); ABA Model Bus. Corp. Act § § 36-37 (1969 rev.).

29. Cf. The Savoy Hotel Limited and The Berkeley Hotel Company Limited: Investigation Under Section 165(b) of the Companies Act, 1948: Report of Mr. E. Milner Holland, Q.C., at 25-26 (Her Majesty's Stationery Office 1954); Gower, Battle for the Berkeley, 68 Harv. L. Rev. 1176, 1185 (1955).

assumes the capacity of officeseeker as well as officeholder. As to policy issues in dispute between incumbents and insurgents, the director is therefore not a decisionmaker, but a proponent who is vitally self-interested in the acceptance of his proposals. Surely it cannot be left to the director to determine whether the future good of the shareholders requires spending corporate money to elect him to a new term. How many officeholders can resist the temptation of deeming themselves indispensable, particularly if the alternative includes not only being dispensable but being dispensed with? The incumbent's judgment concerning the effects of policy proposals must be regarded as the platform of a candidate seeking election, rather than the disinterested policy of a fiduciary, simply because in such matters the incumbent himself cannot say honestly in which capacity he acts.[30] Both in terms of authority and strict fiduciary standards, the presence of a policy issue in a proxy fight should not in itself justify board access to the corporate proxy machinery.[31]

Not surprisingly, considering the substantive defects of the rationale underlying the policy-information-reasonability test, it has proven to be incapable of meaningful application. Although the test is based on a distinction between policy and personnel matters, in fact almost everyone, even courts purporting to apply the test, agrees that this distinction is meaningless, that every contest involves or can be made to involve issues of policy, and that even issues of personnel are often issues of policy.[32] Although the

30. This analysis is applicable whether or not the board is a classified one. Although in elections to a classified board the incumbents may not all be office-seekers, they are typically all campaigners. The members of such boards normally form a cohesive control group, without regard to the classification, and incumbents must back a winning slate at each election or soon lose control.

31. If a doctrine may be judged by its fruits, it need only be added that the policy rationale has been further applied to reach the grotesque result that a board may legally spend corporate funds to buy out potential insurgents in order to prevent a policy issue from ever coming before the shareholders. See Cheff v. Mathes, 41 Del. Ch. 494, 504, 199 A.2d 548, 554 (1964); Kors v. Carey, 39 Del. Ch. 47, 55, 158 A.2d 136, 141 (1960). But see Bennett v. Propp, 41 Del. Ch. 14, 20-22, 187 A.2d 405, 408-409 (1962). See generally Brudney, supra note 21, at 259-285; Note, Buying Out Insurgent Shareholders with Corporate Funds, 70 Yale L.J. 308 (1960).

32. See. e.g., Steinberg v. Adams, 90 F. Supp. 604, 608 (S.D.N.Y. 1950) (Rifkind, J.); Braude v. Havenner, 38 Cal. App. 2d 526, 532, 113 Cal. Rptr. 386, 389 (1974); Hall v. Trans-Lux Daylight Picture Screen Corp., 20 Del. Ch. 78, 84-85, 171 A. 226, 228-229 (1934); McGoldrick v. Segal, 124 N.Y.L.J. 461, col. 2 (Sup. Ct.), affd. mem. sub nom. Blum v. Segal, 277 App. Div. 963, 99 N.Y.S.2d 850 (1950); Brudney,

test requires that the expenses be for the purpose of informing shareholders concerning the policy issue, in fact many common proxy-contest expenses – such as those for proxy solicitors and public-relations counsel[33] – are designed more to persuade than to inform.[34] And although it is intrinsic to the test that the expenses be "reasonable," no workable standard has been enunciated by which such reasonability is to be judged. Apart from a New York lower-court decision adverting to the relationship between the amount involved and the size of the corporation,[35] most of the cases do not bother to state criteria of reasonability, and most of the commentators have supplied either no gloss,[36] or gloss so meaningless as a requirement that the expenses be "ordinary and necessary,"[37] or that they "bear a *substantial relationship* to . . . full information dispersion to the stockholders. . . ."[38]

Thus the three-pronged policy-information-reasonability test is really no test at all, and there seems to be only one modern case[39] which has applied it to restrict board access to the corporate proxy machinery.[40] Some commentators have reacted by suggesting a flat prohibition against charging the corporation for such

supra note 21, at 282-283; Friedman, Expenses of Corporate Proxy Contests, 51 Colum. L. Rev. 951, 952-953 (1951); Machtinger, Proxy Fight Expenditures of Insurgent Shareholders, 19 Case W. Res. L. Rev. 212, 215 (1968); Comment, Expenses of a Proxy Fight – The Problem of Reimbursement by the Corporation, 10 Sw. L.J. 44, 47-48 (1956); Note, Proxy Solicitation Costs and Corporate Control, 61 Yale L.J. 229, 236 (1952).

33. Rosenfeld v. Fairchild Engine & Airplane Corp., 309 N.Y. 168, 177-178, 128 N.E.2d 291, 295-296 (1955) (dissenting opinion).

34. See F. Emerson & F. Latcham, supra note 1, at 72-73; cf. Friedman, supra note 32, at 954-955; Note, Financing Proxy Contests with Corporate Funds, 44 Geo. L.J. 303, 306-307 (1956); 69 Harv. L. Rev. 1132, 1134 (1956).

35. McGoldrick v. Segal, 124 N.Y.L.J. 461, col. 2 (Sup. Ct.), affd. mem. sub nom. Blum v. Segal, 277 App. Div. 963, 99 N.Y.S.2d 850 (1950).

36. E.g., Comment, Corporate Policy, the "Cure-all" for Proxy Solicitation Ailments?, 49 Mich. L. Rev. 605, 610 (1951) ("The most that can be done in the way of asserting a principle is to take sanctuary behind the time-worn generalization that such expenditures as are *reasonably* necessary will be upheld." (emphasis in original)); cf. Note, supra note 32, at 236-237.

37. 24. U. Cin. L. Rev. 606, 607-608 (1955).

38. Comment, supra note 32, at 51 (emphasis in original). See also Machtinger, supra note 32, at 214 ("necessary to the informational process").

39. Rosenthal v. Edwards, 119 N.Y.L.J. 1174, col. 4 (Sup. Ct. 1948); cf. Lawyers' Advertising Co. v. Consolidated Ry. Lighting & Refrigerating Co., 187 N.Y. 395, 80 N.E. 199 (1907); Pittsburgh Steel Co. v. Walker, 92 Pitt. Leg. J. 464 (C.P. 1944).

40. Cf. Brudney, supra note 21, at 282-283; 41 Cornell L.Q. 714, 715 n. 8 (1956).

common campaign techniques as proxy solicitors, public relations counsel, and the like, on the ground that they are not really designed to impart information, and therefore cannot be justified on the basis that the board has authority to inform the shareholders.[41] Since, however, these techniques center on persuasion through rational means, they clearly do have an informational component. The real problem, then, is not whether incumbents should be unable to charge the corporation for the cost of techniques which do not involve imparting information, but whether incumbents should be unable to charge for techniques which provide shareholders with no more information than is already available in the proxy materials.[42]

In considering this problem, three facts must be viewed in conjunction: (1) Personal communication, or even communication through newspapers, is often a much more effective way of reaching shareholders than communication through the proxy statement; (2) Proxy fights involve a lot of money – one informed estimate is 40,000 to 1,000,000 dollars[43] – and most of the expenses are probably incurred in connection with just such techniques; (3) While corporate directorships are unquestionably valuable, in themselves they do not normally pay very much money. A survey of 674 corporations showed that the median annual compensation for outside directorships is in the $3600 to $4800 range, while inside directorships paid little or nothing[44] (although many inside directors of course command high salaries and fringe benefits in their executive capacities). Putting these facts together, most outside directors and many inside directors ordinarily could not be expected to defend a proxy fight in the most effective manner out of their own pockets. Thus a rule which precluded incumbents from using corporate resources for such

41. See F. Emerson & F. Latcham, supra note 1, at 73 (last-minute messages); Friedman, supra note 32, at 954-955 (proxy solicitors); Note, 44 Geo. L.J., supra note 34, at 306-307 (proxy solicitors, public relations counsel, and other "high pressure methods"); cf. Schulman, The Costs of Free Speech in Proxy Contests for Corporate Control, 20 Wayne L. Rev. 1, 17-20 (1973).

42. See Schulman, supra note 41, at 17, 20.

43. Pomerantz, Book Review, 117 U. Pa. L. Rev. 493 (1969).

44. See J. Bacon, Corporate Directorship Practices: Compensation 3 (Chart 1), 46-47 (Conference Board Report No. 596, 1973); cf. M. Mace, supra note 20, at 101-102. But see Korn/Ferry International, Board of Directors Annual Study 12 (1975) (average compensation of $7900); The Corporate Director – A Profile, Financial Executive, Jan. 1974, at 7 (average compensation of $5000-$10,000).

techniques might tend to drive corporate offices into the hands of those who are ready to pay the amounts required.[45] Board access to the corporate proxy machinery in connection with the election of directors may therefore be justified, not because the election of directors is a board function – it is not; and not because typically the issues are policy issues – they are not; but because in the long run the shareholders and the entire economy might suffer if incumbents had to choose between paying for effective proxy campaigns out of their own pockets or confining themselves to the proxy materials.

But this rationale for board access to the corporate proxy machinery also suggests a limitation on that access: since the only sound justification for permitting incumbents to use the corporate proxy machinery is the desirability of neutralizing personal campaign funds as a determinant of corporate office, incumbents should be permitted to use such machinery only to the extent necessary to accomplish that purpose. If the insurgents engage in an advertising campaign, it is reasonable for the incumbents to match them, ad for ad, at the corporation's expense. If the in-

45. Cf. Rosenfeld v. Fairchild Engine & Airplane Corp., 309 N.Y. 168, 173, 128 N.E.2d 291, 293 (1955) (Froessel, J.); Machtinger, supra note 32, at 216; Marsh, Are Directors Trustees? Conflict of Interest and Corporate Morality, 22 Bus. Law. 35, 60 (1966); Note, Reimbursement for Corporate Campaign Expenses Incurred in Proxy Fights, 43 Calif. L. Rev. 893, 899 (1955).

Professor Schulman suggests that management would not be totally disadvantaged, because of "[t]he tendency of shareholders to vote in compliance with the wishes of incumbent management, management's control over corporate records and shareholder lists and its contacts with banks and brokers." Schulman, supra note 41, at 14-15. In this connection, he points to the fact that under the SEC's Rule U-65, the managers of public utility holding companies have been somewhat curtailed in their use of corporate funds for proxy solicitation, and yet proxy contests for control of such companies seldom occur. Id. at 15-16. However, Schulman concedes that "placing limitations on the use of the company treasury for [aggressive campaign techniques] . . . may well produce a somewhat greater degree of success for insurgents." Furthermore, his argument is open to several objections. (i) It is questionable whether "[t]he tendency of shareholders to vote in compliance with the wishes of incumbent management" would hold up under a largely unanswered barrage by insurgents. (ii) The ability of management to keep shareholder lists out of insurgent hands is almost invariably illicit, and is becoming increasingly diluted. See, e.g., Credit Bureau Reports, Inc. v. Credit Bureau of St. Paul, 290 A.2d 691 (Del. 1972); General Tire Corp. v. Talley Industries, Inc., 43 Del. Ch. 531, 240 A.2d 755 (1968). (iii) Insurgents often have contacts with banks and brokers comparable to management's. Cf. Yoran, Restraints on Incumbent Directors in Intracorporate Battles for Control, 7 U. Rich. L. Rev. 431, 454-455, 460 (1973). (iv) There is only limited incentive for seeking control of corporations in an industry as heavily regulated as public utility holding companies.

surgents employ public-relations counsel or proxy solicitors, or if it is reasonably foreseeable that they will,[46] the incumbents should be allowed to do so at the corporation's expense. But incumbents should not be allowed to use the corporate proxy machinery to wage a campaign that substantially exceeds that of the insurgents.[47] Just as the campaign chest of insurgents should not determine corporate elections, neither should the held-in-trust wealth of the corporation.

It appears likely that business mores already reflect such a rule. Comparative spending figures are readily available for 13 contests.[48] In ten of these, the incumbents spent either less or not materially more than did the insurgents. Of the other three cases, in only one were the incumbents' expenses radically disproportionate to those of the insurgents.[49] Thus, the rule proposed would be a shift more in theory than in practice.

What about the other side of the coin? Would a matching test result in an undue drain on the corporate treasury by manage-

46. Normally, the incumbents' access to the corporate proxy machinery should be restricted to defending against and reacting to actual insurgent campaigning. However, there are only a limited number of proxy soliciting firms, which differ in ability and may not be employable on short notice. If the incumbents could not retain such a firm until the insurgents did so, they might be unable to retain the firm of their choice, or perhaps any firm at all. Therefore, reasonable foreseeability of such an insurgent expenditure should be sufficient to justify a defensive expenditure.

47. The possibility that there may be more than one group of insurgents raises the question whether, in such a case, the incumbents should have such access to the corporate proxy machinery as to match the total amount spent by all insurgents, or only that of the highest-spending group. Since the sole purpose of allowing management access should be to neutralize personal campaign funds as a determinant of corporate office, the incumbents should be limited to matching the expenses of the highest-spending group, unless the groups are acting in concert.

48. In response to a senatorial request to ascertain the costs of six of the then most recent proxy battles, the SEC in 1957 reported the following figures:

Company	*Managements' Expenses*	*Insurgents' Expenses*
Alaska Juneau Mining Co.	$ 23,871	$32,795
Fairbanks, Morse & Co.	50,000	50,000
Libby, McNeill & Libby	25,000	19,000
Seiberling Rubber Co.	35,000	35,000
Thermoid Co.	5,000	25,000
Virginia-Carolina Chemical Co.	125,411	83,019

Hearings on SEC Enforcement Problems Before a Subcomm. of the Senate Comm. on Banking and Currency, 85th Cong., 1st Sess. 115 (1957). Similarly, E. Aranow & H. Einhorn, supra note 3, at 543, report comparative spending figures for seven contested elections as follows:

ment? A matching test ties the incumbents' reimbursable expenses to the amount spent by the insurgents, and insurgent spending is likely to be limited by the fact that under present rules of law insurgents are not entitled to reimbursement of their expenses as a matter of right.[50] Furthermore, the theory behind a matching test is that insurgents should not be enabled to win elections simply because they are able to feed more money into a campaign than incumbents. If that theory is sound it should apply regardless of how much the insurgents spend; indeed, the more insurgents are prepared to spend, the greater may be the need for corporate reimbursement of the incumbents' expenses.

While a matching test has not explicitly emerged from the cases, it can be viewed simply as an elaboration of the reasonability prong of the conventional policy-information-reasonability test, and indeed may have been at least subliminally so contemplated by the courts. For example, in *Rosenfeld v. Fairchild Engine & Airplane Corp.*,[51] decided by the New York Court of Appeals, it was said in applying this test:

> In the event of a proxy contest, if the directors may not freely *answer the challenges* of outside groups and in good faith *defend* their actions with respect to corporate policy . . . the corporation may be at the mercy of persons seeking to wrest control for their own purposes, so long as such persons have ample funds to conduct a proxy contest.[52]

Company	*Managements' Expenses*	*Insurgents' Expenses*
Fairchild Engine & Airplane Corp.	$133,966	$ 127,556
Sparks-Withington Co.	51,165	6,000
Thompson-Starret Co.	20,110	25,755
United Cigar-Whelan Stores Corp.	60,159	30,534
New York Central R.R.	875,000	1,308,733
New York, New Haven and Hartford R.R.	94,321	94,834
Republic Corp.	257,000	365,215

49. The management figures, however, probably do not attribute any amount to the labor of corporate personnel and the use of corporate facilities. Thus in a case growing out of the 1967 MGM proxy contest, it was reported that the insurgents spent $175,000 while management spent $125,000 "exclusive of amounts normally expended for a solicitation for an election of directors and costs represented by salaries and wages of regular employees and officers." Levin v. Metro-Goldwyn-Mayer, Inc., 264 F. Supp. 797, 802 (S.D.N.Y. 1967). On the other hand, the insurgent figures probably do not attribute any amount to the value of the insurgents' own time.

50. See text at note 88 infra.

51. 309 N.Y. 168, 128 N.E.2d 291 (1955).

52. Id. at 173, 128 N.E.2d at 293 (Froessel, J.) (emphasis added).

§9.3. Shareholder Access

Management access to the corporate proxy machinery derives essentially from state law, although it is recognized implicitly by the Proxy Rules.[53] As to shareholder access, the Proxy Rules go further, for rule 14a-8[54] provides explicitly that certain types of shareholder proposals must be included in the corporation's proxy materials if they are made by a holder of voting securities subject to the Proxy Rules.[55] However, the access so provided is severely restricted in a variety of ways. Most important for present purposes, rule 14a-8 explicitly excepts from its coverage elections to office,[56] for reasons that have never been explained.[57] However, in the case of shareholder access, as in the case of management access, the Proxy Rules do not preempt the field of proxy regulation to the exclusion of state law, but merely set minimum conditions of fair disclosure and fair conduct; beyond these minimum conditions, questions concerning the allocation of powers between management and shareholders, including questions concerning

53. See Proxy Rules, Schedule 14A, Item 3(a), 17 C.F.R. §240.14a-101(3)(a) (1974).

54. 17 C.F.R. §240.14a-8 (1974).

55. Proxy Rule 14a-7, 17 C.F.R. §240.14a-7 (1974), provides that under certain circumstances a corporation must either furnish a shareholder with a shareholder list or, at its option, mail out materials for him at his expense. Although this provision can be used to facilitate communication among shareholders, it does not really provide meaningful access to the corporate proxy machinery since the shareholder must pay the cost of communication. Furthermore, the machinery provided by rule 14a-7 is frequently unsatisfactory. See 2, 5 Loss 890-894, 2851-2853 (2d ed. 1961, Supp. 1969).

56. Proxy Rule 14a-8(a), 17 C.F.R. §240.14a-8(a) (1974).

57. This exclusion was adopted in 1940, when the SEC first formalized the shareholder-proposal rule. The press release announcing adoption of the rule gave no ground for the exception. See SEC, Securities Exchange Act of 1934 Release No. 2376 (1940). In 1942 the Commission's staff proposed amendments to the Proxy Rules which would have required names of shareholder nominees to be included in the corporate proxy materials. (The proposal limited the number of shareholder nominees to twice the number of directors; if a greater number of nominations were put forward, management was to have power to select from among them "on any equitable basis." See Hearings, supra note 15, at 34-36.) The proposal was circulated for comment, Hearings, supra note 15, at 17-18; 2, 5 Loss 901 n. 178, 2856 (2d ed. 1961, Supp. 1969), but not adopted; again no explanation was given in the relevant press release. See SEC, Securities Exchange Act of 1934 Release No. 3347 (1942). For a critique of the SEC's procedure for adopting rules, see Buxbaum, Securities Regulation and the Foreign Issuer Exemption: A Study in the Process of Accommodating Foreign Interests, 54 Cornell L. Rev. 358, 374-378 (1969).

power over the corporate proxy machinery, must be answered by state law.[58] Let us turn then to an examination, under state law, of the questions: (1) whether shareholders may designate their candidates for directorships in the corporate proxy materials; and (2) whether shareholders may use corporate funds to pay the expenses of a campaign on their candidates' behalf.

A. Designation of Candidates for Directorships

Current practice in connection with the election of directors of publicly held corporations reflects the current assumption that the board has virtually exclusive access to the corporate proxy machinery. The board's candidates for directorships (normally, the members of the incumbent board) are listed and described in a corporate proxy statement prepared in connection with the annual shareholders' meeting; and those same candidates are designated in an accompanying corporate proxy card, in the form of a ballot, which the shareholder is asked to sign and return, thus signifying his vote in favor of the board's candidates. Insurgent shareholders, on the other hand, will normally be forced to send out a separate proxy statement and proxy card listing and describing their candidates, under their own names and at their own expense. Thus, current practice favors an incumbent board in two vitally important ways. First, an incumbent board uses corporate facilities to solicit proxies on its own behalf, while insurgents may have to undertake expensive and time-consuming litigation even to obtain a shareholder list, and must then pay out of their own pockets the expenses of preparing, clearing, printing, and distributing their proxy statement and proxy card. Second, incumbents gain an important psychological advantage in soliciting under the name of "the corporation" rather than under their own names, as insurgents must do.

58. See Securities Exchange Act of 1934, §28(a), 15 U.S.C. §78bb(a) (1970); Wood, Walker & Co. v. Evans, 300 F. Supp. 171, 172-173 (D. Colo. 1969); Kaminsky v. Abrams, 281 F. Supp. 501, 504-505 (S.D.N.Y. 1968); 1, 4 Loss 155-156, 2291-2294 (2d ed. 1961, Supp. 1969); 2, 5 id. 902-903, 2856 ("If Congress had intended to give the Commission power to reallocate functions between the [board and the shareholders], so revolutionary a federal intervention would presumably have been more clearly expressed."); Fleischer, "Federal Corporation Law": An Assessment, 78 Harv. L. Rev. 1146, 1153 (1965) ("The federal securities laws affect a wide range of corporate activities, but generally they do not preempt complementary state laws; they are pervasive but not exclusive"); cf. Diamond v. Oreamuno, 24 N.Y.2d 494, 248 N.E.2d 910 (1969).

Is this practice lawful? While this question must be answered under state law, neither statutes nor cases speak directly to the point.[59] However, several important principles of corporate law each lead to the conclusion that shareholders are entitled to designate candidates for directorships in any proxy card or proxy statement issued by the corporation which lists candidates' names, subject to reasonable restrictions. These principles are: that the exclusive power to elect the board rests with the shareholders; that corporate funds and facilities cannot be applied to the personal benefit of corporate directors or officers except for a clearly defined corporate purpose; and that corporate assets cannot be applied to the benefit of individual shareholders except in an evenhanded manner.

1. The exclusive power to elect the board rests with the shareholders. Under the corporate statutes the power to elect the board is vested exclusively in the shareholders.[60] The board does not have the power to elect its successor board (although it is often empowered to fill interim vacancies caused by death, resignation, or removal),[61] and therefore cannot take actions for the purpose of perpetuating itself in office.[62] "No one would argue

59. The issue of management's right to solicit proxies under the corporate name was raised but not squarely decided in Empire S. Gas Co. v. Gray, 29 Del. Ch. 95, 110, 46 A.2d 741, 748 (1946).

60. See note 22 supra.

61. See, e.g., Cal. Corp. Code §808 (West 1955); Del. Code Ann. tit. 8, §223 (1974); N.J. Stat. Ann. §14A:6-5 (1969); N.Y. Bus. Corp. Law §705(a) (McKinney Supp. 1974); Ohio Rev. Code Ann. §1701.58(D) (Page 1964); Pa. Stat. Ann. tit. 15, §1402(3) (1967); ABA Model Bus. Corp. Act §38 (1969 rev.).

62. See, e.g., A. Berle & G. Means, The Modern Corporation and Private Property 81-88 (1932); cf. Walsh v. State ex rel. Cook, 199 Ala. 123, 74 So. 45 (1917); Coalition to Advocate Public Utility Responsibility, Inc. v. Engels, 364 F. Supp. 1202 (D. Minn. 1973); Schnell v. Chris-Craft Industries, Inc., 285 A.2d 437 (Del. 1971); State ex rel. Ryan v. Cronan, 23 Nev. 437, 452-453, 49 P. 41, 45 (1897); Valle v. North Jersey Automobile Club, 125 N.J. Super. 302, 310 A.2d 518 (1973); Penn-Texas Corp. v. Niles-Bement-Pond Co., 34 N.J. Super. 373, 112 A.2d 302 (Ch. 1955); Commonwealth ex rel. Gallagher v. Knorr, 21 Pa. Dist. 784, 40 Pa. County Ct. 325 (1912); Note, supra note 31, at 313-315. But cf. Northwest Industries, Inc. v. B. F. Goodrich Co., 301 F. Supp. 706 (N.D. Ill. 1969); Adams v. Clearance Corp., 35 Del. 459, 121 A.2d 302 (1956).

In Gallagher a bylaw limited corporate office to persons nominated by (1) a committee consisting of the corporate solicitor and two persons appointed by the president, or (2) 25 percent of the shareholders. The court in striking down the bylaw stated: "The committee of three has the powers of 25 per cent. of the whole number of stockholders in the matter of nominations. If this committee were freely selected by the stockholders from among themselves, something might be said to vindicate it as a mode

that an elected public official should be permitted to extend his own term of office. The same reasoning applies to a corporate director who is also an elected official and a servant of the corporate electorate."[63]

As a corollary to their exclusive power to elect the board, shareholders have at least concurrent power to nominate candidates for directorships.[64] It has already been shown that the proxy system is today's shareholders' meeting. Correspondingly, the designation of candidates in the proxy materials is today's nomination. The shareholder power to make nominations must therefore carry with it access to the basic corporate machinery used to make nominations, that is, the corporate proxy materials. Although it might be objected that nominations are not made in the proxy materials, but rather from the floor at the annual meeting, such an objection at best is based purely on form, and is not well-based even there. Normally, proxies are executed and mailed by shareholders before the date of the meeting, and proxies gathered in a solicitation subject to the Proxy Rules can be voted only in favor of persons named in the proxy.[65] If nominations are not deemed to occur until the meeting, voting would precede nominations – a rather unusual format. Indeed, it appears that in actual corporate practice the bylaws usually do not fix the time for making nomi-

---

of regulating elections. Even then there would be grave objections to be considered. When, however, the solicitor, an officer whose position is pecuniarily advantageous, is made one of the three, and the president, who is the highest functionary, appoints the other two, the liability of the scheme to degenerate into a device for the easy reelection of the incumbents is obvious. This committee of three, brought together by the president, acts easily and smoothly. The stockholders themselves are, however, balked at every step. They must form a kind of subassociation or caucus in order to enable them to exercise their individual rights. If they do not, they will find it impracticable to get each one of 25 per cent. of the stockholders spontaneously and at the same instant to hit upon a list of nominees which will prove to be identical with the lists thought out by the other members of the 25 per cent. club. The conclusion seems obvious that the scheme automatically deprives the stockholders of all practical control of the election." 21 Pa. Dist. at 785-786. Other cases have upheld such bylaws where the minimum number of shareholders required to nominate a candidate was more reasonable. See cases cited in note 74 infra.

63. Penn-Texas Corp. v. Niles-Bement-Pond Co., 34 N.J. Super. 373, 381, 112 A.2d 302, 307 (Ch. 1955).

64. See E. Aranow & H. Einhorn, supra note 3, at 363. Unlike the shareholders' right to elect the board, their right to nominate candidates for the board may not be exclusive. See text at note 68 infra; cf. Poirier v. Welch, 233 F. Supp. 436, 439 (D.D.C. 1964).

65. Proxy Rule 14a-4(d), (e), 17 C.F.R. §240.14a-4(d), (e) (1974).

nations,[66] and that in fact the predominant practice is to treat the proxy materials as the corporation's nominating machinery – so that, for example, persons in whose favor proxies are solicited are normally characterized in the proxy materials as "nominees" rather than merely as "candidates."[67]

In light of the fact that the shareholders have exclusive power to elect the board, it might be questioned on what principle the board may use the corporate proxy machinery to designate candidates at all. Such use might be justified on two bases: as a derivative of a customary concurrent power to nominate,[68] and through application of the principle that as far as reasonably practicable, personal campaign funds should not be permitted to determine corporate office. But neither basis would justify *exclusive* board access to the corporate proxy machinery for this purpose. Even assuming the board has a customary power to nominate candidates, it could not abrogate the shareholders' right to nominate, which inheres by law. And if personal campaign funds should not be permitted to determine corporate office, far less should the funds of the corporation itself, as would tend to be the case if the board's access were exclusive.

2. Corporate funds and facilities cannot be applied to the personal benefit of directors except for a clearly defined corporate purpose. Corporate funds and facilities cannot be applied to the personal benefit of directors, except for a clearly defined corporate purpose, such as compensation for services.[69] But since a

66. See, e.g., By-Laws of AMF, Inc., as amended through Sept. 12, 1972; By-Laws of American Express Co.; By-Laws of The Anaconda Co., as amended to January 7, 1975; By-Laws of Avco Corp., as amended through Oct. 25, 1974; By-Laws of Eastman Kodak Co., as amended through August 19, 1971; By-Laws of General Motors Corp., as amended to 1975; By-Laws of Mobil Oil Corp., as amended to Jan. 25, 1974.

67. See Notice of Annual Meeting and Proxy Statement of AMF, Inc., March 15, 1974, at 1-5; Notice of Annual Meeting of Shareholders and Proxy Statement of American Express Co., March 25, 1975, at 1-7; Notice of Annual Meeting of Shareholders and Proxy Statement of The Anaconda Co., April 8, 1974, at 2-4; Notice of Annual Meeting and Proxy Statement of Avco Corp., March 5, 1974, at 2; Notice of Annual Meeting and Proxy Statement of Eastman Kodak Co., March 29, 1974, at 3-11; Notice of Annual Meeting of Stockholders and Proxy Statement of Eastman Kodak Co., March 29, 1974, at 3-11; Notice of Annual Meeting of Stockholders and Proxy Statement of General Motors Corp., April 18, 1974, at 1-9. But see Notice of Annual Meeting of Stockholders and Proxy Statement of Mobil Oil Corp., March 17, 1975 (referring to "each person to be nominated by management").

68. Poirier v. Welch, 233 F. Supp. 436, 439 (D.D.C. 1964).

69. See, e.g., Diamond v. Oreamuno, 24 N.Y.2d 494, 248 N.E.2d 910 (1969).

corporate directorship is a position of value, to permit incumbent directors to appropriate exclusive access to the corporate proxy machinery to designate themselves as candidates would permit them to apply corporate assets to their own personal benefit for no established corporate purpose – indeed, in violation of the corporate principle that power to nominate and elect resides in the shareholders.[70] A corporate ballot prepared for use at the annual meeting could not validly exclude anyone properly nominated for office, nor could it give favored treatment to one group of nominees. The proxy card and proxy statement, when paid for by corporate funds, become the corporate ballot, and should likewise be open to all persons whose candidacies are properly advanced.

Of course, permitting incumbent directors to designate themselves as candidates for office in the corporate proxy materials even on a nonexclusive basis might be characterized as permitting them to apply corporate funds and facilities to their own personal benefit. However, a nonexclusive right is not only significantly less valuable than an exclusive one, but also serves a corporate purpose, since it tends to maximize the number of potential candidates for office and neutralize personal campaign funds as a determinant of office.

3. Corporate assets cannot be applied to the benefit of individual shareholders in a nonevenhanded manner. Just as corporate funds and facilities cannot be applied to the personal benefit of directors except for a clearly defined corporate purpose, so corporate funds and facilities cannot be applied to the benefit of individual shareholders except in an evenhanded manner.[71] Yet it seems likely that in many or most corporations in which a proxy contest occurs, the incumbent directors originally achieved office

70. A grant of exclusive access could not be justified on the ground that it constituted compensation of the directors, because the "compensation" would in effect consist of a term longer than that legally provided for. Cf. State ex rel. Ryan v. Cronan, 23 Nev. 437, 452-453, 49 P. 41, 45 (1897).

71. Cf. In re San Joaquin Light & Power Corp., 52 Cal. App. 2d 814, 127 P.2d 29 (1942); Iback v. Elevator Supplies Co., 118 N.J. Eq. 90, 93, 177 A. 458, 459 (Ch. 1935); General Inv. Co. v. American Hide & Leather Co., 98 N.J. Eq. 326, 331, 129 A. 244, 246 (Ct. Err. & App. 1925); Theis v. Durr, 125 Wis. 651, 104 N.W. 985 (1905); Herwitz, Stock Redemptions and the Accumulated Earnings Tax, 74 Harv. L. Rev. 866, 894 (1961); Israels, Are Corporate Powers Still Held in Trust?, 64 Colum. L. Rev. 1446, 1452-1453 (1964); Von Falkenhausen & Steefel, Shareholders' Rights in German Corporations (AG and GmbH), 10 A.J.C.L. 407, 408 (1961).

because they held or represented a significant amount of stock.[72] To give "the board" the right to designate candidates in the corporate proxy materials while refusing that right to "shareholders" would, in substance, often be to discriminate among shareholders on the basis of whether they were in or out at the time of the solicitation.

That corporate assets cannot be applied to the benefit of shareholders in a nonevenhanded manner does not mean that each individual shareholder must have the right to designate candidates for director in the corporate proxy materials. No sound reason appears why a bylaw, at least a shareholder-adopted bylaw, could not limit such access, provided that it did so in an evenhanded and reasonable way.[73] Thus bylaws could validly provide that candidates for director may be designated in the corporate proxy materials only by the board (or some committee thereof) or by shareholders holding in the aggregate some minimum percentage of the corporation's outstanding stock – say five percent. The courts have upheld comparable bylaws restricting the shareholders' right to nominate candidates for corporate office,[74] upon which

72. Cf. chapter 5 supra.

73. Cf. Selama-Dindings Plantations, Ltd. v. Durham, 216 F. Supp. 104, 115 (S.D. Ohio 1963), affd. per curiam sub nom. Selama-Dindings Plantations, Ltd. v. Cincinnati Union Stock Yard Co., 337 F.2d 949 (6th Cir. 1964); Conlee Constr. Co. v. Cay Const. Co., 221 So. 2d 792, 796-797 (Fla. Dist. Ct. App. 1969); 8 W. Fletcher, Private Corporations §4191 (rev. vol. 1966); 1 G. Hornstein, Corporation Law and Practice §265 (1959).

74. See In re Flushing Hosp. & Dispensary, 288 N.Y. 125, 41 N.E.2d 917, modified, 288 N.Y. 735, 43 N.E.2d 356 (1942) (upholding, sub silentio, a bylaw restricting nominations to those made by a board-appointed nominating committee or by fifteen members); Stuberfield v. Long Island City Sav. & Loan Assn., 37 Misc. 2d 811, 235 N.Y.S.2d 908 (Sup. Ct. 1962) (upholding a bylaw restricting nominations to those made by a board-appointed nominating committee or by five percent of the shareholders); cf. Booker v. First Fed. Sav. & Loan Assn., 215 Ga. 277, 110 S.E.2d 360, cert. denied, 361 U.S. 916 (1959); In re Hamilton, 5 N.J. Misc. 660, 137 A. 843 (Sup. Ct. 1927); In re City Sav. & Loan Assn., 123 N.Y.S.2d 852 (Sup. Ct. 1953); In re O'Shea, 241 App. Div. 699, 269 N.Y.S. 840 (1934); Pa. Stat. Ann. tit. 15, §1505(A) (Supp. 1969). But see Commonwealth ex rel. Gallagher v. Knorr, 21 Pa. Dist. 784, 40 Pa. Cty. 325 (1912) (n. 62 supra); cf. In re Farrell, 205 App. Div. 443, 445, 200 N.Y.S. 95, 96, affd. per curiam, 236 N.Y. 603, 142 N.E. 301 (1923); Commonwealth ex rel. Laughlin v. Green, 351 Pa. 170, 40 A.2d 492 (1945); Commonwealth ex rel. Grabert v. Markey, 325 Pa. 433, 190 A. 892 (1937); Commonwealth ex rel. Goldstein v. Copperman, 26 Pa. Dist. 763 (1917).

A five percent requirement would not necessarily be reasonable in every situation; for example, it would be unduly burdensome in a very large membership corporation where it would require concerted action by five percent of the total number of members,

the right to designate candidates in the corporate proxy materials is partially based.

The conclusion drawn so far is a very limited one: shareholders have the right to designate candidates for office in the corporate proxy materials, but this right may be circumscribed by reasonable bylaws. It does not necessarily follow that shareholders can use the corporate proxy machinery to pay the expenses of a proxy campaign, a question which will be discussed below. Nor does it follow that management is prohibited from grouping its candidates together and designating these candidates as the management slate – a slate that would probably be elected in the normal course of things. I recognize, however, that this conclusion will nevertheless strike many as unconventional – unconventional perhaps to a fault.[75] Let me therefore attempt to anticipate three kinds of argument that might be made against it.

One argument, which stems from the conclusion's apparent unconventionality, is that even if shareholders might once have claimed the right to designate candidates in the corporate proxy materials, a contrary practice of denying that right has grown up which it is now too late to challenge.[76] In fact, however, it seems highly unlikely that such a practice could be proved, if only because the assertion of the right is so seldom made. True, management has probably assumed that shareholders do not have access to the corporate proxy machinery except under rule 14a-8, and others, including shareholders, have probably assumed either that management's assumption was correct or that in any event management would deny shareholders' requests for such access. But an assumption hardly constitutes a practice. Furthermore, the assumption has for most purposes not been relied upon by those who might set it up as a defense, has not been universally accepted,[77] and where accepted has been accepted uncritically. Finally, even if a practice of denying access to shareholders could be proved, it should not be enshrined as a rule of law, given its

rather than by persons holding five percent of total ownership. See Valle v. North Jersey Automobile Club, 125 N.J. Super. 302, 310 A.2d 518 (1973). But see Dozier v. Automobile Club of Michigan, No. 178 638 (Mich. Cir. Ct. Wayne Cty., Nov. 12, 1974).

75. Such a conclusion is not, however, unprecedented. Cf. Brudney, supra note 21, at 284; Caplin, Shareholder Nominations of Directors: A Program for Fair Corporate Suffrage, 39 Va. L. Rev. 141, 151-154, 159-161 (1953); Friedman, supra note 32, at 959 n. 31; Stifel, supra note 8, at 348; Note, supra note 8, at 1168 n. 23.

76. Cf. Manacher v. Reynolds, 39 Del. Ch. 401, 418, 165 A.2d 741, 751 (1960).

77. See note 75 supra.

self-serving nature, its conflict with significant principles of corporate law, and its own lack of principled justification.

> [A] large portion of that legal opinion which has passed current for law, falls within the description of "law taken for granted." If a statistical table of legal propositions should be drawn out, and the first column headed "Law by Statute,"and the second "Law by Decision;" a third column, under the heading of "Law taken for granted," would comprise as much matter as both the others combined. But . . . the mere statement and restatement of a doctrine, — the mere repetition of the *cantilena* of lawyers, cannot make it law, unless it can be traced to some competent authority, . . . if it be irreconcilable to some clear legal principle.[78]

A second possible argument against the right of shareholders to designate candidates in the corporate proxy materials is that such a result would be impracticable. Certainly, practicability should be considered in determining the rules governing access to the corporate proxy machinery. It does not seem impracticable, however, to permit the shareholders to designate candidates through that machinery. Such access need be triggered only when the corporate proxy machinery is set in motion for a similar purpose by management, and therefore would not entail the distribution of corporate proxy materials that would not otherwise be distributed; all that would be required is the addition of extra names to a proxy card and extra names and descriptions to a proxy statement being distributed anyway. Furthermore, since the corporate proxy machinery will predictably be set in motion at approximately the same date every year, a shareholder's exercise of this right could be conditioned on the submission of the names of his candidates a reasonable time in advance of this date.[79] Thus where the right is exercised — and it will not always be exercised — it is doubtful that it would add materially to the basic solicitation cost. And corporations which deem an unrestricted shareholder right to designate candidates impracticable can adopt a bylaw limiting the right to shareholders owning in the aggregate some minimum percentage of the corporation's stock, say five percent. If it is practicable to spend corporate funds to designate management candidates for office, it is not impracticable to spend

78. O'Connell v. Queen, 8 Eng. Rep. 1061, 1143 (H.L. 1844) (Lord Denman). See also C. Allen, Law in the Making 329-334 (7th ed. 1964).

79. Cf. Proxy Rule 14a-8(a), 17 C.F.R. § 240.14a-8(a) (1974).

some small additional funds to designate the candidates of a shareholder group owning such a percentage of the corporation's stock.

A third possible argument is that as a matter of policy it is preferable to maximize managerial power and minimize the power of shareholders. Such an argument is normally made to rest on one of two different premises: (1) That management knows better than the shareholders themselves what is good for the shareholders, so that the shareholders' own best interests are promoted by limiting shareholders' rights;[80] or (2) That the public interest is best advanced by scaling down the shareholders' interests in favor of corporate client-groups, such as labor or consumers, and that to accomplish this purpose it is necessary to weaken shareholder control over management, which is then in a position to recognize client-group claims.[81] The first premise assumes that the average shareholder is economically naive. However, as pointed out earlier, while the average *shareholder* may be economically naive (although even this has not been proved), the great bulk of *shareholdings* are controlled by sophisticated and wealthy individual or institutional investors who are very well able to calculate their own interests.[82] The second premise assumes that ultimate shareholder control prevents management from being responsive to the due interests of others. In fact, however, even if ultimate shareholder control reinforces a corporate orientation toward profit maximization, it does not prevent management from behaving decently.[83] In the long run, the public interest might better be served by a corporate orientation toward maximizing profits within the limits of decent behavior[84] than by dropping profit

80. Cf. Ruml, Corporate Management as a Locus of Power, 29 Chi.-Kent L. Rev. 228, 238 (1951).

81. See A. Berle & G. Means, supra note 62, at 356; A. Berle, The 20th Century Capitalist Revolution 61-115, 164-188 (1954); R. Eells, The Government of Corporations 74-75, 105-117 (1962).

82. See chapter 5 supra.

83. See A. P. Smith Mfg. Co. v. Barlow, 13 N.J. 145, 154, 98 A.2d 581, 586 (1953); cf. Scott v. Stanton Heights Corp., 388 Pa. 628, 131 A.2d 113 (1957); Hayek, The Corporation in a Democratic Society: In Whose Interest Ought It and Will It Be Run?, in Management and Corporations 1985, at 99, 100 (M. Anshen & G. Bach eds. 1960); Katz, Responsibility and the Modern Corporation, 3 J. Law & Econ. 75, 78-79 (1960).

84. Cf. Hayek, supra note 83; Katz, supra note 83; Rostow, To Whom and For What Ends Is Corporate Management Responsible?, in The Corporation in Modern Society 46, 69-71 (E. Mason ed. 1959).

maximization as the principal corporate goal. But in any event, there is no sound basis for believing either that ultimate shareholder control significantly affects corporate orientation toward profits, or that present-day management could or would use a less circumscribed power selflessly and wisely. Managers are no less self-interested than shareholders, and no more expert on the public interest, and whether shareholders are less apt to vote in the public interest than directors is presently indeterminable.[85]

B. Payment of Campaign Expenses

Assuming that shareholders have the right to designate candidates in the corporate proxy materials, do they also have the right to use corporate funds to wage a campaign on their candidates' behalf? Preliminarily, it should be observed that under the rules delineated so far, this question may have a more limited significance than is usually assumed. If shareholders have access to the corporate proxy machinery to designate their candidates for directorships, and if the board may spend corporate funds for a campaign only to match insurgent campaign spending, the incumbents' access to the corporate treasury to pay for a proxy campaign would not become operative if the insurgents limited their attack to the designation of their own candidates in the corporate proxy materials. Admittedly, however, given the momentum of power, most insurgents probably would be unwilling to run a proxy fight on such a modest basis; and if they do campaign, the incumbents would have a right to use corporate funds and facilities for a counter-campaign. Strict elaboration of the principles applicable to designation of directorial candidates in the corporate proxy materials might then seem to require that the insurgent shareholders should have a comparable right to be reimbursed for their campaign expenses.[86] Furthermore, a proxy fight, even if unsuccess-

85. See chapter 4 supra.

86. Cf. Steinberg v. Adams, 90 F. Supp. 604, 608 (S.D.N.Y. 1950); F. Emerson & F. Latcham, supra note 1, at 75-79; Brudney, supra note 21, at 284; Friedman, supra note 32, at 956.

A distinction is sometimes drawn between management and insurgents on the ground that management has a duty to fight off insurgents advocating a policy which management believes ill-advised, while insurgents have no duty to begin a proxy fight. See, e.g., Note, supra note 34, at 309-310. This argument is essentially a variant of the policy rationale for board access, discussed in text at notes 27-40 supra. Perhaps incum-

ful, may produce discernible corporate benefits, such as providing the body of shareholders with an opportunity to choose between competing philosophies and personnel, keeping management generally responsive to that body, and exposing management shortcomings which would not otherwise come to light and management policies which may be improved by close scrutiny.[87] Yet the little authority in point indicates that insurgents are not entitled to reimbursement of campaign expenses as a matter of right.[88] Is this authority sound?

Unlike a shareholder right to designate candidates in the corporate proxy materials, a shareholder right to reimbursement of campaign expenses would raise severe prudential problems. A right to *full* reimbursement of expenses might cause substantial drains on the corporate treasury, for many shareholders would undoubtedly regard such as right as an invitation to wage proxy fights annually at the corporation's expense.[89] But the establishment of a principle by which to delimit insurgent reimbursement is no easy task. A defensive matching concept, such as that applied to management, would obviously be inappropriate for application to insurgents. Theoretically, perhaps, reimbursement might be limited to the benefit resulting from the insurgents' campaign; but

---

bents are under a duty to call to the shareholders' attention misrepresentations by persons seeking corporate office; but they are under no duty either to stand for reelection, or to challenge merely problematical assertions, concerning business policy, made by opposing candidates.

87. Cf. Steinberg v. Adams, 90 F. Supp. 604, 607-608 (S.D.N.Y. 1950); N. Lattin, R. Jennings & R. Buxbaum, supra note 8, at 497; Stifel, supra note 8, at 345-346; Comment, Proxy Contests: Corporate Reimbursement of Insurgents' Expenses, 23 U. Chi. L. Rev. 682, 686, 690 (1956); 1965 Duke L.J. 412, 415-416; Note, supra note 32, at 234.

88. See Phillips v. United Corp., 5 S.E.C. Jud. Dec. 758, 765 (S.D.N.Y.), appeal dismissed sub nom. Phillips v. SEC, 171 F.2d 180 (2d Cir. 1948); Grodetsky v. McCrory Corp., 49 Misc. 2d 322, 267 N.Y.S.2d 356 (Sup. Ct.), affd. mem., 27 App. Div. 2d 646, 276 N.Y.S.2d 841 (1966), motions for leave to appeal denied, 19 N.Y.2d 582, 226 N.E.2d 708, 20 N.Y.2d 644, 230 N.E.2d 740 (1967).

In Campbell v. Loew's, Inc., 36 Del. Ch. 563, 134 A.2d 852 (Ch. 1957) a faction consisting of only a minority of the directors, including the corporation's president, was held entitled to reimbursement for proxy fight expenses. However, Campbell was highly unusual in that due to board vacancies neither of the two contesting factions had enough directors to call a board meeting and carry a motion. It seems unlikely that a similar result would be reached in a more typical context. Cf. Empire S. Gas Co. v. Gray, 29 Del. Ch. 95, 110, 46 A.2d 741, 748 (1946).

89. See Comment, supra note 87, at 686; 43 Calif. L. Rev. 893, 903 n. 53 (1955).

since such benefits are normally intangible and unquantifiable by a judge or jury, this concept could not be applied in practice.[90] As a fallback, reimbursement might be limited to that portion of the insurgents' expenses allocable to an informational function.[91] This kind of allocation would often be very difficult to make, however, and even such a limited right could easily drain the corporate treasury when there was more than one insurgent group, as would often be the case if such a rule were adopted.[92]

Commentators favoring insurgent reimbursement have proposed various implementing formulas which seem to be constructed with at least one eye on the prudential problem. Under one formula, for example, insurgents would be reimbursed if, but only if, they achieved some minimum amount of voting support, say 10 or 15 percent.[93] Under another, each insurgent group would be reimbursed an amount bearing the same relation to the number of votes achieved by its slate as reimbursement of the incumbents bears to votes for the incumbent slate.[94] Under still a third, each group would be reimbursed a percentage of its expenses which depended on its percentage of total votes – for example, full reimbursement if it gathered 50 percent of total votes, 10 percent reimbursement if it gathered 5 percent of total votes.[95]

Generally speaking, these formulas do not fully solve the multi-insurgent problem. Permitting reimbursement of any insurgent group which gathered ten percent of the votes could result in cases where several groups might so qualify. Limiting reimbursement to an amount based on the ratio between incumbent reimbursement and incumbent votes would provide no effective ceiling where the incumbent vote was very low. Even the third test,

90. Cf. 43 Calif. L. Rev. 893, 903 (1955); 36 Cornell L.Q. 558, 563-564 (1951).

91. Cf. Stifel, supra note 8, at 347; 41 Cornell L.Q. 714, 718-719 (1956).

92. See Stifel, supra note 8, at 347.

93. See, e.g., F. Emerson & F. Latcham, supra note 1, at 76-78; Emerson & Latcham, Proxy Contests: A Study in Shareholder Sovereignty, 41 Calif. L. Rev. 393, 435 (1953); Friedman, supra note 32, at 963.

94. Emerson & Latcham, supra note 93, at 435-436.

95. See Comment, supra note 87, at 691-692.

Professor Schulman points out that in applying such formulas, "[t]he determination of the percentage of votes cast in favor of the insurgents should be made without regard to votes cast representing shares owned by the insurgents. Otherwise a group owning a substantial block could receive reimbursement without having obtained the support of any other shareholder." Schulman, supra note 41, at 37.

although a considerable improvement in this respect over the first two, could result in reimbursement of substantially all the expenses of two insurgent groups where the incumbents received a very low vote. This contingency, however, is probably so remote that legislative adoption of this formula, or some analog, would be desirable. Nevertheless, neither this formula nor the others seem appropriate for *judicial* adoption, since all find expression in mathematical formulas rather than in principled terms.[96] And this difficulty seems indigenous to the problem rather than unique to these particular tests.

There is, however, a more modest approach to the problem, which is within judicial competence, and which has in fact been adopted in judicial decisions. In *Steinberg v. Adams*[97] and *Rosenfeld v. Fairchild Engine & Airplane Corp.*[98] it was held that although insurgents may not be entitled to reimbursement of their expenses as a matter of right, the corporation has *power* to reimburse such expenses.[99] This rule tends toward the equalization of management and shareholder access to the corporate proxy machinery, yet satisfies, without resort to formulas, the prudential considerations discussed above. The rule would seldom, if ever, result in reimbursement of more than one insurgent group, because as a practical matter the corporation will seldom exercise such a power except in favor of successful insurgents.[100] Of course, even reimbursement of one insurgent group may cause an undue drain on the corporate treasury. In most cases, however,

96. See Friedman, supra note 32, at 963; cf. E. Freund, Legislative Regulation 1, 9-10 (1932); H. M. Hart & A. Sacks, The Legal Process: Basic Problems in the Making and Application of Law 665-669, 871 (tent. ed. 1958); Fuller, The Forms and Limits of Adjudication, in id. at 421-426.

97. 90 F. Supp. 604 (S.D.N.Y. 1950).

98. 309 N.Y. 168, 128 N.E.2d 291 (1955).

99. See Steinberg v. Adams, 90 F. Supp. 604, 607-608 (S.D.N.Y. 1950) (Rifkind, J.); Rosenfeld v. Fairchild Engine & Airplane Corp., 309 N.Y. 168, 173, 128 N.E.2d 291, 293 (1955). In Rosenfeld, four judges concurred in holding that such payments were not necessarily illegal; three dissented. See also Central Foundry Co., 49 T.C. 234 (1967).

100. In some cases insurgents may be reimbursed where they are only partially successful. Cf., e.g., Sunshine Mining Staves Off Proxy Fight, Agrees to Name Dissident to Board Slate, Wall St. J., Aug. 28, 1974, at 5, col. 2; Vikoa Settles Dispute With Dissidents Seeking Management Take-Over, Wall St. J., May 4, 1973, at 17, col. 1; Reading to Ask Holders to Approve Payments of $79,000 to Dissidents, Wall St. J., May 19, 1966, at 8, col. 1. But it is unlikely even in these cases that more than one group would be so reimbursed.

undue spending would not be encouraged by the rule itself; since reimbursement under the rule is not a matter of right, insurgents must initially risk their own money,[101] and this risk normally should serve to check their spending, except in a case where the insurgents regarded the possibility of losing the election as minimal. The latter case, however, would normally occur only if the insurgents held a substantial amount of stock. High campaign spending would be counterproductive for such insurgents, since it would drain cash out of the corporate treasury – not only the cash the insurgents spent, but that spent by incumbents. Insurgents who regard the possibility of loss as minimal should therefore tend to underspend rather than overspend.

A more likely case for unduly high insurgent spending would occur where the insurgents were unsure of victory, but the rewards of victory would be very great.[102] Even in this case, since the prize may not be won (and if won may be decreased in value by the very campaign to achieve it), the insurgents' self-interest should normally serve as a check on their spending. Nevertheless, many would probably feel that a check other than the insurgents' own self-interest is necessary, and support for such a position can be drawn from *Rosenfeld* and *Steinberg,* both of which indicate that only the insurgents' "reasonable" expenses may be reimbursed.[103] Reasonability in this context might be measured by taking as a yardstick the amounts spent by insurgents in other corporations which are similar in terms of assets and number of distribution of shareholdings.[104]

A final question: which corporate organ must approve reim-

101. If the solicitation comes under the Proxy Rules, the insurgents are also subject to the check of prospective disclosure, since they must state in their proxy statement "the total amount estimated to be spent and the total expenditures to date for, in furtherance of, or in connection with the solicitation of security holders" and "whether reimbursement will be sought from the issuer. . . ." Proxy Rule 14a-3(a), Schedule 14A, Items 3(b)(4), (5), 17 C.F.R. § §240.14a-3(a), 240.14a-101(3)(b)(4), (5) (1974).

102. Cf. Rosenfeld v. Fairchild Engine & Airplane Corp., 309 N.Y. 168, 186, 128 N.E.2d 291, 301 (1955) (dissenting opinion).

103. Steinberg v. Adams, 90 F. Supp. 604, 608 (S.D.N.Y. 1950); Rosenfeld v. Fairchild Engine & Airplane Corp., 309 N.Y. 168, 173, 175, 128 N.E.2d 291, 293, 294 (1955).

104. Some figures on the cost of past fights have already been published. See notes 48-49 supra. Other figures are available from proxy statements on file with the SEC. See note 101 supra.

bursement of proxy-fight expenses? The case law seems to assume that the board has power to reimburse management.[105] This squares with the underlying substantive rule that the incumbents have a right to reimbursement, provided their expenses are reasonable. Reimbursement then merely constitutes the discharge of a claim, and therefore falls within the board's power to manage the corporation's business. Indeed, if such reimbursement required shareholder approval it would not be a right at all, since approval might not be forthcoming where the insurgents won.

Some commentators have argued that the board should also have power to reimburse insurgents,[106] apparently on the theory that the treatment of management and shareholders should be equalized as far as possible. But the exercise of a discretionary power to reimburse persons for expenses incurred in gaining control of the corporation does not seem to constitute management of the corporation's business in any ordinary sense of that term. Both *Rosenfeld*[107] and *Steinberg*[108] indicate that the reimburse-

105. See Hand v. Missouri-Kansas Pipe Line Co., 54 F. Supp. 649 (D. Del. 1944); Hall v. Trans-Lux Daylight Picture Screen Corp., 20 Del. Ch. 78, 171 A. 266 (1934); Streett v. Laclede-Christy Co., 409 S.W.2d 691, 698-699 (Mo. 1966). In each of these cases shareholder approval had not occurred, nor was it in prospect, but the court nevertheless held that management access to the corporate proxy machinery was proper if the policy-information-reasonability test could be met. In Rosenfeld v. Fairchild Engine & Airplane Corp., 309 N.Y. 168, 173, 128 N.E.2d 291, 293 (1955), shareholder approval had occurred, but the language of Judge Froessel's opinion indicated fairly clearly that he did not regard such approval as a necessary condition to management access:

"The rule then which we adopt is simply this: In a contest over policy, as compared to a purely personal power contest, *corporate directors have the right* to make reasonable and proper expenditures, subject to the scrutiny of the courts when duly challenged, from the corporate treasury for the purpose of persuading the stockholders of the correctness of their position and soliciting their support for policies which the directors believe, in all good faith, are in the best interests of the corporation. *The stockholders, moreover, have the right* to reimburse successful contestants for the reasonable and bona fide expenses incurred by them in any such policy contest, subject to like court scrutiny." (Emphasis added.)

106. See Machtinger, supra note 32, at 217; Note, supra note 32, at 234-235; 24 U. Cinn. L. Rev. 606, 609 (1955).

107. 309 N.Y. 168, 173, 128 N.E.2d 291, 293 (1955).

108. 90 F. Supp. 604, 607-608 (S.D.N.Y. 1950). Later in the opinion Judge Rifkind indicated that he might require board as well as shareholder approval: "[I]t seems permissible to me that those who advocate a contrary policy and succeed in securing approval from the stockholders should be able to receive reimbursement, at least where there is approval by both the board of directors and a majority of the

ment of insurgents requires shareholder approval, and this seems proper if insurgent reimbursement is regarded as a corporate power rather than as a matter of right.

stockholders." Id at 608. See also Grodetsky v. McCrory Corp., 49 Misc. 2d 322, 323-324, 267 N.Y.S.2d 356, affd. mem., 27 App. Div. 2d 646, 276 N.Y.S.2d 841 (1966), motions for leave to appeal denied, 19 N.Y.2d 582, 226 N.E.2d 708, 20 N.Y.2d 644, 230 N.E.2d 740 (1967).

10

Access to the Corporate Proxy Machinery in Connection With Matters Other Than Election to Office

§10.1. Management Access

Management access to the corporate proxy machinery in connection with matters other than election to office is not as difficult to rationalize as its access in connection with election matters. In soliciting votes on a nonelection matter, the board normally acts within its explicit authority: under the statutes, many matters which require shareholder approval must be initiated by the board and then submitted by the board to the shareholders,[1] and even in the absence of statute most recommendations to shareholders on nonelection matters would probably fall within a residual power to advise the shareholders on corporate affairs. Furthermore, since most actions requiring shareholder approval must be approved by a percentage of shares outstanding, rather than merely a percentage of shares actually voting, lack of a solicitation might often result in a failure to consummate advantageous corporate actions.[2]

1. See Chapter 1 supra.

2. In contrast, usually only a plurality of the votes cast, or a majority of the votes cast or present, is required to elect directors, provided a quorum is present. See generally ABA Model Bus. Corp. Act §32 (1969 rev.); Caplin, Proxies, Annual Meetings and Corporate Democracy: The Lawyer's Role, 37 Va. L. Rev. 653, 689 n. 82 (1951). Quorum requirements for regular shareholder meetings vary among publicly held corporations, but few if any would require more than a majority of outstanding shares, and many require less. See, e.g., By-Laws of AMF, Inc., as amended through Sept. 12, 1972, Article I, §5 (majority); By-Laws of American Express Co. §2.4 (majority); By-Laws of Avco Corp., as amended through Oct. 25, 1974, art. II, §3 (majority); By-Laws of Eastman Kodak Co., as amended through August 19, 1971, art. I, §5 (majority); By-Laws of General Motors Corp., as amended to 1975, §11 (thirty percent); By-Laws of Mobil Oil Corp., as amended to Jan 25, 1974, art. II, §4 (one-third).

Similarly, in terms of fiduciary concepts, nonelection matters do not involve an inherent conflict of interest, as election matters do. Normally, then, in nonelection matters the board should be able to prepare and mail a notice of meeting, proxy card, and proxy statement describing the proposed transaction, at corporate expense;[3] and since the affirmative vote of at least a majority of outstanding shares must ordinarily be obtained, the board should also normally be able to utilize the corporate proxy machinery for follow-up techniques such as mailings and phone calls to shareholders, advertisements, and the use of professional proxy solicitors.[4]

But what if the matter is one in which the board is interested? If the usual legal rules governing self-interested transactions were applicable to the board's use of the corporate proxy machinery in such cases,[5] the burden might be on the board to defend that use. In the long run, therefore, such treatment might work against the interest of shareholders as a class by discouraging management from submitting proposals to shareholders. Furthermore, the usual self-interested transaction is fully consummated by management, while in cases involving access to the corporate proxy machinery, final action is by hypothesis in the shareholders' hands.

A distinction might be drawn, however, between cases where a matter being submitted to the shareholders carries a benefit to management in its train, and cases in which the very purpose of the submission is to benefit management. An example of the former would be a merger involving retention of members of the board as officers and directors of the reconstituted corporation; an example of the latter would be a recommendation that the shareholders ratify a questionable board action. Even in the latter case it might be inappropriate to apply the usual rules governing self-

3. Cf. Hall v. Trans-Lux Daylight Picture Screen Corp., 20 Del. Ch. 78, 171 A. 226, 227-228 (Ch. 1934).

4. See Rosenfeld v. Fairchild Engine & Airplane Co., 309 N.Y. 168, 172-173, 128 N.E.2d 191 (1955) (Froessel, J.); E. Aranow & H. Einhorn, Proxy Contests for Corporate Control 558 (2d ed. 1968); Friedman, Expenses of Corporate Proxy Contests, 51 Colum. L. Rev. 951, 953-954 (1951).

5. By "the usual rules" I mean those rules applicable to a classical self-dealing transaction; the precise content of such rules varies from state to state. See W. Cary, Cases and Materials on Corporations 557-559, 565-566 (4th ed. 1969); G. Hornstein, Corporation Law and Practice §439 (1959); Marsh, Are Directors Trustees? Conflicts of Interest and Corporate Morality, 22 Bus. Law. 35, 36-48 (1966).

interested transactions to the distribution of routine corporate proxy materials required to present the proposal fairly – specifically, the proxy statement and proxy card. But if the board goes further, and engages in a solicitation campaign at corporate expense, the usual self-interest rules might very well be appropriate.

§10.2. Shareholder Access

A. Shareholder-Initiated Proposals

1. *Right to access.* Proxy Rule 14a-8 gives shareholders access to the corporate proxy materials in order to submit certain proposals on matters other than election to office. However, the access so provided is restricted in important ways. For one thing, the Proxy Rules are not applicable to all corporations which solicit proxies.[6] For another, rule 14a-8 does not cover all shareholder proposals which are proper subjects for shareholder action under state law. For example, management may refuse to include a proposal without violating rule 14a-8, even though the proposal is a proper subject for shareholder action under state law, if it "consists of a recommendation or request that the management take action with respect to a matter relating to the conduct of the [corporation's] ordinary business operations."[7] In light of these

6. Proxy Rule 14a-2, 17 C.F.R. §240.14a-2 (1974); see, e.g., Carter v. Portland Gen. Elec. Co., 227 Ore. 401, 362 P.2d 766 (1961).

7. Proxy Rule 14a-8(c)(5), 17 C.F.R. §240.14a-8(c)(5) (1974). Compare Proxy Rule 14a-8(c)(1), 17 C.F.R. §240.14a-8(c)(1) (1974), with Proxy Rule 14a-8(c)(5), 17 C.F.R. §240.14a-8(c)(5) (1974), and Auer v. Dressel, 306 N.Y. 427, 118 N.E.2d 590 (1954).

A proposal may also be omitted under rule 14a-8 if it consists of a recommendation, request, or mandate that action be taken with respect to any matter, including a general economic, political, racial, religious, social, or similar cause, that is not significantly related to the business of the issuer or is not within the control of the issuer, Proxy Rule 14a-8(c)(2)(ii), 17 C.F.R. §240.14a-8(c)(2)(ii); or if "the management has at the security holder's request included a proposal in its proxy statement [during the previous two years] and such security holder has failed without good cause to present the proposal, in person or by proxy, for action at the meeting," Proxy Rule 14a-8(c)(3), 17 C.F.R. §240.14a-8(c)(3) (1974); or the proposal has been submitted to the shareholders within the previous five years and has failed to receive a specified percentage of the total votes cast, the exact percentage depending on the number of times the proposal was submitted during the relevant period, Proxy Rule 14a-8(c)(4), 17 C.F.R. §240.14a-8(c)(4) (1974). Even where a proposal must be included under rule 14a-8, if management is opposed the shareholder's supporting statement is limited to two hundred words. Proxy Rule 14a-8(b), 17 C.F.R. §240.14a-8(b) (1974).

limitations on the ambit of rule 14a-8, the question arises whether *state* law gives shareholders access to the corporate proxy materials for the purpose of submitting proposals on nonelection matters.

If it is lawful for the board to use the corporate proxy machinery to submit proposals to shareholders which are within the board's authority to initiate, it should follow that it is lawful for shareholders to use that machinery to submit proposals which are within the shareholders' authority to initiate — at least in a corporation in which there is a practice of submitting proposals to shareholders through the proxy materials. To take a case in which the propriety of shareholder access is relatively clear, under some corporate statutes voluntary dissolution is completely within the shareholders' power — the board is given no statutory role either in initiating or consummating the transaction.[8] Suppose that shareholders of a corporation governed by such a statute wish to have it dissolved. Surely if the corporate proxy materials had been used in the past to present proposals to shareholders, they could be used for a dissolution proposal; and surely too, the members of the corporate organ with exclusive statutory power to consummate voluntary dissolution would have the right to use the materials for this purpose.

But suppose a case in which the question is not so clear. In *Carter v. Portland General Electric Company,*[9] several shareholders of a corporation which was not subject to the Proxy Rules, but which solicited proxies, requested that resolutions opposing management's plans to construct a dam be included in the proxy materials for a forthcoming annual meeting. Management refused. When one of the shareholders attempted to present the resolutions from the floor at the annual meeting, the chairman ruled him out of order. An action was then brought to restrain management from making any future proxy solicitation at corporate expense which did not include shareholders' resolutions of which it had reasonable notice.[10] The Oregon Supreme Court believed that the plaintiffs were asking it to "judicially adopt rules promulgated by the Securities Exchange Commission in respect to proxy solicitation."[11] This the court refused to do:

8. E.g., N.Y. Bus. Corp. Law §1001 (McKinney 1963).
9. 227 Ore. 401, 362 P.2d 766 (1961).
10. See Appellant's Abstract of Record and Brief 14-15, 26-27.
11. 227 Ore. at 403, 362 P.2d at 767.

> Here, if we adopt the rule it would be without limitation. It would apply to any stockholder of any corporation. Nor does there exist any administrative body to make any preliminary determination that a stockholder's proposal is a "proper" one. In simple reality we would be acting in a void. We do not nor is there any means by which we could know the ultimate repercussions of such a rule. We know that it could be invoked for harassing purposes that could only be avoided by extensive litigation. We must be aware that to judicially impose the suggested rules in these circumstances might well impair rather than benefit the orderly development of this important area of the law of corporations.
>
> Secondly, we do not think that the proposal in this case was one that was necessarily proper for the stockholders to give an advisory opinion about. . . .[12]

Understandably, a state court would be leery of embracing the detailed regulatory scheme embodied in the Proxy Rules. Although this was not in fact what plaintiffs were suggesting,[13] the court thought it was, and to the extent that the decision turned on this theme its precedential value on the state-law issue is questionable. Similarly, that portion of the opinion relating to a shareholder's right to require inclusion of proposals concerning a proper subject for shareholder action seems to have been infected by the court's determination that the proposal at issue was not proper.

12. Id. at 406-407, 362 P.2d at 769.

In Dyer v. SEC, 289 F.2d 242 (8th Cir. 1961) and Dyer v. SEC, 266 F.2d 33, 41-44 (8th Cir. 1959), Dyer, a shareholder in Union Gas, sought review of SEC orders permitting Union Gas proxy materials to become effective, on the ground, inter alia, that the materials did not include various proposals made by Dyer pursuant to rule 14a-8. The Eighth Circuit held that rule 14a-8 did not require inclusion of the proposals in question. In the course of its opinions it stated that the rule "affords a privilege, which does not otherwise ordinarily exist in favor of stockholders," 266 F.2d at 41, and is "not an inherent stock-ownership right," 289 F2d at 245. Cf. Campbell v. Australian Mutual Provident Socy., 99 L.T.R. 3 (Privy Council 1908). The Eighth Circuit's statements must be evaluated in the context in which they were made. The issue was not what state law required, but what rule 14a-8 required. The statements were laid down as ipse dixit, neither authority nor reasoning being advanced in their support. The court's purpose in making these statements was primarily to set a tone: shareholders should consider themselves lucky that the SEC adopted rule 14a-8 and should not carp at their benefactor's techniques of dispensation. It may be relevant that Dyer was apparently a rather litigious individual whom the Eighth Circuit openly regarded as vexatious, not to say irritating. See Dyer v. SEC, 289 F.2d 242, 244-245 (8th Cir. 1961); Dyer v. SEC, 287 F.2d 773, 775-777, 782 (8th Cir. 1961); Dyer v. SEC, 266 F.2d 33, 37, 46 (8th Cir. 1959). See also Dyer v. SEC, 291 F.2d 774 (8th Cir. 1961); Dyer v. SEC, 290 F.2d 534 (8th Cir. 1961).

13. See Appellant's Abstract of Record and Brief.

Although couched in terms of an alternative holding, the point might have gone the other way if the court had viewed the proposal as a proper one.

But insofar as *Carter* does hold that under state law a shareholder has no access to the corporate proxy machinery to make proposals which are proper subjects for shareholder initiation, it is unpersuasive. The court placed some weight on the argument that there is no "administrative body to make any preliminary determination that a stockholder's proposal is a 'proper' one."[14] If this is really relevant, it would also follow that management could foreclose judicial review of its refusal to recognize a shareholder's motion made from the floor, or to call a duly requested shareholders' meeting, simply by resting its refusal on the talismanic ground that the proposal does not concern a proper subject for shareholder action. Too bad for shareholders in Oregon corporations! Ironically, the *Carter* court itself found the proposal at issue to be improper for shareholder action, thus belying its claim to need an administrative predetermination of the propriety question.

Apart from the opinion's confusion, moreover, there does exist an organ, albeit imperfect, which is capable of making a "preliminary determination that a stockholder's proposal is a 'proper' one" – management, acting on the advice of corporate counsel.[15] In the first instance, that is to say, a shareholder proposal is not filed with a court but submitted to the corporation. If management determines that it concerns a proper subject, that will end the matter. Only if management determines that it does not concern a proper subject will the court itself be faced with a need to make a proper-subject determination. And in reviewing a negative decision by management, a court would not be tilling unplowed soil, as the Oregon court seemed to believe, since it would be guided by a number of SEC administrative decisions,[16] the

14. 227 Ore. at 406, 362 P.2d at 769.

15. Cf. Monaghan, Annual Stockholders' Meetings: Some Legal and Practical Problems, 16 Baylor L. Rev. 129, 131 (1964).

16. Many such decisions are reported in Clusserath, The Amended Stockholder Proposal Rule: A Decade Later, 40 Notre Dame Law. 13, 17-39 (1964); cf. Hearings on SEC Enforcement Problems, Before a Subcomm. of the Senate Comm. on Banking and Currency, 85th Cong. 1st sess. 78-92 (1957); 2, 5 Loss 901-909, 2855-2859 (2d ed. 1961, Supp. 1969); Bayne, The Basic Rationale of Proper Subject, 34 U. Det. L. Rev. 575, 595-599 (1957); Emerson, The Shareholder Proposal Rule, Analysts J., Nov. 1953,

thinking of many commentators,[17] and even decisional law.[18]

Finally, although the *Carter* court indicated some concern with the shareholder-harassment strawman propped up by the defendants, few shareholders and even fewer attorneys would be willing to invest their time, effort, and dollars in litigation of this kind unless it was meritorious.[19] In sum, then, *Carter* must be deemed an inauthoritative precedent.[20]

2. Reimbursement of expenses. Assuming that shareholders are entitled to insert a proper proposal in the corporate proxy statement and proxy card, the question arises whether they should also be entitled to reimbursement for the expense of follow-up techniques used to solicit votes for the proposal. This problem is comparable to that posed by insurgent campaign expenses, and a comparable rule therefore seems appropriate: that shareholders do not have a right to be reimbursed for such expenses, but that the corporation (acting through its shareholders) has the power to make reimbursement, at least to the extent that similar expenses have been incurred in advancing proposals in similar cases.[21]

---

at 87; Emerson & Latcham, The SEC Proxy Proposal Rule: The Corporate Gadfly, 19 U. Chi. L. Rev. 807 (1952); Heller, Stockholder Proposals, 4 Va. L. Weekly Dicta Compilation 72, 76-77 (1953); Ledes, A Review of Proper Subject Under the Proxy Rules, 34 U. Det. L. Rev. 520, 524-527 (1957).

17. See the commentaries cited in note 16 supra.

18. See the Dyer litigation, note 12 supra; Medical Committee for Human Rights v. SEC, 432 F.2d 659 (D.C. Cir. 1970), judgment vacated and dismissed as moot, 404 U.S. 403 (1972); SEC v. Transamerica Corp., 163 F.2d 511 (3d Cir. 1947), cert. denied, 332 U.S. 847 (1948); Brooks v. Standard Oil Co., CCH 1969 Fed. Sec. L. Rep. ¶92,545 (S.D.N.Y. 1969); Auer v. Dressel, 306 N.Y. 427, 118 N.E.2d 590 (1954).

19. Since such litigation does not aim at a recovery from management, it would not normally lend itself to strike suits.

20. Access to the proxy materials for purposes of making a proposal, like access for the purpose of designating candidates for office, may be limited by reasonable bylaws, see chapter 9 supra, but would be practicable even if not so limited. Proxy Rule 14a-8(a), 17 C.F.R. §240.14a-8(a) (1974), has long required inclusion of most shareholder proposals in the proxy materials for annual meetings of corporations, with no discernible practicability problems. Although the shareholders' right under state law would also extend to special meetings, such meetings can normally be called only by some minimum percentage of the shareholders, usually a fairly high percentage, see, e.g., Cal. Corp. Code §2002(c) (West 1955) (20 percent of the voting power); Ohio Rev. Code Ann. §1701.40(a)(3) (Page 1964) (25 percent, unless charter specifies otherwise); or only by the board and by such other persons as may be authorized by the certificate or bylaws, see Del. Code Ann. tit. 8, §211(d) (1974); N.Y. Bus. Corp. Law §602(c) (McKinney Supp. 1974).

21. Cf. Grodetsky v. McCrory Corp., 49 Misc. 2d 322, 267 N.Y.S.2d 356 (Sup. Ct.), affd. mem., 27 App. Div. 2d 646, 276 N.Y.S.2d 841 (1966), motions for leave to

B. Counter-Arguments to Management Proposals

A related problem is whether shareholders have access to the corporate proxy materials in order to argue against nonelection proposals submitted by management. Since rule 14a-8 expressly excludes counter-proposals,[22] this question is strictly one of state law.

Assuming that shareholders have access to the corporate proxy machinery for the purpose of submitting proposals which are within their authority to initiate, access for the purpose of arguing against nonelection proposals submitted by management would not be necessary for the effectuation of the shareholders' legal powers. Such access might nevertheless be useful: management proposals often involve conflicts of interest,[23] and shareholder access for the purpose of making counter-arguments would help insure that such conflicts, and the proposals themselves, were fully explored. On the other hand, the absence of such access does not necessarily lead to a one-sided picture. A duty to disclose in

---

appeal denied, 19 N.Y.2d 582, 226 N.E.2d 708, 20 N.Y.2d 644, 230 N.E.2d 740 (1967); Schulman, The Costs of Free Speech in Proxy Contests for Corporate Control, 20 Wayne L. Rev. 32-33 n. 97 (1973).

22. Rule 14a-8(a), 17 C.F.R. §240.14a-8(a) (1974). The counter-proposal exception was adopted in 1967. In the previous year the SEC had issued a press release requesting comments from the public on a series of proposed amendments to various Proxy Rules, including rule 14a-8. SEC, Securities Exchange Act of 1934 Release No. 8000, at 3-4, 13-14, 31 Fed. Reg. 15750-15751, 15753-15754 (1966). Nothing was said in this release concerning the possibility of adding a counter-proposal exception to rule 14a-8, and no notice was ever given that such an amendment was being contemplated. Nevertheless, such an amendment was included when the SEC published a final version of the amendments it had proposed in 1966. SEC, Securities Exchange Act of 1934 Release No. 8206, 32 Fed. Reg. 20960, 20961, 20964 (1967). The release gave no reason for the exception. Id. at 20961.

Section 4(b) of the Administrative Procedure Act, 5 U.S.C. §553(b) (1970), provides: "General notice of proposed rule making shall be published in the Federal Register. . . . The notice shall include . . . either the terms or substance of the proposed rule. . . . [T] his subsection does not apply . . . to interpretative rules. . . ." In response to a question concerning the procedure by which the counter-proposal amendment was adopted, the Commission replied: "This amendment was included in the adopted proposals on the basis that it was merely a codification of the proper interpretation of Rule 14a-8 and therefore involved no substantial change in the rule. The reason for this position is that counter proposals are, in effect, a solicitation of a vote against the management's proposal." Letter to the author from Charles J. Sheppe, Chief, Branch of Forms, Rules, Regulations and Legislative Matters, May 21, 1969.

23. See chapter 4, supra.

the proxy materials all material facts relevant to a management proposal is imposed on management itself by state law,[24] by the Proxy Rules (if the solicitation falls under those Rules),[25] and by rule 10b-5 (if the proposal is "in connection with the purchase or sale of any security").[26] Failure to make the necessary disclosure may not only be a ground for setting aside the action taken pursuant to the solicitation,[27] but may result in civil[28] or even criminal[29] liability. When the solicitation falls under the Proxy Rules, the disclosure obligation is also backed up by administrative review of the proposed proxy materials.[30]

Furthermore, shareholder access for the purpose of arguing against management proposals would raise substantial problems of feasibility. Since shareholders frequently could not be expected to anticipate a management solicitation relating to a nonelection proposal, such access would often require a second round of proxy materials, entailing not only substantial expense, but substantial delay. Particularly where the management proposal concerned an action to be taken in conjunction with another business enterprise, as in the case of a merger or a sale of substantially all assets, such delay might prove intolerable.

24. See cases cited in chapter 9, note 10 supra.

25. See Proxy Rules 14a-3, 14a-9, Schedule 14A, 17 C.F.R. §§240-14a-3, 240.14a-9, 240.14a-101 (1974).

26. See Securities Exchange Act of 1934, §10(b), 15 U.S.C. §78j(b) (1964); SEC Rule 10b-5, 17 C.F.R. §240.10b-5 (1974).

27. See Wyatt v. Armstrong, 186 Misc. 216, 59 N.Y.S.2d 502 (Sup. Ct. 1945) (setting aside election of directors).

28. See SEC v. National Securities, Inc., 393 U.S. 453, 464-469 (1969); J. I. Case Co. v. Borak, 377 U.S. 426 (1964); Gerstle v. Gamble-Skogmo, Inc., 478 F.2d 1281 (2d Cir. 1973); Dasho v. Susquehanna Corp., 380 F.2d 262 (7th Cir.), cert. denied, 389 U.S. 977 (1967); Gould v. American Hawaiian S. S. Co., 331 F. Supp. 981 (D. Del. 1971), 351 F. Supp. 853 (D. Del. 1972), 362 F. Supp. 771 (D. Del 1973); Simon v. New Haven Board & Carton Co., 250 F. Supp. 297 (D. Conn. 1966); Eagle v. Horvath, 241 F. Supp. 341 (S.D.N.Y. 1965); R. Jennings & H. Marsh, Securities Regulation – Cases and Materials 1351-1360 (3d ed. 1972).

29. See Securities Exchange Act of 1934, §32(a), 15 U.S.C. §78ff(a) (1964); Bromberg, supra note 28, at 233-241.

30. See Proxy Rule 14a-6, 17 C.F.R. §240.14a-6 (1974).

III
Management Structure

11
Officers and Directors

§11.1. Who Manages the Business of a Corporation? Law and Practice

A. The Received Legal Model and the Working Model

Under the received legal model of the corporation, the board of directors manages the corporation's business and sets business policy; indeed, this aspect of the model is reflected in a central provision of the traditional corporate statutes: "The business and affairs of a corporation shall be managed by a board of directors."[1] It has become increasingly clear over the years, however, that in practice the board rarely performs either the management or the policymaking functions. It is, for example, well accepted that in closely held corporations the business is typically managed by owner-managers,[2] pretty much without any regard to formal capacities. Since, despite some earlier cases to the contrary,[3] there is no reason why they should not be permitted to do so, the major questions in this area concern the role of the board in the publicly held corporation; and it is with these questions that this chapter shall be concerned.

1. Ill. Stat. Ann. ch. 32, §157.33 (Supp. 1974). See also N.J. Stat. Ann. §14A:6-1 (Supp. 1968); N.Y. Bus. Corp. Law §701 (McKinney Supp. 1974).

2. See, e.g., M. Mace, The Board of Directors in Small Corporations 87 (1948).

3. E.g., Jackson v. Hooper, 76 N.J. Eq. 592, 75 A. 568 (Ct. Err. & App. 1910); Long Park, Inc. v. Trenton-New Brunswick Theatres Co., 297 N.Y. 174, 77 N.E.2d 633 (1948).

To begin with, all serious students of corporate affairs recognize that notwithstanding the statutory injunction, in the typical large publicly held corporation the board does not "manage" the corporation's business in the ordinary meaning of that term. Rather, that function is vested in the executives. "Under the system of directorates which has developed in this country among large, listed companies, directors are unable to 'manage' corporations in any narrow interpretation of the word. . . . Directors do not and cannot 'direct' corporations in the sense of operating them."[4] It is often said, however, that the board *does* make business policy,[5] and it is frequently implied that by making business policy the board fulfills the statutory command.[6] In fact, of course, policymaking is not equivalent to management: for example, although civilians may make policy for the Army, they certainly do not manage the Army. But in any event, the typical board no more makes business policy than it manages the business. In the large, publicly held corporation, policymaking, like management, is an executive function. As early as 1945 the economist Robert Aaron Gordon reported in *Business Leadership in the Large Corporation* that in both financial and nonfinancial matters there was little or no indication that the boards of large companies initiated decisions on either specific matters or broad policies. While the board's approval function was more important than its initiating activities, Gordon found that "even with respect to approval, many boards in these large companies are almost completely passive," and that the final approval function was usually exercised by the chief executive in conjunction with either his immediate subordinates, an executive or finance committee of the board, or a few influential directors acting as his informal advisors.[7] Similarly, John C. Baker of the Harvard Business School

4. J. Baker, Directors and Their Functions – A Preliminary Study 12 (1945) [hereinafter cited as Baker]. See also R. Gordon, Business Leadership in the Large Corporation 79-90, 114-115, 128, 134, 143-146 (2d ed. 1961) [hereinafter cited as Gordon]; H. Maurer, Great Enterprise – Growth and Behavior of the Big Corporation 195 (1955) (" 'If outside directors really try to manage, there is hell to pay' ") [hereinafter cited as Maurer].

5. See, e.g., J. Bacon, Corporate Directorship Practices 93 (Natl. Indus. Conference Bd. Studies in Business Policy No. 125, 1967) [hereinafter cited as 1967 Conference Board Survey]; 1 G. Hornstein, Corporation Law and Practice 526 (1959).

6. See, e.g., 1967 Conference Board Survey, supra note 5, at 96; Baker, supra note 4, at 12, 131-132; H. Koontz, The Board of Directors and Effective Management 33-44, 46-58 (1967) [hereinafter cited as Koontz].

7. Gordon, supra note 4, at 128-129, 131. See also id. at 114.

reported the same year that major policies in production, marketing, finance, and personnel were usually formulated by the executives and not even formally confirmed by the board (although there was often consultation with individual directors), while in such matters as addition of new products, preparation of operating budget, and negotiation of collective bargaining agreements, the board's role was limited to receipt and consideration of after-the-fact reports.[8] More recent studies, particularly that of Professor Myles Mace,[9] have confirmed these earlier findings.[10]

In short, under what might be called the working model of management structure — that is, the model which embodies actual corporate practice — most of the powers supposedly vested in the board are actually vested in the executives.

B. Modern Board Practice

The drastic skew between the received and working models of management structure is not simply an accident of time or temper. Rather, it is the virtually inevitable result of several critical constraints imposed by modern board practice.

1. Constraints of time. Some simple statistics: although a board of directors normally can act only at meetings, a 1967 Conference Board study of 454 manufacturing and mining corporations found that the boards of 45 percent of the surveyed corporations met no more than six times a year, and the boards of 96 percent met no more than twelve times a year.[11] Virtually

8. Baker, supra note 4, at 131-132.

9. M. Mace, Directors: Myth and Reality 47-48 and passim (1971) [hereinafter cited as Mace].

10. See, e.g., J. Bacon & J. Brown, Corporate Directorship Practices: Role, Selection and Legal Status of the Board 16-17 (Conference Board Rep. No. 646, 1975) [hereinafter cited as 1975 Conference Board Survey]; C. Brown & E. Smith, The Director Looks At His Job 24-26 (1957) [hereinafter cited as Brown & Smith]; Maurer, supra note 4, at 200-202. But see P. Holden, L. Fish & H. Smith, Top Management Organization and Control 17, 214 (enlarged ed. 1948) [hereinafter cited as Holden, Fish & Smith]; Investor Responsibility Research Center, Changes in the Corporate Board Room: What Should Be Done? Who Should Do It? 5-6 (1974) [hereinafter cited as IRRC].

The same analysis is generally applicable to nonbusiness corporations. See H. Wilensky & C. Lebeaux, Industrial Society and Social Welfare 272-273 (1958); Kerr, The School Board as an Agency of Legitimation, Sociology of Education, Fall 1964, at 34, 49-55.

11. 1967 Conference Board Survey, supra note 5, at 127 Table 21. The figures for other types of corporations surveyed were generally comparable, except for the

identical findings emerged in a 1970 survey of 474 industrial corporations by the management-consulting firm of Heidrick & Struggles.[12] Since board meetings usually last only a few hours,[13] the upshot is that few boards spend more than 36 hours a year in meeting time, and about half spend only 18 hours a year or less.[14] Since time spent preparing for meetings is roughly comparable to meeting time,[15] it is obvious that by reason of time constraints

---

public utilities (of 81 surveyed, 9.9 percent met more than 12 times a year – but none met more than 15 times – and 29.6 percent met six times or fewer) and the banking corporations (of 40 surveyed, 65 percent met 10 to 12 times a year, 30 percent met 13 to 25 times, and only 2.5 percent met fewer than 10 times). Id.

A more recent Conference Board survey of a smaller population – 129 industrials – reported that just over 40 percent held 10 or more meetings per year; no breakdown was given for the 60 percent holding fewer than 10 meetings. See Brown, The Board of Directors and Its Work Routine, Conf. Bd. Rec., March 1972, at 36.

12. Heidrick & Struggles, Profile of the Board of Directors 5 (1971) [hereinafter cited as Heidrick & Struggles]. The percentages for merchandising, insurance, and transportation companies were similar to those for industrials. Among the utilities, 27.8 percent held six or fewer meetings a year, and 11.1 percent held more than 12 meetings a year. Among the banking corporations, 4.4 percent held six or fewer meetings a year, and 26 percent held more than 12 meetings a year.

The Heidrick & Struggles survey was conducted by a questionnaire sent to the 1,000 largest industrial companies, 50 largest merchandising companies, 50 largest transportation firms, 50 largest life-insurance companies, and 50 largest utilities, as ranked by sales volume in Fortune magazine, and 300 largest commercial banks, as ranked by deposits in Polk's World Bank Directory. Id. at 2. Of the corporations surveyed, 750 provided usable responses, including 474 industrials, 158 banks, 26 transportation companies, 23 merchandisers, 33 insurance companies, and 36 utilities. Letter from Heidrick & Struggles to the author, Sept. 30, 1972.

See also Korn/Ferry International, Board of Directors Annual Study 18 (1975) (51 percent of 394 surveyed boards met nine times a year or less, and the average board met seven times a year) [hereinafter cited as Korn/Ferry].

13. See Koontz, supra note 6, at 158; 'Outside' Directors are 'In,' Chemical Week, Aug. 18, 1971, at 57 [hereinafter cited as 'Outside' Directors Are 'In']; cf. Nutt, A Study of Mutual Fund Independent Directors, 120 U. Pa. L. Rev. 179, 221 (1971); Townsend, Let's Install Public Directors, Bus. & Soc'y. Rev., Spring 1972, at 69.

14. Some directors may put in additional time on committee work, but this is normally relatively limited. For example, although the most common board committee has been the executive committee, one-fourth of the 512 manufacturing companies included in a recent Conference Board survey did not have such a committee. J. Bacon, Corporate Directorship Practices: Membership and Committees of the Board 50, 54 Table 13 (Conference Board Report No. 588, 1973) [hereinafter cited as 1973 Conference Board Survey]. In those which did, one-fourth of the committees had no outside directors, and one-fourth had only a minority of outside directors. Id. at 56 Table 15. Almost 10 percent of the executive committees never met. The median number of meetings for those which did meet was seven per year. Id. at 55 Table 14.

15. A study conducted by the Conference Board reported that of 93 responding companies only 19 believed directors spent more time on corporate affairs outside than inside meetings. Of the remaining 74 respondents, 36 believed about as much time was

alone the typical board could not possibly "manage" the business of a large, publicly held corporation in the normal sense of that term:[16] such businesses are far too complex to be managed by persons who put in the equivalent of five to ten working days a year. Furthermore, the same imperative precludes the board from making business policy: in a complex organization concerned with complex choices, policy cannot be developed on a part-time basis.[17]

2. Constraints of information. Some further statistics: although an opportunity to consider relevant data is obviously essential to meaningful decisionmaking, of 474 industrials surveyed by Heidrick & Struggles only 17.2 percent sent directors manufacturing data prior to the meeting, only 21.3 percent sent marketing data, only 5.7 percent sent an agenda, and 11 percent sent no information at all.[18] In many corporations the executives go so far as to wholly deny the board — supposedly entrusted with supreme power over the corporation — access to certain categories

---

spent outside as inside, and 38 believed less time was spent — usually much less. Brown, supra note 11, at 37; cf. 'Outside' Directors are 'In,' supra note 13, at 60. See also Garrett, The SEC Study of Directors' Guidelines, Conf. Bd. Rec., July 1974, at 57, 58. A survey of directors of 46 of the largest companies in the 1973 Fortune 500, conducted by Lamalie Associates, reported that three-fourths spent less than ten hours a month on board activities. The Corporate Director — A Profile, Financial Executive, Jan. 1974, at 7, 53 [hereinafter cited as Lamalie Associates].

16. Of course, if the board consists of officer-directors, then the individuals who do manage the corporation's business are also directors, but they do not manage the business by virtue of their directorial capacities. Similarly, large shareholders may utilize the board as a means of exercising control without actually taking a managerial role, see text accompanying notes 75-77 infra, and the board may then play an active role. But in this case too the board's force derives from nondirectorial capacities.

17. Mace, supra note 9, at 185; Maurer, supra note 4, at 200-201. Even where a part-time board does purport to make policy, the meaningfulness of its decisions may be questionable. "One executive . . . remarked that he did not care who formulated the policy so long as he was left to carry it out, because he knew that by the time the operating organization had modified the so-called major policy decision to meet realities, he would have pretty much his own way." M. Copeland & A. Towl, The Board of Directors and Business Management 66 (1947) [hereinafter cited as Copeland & Towl].

There are, of course, cases where the board does play a meaningful role in making business policy, see Mace, supra note 9, at 48-52, but in many or most of these cases it will probably be found either that the board is dominated by executives or important shareholders, see note 16 supra, or that the business of the corporation does not involve many operating decisions. Cf. SEC, Institutional Investor Study Report, H.R. Doc. No. 64, 92d Cong., 1st Sess. 811-814 (1971) [hereinafter cited as SEC, Institutional Investor Report].

18. Heidrick & Struggles, supra note 12, at 5.

of information. One-fifth of the executives questioned on this subject in both the Conference Board and Heidrick & Struggles surveys responded that directors should not have unrestricted access to company plans and operating data.[19]

Furthermore, the board normally has no staff of its own to evaluate the information it does receive or to gather information directly. Instead, the board must rely on the executives to perform those functions, either directly or through the executives' own staff.[20] Getting additional information is frequently very difficult. In many cases a director does not know what additional information he should request. Even if he does, it is regarded as improper – "just plain bad manners"[21] – to ask executives challenging questions at board meetings.[22] Thus the amount, quality, and structure of the information that reaches the board is almost wholly within the control of the corporation's executives.[23] It need hardly be added that this kind of power over information flow is virtually equivalent to power over decision.[24]

3. Constraints of composition, selection, and tenure. While constraints of time and information restrict the board's ability to manage the business or make policy, they do not directly subordinate the board to the corporation's executives. Direct subordination does necessarily follow, however, from a cluster of elements relating to the composition, selection, and tenure of directors.

a. Composition of the board. The most striking of the compositional elements is the degree to which the typical board

19. 1967 Conference Board Survey, supra note 5, at 132; Heidrick & Struggles, supra note 12, at 6. See also Koontz, supra note 6, at 161; Weinberg, A Corporation Director Looks at His Job, 27 Harv. Bus. Rev. 585, 588-589 (1949). A note accompanying the Heidrick & Struggles data states that "[a] mong [those corporations which do not give unrestricted access] . . . are organizations involved in government work, since exposure to their data necessitates security clearance," but it does not explain how many corporations have this problem or why the directors are not cleared.

20. See J. Juran & J. Louden, The Corporate Director 287 (1966) [hereinafter cited as Juran & Louden].

21. Mace, supra note 9, at 54.

22. See id. at 52-61, 186-188; Nutt, supra note 13, at 221-222. One chief executive told Mace that he liked to have insiders on the board so that he could take advantage of the "commonly observed courtesy" that the president will not be asked embarrassing questions in the presence of his subordinates. Mace, supra note 9, at 124; cf. id. at 54.

23. Cf. Copeland & Towl, supra note 17, at 169; Juran & Louden, supra note 20, at 288; Mace, supra note 9, at 30; Zald, The Power and Functions of Boards of Directors: A Theoretical Synthesis, 75 Am. J. Soc. 97, 104 (1969).

24. Cf. Kerr, supra note 10, at 51; Zald, supra note 23, at 104.

includes persons who are economically or psychologically dependent upon or tied to the corporation's executives, particularly its chief executive. Indeed, a substantial number of seats are held by executives themselves. Employee-directors held half or more of the board's seats in 29 percent of the approximately 500 manufacturing corporations included in a 1973 Conference Board survey,[25] 49.8 percent of the industrials in the Heidrick & Struggles sample,[26] and 55.9 percent of the 1970 *Fortune* 500.[27] Dependent on the chief executive for both retention and promotion,[28] and on other executives for day-to-day support, the inside director is highly unlikely to depart at a board meeting from the inside line determined by management prior to the meeting. As the corporate figures interviewed by Mace reported:

> The vice president inside-director type is in a precarious position at a board meeting. He just can't say anything in disagreement with his boss, so what he usually does is sit quietly and wait until he is called upon to speak.[29]
>
> Insiders don't ask questions or raise issues at board meetings because their points of view and contributions have all been expressed at meetings of management prior to the board meeting. All the insiders have been through the monthly performance review. Rarely — no, *never* — does the head of one operating group raise a question at the board meeting concerning the performance of another operating group. He would not do that at a board meeting.[30]
>
> . . . We have a sort of rule around here — we've even formalized it in a sense. Now, we fight like cats at the management meetings. But if any of our key inside people on the board feels strongly opposed to

25. 1973 Conference Board Survey, supra note 14, at 2, 3. Among approximately 340 nonmanufacturing corporations only 14 percent had boards with insider majorities. Id. Financial institutions in particular have traditionally had a low proportion of inside directors. Cf. id. at 3 Chart 3.

26. Heidrick & Struggles, supra note 12, at 4. In the nonindustrial categories, less than 20 percent of the banking, insurance, transportation, and utility corporations, but 65 percent of merchandising corporations, had insider majorities or evenly divided boards. Id. at 4.

27. Smith, Interlocking Directorates Among the 'Fortune 500,' Antitrust L. & Econ. Rev., Summer 1970, at 47, 49-50. Smith's data actually covered only 495 of the Fortune 500, since information on five corporations was unavailable. Of the 495 corporations, 49.7 percent had a majority of insiders and 6.2 percent were split evenly between insiders and outsiders. Id. at 50. Of the aggregate seats in the 495 corporations, 57.5 percent were held by insiders and 43.5 percent by outsiders. Id. at 47-48 & Table 1. See also Lamalie Associates, supra note 15, at 7. But see Korn/Ferry, supra note 12, at 7.

28. See note 88 infra.

29. Mace, supra note 9, at 119-120.

30. Id. at 120.

> something the president is asking the board to approve – and again, this doesn't happen very often – rather than go to the meeting and vote for it contrary to his judgment, he just doesn't go to that particular board meeting. This is sort of a screwy idea, but that's the way it's done here.[31]

Nor is dependence on the corporation's chief executive confined to inside directors. Recent surveys suggest, for example, that approximately one-fifth to one-fourth of the outside directors in large American corporations are lawyers or investment bankers.[32] Probably most of these are suppliers of services to the corporations on whose boards they sit, and are therefore highly interested in retaining the good graces of the chief executive, who normally has control over the purchase of such services. These surveys also indicate that approximately 12 to 15 percent of outside directors are commercial bankers, who are also often intent on retaining the corporation's business.[33] Many if not most of the remaining directors are psychologically tied to the chief executive by friendship, former collegueship, or both.[34]

b. Selection and tenure. As a result of current practices on selection and tenure, even those directors who are not bound to incumbent management by economic or psychological ties are unlikely to be truly independent. To begin with, directors are typically selected not by the board, as might be expected, but by the chief executive.[35] In making these selections most chief executives will take into consideration whether the candidate can be counted on not to rock the boat.

31. Id.

32. Lamalie Associates, supra note 15, at 7; Smith, supra note 27, at 48-49 & Table 2; 1973 Conference Board Survey, supra note 14, at 29 Table 6. The Conference Board data is somewhat ambiguous: of 2914 outside directors, 359 listed their principal affiliation as "law," and 299 as "investments." The Heidrick & Struggles data does not break out figures for the occupation of outside directors.

33. Smith, supra note 27, at 48-49 & Table 2 (12 percent); 1973 Conference Board Survey, supra note 14, at 29 Table 6 (15 percent).

34. See 1973 Conference Board Survey, supra note 14, at 28 Table 4; Cabot, Management and the Director, Conf. Bd. Rec., April 1974, at 50.

35. See 1975 Conference Board Survey, supra note 10, at 6, 10, 12; Brown & Smith, supra note 10, at 109-110; Gordon, supra note 4, at 109, 121, 130 & n. 24, 131; Mace, supra note 9, at 94-95; Maurer, supra note 4, at 201; Pfeffer, Size and Composition of Corporate Boards of Directors: The Organization and its Environment, 17 Ad. Sci. Q., June 1972, at 218, 220.

> The retired chairman of a medium-sized company in the mid-west stated: "In the companies I know, the outside directors always agree with management. That's why they are there. I have one friend that's just the greatest agreer that ever was, and he is on a dozen boards. . . ."[36]

Beyond the fact that he is usually selected in part because he can be counted on to go along, a new director is likely to be aligned with the chief executive simply by virture of the fact that he owes the latter his appointment[37] — an element reinforced by the chief executive's role in orienting new directors to the board.[38]

Perhaps even more important than the power of selection, in vesting the chief executive with control over outside directors, is the fact that in life as in law the power to hire implies the power to fire. A director who has been brought on the board by a chief executive — as outside directors typically are — is therefore likely to regard himself as serving at the latter's sufferance. "Also communicated to, and generally accepted by, directors was the fact that the president possessed the complete powers of control. Those members of the board who elected to challenge the president's powers of control were advised, usually outside the board meetings, that such conduct was inappropriate or they were asked to resign."[39] Nor is this power exercised infrequently: almost 37 percent of the industrial respondents in the Heidrick & Struggles survey reported that they had fired directors.[40]

36. Mace, supra note 9, at 99; cf. Mutual Funds 285 (R. Mundheim & M. Werner eds. 1970) (remarks of Allan F. Conwill); University of Pennsylvania Law School Conference on Mutual Funds, 115 U. Pa. L. Rev. 663, 739 (1967) (remarks of Abraham L. Pomerantz). As one executive was quoted: "Here in New York it's a systems club. There is a group of companies . . . where the chief executive of Company A has B and C and D on his board. They are all members of the Brook Club, the Links Club, or the Union League Club. Everybody is washing everybody else's hands." Mace, supra, at 99.

37. Cf. 1975 Conference Board Survey, supra note 10, at 25; Moscow, The Independent Director, 28 Bus. Law. 9, 11 (1972); Nutt, supra note 13, at 219.

38. Cf. Brown & Smith, supra note 10, at 88-89; Nutt, supra note 13, at 219.

39. Mace, supra note 9, at 80. See also id. at 79, 80-81; 1975 Conference Board Survey, supra note 10, at 10.

40. Heidrick & Struggles, supra note 12, at 11. Some of these firings may have been attributable to poor performance rather than insubordination.

The percentage of other types of companies which had fired directors ranged from 32.3 to 38 percent, except for the utilities, only 11.1 percent of which reported such firings.

Because it is inherently undesirable for law and practice to be in a state of visible opposition, the drastic skew between the legal and working models of the board would be of serious concern even if no specific dysfunctional consequences could be perceived. In fact, however, a number of such dysfunctions can be identified. On a relatively particularistic level, many legal rules have been shaped on the premise that the board manages the corporation's business in fact as well as in law. For example, by proceeding from the assumption that officers play a subordinate role to the board, the rules governing the authority of officers frequently embody an unrealistically restrictive view of an officer's power of position.[41] Standards of care, by the same token, often seem to be pitched to the outside director rather than the executive, as if the former were really running the business.[42] In duty-of-loyalty cases the courts have often given disproportionate weight to the fact that outside directors have approved a transaction in which executives are interested,[43] while the legislatures have sometimes gone so far as to provide that approval by outside directors is sufficient to sterilize an otherwise infected transaction.[44] In a wider context, the skew between belief and reality has led to what might be called the quack-cure problem – the danger that belief in the validity of the received legal model will forestall meaningful regulation by lulling shareholders, legislators, and the public into the illusion (which often seems deliberately conjured-up[45]) that a disinterested board is supervising the corporation's affairs.[46]

Legally, of course, the chief executive does not have power to discharge a director; however, a recalcitrant director can be dropped simply by arranging that he is not renominated when his term expires.

41. See, e.g., Schwartz v. United Merchants & Mfrs., Inc., 72 F.2d 256 (2d Cir. 1934); Phoenix Western Holding Corp. v. Gleeson, 18 Ariz. App. 60, 500 P.2d 320 (1972); Hurley v. Ornsteen, 311 Mass. 477, 42 N.E.2d 273 (1942); Douglass v. Panama, Inc., 504 S.W.2d 776 (Tex. 1974).

42. See, e.g., Graham v. Allis-Chalmers Mfg. Co., 41 Del. Ch. 78, 188 A.2d 125 (Sup. Ct. 1963); Glassberg v. Boyd, 35 Del. Ch. 293, 116 A.2d 711 (Ch. 1955).

43. See, e.g., Meiselman v. Eberstadt, 39 Del. Ch. 563, 568, 170 A.2d 720, 723 (Ch. 1961); Beard v. Elster, 39 Del. Ch. 153, 164-165, 160 A.2d 731, 738 (Sup. Ct. 1960).

44. See, e.g., Del. Code Ann. tit. 8, § 144(a)(1) (1974).

45. Cf. Amex Votes to Reshape its Structure, N.Y. Times, June 8, 1972, at 69, col. 6; Exchange Members Grant the Public a Louder Voice, N.Y. Times, March 2, 1972, at 55, col. 7; Metz, Directors' Role at Exchanges, N.Y. Times, Dec. 26, 1972, at 54, col. 4; Price of Friendship: How Rich Acquaintances of California Publisher Evidently Lost Bundle, Wall St. J., Aug. 11, 1972, at 1, col. 1; Public Directors Cautious at Big Board, N.Y. Times, May 21, 1973, at 51, col. 5.

46. See Mace, supra note 9, at 107-108; S. Vance, The Corporate Director – A

§11.2. Proposals for Reform of the Board: Bringing the Working Model into Line with the Received Legal Model

Given the skew between the legal and working models of management structure, and the resulting dysfunctions, it is not surprising that proposals for reform of the board have become a permanent part of the American corporate scene. Most of these take the received legal model as a starting point and seek to bring corporate practice into line. From that point on, however, the proposals show wide variation, falling into three broad categories: those calling for professional directors; those calling for full-time directors; and those calling for fully-staffed boards.

Critical Evaluation 63-68 (1968) [hereinafter cited as Vance]; Cary & Harris, Standards of Conduct under Common Law, Present Day Statutes and the Model Act, 27 Bus. Law., Feb. 1972, at 61, 65-66 (special issue) (remarks of Professor Cary); Heineman, What Does and Doesn't Go On in the Boardroom, Fortune, Feb. 1972, at 157, 159; Zald, supra note 23, at 103; Townsend, Book Review, N.Y. Times, Dec. 12, 1971, §7 (Book Review), at 3.

For example, in the Investment Company Act of 1940 Congress sought to regulate conflicts of interest between investment companies and their investment advisers, which were typically under common control, primarily by directing that no more than 60 percent of an investment company's board could be affiliated with its investment adviser in specified ways, and that contracts between an investment company and its adviser required periodic approval by either the shareholders or a majority of the unaffiliated directors. Investment Company Act of 1940, §§2(a)(3), 10(a), 15(a)-(c), 54 Stat. 790, 806, 812-813 (1940). In practice this technique of regulation turned out to be virtually worthless, because the unaffiliated directors of investment companies, like the outside directors of other corporations, were not in control of the board, were selected and indoctrinated by insiders who represented the investment adviser, and were often closely tied to insiders even though not technically "affiliated." See SEC, Institutional Investor Report, supra note 17, at 207-215, 363-364; SEC, Report on Public Policy Implications of Investment Company Growth, H.R. Rep. No. 2337, 89th Cong., 2d Sess. 10-17, 94-125, 150-151, 162-178 (1966); Wharton School of Finance & Commerce, A Study of Mutual Funds, H.R. Rep. No. 2274, 87th Cong., 2d Sess. 27-36, 463-466, 475-539 (1962) [hereinafter cited as Wharton Report]; Nutt, supra note 13, at 184, 215-220. But see University of Pennsylvania Law School Conference on Mutual Funds, supra note 36, at 741, 755 (remarks of Joseph E. Welch).

The Investment Company Act was overhauled in 1970. Among other things, a specific duty was imposed on investment company directors "to request and evaluate . . . such information as may reasonably be necessary to evaluate the terms" of the investment-adviser contract, and a fiduciary duty was explicitly imposed on the adviser with respect to its compensation. 15 U.S.C. §§80a-15(c), 35(b) (1970). See Nutt, supra note 13, at 265.

A. Professional Directors

One common type of proposal calls for filling board places with persons who would make a career out of serving as directors in a number of corporations, and would therefore presumably be more expert in and more attentive to their directorial obligations than those with another vocation.[47] It is unlikely that private action could be depended upon to effectuate such a reform. Over 88 percent of the corporations in the Heidrick & Struggles survey, including 85 percent of the industrials, reported that they had no interest in using professional directors.[48] Yet it is equally unlikely that such a reform could be effected by law. For one thing, it would be extremely difficult to define the term "professional director" statutorily. For another, it is questionable whether a suitable population of potential appointees presently exists; in a 1973 Conference Board survey of 851 boards, for example, only 75 seats were held by persons who considered themselves to be professional directors.[49] Although the population problem might be mitigated by extensive use of retired executives, that solution would simply foster another, equally difficult problem: the creation of a corporate gerontocracy, in conflict with the recent trend toward setting a retirement age for directors as well as executives.[50]

Even putting aside the difficulties of making such a proposal operational, the wisdom of putting it into effect seems very doubtful when its implications are considered. Because directorships

47. See, e.g., W. Douglas, Democracy and Finance 52-55 (1940); Holden, Fish & Smith, supra note 10, at 225; Juran & Louden, supra note 20, at 331-333; cf. Bacon, Directors Under Pressure, Conf. Bd. Rec., Feb. 1972, at 44, 44-45 (remarks of James E. Robison).

48. Heidrick & Struggles, supra note 12, at 10. See also Juran & Louden, supra note 20, at 333-335.

In addition, 64.5 percent of the surveyed corporations, including 56.7 percent of the industrials, had no interest in using retired executives as directors, and most of the remaining corporations had no interest unless there was an age restriction. Heidrick & Struggles, supra note 12, at 10.

49. 1973 Conference Board Survey, supra note 14, at 29 Table 5, 39 Table 9. See also 1975 Conference Board Survey, supra note 10, at 40.

50. See 1973 Conference Board Survey, supra note 14, at 42-47; Heidrick & Struggles, supra note 12, at 10; Juran & Louden, supra note 20, at 182-183; cf. Brown & Smith, supra note 10, at 117; Companies Act of 1948, 11 & 12 Geo. 6, c. 38, § 185 (special notice required for resolution appointing a director over the age of 70).

under present corporate practice are part-time positions, directorship fees are relatively low: median annual compensation for board service is in the $3400-4800 range.[51] To earn a living as a professional director commensurate with the skills required, an individual would therefore need to hold upwards of a dozen directorships.[52] Assuming that the number of large publicly held corporations for which such a reform might sensibly be required is approximately 2750,[53] that the average number of outside directorships in such corporations is six,[54] and that all outside seats would be filled by professional directors, approximately 15,000-16,000 seats would have to be filled in this manner. If each director were to hold a dozen seats, all of these directorships would be filled by just 1300 individuals. Not only would this generate an enormous and institutionalized conflict-of-interest problem but, what is worse, the professional directors would form an interlocking communication network tying the country's major corporations together in a wholly undesirable way.[55]

51. J. Bacon, Corporate Directorship Practices: Compensation 3 Chart 1 (Conference Board Rep. No. 596, 1973). This range includes both manufacturing ($4800) and nonmanufacturing ($3400) corporations. But see Korn/Ferry, supra note 12, at 12 (average compensation of $7900); Lamalie Associates, supra note 15, at 7 (average compensation of $5000-$10,000).

52. Cf. Vanderwicken, Change Invades The Boardroom, Fortune, May 1972, at 156, 282.

53. This figure is based on the number of common stock issues traded on the New York and American Stock Exchanges. Letter to the author from Dorothy Geraghty, Research Associate, New York Stock Exchange, Mar. 3, 1975 (1542 issues); Letter to the author from Robert A. Coplin, Vice-President, Information Services Division, American Stock Exchange, Feb. 27, 1975 (1222 issues).

54. The data permits only an estimate on this point, but the figure of six seems fairly reliable, and a range of five to eight would be highly reliable. See 1973 Conference Board Survey, supra note 14, at 1-2; Heidrick & Struggles, supra note 12, at 4; Korn/Ferry, supra note 12, at 7; Smith, supra note 27, at 48.

55. Cf. Smith, supra note 27; Smith & Desfosses, Interlocking Directorates: A Study of Influence, Miss. Vall. J. Bus. & Econ., Spring 1972, at 57. See also Clayton Act §19, 15 U.S.C. §19 (1970) (". . . No person at the same time shall be a director in any two or more corporations, any one of which has capital, surplus, and undivided profits aggregating more than $1,000,000 . . . if such corporations are or shall have been theretofore . . . competitors. . . ."); Protectoseal Co. v. Barncik, 484 F.2d 585 (7th Cir. 1973); F.T.C. Says 3 Concerns Violate Law on Directors, N.Y. Times, Nov. 25, 1972, at 1, col. 2; Goodyear Chairman Quits Alcoa Board; FTC is Notified, Wall St. J., Dec. 1, 1972, at 6, col. 1; Kerr-McGee's Head Leaves Outside Board, N.Y. Times, July 11, 1974, at 48, col. 1; Legal Actions Prompt Directors to Reassess Their Corporate Roles, Wall St. J., Sept. 17, 1974, at 1, col. 6; Littlefield Quits Board at Chrysler, Remains at GE After FTC Move, Wall St. J., March 23, 1973, at 9, col. 1; Second Alcoa Director Cited by FTC Quits a Post, Case Against 3 Firms May Go On, Wall St. J., Dec. 4, 1972, at 7, col.

Finally, one may doubt the accuracy of the premise that professional directors are more likely than nonprofessionals to be meaningfully involved in managing the corporation's business or making business policy:

> In England, where they have a "profession" known as "company director," the boardroom life is popularly regarded as a cushy sinecure. Said Lord Boothby, a life peer, in a reflective moment: "If you have five directorships it is total heaven, like having a permanent hot bath. . . . No effort of any kind is called for. You go to a meeting once a month in a car supplied by the company, you look grave and sage, on two occasions say 'I agree,' say 'I don't think so' once, and if all goes well you get 500 pounds a year."[56]

B. Full-Time Directors

A second type of proposal for bringing board practice into line with the received legal model is the restriction of board membership to "full-time directors," that is, individuals who are in the corporation's employ on a full-time basis, but differ from executives in that they do not have operating responsibilities.[57] Such a model lifts from the board the time constraint that in itself debars most directors from making business policy. An official of Standard Oil of New Jersey, which had such a board for many years,[58] put the argument as follows:

> [I] t's just inconceivable that a director in a corporation can discharge the [director's] responsibilities . . . unless he does more than attend a board meeting once a month. Unless he works in between those monthly board meetings very hard, he'd come up with a lot of statistics and have a lot of office traffic, but the real issue is whether a director of a corporation can or cannot discharge his responsibilities adequately . . . if he does not know enough about the functioning of the managers who are implementing board policy, and the results that they obtain, to form of his own knowledge proper opinion about what's going on.

1; 25 on Boards of Oil Companies Scrutinized in Antitrust Inquiry, N.Y. Times, March 12, 1974, at 1, col. 8. But cf. Towl, Outside Directors Under Attack, Harv. Bus. Rev., Sept.-Oct. 1965, at 135.

56. Chamberlain, Why It's Harder and Harder to Get a Good Board, Fortune, Nov. 1962, at 109.

57. See generally Brown & Smith, supra note 10, at 57-93.

58. See id. at 57; Vance, supra note 46, at 190-191.

> Now that means, as I say, he's got to be something more than a once-a-month director.[59]

As with the professional director, however, it is doubtful that the full-time director concept could be implemented by law. The distinction between operating and nonoperating decisions is not sufficiently clear to be the subject of legislative mandate, and even if it were, most corporations could not easily develop or afford a complete set of full-time top managers who had no operating responsibilities.[60] Finally, even if problems of statutory definition were overcome and the requirement restricted to those corporations which could afford it, the wisdom of precluding corporations from combining operating and nonoperating functions in the same individuals is doubtful, since in many businesses the major nonoperating functions (such as measurement of divisional performance, allocation of resources among divisions, determination of corporate-wide business principles, and establishment or acquisition of new businesses) cannot be compartmentalized from operating decisions.[61]

59. Brown & Smith, supra note 10, at 58.

60. See id. at 62-63; Juran & Louden, supra note 20, at 170-171.

61. In 1966 Jersey itself significantly changed its full-time director concept by adding part-time outsiders to its board and transferring the old board's functions to a reconstituted full-time executive committee. Vance, supra note 46, at 191.

Perhaps partially in recognition that a board consisting solely of full-time directors is unfeasible in most cases, a variant of the full-time director concept has come into prominence within the last several years. Under this variant, a few (but less than all) of the directors, without taking on management responsibilities, would spend a significant portion (but less than all) of their time directly on the corporation's business. See, e.g., Patton, The Working Director – Management's Middleman, Conf. Bd. Rec., Oct. 1972, at 36. Several major corporations have put such a concept into practice. For example, Westinghouse announced in 1972 that its top executives would retire from their managerial positions at 60, rather than at 65, and would then "be retained as 'officer-directors,' reporting to the board on a variety of significant long-range problems. The 'officer-directors' would spend two-thirds of their time on corporate business until the normal retirement age of 65, and would draw two-thirds of their previous salaries. . . ." Westinghouse to Cut Top Officers' Duties at Age 60 to Facilitate Succession Process, Wall St. J., July 12, 1972, at 8, col. 2; see 1975 Conference Board Survey, supra note 10, at 36. See also id. at 37-39; Vanderwicken, supra note 52, at 282, 290. Again, such a practice would be difficult to require in operative statutory terms. Furthermore, such arrangements in themselves seem to hold out little gain over present practice, since such special directors are likely to be super-consultants, dependent on management for their positions, for their support, and for acceptance of any proposals they might make. Cf. Patton, supra, at 38.

A variant of the variant calls for a special director who would be nominated or approved by some organ independent of the corporation and who would have special

C. Fully Staffed Boards

Still a third type of proposal calls for equipping the board with a substantial staff of its own to advise it in reviewing management proposals and thereby allow it to exercise at least a policy-making – if not a managerial – role.[62] The best known and most complete proposal of this type was made by Arthur J. Goldberg in 1972 at the time of his resignation from the board of TWA.

The Goldberg proposal begins by pointing up the skew between the received and working models of the board, and the inevitability of such a skew under current corporate practice. Since outside directors "cannot acquire more than a smattering of knowledge about any large and far-flung company," the board "is relegated to an advisory and legitimizing function that is substantially different from the role of policy maker . . . contemplated by the law of corporations." As a result, "[i]t is difficult, if not impossible . . . for the most dedicated director to have much impact on policy decisions." Thus the outside director is not fulfilling the policy-making role contemplated by corporate law, leaving him "open to justifiable criticism and legal recrimina-

---

responsibilities and special facilities. See Moscow, supra note 37; Townsend, supra note 13. Under Moscow's proposal such a director would be expected to devote at least 12 working days annually to the corporation's business (in addition to attending board meetings), and would have the purpose of promoting "the long term business success of the corporate enterprise ... [and representing] the collective body of future shareholders. . . ." Moscow, supra note 37, at 12. This seems like quite a lot to do in 12 days. Townsend's proposal, which would apply only to corporations with over a billion dollars in assets, calls for the appointment of a full-time "public director" by an ad hoc committee of congressional members. The corporation would give this official an office on its premises and a million dollars a year with which to pay his own salary and hire staff. He would "receive notice of *all* meetings conducted throughout the company [which would be] automatically open to attendance by him or one of his staff members." Townsend, supra note 13, at 69 (emphasis in original). He and his staff would have access to all files. He would be required to call two press conferences a year to "report on the company's progress or lack of progress on issues of interest to the public. It will be argued that he will reveal company secrets. Let us pray he will." Essentially, this is not an idea for a new kind of director, but for an observer posted at the corporation by the state. The staff would be the observer's, not the board's; the obligations would run to the public, not to the corporation. While the title of "director" might flow from the historical evolution of Townsend's proposal, it is irrelevant to the proposal's substance. For the kinds of difficulties such a proposal might involve, see note 106 infra.

62. See, e.g., Koontz, supra note 6, at 169-170.

tions."[63] The cure proposed for these ills is the establishment of "a committee of overseers of outside directors" which "would be generally responsible for supervising company operations on a broad scale and make periodic reports to the board." This committee would be authorized to hire a small staff of experts "who would be responsible only to the board and would be totally independent of management control," and to engage highly skilled consultants – such as scientific advisors, demographic experts, consumer advisors, advertising consultants, and financiers – to provide an independent source of expertise for the board. Together, the staff and consultants "would look into major policy questions and report to the committee and through them to the board as a whole before decisions are taken on management recommendations." This assistance "would reassert the position of the board as a focal point for creative policy input for corporate decisions."[64]

The Goldberg proposal carries to its logical conclusion the proposition that the working model of the board must be brought into line with the received legal model. Given the premise that the board is to manage the business of the corporation (or at a minimum make business policy), it follows that unless the board is to consist of full-time corporate employees, which would be prohibitively costly and possibly inefficient in most corporations, it must have at its disposal a staff and consultants to scrutinize management's activities, policies, and proposals preliminary to review and revision by the board.

Notwithstanding its logic, however, the Goldberg proposal is both unsound and unworkable. Stripped of its trappings, it would create a shadow staff with an institutionalized obligation to second-guess the management, but with very limited responsibility for results. Assuming that the directors are part-time, in cases where the recommendations of staff and management diverged, they would have little choice except to adopt one set of recommendations or the other. Yet absent self-dealing on the part of management, the board's staff could normally be expected only to decide again – with much more limited facilities and feel for

63. Goldberg, Debate on Outside Directors, N.Y. Times, Oct. 29, 1972, § 3, at 1, col. 3. See also N.Y. Times, Oct. 19, 1972, at 69, col. 5.

64. Goldberg, supra note 63, at 3.

the business, and at the price of additional expense and time – issues which management and the corporate staff have already once decided. If the conclusions of management and staff are the same, nothing will have been gained for this price. If they differ, it is far from clear how the board will choose between them. In short, the proposal would add a further and unnecessary level of decision-making to corporations which already tend toward overbureaucratization; would add immensely to the difficulties of running the corporation's business; and would produce a wholly undesirable diffusion of responsibility as among the executives, the shadow staff, the overseeing committee, and the board itself.[65]

§11.3. The Functions of the Board

Given that the Goldberg proposal carries to its logical conclusion the premise that the working model of the board should be brought into line with the received legal model, and given further that the proposal is both unworkable and unsound, its ultimate thrust is to demonstrate, however inadvertently, the invalidity of the premise from which it proceeds: since the board cannot be expected either to manage the business or make business policy, the task of reform must lie not in aligning the working model of the board with the received legal model, but in structuring the board to ensure effectuation of any meaningful functions it *can* perform, and particularly any functions it is uniquely qualified to perform.

65. Cf. Blough, The Outside Director at Work on the Board, 45 N.Y. State B.J. 467 (1973); Smith, The Goldberg Dilemma: Directorships, Wall St. J., Feb. 7, 1973, at 14, col. 4. Blough points out that while the Goldberg proposal is grounded in significant part on protecting the director against liability for failure to obey the statutory mandate that he manage the corporation, it "would raise as many legal problems for a safety-first minded outside director as it would settle. If a conflict among staffs arose, some comfort could be taken legally in the board's having considered all viewpoints and its conclusion thus should not ordinarily be questioned by a court under the 'business judgment' rule. But the directors would also have to consider . . . the comparability of the quality of the outside staff with the inside group, the possibility that a dissident stockholder would claim that because of a disclosed adverse report the board knew or should have known the investment would turn sour, or that confronted by conflicting views the board did nothing when it should have taken advantage of a golden opportunity." Blough, supra, at 470.

For a more sympathetic view of the Goldberg proposal, see Schwartz, A Plan to Save the Board, 28 Record of N.Y.C.B.A. 279 (1973).

With management and policymaking beyond the board's reach, four clusters of functions remain: providing advice and counsel to the office of the chief executive; authorizing major corporate actions; providing a modality by which persons other than executives can be formally represented in corporate decision-making; and selecting and dismissing the members of the chief executive's office and monitoring that office's performance.[66] In considering the bearing of each of these functions on the structure of the board, two related questions must be asked: how important is the function; and to what extent is the board uniquely qualified to perform it?

A. Advice and Counsel

It is commonly stated that a major function of the board is to provide advice and counsel to the corporation's chief executive.[67] Certainly a director is in many ways ideally suited to fill such a role. As a member of the corporate institution he has both a reasonable degree of familiarity with its business operations and a special set of loyalties to its welfare. And because he is a formal equal of the chief executive, he may be free to speak his mind in a way that is closed to the chief executive's subordinates, while the chief executive may be able to discuss with him matters that could not easily be raised with subordinates.[68] On the other hand, the advice-and-counsel function is hardly essential to the corporation's operation. The chief executive could perform his own functions with advice only from staff and line. If the chief executive does

66. Another function sometimes attributed to the board is handling crisis situations. See, e.g., Mace, supra note 9, at 27. On examination, however, this function invariably boils down to selecting a new chief executive when the incumbent dies unexpectedly or when the corporation is in deep trouble due to his inadequacy, see id., and is therefore really a special case of the selection-and-dismissal function.

The asking of pertinent questions is also sometimes listed as an important board function. See Baker, supra note 4, at 19; Copeland & Towl, supra note 17, at 95-114; Koontz, supra note 6, at 39-40. In fact boards seldom ask such questions, see text accompanying notes 21-22 supra, but even if they did it would simply be an application of the functions described in the text.

67. See Brown & Smith, supra note 10, at 19 (remarks of unidentified director); Gordon, supra note 4, at 135-137; Mace, supra note 9, at 13-22; Bacon, supra note 47, at 44 (remarks of Gustave L. Levy); Vanderwicken, supra note 52, at 157; Weinberg, A Corporation Director Looks at His Job, Harv. Bus. Rev., Sept. 1949, at 591.

68. See 1975 Conference Board Survey, supra note 10, at 18; Vanderwicken, supra note 52, at 157-158.

want outside advice, he can and frequently will obtain it from the corporation's lawyers, accountants, or bankers, rather than from the board. Indeed, the fact that a given director is a professional often better accounts for his advice being sought than the fact that he is a director.

B. Authorization of Major Corporate Actions

Many kinds of corporate actions require authorization by the board of directors as a matter of either law or practice. The statutory direction that the corporation's business be managed by the board serves to impose a requirement of board authorization for transactions of a certain quantitative magnitude, regardless of type – a requirement normally policed by third persons involved in such transactions. The statutes also commonly require board authorization of certain types of transactions regardless of quantitative magnitude – typically, dividend declaration, certificate amendment, merger, sale of substantially all assets, and dissolution.[69] Furthermore, the internal operating procedures of many corporations require board authorization for capital investments, acquisitions, long-term commitments, and other defined types of transactions involving some designated dollar amount.[70]

Certainly the authorization function may be a useful one. Even pro forma review is likely to inhibit practices which cannot stand even superficial scrutiny.[71] Moreover, the mere expectation that review is required before a plan can become effective probably heightens the rationality of the decision process by inducing extra care in the preparation of proposals.[72] Finally, providing the chief executive with an organ to which he is accountable, even in form, may dissipate somewhat the strains which accompany ultimate substantive responsibility. A leading executive has remarked that the board "buffers and protects the chief executive and provides him and his subordinate management with a sheltered and supportive environment in which to function."[73]

69. See Eisenberg, The Legal Roles of Shareholders and Management in Modern Corporate Decisionmaking, 57 Calif. L. Rev. 1, 60-68 (1969).

70. See, e.g., 1967 Conference Board Survey, supra note 5, at 97; Koontz, supra note 6, at 45-53.

71. Nutt, supra note 13, at 223.

72. See Koontz, supra note 6, at 24; cf. id. at 23-24; H. Wilensky & N. Lebeoux, Industrial Society and Social Welfare 273 (1958).

73. Heineman, supra note 46, at 157.

On the other hand, beyond serving as an audience, and a generally agreeable one at that, the board's reviewing role is usually quite limited, since its decisions must normally turn on analyses prepared by the very executives who formulate that which is being analyzed. Furthermore, the audience role itself can be played with more effectiveness elsewhere in the corporate structure, and it generally is. Since the modern corporation is highly bureaucratic, most plans must go through several layers of review even in the absence of a requirement of board approval. In all likelihood any one of these reviews has greater potential for disclosing a proposal's weaknesses than does review by the board. Indeed, for most or all practical purposes the last real authorization level is the office of chief executive.[74] Thus, aside from the potential check it provides in conflict-of-interest cases, the board's authorization function, like its advice-and-counsel function, is of limited importance, except where the board includes major shareholders or creditors who wish to play an active role in corporate affairs without assuming corporate office.

C. A Modality for Exercising Influence or Control

A third function served by the board is the provision of a modality through which classes of persons other than the corporation's executives can influence or control corporate action. For example, major shareholders may want to become meaningfully involved in corporate decisions, yet may not wish to take on an executive position. Exercise of control through formal shareholder channels is likely to be unsatisfactory in such cases because the body of shareholders may not be legally permitted to make the relevant decisions,[75] and in any event may constitute too clumsy an instrument for this purpose. Exercise of control through informal channels may be undesirable because such a role may subject the shareholder to individual liability,[76] and in any event may be unsatisfactory just because of its informality. For such shareholders the board provides an ideal modality, since internal corporate processes can be so structured that all transactions of a

74. See Gordon, supra note 4, at 131-133.

75. See, e.g., Charlestown Boot & Shoe Co. v. Dunsmore, 60 N.H. 85 (1880).

76. See Kingston Dry Dock Co. v. Lake Champlain Transp. Co., 31 F.2d 265 (2d Cir. 1929) (L. Hand, J.).

given class must go through the board or a board committee on which the shareholder sits.[77]

Major shareholders are not the only persons who want to use the board as a modality for involvement in corporate decisionmaking. Major creditors often make similar use of the board for similar reasons,[78] and lately much consideration has been given to the desirability of providing various corporate client-groups (for example, employees, suppliers, consumers), and certain disadvantaged social groups (such as blacks and women) with access to the corporate decisionmaking process through board membership.[79]

How important is the modality function? For a major shareholder or creditor the mechanism is certainly useful. For the other groups the answer is less clear. Membership in such groups does not guarantee either the financial and business skills or the time required to exert a meaningful say in corporate decisionmaking. In all probability, some client and social groups press for board representation because they fail to realize this and also overvalue the board's role. But even a group that is aware of the limited utility of board membership might want such representation. While normally the board can, as a practical matter, neither manage the business nor make business policy, it may be able to impress upon those who do the importance of taking particular kinds of values into account. At a minimum, the allocation of directorships to certain groups may concretely symbolize, to middle and lower management, top management's commitment to the values that the group represents.[80]

77. See, e.g., O. Williamson, The Economics of Discretionary Behavior: Managerial Objectives in a Theory of the Firm 105 (1964); cf. Great Western United's Board Reestablishes Executive Committee, Wall St. J., July 31, 1972, at 12, col. 4; Great Western United Faces Proxy Fight as Director Backs Disposal of Some Units, Wall St. J., Aug. 23, 1972, at 6, col. 1.

78. As in the case of a shareholder, direct involvement in corporate decisionmaking by a creditor may result in the imposition of individual liability. Cf. Connor v. Great W. Sav. & Loan Assn., 69 Cal. 2d 850, 447 P.2d 609, 73 Cal. Rptr. 369 (1968) (Traynor, C.J.).

79. See Blumberg, Reflections on Proposals for Corporate Reform Through Change in the Composition of the Board of Directors: "Special Interest" or "Public" Directors, 53 B.U.L. Rev. 547 (1973); Bunting, Conard, Deutsch, Farrell & Hickman, The Corporate Machinery for Hearing and Heeding New Voices, 27 Bus. Law. 195, 197-208 (remarks of Professor Alfred F. Conard), 214-218 (remarks of John R. Bunting) (1971); PoKempner, The More Representative Board, Conf. Bd. Rec., Feb. 1972, at 42; Vanderwicken, supra note 52, at 285-290; cf. Firms Find Integration in their Boardrooms is Working Quite Well, Wall St. J., Oct. 5, 1972, at 1, col. 6.

On the other hand, there are alternative modalities through which the ends desired by such groups can be achieved. These alternatives can be ranged along a continuum, with informal channels of influence at one extreme and direct government regulation at the other. Between these poles lie a great variety of formal modalities. For example, labor can gain a say in corporate decisionmaking through collective bargaining and the grievance machinery.[81] Creditors can exercise control through restrictive covenants.[82] Suppliers and consumers can be organized either through private action, as in the case of American automobile dealers,[83] or under legal auspices, as in the case of the consumer councils created by statute in connection with socialized industries in Great Britain.[84] Social groups can gain a say through working relationships developed between the corporation and representative organizations.[85] These modalities may be more effective mechanisms than board membership for the exercise of influence by client and social groups, since they can be closely tailored to the substantive and procedural needs of each group, while the board's form is relatively fixed, its jurisdiction necessarily diffuse, and its effective power very limited.

Furthermore, board representation by such groups entails costs that may outstrip any potential benefits. For one thing, a director appointed to represent such a group may face the difficult and at times irreconcilable problems which result from attempting to promote two potentially conflicting objectives: the best interest of the corporation, and the special interests of those whom the director represents.[86] Moreover, the special interests of the various groups represented under such a concept are themselves likely to

80. See Blumberg, supra note 79, at 552; Bunting, et al., supra note 79, at 201 (remarks of Prof. Conard), 215-217 (remarks of Mr. Bunting); Vanderwicken, supra note 52, at 290; cf. City to Add Nurses to Hospital Boards, N.Y. Times, Aug. 2, 1966, at 1, col. 7.

81. See J. Kuhn, Bargaining in Grievance Settlement (1961); Feller, A General Theory of the Collective Bargaining Agreement, 61 Calif. L. Rev. 663 (1973).

82. Cf. American Bar Foundation, Corporate Debt Financing Project, Commentaries on Indentures 312-473 (1971).

83. Cf. S. Macaulay, Law and the Balance of Power (1966).

84. See W. Robson, Nationalized Industry and Public Ownership 243-277 (1960).

85. Cf. R. Walton & R. McKersie, A Behavioral Theory of Labor Negotiations 391-398 (1965).

86. Cf. Vagts, Reforming the "Modern" Corporation: Perspectives From the German, 80 Harv. L. Rev. 23, 52-53 (1966).

conflict, with consequences that have been pointed up by Professor Vagts:

> The system [adopted under German law and practice, under which the supervisory board includes labor, banking, supplier, and big-consumer representatives] has . . . special dangers. By bringing the public and the employees into the inner councils of the corporation it tends to screen both the conflicts between the interests involved and their resolution from public view. Thus it causes power to be exercised by a relatively closed group that tends to develop common alliances within itself at the expense of those whom it represents.[87]

In short, while the problem of board representation by client and social groups is a complex one, for present purposes it seems fair to conclude that some benefits derive from such representation; that the benefits probably consist of marginal changes in decisionmaking input, rather than gross changes in decisionmaking output; that most of the benefits can be achieved, perhaps more effectively, through means other than board representation; and that costs as well as benefits result. On balance, therefore, the importance of the board's modality function may be considerable as to major shareholders and perhaps creditors, but is questionable as to client and social groups.

D. Selection and Removal of the Chief Executive; the Monitoring Function

A fourth cluster of functions served by the board consists of selecting and dismissing the members of the chief executive's office, and monitoring that office's performance. Unlike the advice, authorization, and modality functions, the elements of this fourth cluster are both of critical importance to the corporation and uniquely suited for performance by the board.

1. Selection. By law and practice the corporation's chief executive is formally chosen by the board.[88] Of course, an out-

87. Id. at 88.

88. In most cases the board also formally chooses other major officers, and often minor officers as well. Both statutes and practice show considerable variation in this regard. As to the major officers (usually president, vice-presidents, treasurer, and secretary): some statutes provide that these officers shall be chosen by the board. See Cal. Corp. Code §821 (West 1955); Ill. Ann. Stat. ch. 32, §157.43 (Smith-Hurd 1963); N.Y. Bus. Corp. Law §715(a) (McKinney 1963); Ohio Rev. Code Ann. §1701.64(A)

going chief executive will have a great deal to say in the selection of his successor.[89] Typically a successor will be sought from within the ranks, and in such cases the outgoing chief executive has far better information on candidates than the board.[90] Frequently he will have designated a crown prince, either by title (for example, executive vice-president), or otherwise; appointment of anyone else is then rendered difficult by the personal and institutional expectations such a designation creates.[91] And if the chief executive has managed the business well, the board will normally be hesitant to override his judgment as to who can best perpetuate the corporation's prosperity.[92]

Nevertheless, despite significant input from the outgoing chief executive, the board's role in selecting a successor is often considerably more than a formality.[93] The elements that prevent the board from making business policy, for example, do not prevent it from taking a meaningful role in selection of a new chief executive. Policymaking for a complex enterprise is a full-time occupation; selecting a chief executive is not. Policymaking requires intimate involvement with the business; selecting a chief executive does not. Policymaking depends on a body of sub-

---

(Page Supp. 1973); ABA Model Bus. Corp. Act §50 (1969 rev.). Others provide that such officers shall be chosen by the board unless otherwise provided by the bylaws, see N.J. Stat. Ann. §14A:6-15(1) (Supp. 1974), or as prescribed by the bylaws or as the board of directors determines, see Del. Code Ann. tit. 8, §142(b)(2) (1974). The statutory variations as to minor officers (assistant secretary, assistant treasurer, etc.) are comparable. Whatever the form, however, the board normally just rubberstamps the chief executive's selections in the case of all officers below the chief executive's level. See Gordon, supra note 4, at 107-108; Juran & Louden, supra note 20, at 88, 91-92; M. Newcomer, The Big Business Executive 40 (1955).

89. See 1975 Conference Board Survey, supra note 10, at 24; Gordon, supra note 4, at 129 n. 21; Mace, supra note 9, at 65-68, 70-71; Heineman, supra note 46, at 159; cf. Zald, Who Shall Rule? A Political Analysis of Succession in a Large Welfare Organization, Pac. Soc. Rev., Spring 1965, at 52. An extreme example is recorded by Juran and Louden:

"Some [chief executive officers] have resorted to the 'sealed letter' method for selecting their successors in an emergency. They have named their successors and the reasons for their choice but have not announced this. Instead, they have recorded it in a sealed letter which is not to be opened unless they meet with some sudden emergency." Juran & Louden, supra note 20, at 104.

90. See Mace, supra note 9, at 70-71.

91. Cf. Zald, supra note 23, at 109.

92. Cf. Zald, supra note 89, at 58-59.

93. See 1975 Conference Board Survey, supra note 10, at 26; Gordon, supra note 4, at 107-108; Juran & Louden, supra note 20, at 88, 91-92; M. Newcomer, supra note 88, at 40.

stantive knowledge possessed only by those in the field; in the selection of a chief executive, however, outside directors, who are themselves often chief executives,[94] are likely to be as qualified in evaluating candidates as the outgoing chief executive. Thus the board can be expected to and frequently does play a real albeit restrained role in the selection of a new chief executive.

How important is the selection function? It has been argued that in a large, publicly held corporation the chief executive, or even the top executives taken as a group, cannot determine policy, and that instead this power inheres in the technocrats inhabiting the middle cells of the organization chart.[95] Although this proposition contains a significant element of truth, it is nevertheless greatly overstated. While it may well be that day-to-day policy can be made only on lower levels, the office of the chief executive (that is, the individual or individuals[96] who fill that office together with associated cabinet and staff) will normally be the locus of final decision on most important policies, and will have an indirect voice in other policies through the selection and domination of the other executives. With its large powers over policy, selection, promotion, and budget, that office can do much to determine the profitability and direction of the enterprise; it is, therefore, generally appropriate to give that office credit when the enterprise operates efficiently, and to hold it responsible when the enterprise does not.[97]

2. Removal and monitoring. The removal power is a concomitant of the selection power. In terms of ongoing corporate activities taken as a whole, the selection power is probably the more important of the two. In terms of the special role the board can play, however, the removal power is preeminent – not because removal is so important in itself, but because it subsumes a third, semi-autonomous function: monitoring the results achieved by the chief executive's office to determine whether the incumbent

94. See 1973 Conference Board Survey, supra note 14, at 29 Table 5; Mace, supra note 9, at 87-89.

95. J. Galbraith, The New Industrial State 59-71 (2d ed. 1971).

96. See Second Thoughts on the 'Office of the President,' Business Week, Oct. 3, 1970, at 42; Vance, Toward a Collegial Office of the President, Calif. Mgmt. Rev., Fall 1972, at 106; Yunich to Retire at 55 from R. H. Macy, N.Y. Times, Sept. 27, 1972, § 2, at 63, col. 5; Some Large Firms Find Operations Are Simplified By Group Takeover of the Chief Executive's Role, Wall St. J., July 7, 1972, at 22, col. 1.

97. Cf. Gordon, supra note 4, at 91-97, 106-115.

should remain in place. A structure which emphasizes the preeminence of this function may be referred to as a monitoring model.

Unlike the received legal model, which, as elaborated, stresses the policymaking function and therefore assumes the board is an integral part of the corporation's management structure, the premise of a monitoring model is that management is a function of the executives, with ultimate responsibility located in the office of the chief executive. Under a monitoring model, therefore, the role of the board is to hold the executives accountable for adequate results (whether financial, social, or both), while the role of the executives is to determine how to achieve such results.[98] Of course, the board cannot perform this function without regard to policy: objectives must be set, explicitly or implicitly, against which to measure management's results, and the selection of objectives will partly depend on the directors' broad notions of policy and will interact with the question of what business policies are suitable for the particular firm. Nevertheless, the selection of an objective is distinguishable not only in theory but pretty largely in practice from the determination of how an objective will be met: it is one thing, for example, to demand a certain return on capital; it is another to decide upon the strategy and tactics which promise to yield that return.

The monitoring model, moreover, is not simply mechanistic; monitoring must begin with results, but it cannot end there. Apparently satisfactory profits, for example, may have been purchased by skimping on maintenance or research, or may flow from a windfall. Similarly, profits which seem unsatisfactory may be the product of an acceptable risk which did not bear fruit, of heavy start-up costs, or of a natural catastrophe. The concept of monitoring for results thus does not preclude the monitors from going behind the result and either accepting as satisfactory a level of performance which falls short of the applicable objective, or criticizing as unsatisfactory a level of performance which exceeds it. What the concept of monitoring does require is the availability of sophisticated and independent information-gathering systems — a matter which will be discussed in chapter 12 — and directors who

98. See Conard, A Behavioral Analysis of Directors' Liability for Negligence, 1972 Duke L.J. 895, 916-919; IRRC, supra note 10, at 16-19.

are equally sophisticated in interpreting both financial and non-financial data.

The critical importance of monitoring as a board function rests on two elements. First, in the exercise of many of its other functions, including even its power of selection, the board must properly pay great deference to the incumbent chief executive. In the exercise of its monitoring function, however, the board must be completely independent of the chief executive, since he is the very person whose results are being monitored. Second, the very premise of the corporate system, in which control of the factors of production and distribution is vested in the hands of privately appointed corporate managers, is that it can be expected to attain a more efficient utilization of economic resources than that achievable under alternative economic constitutions. Given that premise, however, the legal system may and even must insist on some structural assurance that such efficiency will be forthcoming, and under appropriate conditions the board's monitoring function can help provide that assurance.

Since those who manage obviously cannot be trusted to assure their own efficiency, the removal of inefficient managers requires some mechanism external to the managers themselves. One such mechanism is the market in which the corporation operates, with its attendant sanction of corporate failure. But this mechanism permits substantial inefficiency, since given the structure of most markets, a firm can usually remain in business for a protracted period of time if it has even the most meager returns.[99] A second such mechanism is the takeover bid: if the corporation's assets are inefficiently utilized, its shares will normally be underpriced, tempting outsiders to acquire control through stock purchases.[100] This mechanism, however, also provides excessive leeway for managerial inefficiency, because of the high transaction costs of takeover bids resulting from their inherent mechanics,[101]

99. See, e.g., Publicker Industries' Losses on Operations Irk Critics; Firm Manages by Selling Assets, Wall St. J., April 24, 1972, at 30, col. 1.

100. Cf. D. Austin & J. Fishman, Corporations in Conflict – The Tender Offer 43-45 (1970); Fleischer & Mundheim, Corporate Acquisition by Tender Offer, 115 U. Pa. L. Rev. 317, 324-325 (1967); Hayes & Taussig, Tactics of Cash Takeover Bids, Harv. Bus. Rev., March-April 1967, at 135, 139-140; Manne, Mergers and the Market for Corporate Control, 73 J. Pol. Econ. 110, 112-113 (1965).

101. Cf. O. Williamson, Corporate Control and Business Behavior 99-100 (1970).

the barriers to success thrown up by the Williams Act,[102] and the ability of incumbent executives to oppose such bids through use of the target corporation's own resources.[103] Some further constraint on managerial inefficiency is therefore required to assure the most efficient utilization of economic resources. An agency that could monitor the efficiency of the chief executive's office on a regular basis, and remove the inhabitants of that office for inadequate performance, would be ideally suited to aid in the implementation of this critical social function.

Such a power might, of course, be vested in some agency other than the board. But what are the alternatives? The body of shareholders is too disparate, shifting, and clumsy to conduct the type of inquiry involved. Effective replacement would be highly improbable; monitoring in any sense would be all but impossible; and removal situations would be turned into semi-public quasi-trials, involving intolerable cost, rigidity, embarrassment, and delay. Client-groups cannot be assigned this function, partly because of administrative considerations, but also on the ground that such groups often have special interests which are inconsistent with the general corporate welfare. A council of corporate executives would not present administrative problems, but vesting the power to remove the chief executive in such an organ would put enormous pressure on the chief executive to select subordinates purely on the basis of their subordination.[104] A governmental

102. Pub. L. No. 90-439, 82 Stat. 454 (1968), 15 U.S.C. §§78m(d), (e), 78n(d)-(f) (1970). See Manne, Cash Tender Offers for Shares – A Reply to Chairman Cohen, 1967 Duke L.J. 231.

103. See E. Aranow & H. Einhorn, Tender Offers for Corporate Control 219-274 (1973); Schmults & Kelly, Cash Take-over Bids – Defense Tactics, 23 Bus. Law. 115 (1967); Note, Defensive Tactics Employed by Incumbent Managements in Contesting Tender Offers, 21 Stan. L. Rev. 1104 (1969); cf. Austin, Tender Offers Revisited: 1968-1972 Comparison with the Past and Future Trends, Merger & Acquisitions, Fall 1973, at 16; Hindley, Separation of Ownership and Control in The Modern Corporation, 13 J. Law & Econ. 185 (1970); Armada Pauses on Acquisition Trail to Bolster Own Take-Over Defenses, Wall St. J., June 3, 1974, at 17, col. 1; CNA Financial Corp., Once the Avid Hunter, Now is Worried Prey, Wall St. J., July 22, 1974, at 1, col. 6; Market Place – Obstacles Cited on Take-Overs, N.Y. Times, May 28, 1970, at 52, col. 5; Shelters Impede Takeovers, N.Y. Times, Mar. 29, 1970, §3, at 1, col. 1; cf. Del E. Webb Corp. To Seek Bylaw Change on Director Elections, Wall St. J., April 8, 1975, at 14, col. 4; Jorgensen Co. Proposes Delaware Rechartering as Take-Over Defense, Wall St. J., April 4, 1974, at 8, col. 5; Instrument Systems Is Asking Its Holders To Make It Even Harder to Oust Directors, Wall St. J., Feb. 24, 1975, at 9, col. 1.

104. This difficulty might be overcome by also vesting such a council with the

agency[105] would almost surely serve to politicize the selection and removal of corporate executives, in the narrowest sense of that term;[106] in any event it is unlikely that any single agency could effectively screen candidates for executive office in hundreds or thousands of corporations, let alone effectively monitor the performance of those it had chosen. Optimal performance of the selection, monitoring, and removal function requires an agency, like the board, which is compact and cohesive, relatively free of conflicting interests, and individualized to the corporation, yet capable of being made independent of executive control.

---

power to select and dismiss its own members, but divesting the chief executive of those powers would be both impracticable and unwise.

105. See, e.g., Roth, Supervision of Corporate Management: The "Outside" Director and the German Experience, 51 N.C.L. Rev. 1369, 1382 (1973); Townsend, supra note 13, at 69-70.

106. The history of General Aniline is instructive. In 1942 the U.S. Government took over General Aniline's stock as enemy property, and the Secretary of the Treasury, Henry Morgenthau, who was then in charge of alien property, designated a new president and board. In 1943 Leo Growley was appointed Alien-Property Custodian. He forced out Morgenthau's president and half of Morgenthau's board and installed his own designees in their places. In 1947, when Growley's president retired, his successor came to General Aniline through the chairman of the Democratic National Committee. In 1953, when the Republicans came into office, they reappointed only five of 11 outside directors. Only one of these five was a Democrat. Of the six new outside directors appointed by the Republicans, five were Republicans and the sixth was an independent. In 1955 a friend of Eisenhower was named as General Aniline's new president. In 1961, when the Democrats regained office, they ousted all the outside directors except the Democrat the Republicans had left in. Of 15 new outside directors, two were employees of the Justice Department, and the other 13 were either Democrats or independent Kennedy supporters, including the principal lawyer for the Kennedy enterprises, prominent Democratic fund raisers, and an old friend of Joseph Kennedy.

Over the years, similar shifts were made in the position of counsel. During the Truman administration General Aniline's general counsel was Steptoe & Johnson, in which Louis A. Johnson, a prominent Democrat and former Secretary of Defense, was a leading partner. During the Eisenhower administration Steptoe & Johnson was replaced by Winthrop, Stimson, Putnam & Roberts, a firm with strong Republican connections. During the Kennedy administration, Winthrop, Stimson was replaced by Manes, Sturim & Laufer, which was chosen by one of Robert Kennedy's chief assistants, who was a longtime friend of one of the firm's senior partners. (The Kennedy administration also dismissed General Aniline's auditors and advertising agency, retaining in their places firms which had connections to the President or Robert Kennedy.) Ross, General Aniline Goes Private, Fortune, Sept. 1963, at 127, 128-129, 144. See also Schwartz, Governmentally Appointed Directors in a Private Corporation – The Communications Satellite Act of 1962, 79 Harv. L. Rev. 350, 357-361 (1965) (experience with government-appointed directors on the board of Union Pacific); Nixon Eyes Fitzsimmons for Meany Comsat Seat, Wall St. J., May 19, 1972, at 5, col. 4 (Frank Fitzsimmons to replace George Meany as a government-appointed director of Comsat, after Meany quit President Nixon's Pay Board while Fitzsimmons stayed on as the Board's only union official).

E. Summary

Many of the modern board's functions — providing advice and counsel to the chief executive's office, playing a formal role in the authorization of major corporate projects, and providing a modality for the exercise of influence and control by nonexecutives — are for the most part relatively unimportant, or can easily be located elsewhere. Making business policy, although widely held to be a central board function, is usually beyond the competence of the board, since a corporate organ cannot be meaningfully involved in making business policy unless its members are highly active, and it is not realistic to expect a high degree of activity from the board. Directors may be highly active because they are executives; but in that case their activity does not derive from their directorial capacities, and the board cannot meaningfully be considered as a separate corporate organ. Directors may be highly active because they work at their directorships full-time, although they are not involved in operations; but this type of board is unsuitable for many or most corporations. Directors may be highly active because they are professional directors who make a career out of a dozen or so directorships, and are therefore able

---

Government-appointed directors may also raise other problems. For example, they may tend to adopt unduly cautious business policies, cf. Ross, supra, at 148, and may be unduly responsive to presidential jawboning, cf. 1948 Office of Alien Property Annual Report 34-37, to the needs of American foreign policy, cf. 1943 Office of Alien Property Custodian Annual Report 67-68, and to challenges to corporate practices issued by government agencies, cf. 1944 Office of Alien Property Custodian Annual Report 65-66. These, in turn, are specific instances of a more general problem identified by Professor Vagts:

"The effect on a firm of having a partially public management may be compared with that of being subject to regulation. In both cases the tendency of management to maximize profits is subject to restraints designed to further other interests. The restraints imposed by public representatives are not, however, exerted in as plainly visible a fashion and there is less need for the government to take as clear and reasoned a stand. Thus on the one hand there is considerable danger that the government may seek to achieve in the quiet of the conference room what it cannot achieve in the normal administrative process. On the other hand, the asserted tendency of administrative agencies to fall under the influence of the industry they regulate is apt to reveal itself even more with government board members who work together with the regular management and develop a common set of attitudes and a common esprit de corps. On the whole, one is inclined to believe that a more rational and orderly development of economic law is apt to be achieved by pursuing the American pattern of open regulation rather than the German form of operating through undisclosed negotiations between private and public representatives." Vagts, supra note 86, at 86-87. See also Schwartz, supra, at 363-364.

to devote significant time to each one; but there is no suitable population from whom the necessary number of professional directors can be drawn, and even if there were the logistics would inevitably involve either very heavy use of aged directors or massive board interlocks.

The major effect of according central importance to the policymaking function, therefore, has been to divert legal and corporate institutions from implementing a cluster of functions which the board can perform, and which cannot easily be performed by any corporate organ except the board: selecting, monitoring, and removing the members of the chief executive's office.[107] Unlike policymaking, performance of these functions does not presuppose a high level of board activity. It does presuppose that the board has an adequate flow of objective information, and that the directors — or at least a clear majority of them — are independent of the chief executive. Given the importance of this cluster of functions, it therefore follows that the primary objective of the legal rules governing the structure of corporate management should be to maximize the likelihood that these conditions will obtain. Specifically, these rules must, to the extent possible: (1) make the board independent of the executives whose performance is being monitored; and (2) assure a flow of, or at least a capability for acquiring, adequate and objective information on the executives' performance. The former objective will be explored in the next section; the latter, in chapter 12.

§11.4. The Legal Rules Governing the Composition and Structure of the Board: Independence of Directors

Although the monitoring role of the board is crucial as a theoretical matter, the available evidence admittedly suggests that in practice boards do not perform this function well. Most boards will not remove a chief executive for inefficiency unless the corporation has entered the crisis zone, and cases such as Penn

107. Cf. Bacon, supra note 47, at 44 (remarks of Gustave L. Levy); PoKempner, supra note 79, at 42 (remarks of John R. Bunting).

Central,[108] L-T-V,[109] Ampex,[110] and Memorex[111] indicate that many boards will not act until the crisis has become virtually irredeemable. Indeed, outside directors will often resign rather than attempt to remove an inefficient management.[112]

One interpretation of this behavior, of course, is that the concept of the monitoring function is an illusion. An alternative interpretation, however, is that effective monitoring has been all but precluded by current corporate ideology and practice. The ideological problem is that the board is commonly conceived as an agency whose primary obligation is not to monitor management, but rather to make policy as an integral part of management.[113] The problem of corporate practice is that while effective performance of the monitoring function is conditioned on monitors who are (i) independent of those who are monitored, and (ii) capable of obtaining adequate and objective information concerning management, in the case of most boards neither condition is presently fulfilled. First, state corporation law has done little or nothing to insure board independence, and as a result most directors in most publicly held corporations are closely tied to the chief executive – either economically, through an employment, professional, consulting, or supplier relationship with the corporation,[114] or psychologically, through friendship, prior employment, or the

108. See J. Daughen & P. Binzen, The Wreck of the Penn Central (1971); Townsend, Book Review, N.Y. Times, Dec. 12, 1971, §6 (Book Review), at 3.

109. See LTV Recounts Its Many Ills, Business Week, Dec. 19, 1970, at 42.

110. See How Ampex Saturated Recorded Tape Market and Got Soaked Itself. Wall St. J., March 9, 1972, at 1, col. 6; Ampex Corp. Had Loss Totaling $3.2 Million in Fiscal First Period, Wall St. J., August 23, 1972, at 19, col. 6; Ampex Expects $40 Million Loss For Fiscal 1972, Wall St. J., Jan 12, 1973, at 4, col. 2.

111. Memorex Concedes It's in Financial Morass and That Bank of America Has Intervened, Wall St. J., May 16, 1973, at 4, col. 2.

112. "[F]ar more dangerous than the general ineffectiveness of boards in disaster situations . . . is the lack of any mechanism for identifying and eliminating mediocrity of management. . . . [D]irectors are far more likely to 'go along,' or resign, than to demand changes because of mediocre performance." Heineman, supra note 46, at 157. See also Mace, supra note 9, at 15, 33-36, 61, 187; Ludlow, The Board of Directors Faces Challenge and Change, Conf. Bd. Rec., Feb. 1972, at 39, 41 (remarks of Harleston R. Wood).

113. Cf. Heidrick & Struggles, supra note 12, at 5.

114. See text accompanying notes 27-33 supra; cf. Juran & Louden, supra note 20, at 164-170, 203-204; Kilborn, Singer's High-Key Diversification Hits a Sour Note, N.Y. Times, Oct. 24, 1974, at 61, col. 3.

fact that they have been selected and indoctrinated by the chief executive and hold their seats at his pleasure.[115] Second, most boards have had no independent mechanism for obtaining adequate and objective information. Instead, directors are almost wholly dependent for information either on the very executives whose performance the information is supposed to describe, or on accountants who are themselves dependent on those executives.[116] Although it may be that even independent and fully-informed boards cannot be expected to perform a monitoring function,[117] that proposition cannot be established on the basis of the existing record.

If the monitoring function is to be effectively performed, then, the first task of the legal rules governing the composition of the board must be to ensure that it is independent of management. The problem is how to achieve that independence consistent with the best effectuation of the monitoring function and, to the extent possible, the board's remaining functions as well. At least three alternative models must be considered: (1) a single-board system in which all directors are required to be independent of management; (2) a single-board system in which independent directors constitute a clear majority; and (3) a dual-board or two-tier system in which managers and supervisors are members of separate corporate organs.

A. A Single Board Comprised Wholly of Independent Directors

Assuming that the present single-board system is retained, the advantages of requiring all directors to be independent are obvious. Since the board's principal function is to monitor management's performance, and since a director who is not independent can scarcely be trusted to perform that function, board membership for such persons seems counterproductive. Nor, in most cases, would exclusion of non-independent directors hamper the board's performance of its other functions. To the contrary, permitting the corporation's executives to sit on the board is in-

115. See text accompanying notes 35-40 supra.

116. See chapter 12 infra.

117. Cf. Mace, supra note 9, at 195; Roth, supra note 105, at 1381-1382.

consistent with the board's advice-and-counsel function, since the executives are already paid to give advice and counsel in their executive capacity; inconsistent with the authorization function, since the board is usually called upon to authorize only what the executives themselves have proposed; and inconsistent with the modality function, since the purpose of that function is to give nonexecutives a voice in corporate decisionmaking.[118] Similarly, permitting outside counsel to sit on the board severely compromises his objectivity, since he is then simultaneously attorney and client,[119] and permitting the corporation's investment banker to sit on the board often gives rise to severe conflict-of-interest problems,[120] and may impair the corporation's ability to raise

118. Cf. Mace, supra note 9, at 119, 126-127. Against this view it has been argued that board membership for executives (i) aids in recruitment; (ii) educates executives in board-level management processes; (iii) enables outside directors to evaluate executives who may eventually be candidates for chief executive; and (iv) ensures the presence at board meetings of persons who can answer questions concerning corporate operations. See Mace, supra note 9, at 111-119 (quoting corporate executives); cf. 1975 Conference Board Survey, supra note 10, at 63-65. None of these arguments will withstand analysis. The first and second are essentially circular, for if executives were barred from the board it would be unnecessary to educate them to board-level processes, and directorships would cease to be a part of the recruitment apparatus. Additionally, the second rests on the doubtful premise that there is such a thing as board-level management. The premise behind the third is similarly dubious. Where promotion is from within, as it usually is, the recommendation of the outgoing chief executive will normally be a good deal weightier than the casual evaluations of outside directors. Furthermore, the board-meeting context may provide "an artificial, synthetic exposure" in which to measure ability. Mace, supra, at 117. The fourth supports the *presence* of executives at board meetings, not their membership.

It is sometimes said that executives will speak out more freely at board meetings if they are members rather than merely invited guests. See id. at 115 (quoting a corporate executive). But on what subjects will they speak out? Certainly they are not going to criticize each other or the chief executive.

"If you watch what happens at board meetings, you will observe that any questions are asked by outside directors and never by insiders. And it's a little bit like a tennis match — if a questioning outside director is at one end of the board table, and the president is at the other end, the question and response results in all eyes moving in unison to whoever is speaking." Id. at 119-120 (quoting a corporate executive).

119. See Swain, Impact of Big Business on the Profession: An Answer to Critics of the Modern Bar, 35 A.B.A.J. 89, 170 (1949); Gartner, A Question for Mr. Casey, Wall St. J., March 3, 1971, at 10, col. 3; SEC Head to be Sued for Role as Director of Small Firm in '68-'70, Wall St. J., Jan. 16, 1973, at 1, col. 1; Redcay, Corporate Counsel on His Client's Board of Directors, March 8, 1973 (unpublished paper); cf. Investment Company Act, 15 U.S.C. §§80a-2(19)(A)(iv), (B)(iv) (1970). For data concerning the extent to which counsel for publicly held corporations double as directors, see W. Hudson, Outside Counsel: Inside Director (1973).

120. See Mace, supra note 9, at 133-134; Slade v. Shearson, Hammill & Co.,

capital on the most advantageous terms, since the investment-banking community frequently views such a membership as a territorial signal.[121]

B. A Single Board with a Clear Majority of Independent Directors

Despite the advantages of a rule mandating complete independence, a rule requiring that only a clear majority of the board be independent would probably be preferable, at least today. First, the former rule would in the minds of many persons represent an unacceptably sharp break with tradition in a social sector which puts a premium on stability. The latter rule, on the other hand, is already almost within reach. Partly as a result of a policy adopted in the mid-1960s by the New York Stock Exchange,[122] all but a dozen or so of the 1400 corporations listed on that Exchange already have at least one or two outside directors,[123] 94 percent have at least three,[124] and half have at least seven.[125]

[1973-1974 Transfer Binder] CCH Fed. Sec. L. Rep. ¶94,329 (S.D.N.Y. 1974), question certified, [1973-1974 Transfer Binder] CCH Fed. Sec. L. Rep. ¶94,439 (S.D.N.Y. 1974), interim appeal denied, 517 F.2d 398 (2d Cir. 1974), on remand sub nom. Odette v. Shearson, Hammill & Co., 394 F. Supp. 946 (S.D.N.Y. 1975); Black v. Shearson, Hammill & Co., 266 Cal. App. 2d 362, 72 Cal. Rptr. 157 (1st Dist. 1968).

121. See Mace, supra note 9, at 132, 144-148; cf. Juran & Louden, supra note 20, at 202. But see Mace, supra note 9, at 148-149; Robertson, The Underwriters Have to Offer Even More, Fortune, Jan. 1973, at 116, 117-118.

122. New York Stock Exchange, Company Manual B-23; New York Stock Exchange, The Corporate Director and the Investing Public 7 (1965). Until recently, the Exchange required two outside directors for newly-listed companies, but it now recommends a minimum of three. New York Stock Exchange, Recommendations and Comments on Financial Reporting to Shareholders and Related Matters 5-6 (1973).

A requirement of two outside directors is statutorily imposed by the new Ontario statute. Ontario Business Corporations Act, ch. 53, §122(2), [1970] Ont. Rev. Stat. 427-428. The proposed new Canadian Business Corporations law would also require two outside directors for publicly-held corporations. Bill C-29, §97(2), House of Commons, 1st Sess., 30th Parl. (Can. 1974). See also Law No. 66-537 of July 24, 1966, on Commercial Companies, Art. 93, [1966] J.O. 6402, [1966] B.L.D. 353 [hereinafter cited as French Commercial Companies Law], translated in CCH, French Law on Commercial Companies (1971).

123. See Publicker Industries' Losses on Operations Irk Critics, Wall St. J., April 24, 1972, at 28, col. 1; Vance, supra note 46, at 198.

124. New York Stock Exchange, Response to White Paper Questionnaire Concerning "Recommendations and Comments on Financial Reporting to Shareholders and Related Matters" 1 (1974) [hereinafter cited as White Paper Response].

125. Id.

Similarly, nonemployee directors held half or more of the seats in approximately 44 percent of the *Fortune* 500, 50 percent of the industrials in the Heidrick & Struggles survey, and 71 percent of the industrials in the Conference Board survey.[126] Another advantage of a clear-majority rule is that it would not in itself exclude any category of persons from board membership, and therefore would moot arguments that certain types of persons are valuable board members despite their lack of independence. Correspondingly, a clear-majority rule would put much less strain on the statutory definition of independence in the case of persons whose independence is debatable, such as commercial bankers and retired executives.[127] Finally, permitting a structural overlap between the managerial group and the reconstituted board would encourage management to continue to take important issues to the board on at least a pro forma basis – a practice which is extremely desirable, since it significantly augments the board's capability for effective monitoring.

But a clear-majority rule would be effective only if two conditions are met. First, the definition of independence must be rigorous. For example, any person who is an executive of the corporation, or who has a professional relationship or material business dealings with the corporation, and any close relatives of such persons, must be treated as not independent.[128] Second, the inde-

126. See text accompanying notes 25-27 supra. Of course, many of the directors now classified as "outside" are not really independent. See text accompanying notes 32-34 supra. Therefore, some outside seats would have to be shifted to achieve de jure independence, and other steps would have to be taken to achieve de facto independence. See text accompanying notes 129-130 infra.

127. Compare Mace, supra note 9, at 123, with id. at 192 and Moscow, supra note 37, at 11.

128. It may be that any director proposed by management should also be considered not independent for these purposes. Cf. Wharton Report, supra note 46, at 465-466.

Two important recent cases, SEC v. Mattel, Inc., CCH Sec. Reg. Rep. ¶94,807 (D.D.C. 1974), and Springer v. Jones, Civ. No. 74-1455-F (C.D. Cal. Nov. 23, 1974), terminated in settlements involving the restructuring of the board to ensure a clear majority of independent directors. The Mattel action was based on violations of the SEC's antifraud and corporate-reporting requirements. A consent decree required Mattel to appoint additional unaffiliated directors, who are approved by the SEC and the court, in sufficient number to constitute a majority of the board. Mattel also agreed to maintain an executive committee consisting of three or more members, "a majority of whom shall at all times consist of additional directors."

Springer v. Jones was a derivative action against officers of Northrop Corporation

pendent directors must be independent in fact as well as in form, and must have effective power to select and remove the members of the chief executive's office.

These two objectives can be achieved only if the board's control of the corporate proxy machinery is vested exclusively in the independent directors as a group.[129] Where control of the proxy machinery carries the de facto power to select and dismiss members of the board, who in turn have the power to select and dismiss the executives, whoever has that control has ultimate control over the corporation. At present, the power to select and dismiss directors is typically vested in the chief executive. Since the full board has control of the proxy machinery, and since the chief executive usually dominates at least a majority of the board, he can effectively remove any single board member who opposes him by wielding his power over the board majority to prevent that director's renomination. A director who would otherwise oppose the chief executive will therefore normally either remain silent or resign, unless he can somehow himself mobilize a majority cabal,

---

based on illegal political contributions, and a class action against Northrop itself based on violations of the proxy rules. The settlement requires a number of important changes in Northrop's board. First, the size of the board must be increased by the addition of four new directors, who are to be approved by the court as qualified in terms of experience, independence, integrity, and ability. Second, 60 percent of the board must consist of "Independent Outside Directors," defined to mean "any person who (i) is not an officer of the Company; (ii) has not individually received from the Company in any of the preceding four . . . years or is not presently proposed to receive in the next year in excess of $25,000 (other than fees as a director) for services rendered or from the sale of material; and (iii) is not associated with a company or firm which has in any of the four . . . preceding years received or is not presently proposed to receive in the next year in excess of one percentum . . . of its gross sales from transactions with the Company." The four new directors are specifically required to meet this test. In addition, no lawyer who serves as (or is associated with a law firm serving as) outside counsel to Northrop can be a director. Finally, Northrop must reconstitute its executive committee so that seven of its eight members, including its chairman, are independent outside directors, as defined.

As a matter of full disclosure: the plaintiff in Springer v. Jones was represented by the Center for Law in the Public Interest, a public interest law firm in Los Angeles, and I served as a consultant to the Center in connection with that action.

129. See Conard, A Behavioral Analysis of Directors' Liability for Negligence, 1972 Duke L.J. 895, 917-918; cf. Comment, Duties of the Independent Director in Open-End Mutual Funds, 70 Mich. L. Rev. 696, 724 (1972).

Some investment companies have already begun on an informal basis to follow similar practices in selecting outside directors. See Glazer, A Study of Mutual Fund Complexes, 119 U. Pa. L. Rev. 205, 234-235 (1970); Nutt, supra note 13, at 216. However, since the arrangement is voluntary, and the independent directors need only make up 40 percent of such boards, see note 46 supra, the practice stops considerably short of what is necessary to vest control of the board in independent directors.

which is rarely possible. As a result, the external sources of the chief executive's dominance over individual directors, whether economic or psychological, are reinforced by internal political realities, which in turn reinforce his economic and psychological dominance. In order to break this circle it is necessary not only to strike at the externals, by ensuring that a majority of the board is not economically tied to the chief executive, but to recast the internal realities as well. Vesting control of the corporate proxy machinery in the independent directors would facilitate their structural and psychological independence by locating the source of their appointment and the power of their removal elsewhere than in the chief executive. Only so can the monitoring function be made fully effective.[130]

C. The Two-Tier System

A third alternative remains to be considered: the dual-board or two-tier system, in which the functions supposedly performed by the single board under the received legal model are distributed between two corporate organs, one entrusted with management and the other with supervision. Originating in Germany in the second half of the nineteenth century,[131] the two-tier system has been spreading throughout Europe in recent years. The Nether-

130. As part of the settlement of Springer v. Jones, see note 128 supra, Northrop Corporation agreed to create a board nominating committee, consisting entirely of independent directors, which "shall nominate all candidates for directors on the Board's behalf; shall cause the names of those candidates to be listed in the proxy materials of this Corporation prepared in connection with any meeting at which directors are to be elected; shall be empowered to expend corporate funds to support those candidacies, to the extent permitted by law; and shall appoint the persons who shall serve as proxies to vote the proxies solicited by management. . . ." Civ. No. 74-1455-F (C.D. Cal. Nov. 23, 1974).

The technique of treating independent directors as a separate corporate organ for certain purposes also finds precedent in the Investment Company Act, which provides that certain types of matters require approval by a majority of the independent directors, rather than a majority of the board. See 15 U.S.C. §80a-15(c) (1970) (contracts between the fund and an investment adviser or principal underwriter); 15 U.S.C. §80a-31(a) (1970) (retention of accountant).

Probably the law should also require the chairman of the board to be an independent director, since this position provides a potential focal point for leadership of the board, not only because of the title, but also through the power to call, agenda, and chair board meetings. Cf. 1975 Conference Board Survey, supra note 10, at 25-26.

131. Conard, Company Laws of the European Communities from an American Viewpoint, in The Harmonisation of European Company Law 45, 52 (C. Schmitthoff ed. 1973); Vagts, supra note 86, at 50-51.

lands has already adopted a variant,[132] Belgium and Luxembourg are expected to do so,[133] and France has permitted use of the system on an optional basis since 1966.[134] In addition, the system is embodied in the current draft of the proposed European Stock Corporation Law,[135] and is presently reflected in the proposed Fifth Directive for the Harmonization of Company Law of the Member States of the European Economic Community.[136]

While details vary, the German version may be regarded as prototypical. Under that version, in all stock corporations and in the larger limited liability companies, direct control of the corporate enterprise is vested in an organ known as the *Vorstand,* or managing board,[137] which is comprised of the corporation's top

132. Sanders, The Reform of Dutch Company Law, in The Harmonisation of European Company Law 133, 134-135 (C. Schmitthoff ed. 1973); Van De Ven, Corporate Developments in the Netherlands, 27 Bus. Law. 873, 875-877 (1972).

133. See E. Stein, Harmonization of European Company Laws 154 (1971); Conard, Mace, Blough, & Gibson, Functions of Directors Under the Existing System, 27 Bus. Law., Feb. 1972, at 23, 25 (special issue).

134. French Commercial Companies Law, supra note 122, Arts. 118-150.

Of 3443 French corporations organized in 1968 and the first half of 1969, only 42 chose the new two-tier form. Approximately 260 corporations already in existence also adopted the new form. E. Stein, supra note 133, at 124-125. For a discussion of some of the differences between the French and German systems, see Will, Recent Modifications in the French Law of Commercial Companies, 18 Int'l & Comp. L.Q. 980, 988-991 (1969). For literature on comparable laws in Norway and Sweden, see Solomon, Toward a Federal Policy on Work: Restructuring the Governance of Corporations, 43 Geo. Wash. L. Rev. 1263, 1321-22 n. 164 (1975).

135. Proposed Statute for the European Company, Arts. 62-79, 13 Journal Officiel des Communautés Européennes, No. C 124, at 14-18 (Oct. 10, 1970), translated in Bull. European Communities, Aug. 1970, Supp., at 55-68. See Sanders, Structure and Progress of the European Company, in The Harmonisation of European Company Law 83, 89-96 (C. Schmitthoff ed. 1973); Vagts & Welde, The Societas Europaea: A Future Option for U.S. Corporations?, 29 Bus. Law. 823, 825-827 (1974).

136. The Commission draft would have made a two-tier system mandatory. Proposal for a Fifth Directive on the Structure of the Company, 15 Journal Officiel des Communautés Européennes, No. C 131, at 49 (Dec. 13, 1972), translated in Bull. European Communities, Oct. 1972, Supp. However, an opinion of the Economic and Social Committee of the European Parliament, rendered at the request of the Council, recommends that it be optional. 17 Official J. European Communities, No. C109, at 9, 10-11 (Dec. 21, 1974). See generally Ficker, The EEC Directives on Company Law Harmonisation, in The Harmonisation of European Company Law 66, 80-81, (C. Schmitthoff ed. 1973).

137. See Law of Sept. 6, 1965, [1965] BGB1. I 1089, §§76-94 [hereinafter cited as Aktiengesetz], translated in CCH, German Stock Corporation Act (F. Juenger and L. Schmidt transl. 1967). See generally Roth, supra note 105; Schoenbaum & Lieser, Reform of the Structure of the American Corporation: The "Two-Tier" Board Model, 62 Ky. L.J. 91, at 95-108 (1973); Vagts, supra note 86, at 48-64.

The two-tier system is mandatory for virtually any "Aktiengesellschaft" (roughly

executives. The managing board, in turn, is supervised by a second organ known as the *Aufsichtsrat,* or supervisory board,[138] which cannot include any members of the managing board.[139] The supervisory board can adopt rules requiring its approval for specific types of transactions, but is not otherwise empowered to involve itself in the management of the corporation,[140] and exercises only indirect control over the managing board. It appoints the members of the managing board for periods not exceeding five years and may revoke such appointments for substantial cause, such as gross breach of duty or inability to conduct the corporation's business properly; it can express disapproval of the managing board in its comments to the shareholders on the results of the annual audit; and it can call a special shareholders' meeting to consider the appointment of special auditors to investigate the managing board's conduct of the business.[141]

Within the last few years there has been much discussion whether the two-tier system should be adopted in the United States.[142] Certainly such a system would be preferable to the

---

speaking, a publicly-held corporation), and any "Gesellschaft mit beschränkter Haftung" (roughly speaking, a close corporation) with over 500 or more employees. Juenger, Introduction to CCH, German Stock Corporation Act at 1, 2-4 (1967); Schoenbaum & Lieser, supra, at 98; Vagts, supra note 86, at 32-35.

138. Aktiengesetz §§95-116.

139. Id. §105.

140. Id. §111(4). Where the supervisory board's approval is required and is not given, the managing board can take the issue to the shareholders, but shareholder approval under these circumstances requires at least three-fourths of the votes cast. Aktiengesetz §111(4).

141. Id. §§84(1), 84(3), 111(3), 142(1), 171(2).

142. See, e.g., Cary & Harris, supra note 46, at 66 (remarks of Professor Cary); Schoenbaum & Lieser, supra note 137. Although such a system is not required under the laws of any state, it might be permissible under some of the more recent state corporations statutes. For example, the Delaware code provides:

"The business and affairs of every corporation . . . shall be managed by or under the direction of a board of directors, except as may be otherwise provided . . . in its certificate of incorporation. If any such provision is made in the certificate . . . the powers and duties conferred or imposed upon the board of directors by this chapter shall be exercised or performed to such extent and by such person or persons as shall be provided in the certificate. . . ." Del. Code Ann. tit. 8, §141(a) (Supp. 1975).

See also Ariz. Rev. Stat. Ann. §§10-122, 10-191 (1956); Wis. Stat. Ann. §180.30 (Supp. 1974); ABA Model Bus. Corp. Act §35 (1974 rev.); cf. N.J. Stat. Ann. §§14A:6-1, 14A:2-7 (1969); N. Lattin, The Law of Corporations 242-243 (2d ed. 1971). Professor Ernest Folk, who served as Reporter to the Committee which drafted the 1967 revision of the Delaware statute, has commented that "the Delaware corporation enjoys the broadest grant of power in the English-speaking world to establish the

present working model, but it would probably not be preferable to a requirement that the board have a clear majority of independent directors vested with control of the proxy machinery. To begin with, it must be borne in mind that despite their apparently great dissimilarity, most of the differences between the single-board and two-tier systems tend to be marginal. In fact, many or most large American corporations have already adopted working structures strikingly similar to the two-tier system.

In one such structure, authority for direction and control of the enterprise is vested in a formally constituted general management committee consisting of top executives.[143] Like the German managing board, this committee "determines operating policies and objectives and concentrates upon the broad direction, coordination and control of the business as a whole."[144] It has been said of corporations utilizing such committees that they "have in effect two boards: an inside working board and an outside board of

---

most appropriate internal organization and structure for the enterprise." E. Folk, Amendments to the Delaware Corporation Law 5 (Corp. Serv. Co. 1969).

Under the more traditional corporate statutes, however, a full-scale two-tier board would probably be impermissible. These statutes typically provide that the board of directors shall manage the business of the corporation, see text accompanying note 1, supra, and a formalized and permanent delegation of that power to a second corporate organ would in all likelihood be deemed invalid. See Jackson v. Hooper, 76 N.J. Eq. 592, 603, 75 A. 568, 573 (Ct. Err. & App. 1910); Long Park, Inc. v. Trenton-New Brunswick Theatres Co., 297 N.Y. 174, 77 N.E.2d 633 (1948); Continental Securities Co. v. Belmont, 206 N.Y. 7, 16, 99 N.E. 138, 141 (1912). The rationale for this view has been stated as follows: "The State, granting to individuals the privilege of limiting their individual liabilities for business debts by forming themselves into an entity separate and distinct from the persons who own it, demands in turn that the entity take a prescribed form and conduct itself, procedurally, according to fixed rules." Benintendi v. Kenton Hotel, 294 N.Y. 112, 118, 60 N.E.2d 829, 831 (1945). But see Kessler, The Statutory Requirement of a Board of Directors: A Corporate Anachronism, 27 U. Chi. L. Rev. 696 (1960).

The English cases reach a similar result, although it is based on a contractual rather than a statutory theory. See Wedderburn, The Relationship of Management and Shareholders in the English Company, in Evolution et Perspectives Du Droit Des Sociétés à la Lumière des Différentes Experiences Nationales 163, 165-169 (1965).

143. See Gordon, supra note 4, at 100-103; P. Holden, C. Pederson & G. Germane, Top Management 71-72 (1968) [hereinafter cited as Top Management]; Holden, Fish & Smith, supra note 10, at 24-26; Maurer, supra note 4, at 201, 207-217.

144. Holden, Fish & Smith, supra note 10, at 24.

Many corporations have adopted a variant of this concept, in which a formally constituted management council serves principally as a communicative rather than a policymaking device. See Top Management, supra note 143, at 72-73; cf. Holden, Fish & Smith, supra, at 22-24.

review."[145] In this type of structure, however, the "outside" board of review is likely to be dominated by members of the inside working board.

A second (and overlapping) type of working structure, in which the board of review is not likely to be dominated by the working managers, is found in the decentralized corporation. In a *centralized* corporation the corporate business is departmentalized on the basis of functions, such as production, marketing, and engineering. Since each department constitutes only a fragment of a business, there are frequently no ready criteria by which to judge a department's performance — certainly not profitability. Headquarters in such corporations typically consists of a central office comprised of the president and the chief of each functional department; it is therefore responsible both for the coordination of corporate operations and for the determination of overall corporate strategy. In contrast, in a *decentralized* corporation the corporate business is divisionalized on the basis of product or geography, and each division includes a substantially complete set of functional departments. The performance of each division (and of its general manager) can therefore be measured by profit criteria and, within the constraints of corporate policies and capital funding set by corporate headquarters, the divisional manager can be given substantial autonomy, at least if divisional profits and market share meet expectations. Headquarters in such cases typically consists of a general office comprised of executives who are relieved of responsibility for operations and functional coordination. Instead, they are charged solely with setting general corporate policy, making strategic corporate decisions, and allocating corporate resources among the operating divisions. The general office exerts control not by directing operations, as does the central office in the centralized corporation, but through budgetary and accounting processes, selection and promotion of personnel, and the establishment and interpretation of corporation-wide principles.[146] In such corporations each division manager is a

145. Maurer, supra note 4, at 201.

146. American Institute of Management, Corporate Structure in the Business Enterprise 121-151 (rev. ed. 1961); A. D. Chandler, Strategy and Structure 10-15, 43-50, 382-389 (Anchor ed. 1966); O. Williamson, Corporate Control and Business Behavior 18-19, 46-49, 113-119, 124-127 (1970); Chandler & Redlich, Recent Developments in

counterpart to the chief executive in the received legal model of the corporation, while the general office is a counterpart to the board:

> The top executive group becomes an "activated board of directors" whether or not they are the legally constituted board. . . . Such an executive group . . . does not "manage" in the usual sense of the word. . . . Instead the role of such a group is more like that of an investment manager with the power to choose the particular users of funds . . . and to judge performance of those whom it authorizes to use the capital.[147]

American Business Administration and Their Conceptualization, Bus. Hist. Rev., Spring 1961, at 1, 4-20; Heflebower, Observations on Decentralization in Large Enterprises, J. Ind. Econ., Nov. 1960, at 7.

The decentralized corporation has been described as follows: "Each division is equipped with a self-contained organization having complete jurisdiction over manufacture, sales, and finance, subject to control from the central authority. The ordinary, everyday questions of policy, embodying even such important matters as production schedules, inventory commitments, design of product, and methods of distribution, are left ordinarily within the consideration and decision of the divisions themselves, under certain general limitations, and in every way the men on the firing line are inspired with a sense of responsibility for results." Brown, Pricing Policy in Relation to Financial Control, 7 Man. & Ad. 195 (1924).

147. Heflebower, supra note 146, at 18. Williamson wrote of the decentralized corporation: "The relationship of the headquarters unit to the operating divisions appears to be largely one where operating divisions are free to conduct their affairs without interference as long as they achieve a certain 'objective' profit goal. This relationship is thus similar to the one that exists between the stockholders and the firm. There are, however, major differences that should be noted. First, the headquarters unit has access to vastly more information than the stockholders and hence is able to make a more exacting appraisal. Second, the machinery for replacing a division head is considerably simpler than that for replacing the company president. In both respects, the division is subject to greater pressure than is the firm." O. Williamson, The Economics of Discretionary Behavior 120 (1964); cf. J. Bower, Managing the Resource Allocation Process 293 (1970).

The resemblance between these working structures and a formal two-tier board is often heightened by constituting the members of the general management committee or general office as the board's executive committee. See Brown & Smith, supra note 10, at 28-30, 94-96; Gordon, supra note 4, at 103-104; Holden, Fish & Smith, supra note 10, at 229; Top Management, supra note 143, at 72; Mylander, Management by Executive Committee, Harv. Bus. Rev., May-June 1955, at 51. Of 508 manufacturing corporations surveyed by the Conference Board, 377 had executive committees; of these, 24 percent were composed entirely of insiders. See 1973 Conference Board Survey, supra note 14, at 55-56 Tables 14, 15. Under modern statutes, such a committee can be vested with extensive powers. For example, the Model Act permits such a committee to exercise all the authority of the board except as to certificate and bylaw amendment, merger, sale of substantially all assets, and dissolution. ABA Model Bus. Corp. Act §42 (1969 rev.). In such cases, therefore, the general management committee or general office is, like the

The major advantage of the two-tier system, therefore, is not that it creates two levels of administration where only one existed before, or that it recognizes management as a separate corporate organ, but that it achieves the separation of those who manage from those who monitor in a particularly sharp manner,[148] and therefore results in extreme organizational transparency.[149] Separation and transparency, however, can both be achieved even without a two-tier system: the former, by requiring a clear independent majority and by vesting control of the corporate proxy machinery in the outside directors to ensure their structural and psychological independence from the chief executive; the latter, by making clear that the board can function as a monitoring rather than a managing organ[150] and by constituting the independent directors as a separate corporate organ for certain purposes, such as control over the proxy machinery.[151]

German managing board, a formally constituted corporate organ vested with both factual and legal power to manage the corporation's business. Cf. L. Gower, Principles of Modern Company Law 141 (3d ed. K. Wedderburn, O. Weaver & A. Park 1969).

148. Under German law and practice, this separation is far from complete. German law bars members of the managing board from serving on the supervisory board, but does not bar other executives from serving on the supervisory board. Cf. Roth, supra note 105, at 1380. Furthermore, it is common for banks to be represented, sometimes heavily, on the supervisory board, and the managing board may have leverage over those banking members as a result of competition between banks for corporate accounts. See note 153 infra.

149. See Will, supra note 134, at 991; cf. Vagts, The European System, 27 Bus. Law., Feb. 1972, at 165, 166 (special issue); Riger, Book Review, 60 Geo. L.J. 859 (1972).

150. For example, under the 1974 amendments to the Delaware corporation law, "[t]he business and affairs of every corporation . . . shall be managed *by or under the direction of* a board of directors." Del. Code Ann. tit. 8, §141(a) (Supp. 1974) (emphasis added). Similarly the Ontario statute provides: "[T]he board of directors shall manage or *supervise the management of* the affairs and business of the corporation." Ontario Business Corporations Act, ch. 53, §132(1), [1970] Ont. Rev. Stat. 430 (emphasis added); cf. ABA Model Bus. Corp. Act §35 (1974 rev.).

151. A corollary advantage of the two-tier system is that the sharp legal allocation of roles between the two boards helps assure that substantive rules of corporation law are based on accurate premises as to the roles of executives and directors; but this advantage too is only marginal, since even without this sharp allocation enough is now known about corporate life to enable American legal institutions to mold corporate rules on the basis of corporate reality. For example, the courts could even now readjust concepts of officers' authority to be more reflective of the truths of corporate life. See, e.g., Lee v. Jenkins Bros., 268 F.2d 357, 365-371 (2d Cir.), cert. denied, 361 U.S. 913 (1959); Gronholz v. Saginaw Sav. & Loan Assn., 41 Mich. App. 735, 201 N.W.2d 98 (1972); Holman-O.D. Baker Co. v. Pre-Design, Inc., 104 N.H. 116, 179 A.2d 454 (1962);

On the negative side, we know very little about the effect of the two-tier system as a structural abstraction. The working of the system in Germany, the only country in which it has an established track history, is integrally related to the German social and economic context. For example, the number of large German commercial banks is relatively small, so that each is very powerful, and because most corporate stock is held in bearer form and deposited with the banks for safekeeping, proxies for a great proportion of the voting stock are in the bankers' hands.[152] Bankers who sit on the supervisory board therefore often carry enormous weight, and their presence helps assure the independence of many supervisory boards.[153] Again, the German two-tier system is intimately related to the principle of codetermination, under which labor is formally represented at the board level. Adoption of the two-tier system in the very different American economic setting might produce results very different from those hoped for.[154]

Yucca Mining & Petrol. Co. v. Howard C. Phillips Oil Co., 69 N.M. 281, 365 P.2d 925 (1961). Similarly, courts could adopt separate standards of care for executive and non-executive directors. See, e.g., Bates v. Dresser, 251 U.S. 524 (1920); Boulecault v. Oriel Glass Co., 283 Mo. 237, 223 S.W. 423 (1920); Cary & Harris, supra note 46, at 64-65; Folk, Civil Liabilities under the Federal Securities Acts: The BarChris Case, 55 Va. L. Rev. 1, 46 (1969); Israels, A New Look at Corporate Directorships, 24 Bus. Law 727 (1969); cf. Lanza v. Drexel & Co., 479 F.2d 1277 (2d Cir. 1973); Feit v. Leasco Data Processing Equip. Corp., 332 F. Supp. 544, 576-578 (E.D.N.Y. 1971); Escott v. BarChris Constr. Corp., 283 F. Supp. 643 (S.D.N.Y. 1968); Bennett v. Propp, 41 Del. Ch. 14, 187 A.2d 405 (Sup. Ct. 1962).

152. See Roth, supra note 105, at 1378-1379; Vagts, The European System, 27 Bus. Law., Feb. 1972, at 165, 169 (special issue); Petrodollar Pressure on Big Three German Banks, N.Y. Times, Jan. 24, 1975, at 41, col. 1.

153. The extent of the bankers' influence may vary substantially according to the financial strength of the corporation, since the management of a strong corporation which does business with several banks may be able to neutralize them by playing one off against the other, or by threatening to shift the corporation's business entirely. Cf. Roth, supra note 105, at 108.

154. Putting these questions aside, a reconstituted single board might have several distinct advantages over the specific two-tier system adopted in Germany. For example, under American law managers can normally be discharged from their positions without cause. Under the German two-tier system, however, the members of the managing board cannot be discharged during their term (which may run up to five years) except for "wichtiger Grund" – substantial cause. See Aktiengesetz, supra note 137, §81; Schoenbaum & Lieser, supra note 137, at 95-96. The German system therefore gives management a security of tenure which tends to defeat one of the very purposes the separation of managers and monitors should be designed to achieve. Again, under American law the intra-executive structure can be made to vary according to the needs of the individual

A second and more important problem with the two-tier system as compared to a reconstituted board is that the former would represent a radical break with present institutional practices, while the latter would not. The tradition of the American corporation is that important business decisions come before the board, even if only by way of post hoc review. Reconstituting the single board would be unlikely to impede this practice, particularly if the reconstituted board included insiders. In contrast, the creation of a wholly new institution in which managers and monitors did not mix might well result in cutting off the flow of business decisions to the outside board on an ongoing basis, thereby reducing that board's capacity to gain the feel for the corporate situation which helps bring the financial data to life. The net result of adopting a two-tier system in this country might therefore actually be a weakening of the crucial monitoring function, as compared with the results achievable through a reconstituted single board.

---

business. Under the German two-tier system, however, a formal collegial structure is imposed on the top executives whether or not it is suitable to the needs of the business. See Aktiengesetz, supra note 137, § 77(1).

12

The Flow of Information to the Board and the Role of the Accountant

To the extent that the autonomy of corporate management ultimately rests on notions of efficiency, it follows that the techniques by which managerial efficiency is measured – whether by the board or by others – must be a central concern of the corporate system. As a practical matter, such techniques must have three interrelated characteristics: (1) the indexes they employ must be numerical in nature; (2) the numbers they generate must be comparable with those generated in measuring the efficiency of management in like enterprises; and (3) the methods by which the numbers are generated must be as objective as possible. The primary techniques used today to measure managerial efficiency center on indexes involving corporate profits. Such indexes obviously meet the first qualification: they are nothing if not numerical. It is widely recognized, however, that the profits of a corporate enterprise can never be determined with complete objectivity and comparability, since they are in significant part a function of the choice of accounting principles employed in the preparation of its financial statements.[1] In theory, a satisfactory

1. See Arthur Andersen & Co., Establishing Accounting Principles – A Crisis in Decision Making 1-2 (1965) [hereinafter cited as Arthur Andersen]; P. Grady, Inventory of Generally Accepted Accounting Principles for Business Enterprises 33-34, 373-397 (AICPA Accounting Research Study No. 7, 1965) [hereinafter cited as Grady]; Graham, Some Observations on the Nature of Income, Generally Accepted Accounting Principles, and Financial Reporting, 30 Law & Contemp. Prob. 652, 669-672 (1965); Even Accountants Find Some Financial Reports of Combines Baffling, Wall St. J., Aug. 5, 1968, at 1, col. 6; Were 'Golden Fleece' Earnings Per Share $3.14 or $1.99? Well . . ., Wall St. J., Aug. 5, 1968, at 14, col. 3. See generally A. Briloff, Unaccountable Accounting

degree of objectivity and comparability is nevertheless achieved through institutional means – the central role given to independent accountants. In practice the theory has not held up, due to a series of institutional failures. First, responsibility for selecting accounting principles has been placed with management rather than with the accountants; second, management has been given enormous discretion in selecting among competing accounting principles; and finally, the accountants have been dependent upon management for their selection, tenure, and dismissal. If the board is to monitor the efficiency of management in a meaningful way, these failures must be clearly perceived and effectively remedied.

§12.1. The Failure of the Accountants

A. Responsibility for Selecting Accounting Principles

Since a major purpose of financial statements is to measure management's performance, and since the financial data reported by a corporation depend in significant part on discretionary choices among competing accounting principles, it is reasonable to expect that the principles employed in the preparation of a corporation's financial statements will be selected by the corporation's outside accountant, and not by its managers.[2] The outside accountant, after all, is a professional, skilled in accounting principles and practice, and presumably objective in the exercise of his discretion. In contrast, the manager typically has no advanced training in accounting and is invariably highly self-interested in selecting those principles that show off his performance in the best possible light.[3]

(1972); A. Briloff, The Effectiveness of Accounting Communication (1967).

Although this chapter will focus on accounting principles, similar observations are applicable to accounting estimates. Cf. Frishkoff, Consistency in Auditing and APB Opinion No. 20, J. Accountancy, Aug. 1972, at 64.

2. Cf. Beck, The Role of the Auditor in Modern Society: An Empirical Appraisal, Acctg. & Bus. Res., Spring 1973, at 117, 122; Letter from E. Feany, J. Accountancy, April 1967, at 27.

3. Cf. D. Ladd, Contemporary Corporate Accounting and the Public 164 (1963) [hereinafter cited as Ladd]; Johnson, Management and Accounting Principles, 30 Law & Contemp. Prob. 690, 693-698, 702-705 (1965); Miller, Audited Statements – Are They Really Management's?, J. Accountancy, Oct. 1964, at 43, 45; Moore, Management

Yet the official position of the American Institute of Certified Public Accountants is that "the accounts of a company are primarily the responsibility of *management.* The [only] responsibility of the auditor is to express his opinion concerning the financial statements and to state clearly such explanations, amplifications, disagreement, or disapproval as he deems appropriate."[4] To put this differently, the accountants' position is that their role is not to determine which accounting principles most appropriately present the financial results, but only to certify that the principles selected by management are not completely inappropriate. As an academic accountant has stated: "An analogy might be having the baseball batter calling the balls and the strikes."[5]

B. Discretion in Selecting Among Competing Accounting Principles; the Test for Certification

Placing responsibility for selecting accounting principles with management rather than with the accountants might perhaps be tolerable if management's discretion in selecting among competing accounting principles were relatively circumscribed. But here too reasonable expectations have been confounded. Since the accountant's major control over the financials is his power to withhold or qualify his certification, the test for determining whether a clean certificate will be granted is critical to the integrity of the process. The test the accountants have formulated is whether the financial statements "present fairly the financial position of [the company] and the results of its operations . . . in conformity with generally

---

Changes and Discretionary Accounting Decisions, 11 J. Acctg. Res. 100 (1973); Sterling, Accounting Power, J. Accountancy, Jan. 1973, at 61, 65; Kripke, Book Review, 73 Colum. L. Rev. 1681, 1688 (1973). See generally, Hayes, Ethical Standards in Financial Reporting: A Critical Review, in Corporate Financial Reporting: Ethical and Other Problems 73, 79-82 (J. Burton ed. 1972).

4. American Institute of Certified Public Accountants [hereinafter referred to as AICPA], Accounting Research and Terminology Bulletins 10 (final ed. 1961) (emphasis added). See also AICPA, Committee on Auditing Procedure, Statement on Auditing Standards §110.02, at 1-2 (1973) [hereinafter cited as Auditing Standards] ("Management has the responsibility for adopting sound accounting policies"); Grady, supra note 1, at 12.

5. Horngren, Accounting Principles: Private or Public Sector?, J. Accountancy, May 1972, at 37, 41. See also Johnson, supra note 3, at 698-699.

accepted accounting principles. . . ."[6] As elaborated and applied this test has been fundamentally defective, because an accounting principle may be "generally accepted" without being fair, and because certification has been deemed permissible even though the corporation's financial statements do not fairly present its financial position and the results of its operations.

1. "Generally accepted accounting principles." It might seem reasonable to expect that the essential standard for certifying the acceptability of an accounting principle would be that the principle presents fairly the transactions it describes. The accountants, however, do not so interpret the matter. In their view, a principle can be certified as "generally accepted" merely on the basis of past use in other financial statements or support in the literature.[7] Since accounting principles are selected by management, however, the test of past use need only mean that a few accountants have agreed not to object to a management decision,[8] while the test of support in the literature need only mean that a single accountant has published his reasons for not objecting to such a decision. Furthermore, when the significance of past use is combined with the power of management to determine what principles are used — subject only to the test of past use by other managements — it follows that an accountant may certify a statement even though he believes that the principles employed in its preparation do not account for the underlying transactions as fairly as competing principles that management has rejected.[9] This

6. Auditing Standards, supra note 4, §511.04 at 81.

The accountants prefer to use the terms "opinion" or "report," rather than "certificate," but the latter is both more meaningful and more prevalent in common usage.

7. See id. §§410.03, 410.04 at 71-72; T. Fiflis & H. Kripke, Accounting for Business Lawyers 86-87 (1971) [hereinafter cited as Fiflis & Kripke]; Grady, supra note 1, at 52-53; Miller, supra note 3, at 44.

8. Cf. Auditing Standards, supra note 4, §410.03 at 71 ("an accounting principle may have only limited usage but still have general acceptance"); Armstrong, Some Thoughts on Substantial Authoritative Support, J. Accountancy, April 1969, at 44, 47-48. Armstrong holds that intraoffice memoranda based on discussions inside the firm and with other accountants can constitute "substantial authoritative support" rendering a principle "generally accepted."

9. See Briloff, Old Myths and New Realities in Accountancy, 41 Accounting Rev. 484, 489 & Table 4 (1966); Hoenemeyer, Compatibility of Auditing and Management Services — II. The Viewpoint of a User of Financial Statements, J. Accountancy, Dec. 1967, at 32, 35; Kripke, Conglomerates and the Moment of Truth in Accounting, 44 St. John's L. Rev., Spring 1970, at 791, 794 (special issue); Kripke, Book Review, supra

certification in turn provides even further support for the principles, and since managers of competing companies are evaluated by comparing their financial results with those of their competitors, there is great pressure for inferior principles to spread throughout an industry. The net result is a frequent tendency toward general deterioration of both accounting principles and financial statements. As one accountant has put it: "[T]his chain reaction . . . leads to a reverse of keeping up with the Joneses; it is a keeping *down* with the Joneses. As Leonard Spacek has observed, the tendency noted by Gresham's Law, that bad money drives out the good, seems to apply to accounting: The bad alternatives drive out the good alternatives."[10]

The rule that "general acceptance" can rest on past use or support in the literature, which is the foundation of this tendency in accounting, was far from inevitable. Even if individual accountants did not want to render a judgment on the fairness of individual accounting principles – notwithstanding the language of their certification – the AICPA's Accounting Principles Board (APB) was empowered to issue authoritative opinions on accounting principles generally. If the principles approved in those opinions had been deemed to preempt competing principles, the criterion of past use might gradually have given way to a criterion

---

note 3, at 1688; cf. Seidler, Auditors Labor Under Mighty Handicaps, Comm. & Fin. Chron., Jan. 13, 1972, at 1, 18.

10. Miller, supra note 3, at 44-45. Another accountant has put it more succinctly: "The development and regulation of accounting theory and practice is basically the result of ad hoc expedients, largely dictated by the very corporations whose affairs are being accounted for." Ladd, supra note 3, at 160. "General acceptance . . . tends to mean 'anything goes.' " Id. at 163.

Consider the following statement by a then-member of the APB:

"A few weeks ago, I received a telephone call from a practicing certified public accountant who was trying to decide whether he should accept a change in an accounting principle proposed by one of his clients . . . [who] had just returned from a convention where a competitor had told how he intended to improve earnings merely by adopting the proposed accounting method. The acceptability of the new method was in doubt.

"I asked whether any authoritative support had been found for the proposed principle and he replied, 'Well, I looked for an example in Accounting Trends & Techniques but found none, so, I thought I should give you a call.'

"Obviously, he was thanked for the expression of confidence and then I proceeded to comment on his failure to undertake a more thorough search for substantial authoritative support concerning the proposed accounting principle." Armstrong, supra note 8, at 44.

of analytical soundness. Unfortunately, the AICPA took just the opposite position:

> 1. "Generally accepted accounting principles" are those principles which have substantial authoritative support.
> 2. Opinions of the Accounting Principles Board constitute "substantial authoritative support."
> 3. *"Substantial authoritative support" can exist for accounting principles that differ from Opinions of the Accounting Principles Board.*[11]

Of course, in some cases an APB opinion would either cast grave doubt on some or all competing principles or explicitly render competing principles unacceptable. But since the APB was practitioner-dominated and notoriously weak,[12] in many areas it did not speak at all,[13] in many others it did not speak decisively, and even where it spoke decisively its opinions often failed to drive out unsound accounting practices.[14]

The accountants' rejection of a standard of fairness in the all-too-frequent absence of an authoritative opinion by an organ of

11. AICPA, Disclosure of Departures from Opinions of the Accounting Principles Board (Special Bull. 1964), reprinted in AICPA, Opinions of the Accounting Principles Board 48 (1965) [hereinafter cited as Special Bull.] (emphasis added). In 1972, the APB was replaced by a board which is expected to narrow the choice of competing principles. See text accompanying notes 32-34 infra. On the status accorded APB opinions prior to 1973, see AICPA, Establishing Financial Accounting Standards 39-43 (1972) [hereinafter cited as Wheat Report]. On their present status, see text at note 35 infra.

12. See Overhaul of Accounting Rule-Making Unit Expected Today, Is Seen Reducing Conflicts, Wall St. J., May 2, 1972, at 42, col. 1: "Do [the members of the APB] speak for their clients?" an APB staff member asks rhetorically. "Every once in a while I sit there and I can tell you *which* client is speaking. It is always big-big. Not only are they speaking for a client. They are speaking for every damn client they have and all the ones they'd like to have."

See also Kripke, The SEC, The Accountants, Some Myths and Some Realities, 45 N.Y.U.L. Rev. 1151, 1184 (1970); Louis, The Accountants Are Changing the Rules, Fortune, June 15, 1968, at 177, 336; Accountants Striking Dry Well in Attempts to Significantly Change Oil-Company Rules, Wall St. J. Feb. 16, 1972, at 32, col. 1; Accountants' Top Rule-Making Body Drops Plan to Limit Pooling-of-Interest Mergers, Wall St. J., Aug. 3, 1970, at 4, col. 2; Accounting Body Fails in Attempts to Change Some Firms' Reporting, Wall St. J., Jan. 8, 1968, at 1, col. 6 (Pacific Coast ed.); Metz, Market Place: Debate Lingers on Accountants, N.Y. Times, Jan. 24, 1973, at 52, col. 3; Metz, Market Place: New Accounting for Land Sales, N.Y. Times, Jan. 4, 1973, at 54, col. 2.

13. Cf. Fiflis & Kripke, supra note 7, at 87.

14. See Arthur Andersen, supra note 1, at 9; Cushing, Accounting Changes: The Impact of APB Opinion No. 20, J. Accountancy, Nov. 1974, at 54, 62; Accounting Panel Seen Curbing Use of Special Items, Wall St. J., March 5, 1973, at 2, col. 2.

the AICPA, and their readiness to rely on past use as the standard in certifying general acceptability, is well-illustrated by the leading case of *Escott v. BarChris Construction Corp.*[15] and the critical comment it engendered. In that case, BarChris was engaged in the construction of bowling alleys and had entered into a transaction under which an alley it built for a wholly-owned subsidiary was "sold" to a factor, which then leased the alley back to a second subsidiary whose obligations to the factor were guaranteed by BarChris. Thus the transaction was in substance (and to a large extent in form) a loan by the factor to BarChris on the security of the alley and BarChris's guarantee. In its financial statements, however, BarChris treated the amount it had received from the factor as sales income and did not show the amount owing to the factor as a direct liability. BarChris's accountants – Peat, Marwick, Mitchell & Co. – certified that the financials were prepared in accordance with generally accepted accounting principles. Obviously, no sound accounting principle would have permitted this transaction to be accounted for as a sale. The cash that changed hands was not the result of an arm's-length price paid by a willing buyer, but simply a loan by a factor engaged in the business of lending, and when all the shooting was over BarChris retained both the use of the property (through its wholly-owned subsidiary) and the economic risks of ownership (through its guarantee). In a private action against Peat, Marwick and others, brought under section 11 of the Securities Exchange Act by purchasers of BarChris convertible debentures, the certification was accordingly found wanting and liability was imposed on the accountants.

Subsequently, an article published in the *Journal of Accountancy* criticized this result. The authors did not specifically assert that the accounting treatment of the transaction was *fair.* Instead they argued, in substance, that in determining whether an accounting principle selected by management is certifiable, fairness is irrelevant:

> In *BarChris* the Court ruled that profits on a sale-leaseback should have been eliminated; however, the AICPA statements on accounting principles at the time of the transaction were silent as to the need for eliminating such profits. . . .
>
> Let us re-examine the BarChris sale-leaseback transaction in the

15. 283 F. Supp. 643 (S.D.N.Y. 1968).

> light of then existing accounting principles to answer the claims of some commentators that the relevant principles were sufficiently defined before the case was brought to trial. One might advance several reasons to explain why BarChris should [not have reported profit from the sale-leaseback transaction].... [T]he overriding doctrine of fairness might be invoked; one might argue profit [from the transaction] should be eliminated so that financial statements would fairly present the financial position and results of operations for BarChris.
>
> But the doctrine of fairness is necessarily egocentric. He who espouses it presumes to know the one and only correct interpretation of a given transaction. Unfortunately, fairness like beauty exists in the eye of the beholder. What appears fair to one often appears unfair to another. No one denies the propriety of fairness, but accountants need more explicit guidelines....
>
> ... [R]easonable doubt existed as to what was required in accordance with the generally accepted principles circa 1960....[16]

Thus the authors' position — which seems to reflect the prevalent attitude of the accounting profession[17] and indeed the official position of the AICPA — appears to be that an accounting principle can be considered generally accepted if it is in use and has not been specifically disapproved by an authoritative institution, whether or not it fairly accounts for the transaction it describes. That position, however, rests on a fallacious premise — that "[h]e who espouses [a test of fairness] presumes to know the one and only correct interpretation of a given transaction." One need not know the "one and only correct interpretation" of a transaction to know when an interpretation is obviously incorrect.[18] This is perfectly illustrated by the *BarChris* case itself, because the possibility that there was more than one fair way to describe the transaction clearly does not mean it could be accounted for in any way management chose. No one would claim, for example, that the transaction could have been accounted for as a gift, and it was equally inappropriate to account for it as a sale yielding sales income. An argument that accounting for the transaction as a sale was permissible because others were doing it and

16. Reiling & Taussig, Recent Liability Cases — Implications for Accountants, J. Accountancy, Sept. 1970, at 39, 41-42.

17. Cf. Carmichael, What Does the Independent Auditor's Opinion Really Mean?, J. Accountancy, Nov. 1974, at 83, 84; Rosenfield & Lorensen, Auditors' Responsibilities and the Audit Report, J. Accountancy, Sept. 1974, at 73, 74, 76-77, 82.

18. Cf. Summers, "Good Faith" in General Contract Law and the Sales Provisions of the Uniform Commercial Code, 54 Va. L. Rev. 195, 199-207 (1968).

the APB had not forbidden it simply demonstrates the moral and intellectual poverty of the term "generally accepted accounting principles" as interpreted by the accountants.

2. "Present fairly." Vesting in management the power to select the principles applied to audit its own performance might perhaps have been made tolerable by narrowly confining management's discretion in selecting among competing principles;[19] this the accountants failed to do. Alternatively, vesting in management wide discretion to select among competing principles might perhaps have been made tolerable by forbidding a clean certificate even though each principle selected by management was generally accepted, if the financial statements *taken as a whole* failed to present fairly the corporation's financial picture. This interpretation of the accountant's role seems called for by the legitimate expectations of the statement-using public and by the very language of the certificate itself – that the company's financial statements "*present fairly* . . . in conformity with generally accepted accounting principles" its financial position and operating results. To read this language as satisfied simply because each principle employed in the preparation of the financial statements is generally accepted would be to read the term "fairly" right out of the certification: if a statement prepared in accordance with generally accepted accounting principles is presented fairly by virtue of that fact alone, there would be no difference between "present . . . in conformity with" and "present *fairly* . . . in conformity with."

But here too, however, the accountants managed to subvert legitimate expectations by interpreting their role in a minimalist way. While the AICPA long failed to give a definitive interpretation of the language in question, many or most accountants took the position that as long as the financials are prepared in accordance with generally accepted accounting principles, certification is proper even if the auditor believes that the statements are not fairly presented.[20] The following exchange illustrates the point:

19. Cf. Ladd, supra note 3, at 163-165.

20. One commentator concluded: "The auditor is not required to state that the principles followed were proper or that, in his opinion, the financial statements give a fair presentation. . . . [I]t is possible that the individual auditor may actually believe that the statements are not fairly presented." Hennessy, Unrealities in Accounting Reporting,

Chairman [of a Practicing Law Institute Panel]: ... Let us assume that a company has a lot of decisions to make on accounting principles and [that in each case] ... the company uses a more liberal method or the one that is least acceptable.... Do you think that while each of these might have been a generally accepted accounting principle, in the aggregate they can so distort the financial statement that you would not be willing to give an opinion that they fairly present the financial condition of the company?

[CPA]: I think that is like being a little bit pregnant; there is no such thing. I think what you do in a case like that would be to take a deep breath, swallow hard, and sign the certificate.

You might try to persuade management that your feeling is that they should not use all of them because of the danger of creating what might be considered a distortion. Under the present rules of the game, if they insist on doing it, you have no alternative.[21]

---

in Proceedings of the Eighth Annual Institute of Accounting 11, 12 (1961); cf. Carmichael, supra note 17; Rosenfield & Lorensen, supra note 17, at 73-77. But cf. United States v. Simon, 425 F.2d 796 (2d Cir. 1969), cert. denied, 397 U.S. 1006 (1970), discussed at text accompanying notes 43-51 infra; Kripke, supra note 9, at 793; Casey Warns Accountants of SEC Action If Industry Doesn't Upgrade Standards, Wall St. J., Oct. 3, 1972, at 3, col. 2.

21. Corporate Accounting Problems 64-65 (PLI Transcript Series No. 5, J. McCord ed., 1969); cf. Carmichael, supra note 17, at 86; Rosenfield & Lorensen, supra note 17, at 81-82. This interpretation of the accountant's certification was explicitly rejected by the Second Circuit in United States v. Simon, 425 F.2d 796 (2d Cir. 1969), cert. denied, 397 U.S. 1006 (1970) discussed at text accompanying notes 43-51, infra. A survey taken by Briloff before *Simon* disclosed the interpretations of the phrase shown in the accompanying tabulation.

	From the Financial Community	*From the Accounting Profession*
The clause "present fairly ... in conformity with GAAP" means that in the auditor's opinion		
The statements are both fair and in accordance with GAAP	44 [%]	34 [%]
The statements are fair because they are in accordance with GAAP	22	30
The statements are fair only to the extent that GAAP is fair	28	20
None of the foregoing	6	16

Briloff, supra note 9, at 488.

C. The Selection and Dismissal of Accountants

Virtually the only substantive limit placed on management's discretion by the accountants is that the principles management selects in preparing its financial statements must be "generally accepted."[22] Virtually the accountant's only mechanism for enforcing this limit is his power to withhold a clean certificate from the corporation's financial statements. Yet by law, and largely by practice, the selection, tenure, and dismissal of an accountant is entirely in the hands of the management. Moreover, management is not hesitant to use this power. During the 18-month period of November 1971 to April 1973 there were approximately 400 accountant changes among the corporations which must file Form 8-K's with the SEC, and during the 18-month period of January 1973 to June 1974 there were approximately 700 such changes. At least 10 percent of these changes, and almost certainly more, were made against a background of disputes over accounting principles.[23]

22. A further limit is the requirement that the financial statements "present fairly [the position of the company] . . . in conformity with [GAAP] applied on a basis *consistent with that of the previous year.*" Auditing Standards, supra note 4, §511.04 at 81 (emphasis added). In practice, however, at least until recently, management has been able to switch principles with virtually no constraint. For example, in 1968-1969 more than 60 corporations, including many of the largest steel companies, switched from accelerated to straight-line depreciation for no apparent reason other than to increase reported earnings. Inland Steel raised its reported 1968 income $17.3 million by the switch, and U.S. Steel raised its 1968 reported income $94 million by this and other switches. Similarly, in 1970-1971 a number of corporations changed their inventory accounting method from LIFO to FIFO to raise reported profits, despite the fact that such a switch results in a very substantial increase in taxes. Allegheny Ludlum, for example, increased its taxes for 1970 by $6 million through this switch. See Fiflis & Kripke, supra note 7, at 83, 196, 264; Frishkoff, supra note 1, at 64-65; Frishkoff, Some Recent Trends in Accounting Changes, 8 J. Accounting Res. 141, 142 (1970); Allegheny Ludlum Asks IRS Approval to Switch System of Accounting, Wall St. J., March 4, 1970, at 4, col. 2; Allegheny Ludlum Plan to Change Accounting Draws Holder's Fire, Wall St. J., April 15, 1970, at 15, col. 1; Inland Steel Changes 2 Accounting Methods, Lifting Net 27%, Wall St. J., Sept. 26, 1968, at 23, col. 1. See also, e.g., First National City Alters Accounting in Chase Race, Wall St. J., Jan. 9, 1969, at 5, col. 3; Metz, Market Place: Swift Net Aided by Accounting, N.Y. Times, Dec. 12, 1972, at 70, col. 2.

In 1971 the APB attempted to tighten up this area with APB Opinion No. 20, but the operational effect of that opinion is not yet clear. See note 31 infra.

23. Hawes, Disclosing Auditor Changes, 7 Rev. Sec. Reg. 837 (1974); SEC Securities Act of 1933 Release No. 5534 (Oct. 11, 1974).

Until 1971, it was almost impossible to gather meaningful information on the real

The accountant's dependence on management for his tenure, when combined with management's discretion in selecting among competing accounting principles and the low standards set by the accountants for determining whether a given principle is "generally accepted," result in an almost irresistible pressure on the accountant to go along with marginal principles.[24] The accountant "can swallow his convictions or he can qualify his opinion, or he can resign. Usually the latter two courses are one and the same."[25]

The pressure on the accountants to go along in marginal (and even less-than-marginal) cases is considerably augmented by the

---

reasons for auditor changes. See Now, When Auditors and Clients Split Up After Feud, The Public Must Be Told Why, Wall St. J., Feb. 23, 1972, at 36, col. 1. In 1971, however, the SEC amended its Form 8-K (which requires registered corporations to report specified types of events within ten days after the close of the month in which they occur) to include a new Item 12, calling for (i) a report when a new accountant is engaged, and (ii) a letter "stating whether in the eighteen months preceding such engagement there were any disagreements with the former principal accountant on any matter of accounting principles or practices, financial statement disclosure, or auditing procedure, which disagreements if not resolved to the satisfaction of the former accountant would have caused him to make reference in connection with his opinion to the subject matter of the disagreement." The registrant was also required to request the former accountant to furnish a comparable letter. Even these provisions did not produce entirely reliable information, and recently the 8-K was further amended to broaden the scope of the disclosure and require that the information called for in the separate letter be supplied in the 8-K itself. Related amendments were made in Regulation S-X and the Proxy Rules. SEC Securities Act of 1933 Release No. 5550 (Dec. 20, 1974); see Hawes, supra.

24. Mautz and Neuman observe:

"One nonofficer director commented to us, 'The independent CPA is like a mayor. His first task is to get reelected.' He asserted this without any intent of vilifying CPAs. His point was that continuity of the auditor-client relationship is necessarily a matter of importance to the independent CPA and is dependent ultimately on the management of the client company. He implied that the CPA's awareness of this situation could enter into his relationship with management personnel of client companies in ways so subtle that the CPA had an almost impossible task in guarding against them." Mautz & Neumann, The Effective Corporate Audit Committee, Harv. Bus. Rev., Nov.-Dec. 1970, at 57, 61. See also Kripke, supra note 12, at 1185. Kripke notes that "[o]ne might suppose that the huge size of the accounting firms (some of them with 4000 or more professionals) would make them independent of even the largest client. But it apparently does not work that way. The thousands of professionals are scattered among numerous local offices, and each office seemingly must show its own profitable operation and keep its clients happy." Id. at 1185 n. 146.

25. Ladd, supra note 3, at 163-165, quoting Leonard Spacek. See also Sterling, supra note 3, at 61-62, 65; cf. Metz, Market Place: Real and Ideal in C.P.A. Audits, N.Y. Times, Nov. 18, 1972, at 52, col. 3; Why Didn't Auditors Find Something Wrong With Equity Funding?, Wall St. J., May 4, 1973, at 1, col. 6; Fewer Companies Get Auditors' Full Okay On Financial Reports, Wall St. J., April 17, 1975, at 1, col. 6.

fact that if an incumbent accountant does balk, a more flexible auditor can almost always be found.[26] The result is that an accountant who uses or threatens to use his only real control over management's selection of accounting principles is likely to lose his own position without materially benefiting those who use the corporation's financial statements. Many accountants appear to regard the withholding of a clean opinion under such circumstances as a quixotic gesture.[27]

§12.2. Structural Reform of the Accountant's Corporate Role

The accountant plays a critical role in the modern corporation: objective auditing of management's performance is and must be a central concern of the corporate system, and only through the accountant can such auditing be achieved. But the structure of the accountant's role is seriously – even fundamentally – flawed. It is impossible to expect objective reporting from an institutional structure which combines (1) power of selection of accounting principles by the very managers whose activities are being ac-

26. For example, in late 1971 Boothe Computer Corporation, which was engaged in the business of leasing computers, prepared a financial statement carrying as assets $2.6 billion in IBM System 360 equipment which was out on lease. Since IBM had begun marketing a newer and more powerful series which would make the 360 equpiment less desirable, and since many of the leases could be canceled by the lessee on short notice, Arthur Andersen & Co. proposed to qualify its opinion by stating that Boothe's financial statements were satisfactory "subject to the effect of the outcome . . . of future events with respect to rental revenues which the computer equipment will produce." Boothe promptly discharged Andersen and retained in its place Touche Ross & Co., which gave a clean opinion. Now, When Auditors and Clients Split Up After Feud, the Public Must Be Told Why, Wall St. J., Feb. 23, 1972, at 36, col. 1. Shortly thereafter another computer lessor, DCL, dismissed Price, Waterhouse & Co., which had insisted on a qualification similar to that desired by Arthur Andersen, and retained Lybrand, Ross Bros. & Montgomery, which did not. Diebold Parent Feels Cash Pinch, N.Y. Times, Sept. 26, 1972, at 63, col. 5.

For other recent cases of discharges based on disputes over accounting principles, see Hawes, Stockholder Appointment of Independent Auditors, 74 Colum. L. Rev. 1, 3 n. 11, 18 & nn. 98 & 99 (1974); Hershman, Companies v. Auditors, 104 Dun's Rev., July 1974, at 33; Allegheny Beverage Fires Auditors Seeking to Force Lower Profit, Wall St. J., April 20, 1972, at 17, col. 2; ICN Pharmaceuticals Fired Its Auditor Peat Marwick, in Dispute Over 1972 Net, Wall St. J., Sept. 6, 1974, at 9, col. 1; Investors Funding Fires Peat Marwick in Dispute Over Real-Estate Accounting, Wall St. J., Feb. 28, 1973, at 12, col. 2. See generally, Bedingfield & Loeb, Auditor Changes – An Examination, J. Accountancy, March 1974, at 66.

27. Cf. Sterling, supra note 3, at 61-63.

counted for, (2) wide discretion in making that selection, and (3) auditing of that selection by persons hired and fired by the very managers who make the selection.[28] As long as management rather than the accountant is empowered to make discretionary choices among competing accounting principles, such choices will often lack soundness and will invariably lack objectivity. As long as management hires and fires those who audit management, there can be no true auditing. To achieve an objective flow of information on the results achieved by management, one of two conditions must prevail. Either accounting principles must be made so narrow and mutually exclusive that selection among them becomes a mechanical rather than a discretionary act, or the power to select applicable accounting principles must be vested in accountants who are truly independent of management.[29] Since the former condition is not practicably attainable, corporate law must aim at establishing the latter.

A. Responsibility for Selecting Accounting Principles

Although at first glance a shift of responsibility for selecting accounting principles from management to the accountants might appear so radical as to be unrealistic, in many respects it would simply carry to their logical conclusion a series of recent developments in the courts, the SEC, and the accounting profession itself. In the accounting profession, for example, in 1964 the AICPA Council issued a Special Bulletin recommending that financial statements disclose any departure from principles recognized by the APB, even where the principle utilized in the statement has

28. Cf. Foster, Securities, Balance Sheets and the Exchange, Com. & Fin. Chron., Sept. 7, 1972, at 1, col. 1; Sterling, supra note 3, at 61; Accounting Profession Assailed by SEC Aidc For Lack of Skepticism, Wall St. J., Jan 9, 1974, at 4, col. 3; Overhaul of Accounting Rule-Making System, Expected Today, Is Seen Reducing Conflicts, Wall St. J., May 2, 1972, at 42, col. 1; SEC Proposes Fuller Disclosure by Public Firms, Wall St. J., Dec. 19, 1972, at 2, col. 2.

29. See A. Briloff, The Effectiveness of Accounting Communication 83-84, 136-137 (1967); Briloff, Corporate Financial Reporting Quagmire, Com. & Fin. Chron., Jan. 13, 1972, at 1, col. 1; Kripke, supra note 12, at 1184-1187; Miller, supra note 3, at 45-46; Sterling, supra note 3, at 66 Expanded Auditors' Role Urged by SEC Official, N.Y. Times, Dec. 20, 1972, at 63, col. 6.

Responsibility for the data underlying the financial statements would of course remain with management, while responsibility for auditing the data would remain with the accountants. See Kripke, supra note 12, at 1187.

substantial authoritative support.[30] In 1971 the APB issued Opinion No. 20, which stated a presumption that an accounting principle once adopted by a firm should not be changed in accounting for later events and transactions of a similar type – a presumption that can be overcome only by the justification that a new principle is preferable to the old one.[31] In 1972 the AICPA replaced the part-time, practitioner-dominated APB with a Financial Accounting Standards Board (FASB),[32] which is expected to narrow the choice of generally accepted accounting principles.[33] In contrast to the APB, three of the FASB's seven members need not be CPA's, and all are to serve full-time five-year terms and must sever their former employment or partnership ties.[34] Finally,

30. Special Bull., supra note 11.

31. AICPA, Opinions of the Accounting Principles Board No. 20, at 390-391 (1971). See also SEC Reg. S-X, Rules 2.02(c)(2), 3.07(a), 17 C.F.R. § §210.2-02(c)(2), 210.3-07(a) (1974). APB No. 20 distinguishes, however, between changes in "accounting principles" and "accounting estimates," and is much less rigorous as to changes in the latter category. (For a critique, see Frishkoff, supra note 1, at 64.) Furthermore, many accountants have failed to follow the rules set out in APB No. 20. See Cushing, supra note 14.

32. AICPA Press Release, CPAs Adopt Wheat Report, May 3, 1972.

33. Wheat Report, supra note 11, at 61-63, 70-75; Overhaul of Accounting Rule-Making System, Expected Today, Is Seen Reducing Conflicts, Wall St. J., May 2, 1972, at 42, col. 1.

34. Wheat Report, supra note 11, at 37-43, 54. Members of the FASB are appointed by a newly created Financial Accounting Foundation, consisting of nine trustees: the president of the AICPA, ex officio, and eight trustees appointed by the AICPA's board for three-year terms, including four CPA's in public practice, two financial executives, a financial analyst, and an accounting educator. The latter four trustees are to be chosen from short lists submitted by certain named organizations. Id. at 69.

A factor which may inhibit the FASB's ability to eliminate unsound accounting principles is that approval of an accounting standard requires the vote of five of its seven members, Wheat Report, supra note 11, at 73-74, and any three members therefore have a veto.

Professor Moonitz has predicted that the FASB will suffer the same fate as the APB:

"The absence of an explicit framework, of a code of generally accepted accounting principles, will continue to frustrate the FASB just as it did the APB. Given such a code, the prognosis would be one of success for the FASB in its technical function of making policy decisions in the area of accounting standards. Without it, the FASB will repeat the experience of the APB. Some of its pronouncements will be inconsistent with other pronouncements. Individual pronouncements will be incomplete or vague, leaving the way open for new variations that will call for additional pronouncements. Partial solutions will parade as general standards and special interest groups will have a field day as loopholes are discovered and exploited." M. Moonitz, Obtaining Agreement on Standards in the Accounting Profession 83-84 (Am. Acctg. Assn. Studies in Accounting Research No. 8, 1974).

in 1973 the AICPA adopted a new rule which makes it unethical for a member to "express an opinion that financial statements are presented in conformity with generally accepted accounting principles if such statements contain any departure from an accounting principle promulgated by [the APB or FASB] which has a material effect on the statements taken as a whole, unless the member can demonstrate that due to unusual circumstances the financial statements would otherwise have been misleading."[35]

A second line of developments leading to increased responsibility for accountants is taking place in the courts and the SEC. To begin with, those accountants who do not meet even the minimum standards of their own profession are being exposed to severe sanctions. Partners in Lybrand, Ross Bros. & Montgomery[36] and Peat, Marwick, Mitchell & Co.[37] have been found guilty of criminal violations. Arthur Andersen & Co. has been censured by the SEC.[38] Private actions against Haskins & Sells, Arthur Andersen, Lybrand, Arthur Young, and Peat, Marwick have been settled for amounts ranging from $300,000 to just under $5 million.[39] As of

35. See AICPA, Restatement of the Code of Professional Ethics, Rule 203 (1972). Where a departure is justified under this test, the accountant's report "must describe the departure, the approximate effects thereof, if practicable, and the reasons why compliance with the [APB or FASB] principle would result in a misleading statement." Predecessor rules had merely required disclosure of a departure from generally accepted accounting principles, without giving any special weight to principles adopted by the APB. See AICPA, Code of Professional Ethics, Rule 2.02(e) (1972 ed.).

Although rule 203 does not explicitly require disregard of authoritative principles whose application would result in unfair presentation, an interpretation issued by the AICPA's Division of Professional Ethics states that "upon occasion there may be unusual circumstances where the literal application of pronouncements on accounting principles would have the effect of rendering financial statements misleading. In such cases, the proper accounting treatment is that which will render the financial statements not misleading." AICPA, Restatement of the Code of Professional Ethics 35 (1972).

The AICPA's trial board is empowered to admonish or expel a member for violations of professional ethics, but has no power to impose fines or to bar a person from the practice of accounting. It has been charged that the AICPA's enforcement of its ethics code has been less than rigorous. Accounting Institute Votes Code Requiring Auditors to Follow Principles Board Rules, Wall St. J., Jan. 22, 1973, at 4, col. 2.

36. U.S. v. Simon, 425 F.2d 796 (2d Cir. 1969), cert. denied, 397 U.S. 1006 (1970).

37. Two Auditors Are Convicted of Stock Fraud, Wall St. J., Nov. 15, 1974, at 8, col. 2.

38. Arthur Andersen Censured by SEC over Whittaker, Wall St. J., July 9, 1974, at 4, col. 1.

39. See L. & J. Gilbert, Thirty-Second Annual Report 248 (1971); Arthur Young Agrees to Settle Suit for $950,000, Wall St. J., Sept. 4, 1973, at 22, col. 1; Louisiana &

1973, claims against accountants involving more than 500 companies were either in process or in litigation,[40] and in 1974 Arthur Andersen alone had lawsuits pending against it involving 34 companies.[41] The heavy pressure exerted by this criminal and civil litigation is causing accountants to be both more careful and more scrupulous in observing their own minimal standards.[42]

Of perhaps greater import, the courts are beginning to upgrade the standards of the profession in the first instance.[43] This upgrading is most dramatically exemplified by *Escott v. BarChris Construction Corp.*[44] and *United States v. Simon.*[45] The *BarChris* case, discussed earlier, focused on liability for certifying a principle that does not fairly account for the transaction being described; *Simon* focused on liability for certifying a financial statement that is unfair taken as a whole.

The problem in *Simon* grew out of the use by Harold Roth of two corporations under his control, Continental and Valley, to finance personal stock-market transactions, by causing Continental to loan money to Valley, which in turn lent the money to him. The purpose of making the loans through Valley, rather than directly from Continental to Roth, was to dress up Continental's balance sheet: the loans were shown on Continental's books as an account receivable from Valley rather than from Roth. At the end of fiscal 1962, Continental's account receivable from Valley arising out of loans destined for Roth exceeded $3.5 million. Before Continental's financial statements for that year were certified, its accountants learned that the Valley receivable was uncollectible

---

Southern, Auditor to Settle Suit with Payout of Stock, Wall St. J., Oct. 6, 1972, at 4, col. 3; Peat Marwick, Allen & Co., Inc., Others, Quietly Settle Fraud Suit for $2.9 Million, Wall St. J., Dec. 9, 1974, at 12, col. 2.

40. Arthur Andersen, & Co., 1973 Annual Report 4. See also Louis, supra note 12, at 177.

41. Arthur Andersen's 1974 Report Indicates it Will Keep Growing, Fight Litigation, Wall St. J., June 24, 1974, at 10, col. 2.

42. See Hershman, supra note 26, at 33, 35; Now, When Auditors and Clients Split Up After Feud, Public Must be Told Why, Wall St. J., Feb. 23, 1972, at 36, col. 1; SEC Jolting Auditors Into a Broader Role in Fraud Detection, Wall St. J., July 6, 1974, at 25, col. 2.

43. Cf. Sommer, Survey of Accounting Developments in the 60's; What's Ahead in the 70's, 26 Bus. Law. 207 (1970).

44. 283 F. Supp. 643 (S.D.N.Y. 1968), discussed at text accompanying notes 15-16 supra.

45. 425 F.2d 796 (2d Cir. 1969), cert. denied, 397 U.S. 1006 (1970).

(and therefore could not be shown on Continental's books as an asset) because Roth was unable to repay Valley the amount it had lent him, an amount far exceeding Valley's net worth. To remedy this, Roth collateralized the Valley receivable, but the collateral consisted principally of stock and convertible debentures in Continental itself. The accountants, aware of all the relevant facts, nevertheless certified the $3.5 million Valley receivable with only the following qualification, which appeared in a footnote:

> The amount receivable from Valley Commercial Corp. (an affiliated company of which Mr. Harold Roth is an officer, director and stockholder) bears interest at 12% a year. Such amount, less the balance of the notes payable to that company, is secured by the assignment to the Company of *Valley's equity in certain marketable securities.* As of February 15, 1963, the amount of such equity at current market quotations exceeded the net amount receivable.[46]

Subsequently the accountants were indicted under the Securities Exchange Act for certifying a false or misleading financial statement.[47] At the trial they called as witnesses eight expert accountants, constituting, in the words of the Second Circuit, "an impressive array of leaders of the profession," who testified that the failure to disclose in the footnote the purpose of the loans to Valley and the nature of the collateral was in no way inconsistent with generally accepted accounting principles.[48] The defendants asked for instructions which, in substance, would have told the jury that "a defendant could be found guilty only if, *according to generally accepted accounting principles,* the financial statements as a whole did not fairly present the financial condition of Continental at September 30, 1962, and then only if his departure from accepted standards was due to willful disregard of those

46. Id. at 800 (emphasis added).

47. The indictment was based on (1) the failure of the note to disclose the purpose of the loans to Valley and the nature of the collateral, and (2) the fact that in determining the value of the collateral and the extent to which the Valley receivable was collateralized, the accountants improperly netted Continental's account payable to Valley against its Valley receivable, failed to discover that there was a lien of $1 million against the pledged securities, and failed to disclose that the amount of the receivable had risen by $400,000 between the end of the fiscal year and the date of certification, while the value of the collateral had declined by more than $270,000 between the date of certification and the date the financial statements were mailed. Id. at 801, 805-808.

48. Id. at 805 (except for the erroneous netting).

standards with knowledge of the falsity of the statements and an intent to deceive."[49] The trial court declined to give such instructions – which would have given the defendants a complete defense in light of the expert testimony – but instead instructed that the critical issue was whether the financial statements *as a whole* fairly presented Continental's financial position and accurately reported its operations. If they did not, the basic issue was whether defendants had acted in good faith. Proof of compliance with generally accepted accounting principles would be "evidence which may be very persuasive but not necessarily conclusive" on that issue.[50]

A jury verdict convicting the accountants was sustained by the Second Circuit in an opinion by Judge Friendly. Thereafter, in a speech to the AICPA, the Chairman of the SEC described the result of the case as follows:

> [T]he court established that it is not enough to merely adhere to rules, even if they are generally accepted principles or standards. Rather a critical test is whether the financial statement, as a whole, fairly presents the position of the company and accurately reports its operation for the period it purports to cover. To meet this test and establish good faith, an accounting report has to reflect pertinent information which those who prepare it have, or in due diligence, should obtain, whether or not the disclosure of that information is required by specific generally accepted principles or standards.[51]

To put the matter differently, just as *BarChris* held, in effect, that an accountant cannot rely on general acceptance to support his certification of a principle that does not fairly account for the transaction being described, *Simon* held that an accountant cannot rely on the general acceptance of each principle employed in the preparation of a financial statement to support his certification of a statement that is not fair as a whole. To comply with these decisions the accountants will need to increase significantly their control over the financial statements they certify. Taken together with the cases holding accountants to their own existing standards, as well as the trends within the accounting profession itself, *BarChris* and *Simon* indicate that a shift of power over the selec-

49. Id. (emphasis added).

50. Id. Cf. Herzfeld v. Laventhol, Krekstein, Horwath & Horwath, [1973-'74 Transfer Binder] CCH Fed. Sec. L. Rep. ¶ 94, 574 (S.D.N.Y. 1974).

51. The Partnership Between the Accounting Profession and the SEC, Address by William Casey, chairman of the SEC, before the AICPA, Oct. 2, 1972.

tion of accounting principles would represent a natural culmination of processes already under way.[52]

B. Selection and Dismissal

Vesting in the accountants responsibility for the selection of accounting principles is a necessary condition to ensure the integrity of financial statements, but not a sufficient one. As long as selection among competing accounting principles is discretionary, the purpose of such a shift could be subverted too easily if management itself retained the power to select and dismiss the accountants. As a second structural reform, it is therefore necessary to shift that power too out of management's hands.[52] One proposal to accomplish this objective is embodied in the thorough and persuasive argument of Douglas Hawes that the power to appoint and dismiss a corporation's accountant should reside in the body of shareholders rather than the board.[53] Left to itself, however, that body would undoubtedly look to the board for guidance on selection and dismissal, could neither determine the scope of the audit nor the compensation of the accountant, and could not give the accountant periodic direction and support. A complementary step is therefore necessary: every publicly held corporation should be required to have an audit committee, comprised entirely of independent directors, which would have the exclusive power (1) to nominate and recommend dismissal of the corporation's accountant on behalf of the board, and (2) to direct the accountant's activities and set the terms of his engagement.[54]

52. In July 1975, the AICPA's Auditing Standards Executive Committee issued Statement on Auditing Standards No. 5, concerning the meaning of "present fairly," which appears to substantially adopt the *Simon* position. Paragraph 7 of this Statement provides that "Generally accepted accounting principles recognize the importance of recording transactions in accordance with their substance. The auditor should consider whether the substance of transactions differs materially from their form." Paragraph 9 provides that "When criteria for selection among alternative accounting principles have not been established . . . the auditor may conclude that more than one accounting principle is appropriate. . . . The auditor should recognize, however, that there may be unusual circumstances in which the selection and application of specific accounting principles from among alternative principles may make the financial statements taken as a whole misleading."

53. Hawes, supra note 26.

54. Hawes also proposes requiring an audit committee in publicly held corporations. His proposal would not, however, require the committee to consist of independent directors, although this was largely because he felt that "the idea of [requiring independent] directors on the boards of all public companies . . . is not central to the

As in the case of responsibility for financial statements, the shift of power here proposed, while new in form, would simply carry to its conclusion a practice that has been gaining momentum as a voluntary institution. Professor Hawes reports that 57 of the 100 largest industrials, and 3121 of the 7000 corporations filing proxy statements with the SEC, already submit the choice of accountant to the shareholders in some fashion.[55] The percentage of publicly held corporations with audit committees composed of outside directors is probably comparable.

Such committees were authoritatively proposed in this country in 1940 by the SEC.[56] The AICPA announced in favor of such committees in 1967,[57] and a number of individual accounting firms have since climbed on board.[58] In 1972 the SEC issued a second release on the subject, which concluded with the statement that "the Commission . . . endorses the establishment by all publicly-held companies of audit committees composed of outside directors," and urged the business and financial communities and shareholders to lend full support to implementation of that endorsement.[59] Finally, in a 1973 White Paper the New York Stock Exchange strongly recommended that every listed company form an audit committee consisting of three to five outside directors, and in 1974 the SEC issued still a third release, requiring registered corporations to disclose in their proxy materials either the composition or nonexistence of an audit committee.[60]

---

proposal [that auditors be elected by the shareholders], and would unnecessarily burden the debate thereon." Hawes, supra note 26, at 37.

55. Hawes, supra note 26, at 12.

56. SEC, Accounting Series Release No. 19 (Dec. 5, 1940). This report, which was a response to McKesson & Robbins' debacle, recommended that a committee of outside directors be established "to make all company or management nominations of auditors and . . . [to arrange] the details of the engagement." The report also called for shareholder election of auditors.

57. AICPA Executive Committee Statement on Audit Committees of Boards of Directors, J. Accountancy, Sept. 1967, at 10.

58. For example, Touche Ross & Co. issued a brochure and a 27-minute color film on audit committees, and the Touche Ross foundation sponsored a major study of such committees by Mautz & Neumann. See Touche Ross & Co., supra note 54; Auditors, Outside Directors Set Up Panels To Find Firms' Woes Before Crises Occur, Wall St. J., May 31, 1972, at 32, col. 1. See also, e.g., Arthur Andersen & Co., The Audit Committee of the Board of Directors (1972); Arthur Andersen & Co., 1974 Annual Report 4.

59. SEC, Accounting Series Release No. 123 (March 23, 1972).

60. New York Stock Exchange, Recommendations and Comments on Financial Reporting to Shareholders and Related Matters 6 (1973); SEC Securities Act of 1933 Release No. 5550 (Dec. 20, 1974).

The results of this developing momentum are reflected in the data. A report by the Conference Board in 1967 found that only 19 percent of the surveyed manufacturing and 21 percent of the nonmanufacturing corporations had audit committees. In a comparable survey in 1973, the figures had jumped to 45 percent and 46 percent respectively.[61] Of these, 97 percent had at least a majority of outside directors, and over 83 percent consisted entirely of outside directors.[62] As of 1972, 35 of the country's 50 largest corporations had audit committees, nine having adopted such a committee between 1967 and 1972.[63] In a recent survey of the 1563 companies listed on the New York Stock Exchange, 80 percent of 1083 respondents reported they had an audit committee, and another 13 percent had plans to establish such a

61. J. Bacon, Corporate Directorship Practices; Membership and Committees of the Board 50-51 (Conference Board Report No. 588, 1973). In other samples during this period, 32 percent of 385 corporate respondents in a survey by Mautz and Neumann reported they had auditing committees, Mautz & Neumann, supra note 54, at 14 Table 2, as did 30 percent of 797 respondents in a survey by the Financial Executives Institute, Hobgood & Sciarrino, Management Looks at Audit Services, Financial Executive, April 1972, at 29-30, and 42 percent of 750 respondents in the Heidrick & Struggles survey, Heidrick & Struggles, Profile of The Board of Directors 6 (1971).

62. J. Bacon, supra note 61, at 64 (Table 21).

63. Vanderwicken, Change Invades the Boardroom, Fortune, May 1972, at 156, 159. See also Auditors, Outside Directors Set Up Panels To Find Firms' Woes Before Crises Occur, Wall St. J., May 31, 1972, at 32, col. 1. Similarly, 40 percent of the 121 committees reported in response to the Mautz & Neumann survey were formed during the period 1965-1970. Mautz & Neumann, supra note 54, at 9.

The Mattel consent decree, see chapter 11, note 128, supra, requires Mattel to establish a Financial Controls and Audit Committee consisting of four directors, at least three of whom are to be independent directors appointed pursuant to the decree's provisions. In case of disagreement or controversy between the accountants and management, "[t]he Committee shall determine the position of Mattel in such disagreement or controversy and Mattel shall abide by and act in accordance with any such determination by the Committee." The Committee also has the duty of approving or disapproving any change of accountants. SEC v. Mattel, Inc., CCH Sec. Reg. Rep. ¶94,807 (D.D.C. 1974).

Similarly, under the Northrop settlement, see chapter 11, note 128, supra, Northrop's Audit Committee is required to consist entirely of independent directors. The Committee:

"1. . . . [S]hall nominate to the shareholders on behalf of the Board, the Corporation's auditors and shall have power, on behalf of the Board, to propose to the shareholders the removal of the auditors at the annual shareholders' meeting or at a special shareholders' meeting called for that purpose.

"2. In case of a vacancy in the position of auditor occurring otherwise than through removal . . . shall appoint an auditor to fill the vacancy until the next annual shareholders' meeting.

"3. . . . [S]hall arrange the details of the auditors' engagement, including fixing the auditors' remuneration." Springer v. Jones, Civ. No. 74-1455-F (C.D. Cal. Nov. 23, 1974).

committee. Of the existing committees, 84 percent consisted exclusively of outside directors, and 95 percent had a majority of such directors.[64]

There are also impressive legislative precedents for shifting the selection and dismissal of the accountant away from the control of management. The Investment Company Act requires that a registered investment company's accountant be selected by a majority of the board's disinterested directors and approved by the shareholders.[65] English statutory law has for many years required that auditors be elected and dismissed by the shareholders;[66] analogous procedures are provided by the Canada Corporations Act[67] and the statutes of most of the Canadian provinces,[68] most notably the Ontario Business Corporations Act.[69] Experience

64. New York Stock Exchange, Response to White Paper Questionnaire Concerning "Recommendations and Comments on Financial Reporting to Shareholders and Related Matters" 3 (1974).

65. 15 U.S.C. §80a-31(a) (1970); cf. Law of Sept. 6, 1965, [1965] BGBl. I 1089, §§124(3), 163, translated in CCH, German Stock Corporation Act (F. Juenger & L. Schmidt transl. 1967). Under the tentative draft of the ALI's Federal Securities Code, the SEC would be explicitly empowered to prescribe comparable requirements (except for the qualifications of directors) for all registered corporations. See ALI, Federal Securities Code §1503(d) (Reporter's Revision of Text of Tentative Drafts Nos. 1-3, 1974).

66. The Companies Act of 1948, 11 & 12 Geo. 6, c. 38, §159(1) [hereinafter cited as Companies Act of 1948]; Hawes, supra note 26, at 5 n. 20. The board may appoint an auditor before the first general shareholders' meeting, and may fill vacancies caused by the auditor's death, disqualification, or legal incapacity. Companies Act of 1948, §159(5)(b), (6). Where dismissal is proposed, the auditor must be given notice of the proposal and is entitled to require the corporation to circulate his written statement to the shareholders, Companies Act of 1948, §160(1)-(3), and then to present his case orally at the shareholders' meeting. The Companies Act 1967, c. 81, §14(7). For a detailed description of the English law, see Hawes, supra note 26, at 4-9. The English statute further strengthens the auditor by giving him a right of access at all times "to the books and records and accounts of the company," a right "to require from the officers ... such information and explanation as he thinks necessary" for the performance of his duties, and a right to attend all shareholders meetings, receive all notices and other communications that a shareholder is entitled to receive, and be heard at any such meetings on any matter which concerns him as auditor. The Companies Act of 1967, c. 81, §§14(5), (7). Gower states that "These legal provisions are supplemented by a strictly observed rule of etiquette of the accountancy profession whereby an auditorship is not undertaken without prior consultation with the former auditor to ensure that there is no reason why the post should not be accepted." L. Gower, Principles of Modern Company Law 469 n. 78 (3d ed. K. Wedderburn, O. Weaver & A. Park 1969).

67. Canada Corporations Act, Can. Rev. Stat. c. C-32, §§130-132 (1970).

68. See Hawes, supra note 26, at 11 n. 56.

69. Ontario Business Corporations Act, ch. 53, §§167-171, [1970] Ont. Rev. Stat. 445-450. The Ontario statute requires publicly held corporations to have audit

under the English statute suggests that this difference in structure is likely to have substantive consequences as to the auditor's independence. In several widely publicized instances accountants in England have successfully resisted management's efforts to discharge them.[70] Comparable results can be expected in this country, because of the increasing pressures toward independence and because resistance to management attempts at discharge would be in the accountants' own financial self-interest.[71]

---

committees consisting of at least three directors, a majority of whom are outsiders, but does not require the committee to play a formal role in the appointment, tenure, and removal of the corporation's accountant. Id. §182. Indeed, the precise role of the committee generally is unclear, although the legislative intent apparently was to insulate the auditor from management pressures. See Iacobucci, The Business Corporations Act, 1970: Management and Control of a Corporation, 21 U. Toronto L.J. 543, 546 (1971). The proposed new Canada Business Corporations Act contains provisions similar to those in Ontario. Bill C-29, §§159-165, House of Commons, 30th Parl., 1st Sess. (Can. 1974).

70. Hawes describes one such case: the 1963 effort by the management of The City of London Real Property Co., Ltd. to replace its auditors. Management settled a dispute over accounting treatment by yielding to the accountants but at the next annual meeting proposed that new auditors be appointed on the ground that mutual confidence no longer existed between the board and the auditors. The English professional accountants' association took sharp exception:

"The existence of such a possibility [of a difference of opinion between the directors and the auditors] is among the reasons why auditors are appointed. The work of the auditors and their freedom to perform it with a sense of complete independence can only continue as long as it is generally accepted that the issue by auditors of a report expressing disagreement with the directors of a company of which they are auditors does not of itself provide a reason for the removal of the auditors from office. The purpose implicit in the appointment of auditors under the Companies Act would be defeated if there were to grow up a practice of displacing auditors whenever a disagreement between them and the directors of a company occurs on a matter of accounting principle."

The Association of Investment Trusts took the accountants' side by recommending that those of its members whose trusts owned stock in the company vote against the proposal. As a result of this stand and shareholder opposition, management withdrew its recommendation. Hawes, supra note 26, at 7-8.

All this is not to say that the accounting scene in England is free from trouble. See E. Stamp & C. Marley, Accounting Principles and the City Code: The Case for Reform 65-154 (1970).

71. From the perspective of investors, freeing the accountant from management's control is a necessary condition to ensuring the integrity of financial statements, but not necessarily a sufficient one, because even independent directors may pressure the accountant to paint an unduly favorable picture for the public eye. This danger should not be exaggerated, however, since independent directors would generally have little reason for exerting such pressure – on the contrary, they would risk exposure to a liability out of all proportion to their directors' fees and perquisites. Nevertheless, the danger, however minimal, still exists, and a restructured role for the accountant should not in itself relieve the FASB and the SEC from responsibility for narrowing the choice of accounting principles.

§12.3. An Auditing Capability for the Restructured Board

Although the primary role of the accountant is to audit management's financial results, once the accountants have been made independent they will provide a capability enabling the board to audit management's performance in other areas as well. Through this capability, for example, the board can acquire objective and reliable data not only on net profits, but on such benchmark indicators as market penetration and comparative costs.[72] Going one step further, through this capability the board can audit the soundness of the corporation's underlying control systems, such as its capital- and operating-budget processes, cash- and sales-forecasting techniques, and conflict-of-interest procedures.[73] Finally,

72. The value of a capability to acquire information of this kind is illustrated by the following examples concerning Standard Oil and Pan Am:

"Standard Oil of New Jersey received . . . a shock not long ago. Says . . . one of its executives . . . : 'You can't begin to tell how good or bad you are until you have figures. A few years ago [Standard Oil] was hard hit by the competition of small local refineries. People started saying that these companies were more efficient than we were, but we wouldn't believe this because it was inconsistent with our self-image. When we got comparative data, management was first incredulous, then astounded. Finally it started doing something about the problem.' " Rose, The News About Productivity Is Better Than You Think, Fortune, Feb. 1972, at 98, 188.

"By last fall, dissatisfaction [with Najeeb Halaby, Pan Am's president] had reached its highest point. A veteran director told Halaby that he was receiving direct reports of problems from several upper-level executives. At about the same time, statistics prepared by Pan Am for the T.W.A. merger negotiations jolted a number of directors into recognizing just how serious the situation had become.

"T.W.A. and Pan Am are by no means perfectly comparable, because T.W.A. has a big domestic network. . . . But over the North Atlantic, where their operations *are* comparable, T.W.A.'s costs per available ton-mile (i.e., the total capacity of all planes multiplied by the number of miles flown) are substantially better. Through nine months of last year, T.W.A.'s costs amounted to 15.74 cents, against Pan Am's 19.01 cents. Had Pan Am's cost ratio been as good as T.W.A.'s it could have converted its operating loss of almost $7 million into a substantial profit." Cordtz, Pan Am's Route Across The Sea of Red Ink, Fortune, Jan. 1972, at 78, 146.

73. See Burton, Management Auditing, J. Accountancy, May 1968, at 41; Campfield, Trends in Auditing Management Plans and Operations, J. Accountancy, July 1967, at 41; Dodwell, Operational Auditing: A Part of the Basic Audit, J. Accountancy, June 1966, at 31; Witte, Management Auditing: The Present State of The Art, J. Accountancy, Aug. 1967, at 54; cf. Auditors, Outside Directors Set Up Panels To Find Firms' Woes Before Crises Occur, Wall St. J., May 31, 1972, at 36, col. 1. But cf. Norgaard, The Professional Accountant's View of Operational Auditing, J. Accountancy, Dec. 1969, at 45, 47-48.

the capability brought to the board by truly independent accountants would enable it to evaluate management's results in meeting relevant nonfinancial objectives, such as compliance with law,[74] due respect for the environment, provision of safe working conditions, nondiscrimination, and fair treatment of the consumer.[75]

These functions would not be completely new to accountants. Comparable audits have long been performed on behalf of government,[76] and the profession has recently begun performing "management" or "operational" audits on behalf of business corporations.[77] Until now, however, such audits have usually been performed as a service to management rather than as a check upon it.

74. Cf. Melamed & Baker, Outside Directors, 6 Rev. Sec. Reg. 915, 921-922 (1973).

75. Under the Northrop settlement, see chapter 11, note 128, supra, Northrop's audit committee, which must consist entirely of independent directors, is given the power "to direct the outside independent auditors and the Corporation's internal audit staff to inquire into and report to it on any corporate contract, transaction, or procedure, the conduct of any corporate office, division, profit center, subsidiary, or other unit, or any other matter having to do with the Corporation's business and affairs." Springer v. Jones, Civ. No. 74-1455-F (C.D. Cal. Nov. 23, 1974).

76. See Morse, Performance and Operational Auditing, J. Accountancy, June 1971, at 46; Inquiry into Democratic Break-In Strips General Accounting Office of Some of Its Anonymity, N.Y. Times, Sept. 3, 1972, at 38, col. 2. For examples, see U.S. Comptroller General, 1974 Annual Report, passim; Lockheed Unit Faces 'Major' Problems on Trident Sub Missile, GAO Study Says, N.Y. Times, April 7, 1975, at 2, col. 3.

77. See articles cited in note 73, supra. Questions have been raised as to whether performance of such services may impinge on an auditor's independence. See Burton, supra note 73, at 45; Hylton, Are Consulting and Auditing Compatible? – A Contrary View, 39 Accounting Rev. 667 (1964); Schulte, Compatability of Management Consulting and Auditing, 40 Accounting Rev. 587 (1965); cf. SEC, Accounting Series Release No. 126 (July 5, 1972). However, these questions should be largely obviated if the services were performed for an independent board. Cf. Carmichael, Some Hard Questions on Management Auditing, J. Accountancy, Feb. 1970, at 72.

IV
Structural Changes

CORPORATION COMBINATIONS

13

The Stock Modes — An Introduction

THE DE FACTO AND EQUAL-DIGNITY THEORIES OF STATUTORY INTERPRETATION

The next five chapters of this book will be concerned with three basic types of events which tend to involve significant changes in corporate structure — combinations, contractions, and divisions. Combinations will be considered in Part IV (chapters 13-15); contractions and divisions in Part V (chapters 16-17).

§13.1. The Stock Modes

The prototypical corporate combination is a transaction which may be referred to as a classical or "statutory" merger. It involves the fusion of two constituent corporations, pursuant to a formal merger agreement executed with reference to the relevant statute, under which the stock of one (the transferor) is converted into stock of the other (the survivor). The survivor then succeeds to the transferor's assets and liabilities by operation of law. Although at one time this type of transaction probably was the dominant mode of corporate combination, in present times its scope has been so reduced that in a study of 1200 combinations during a seven-year period, only "relatively few" were found to be statutory mergers.[1] Broadly speaking, the upstart modes of com-

1. J. Butters, J. Lintner, & W. Cary, Effects of Taxation: Corporate Mergers 316 & n. 1 (1951). See also Heilbrunn v. Sun Chem. Corp., 38 Del. Ch. 321, 325, 150 A.2d 755, 757 (1959); Hills, Consolidation of Corporations by Sale of Assets and Distribution of Shares, 19 Calif. L. Rev. 349 (1931). The classical merger has lately become more popular, due to the advent of the so-called triangular merger. See ch. 18, text at note 80

bination which have shouldered aside the classical merger fall into four categories: stock-for-assets, stock-for-stock, cash-for-assets, and cash-for-stock.[2]

A *stock-for-assets* combination may be said to occur when Corporation *A* issues shares of its own stock to Corporation *B* in exchange for substantially all of *B*'s assets. Typically, *A* agrees to assume *B*'s liabilities, and *B* agrees that it will dissolve and distribute its stock in *A* to its own shareholders. Frequently it is also agreed or understood that some or all of *B*'s officers and directors will join *A*'s management.[3] A *stock-for-stock* combination may be said to occur when Corporation *A* issues shares of its own stock directly to the shareholders of Corporation *B* in exchange for an amount of *B* stock – normally at least a majority – sufficient to carry control. By virtue of such a combination the shareholder groups of the two corporations are combined to a substantial extent, and *B* becomes a subsidiary of *A*. Frequently *B* is then liquidated or merged into *A*, but whether or not this occurs, *B*'s assets will be under *A*'s control for most practical purposes. Although in theory such a combination does not require approval by *B*'s management (since corporate action by *B* is not required), in practice it is not easy to accomplish such a transaction without such approval,[4] at least in the case of a publicly held corporation. Often, therefore, the terms of the exchange of stock are worked out beforehand by the management of both corporations,[5] and often too it is agreed or understood that some or all of *B*'s management will stay on with *B* in its new role as a subsidiary, or will join Corporation *A* itself.[6] (To facilitate comparison of these modes

---

& note 80, infra.

For purposes of simplicity the term "merger" will be used to include consolidations, in which two corporations fuse to form a third, new corporation.

2. Cf. J. Butters, J. Lintner & W. Cary, supra note 1, at 316; A. Wyatt, A Critical Study of Accounting for Business Combinations 11-12 (1963).

3. See, e.g., Rath v. Rath Packing Co., 257 Iowa 1277, 1280-1281, 136 N.W.2d 410, 412 (1965); Farris v. Glen Alden Corp., 393 Pa. 427, 430, 143 A.2d 25, 27 (1958); cf. 59 Colum. L. Rev. 366, 370 (1959).

4. Cf. Fleischer & Mundheim, Corporate Acquisitions by Tender Offer, 115 U. Pa. L. Rev. 317, 348 & n. 119 (1967); Folk, De Facto Mergers in Delaware: Hariton v. Arco Electronics, Inc., 49 Va. L. Rev. 1261, 1282 (1963).

5. Cf. Orzeck v. Englehart, 41 Del. Ch. 361, 195 A.2d 375 (1963); Applestein v. United Board & Carton Corp., 60 N.J. Super. 333, 338-340, 159 A.2d 146, 149-150 (Super. Ct. 1960), affd. per curiam, 33 N.J. 72, 161 A.2d 474 (1961).

6. See cases cited note 5, supra.

with the classical merger, hereafter a corporation which acquires assets or stock in any type of combination will be called "the survivor," and a corporation which transfers assets, or whose stock is transferred by its shareholders, in any type of combination will be called "the transferor" – bearing in mind that in the latter case this terminology is not strictly appropriate, since the stock transfers are made by the shareholders rather than by the corporation.)

Only a few of the corporate statutes have come directly to grips with the newer modes of combination, and even these only recently. Nevertheless, the courts have generally tried to answer questions concerning the requirements for approval of such transactions, and whether they give rise to appraisal rights, on the basis of the statutes. There has, however, been a sharp split between the courts as to which statutory provisions are applicable. A priori, a stock-for-assets combination, for example, might be viewed as either a merger, on the one hand, or a purchase and sale of the transferor's assets, effected through the issuance of stock by the survivor, on the other. But the rights of shareholders will often differ sharply according to which view is taken. For a merger, the traditional statutes usually require approval by a majority or two-thirds of the outstanding voting shares of each constituent, and normally give appraisal rights to shareholders of both constituents.[7] For a sale of substantially all assets, however, the traditional statutes require approval by only the transferor's shareholders, do not give appraisal rights to shareholders of the survivor, and may not give appraisal rights to shareholders of the transferor.[8] Moreover, for a purchase of assets or issuance of stock the traditional statutes are completely silent as to both shareholder approval and appraisal rights – except insofar as they confer on the board the power to issue authorized but unissued stock[9] or the power to determine the consideration for which stock can be issued.[10] Critical shareholder rights may therefore depend on precisely how a corporate combination is viewed. In fact, the

7. See, e.g., Ill. Ann. Stat. ch. 32, §§157.63, 157.64, 157.70 (Smith-Hurd 1954 & 1974 Supp.). But see N.J. Stat. Ann. §14A:10-3(2) (Supp. 1974) (majority of votes cast).

8. See, e.g., Del. Code Ann. tit. 8, §§262, 271 (1974).

9. See, e.g., Del. Code Ann. tit. 8, §161 (1974).

10. See Ill. Ann. Stat. ch. 32, §157.17 (Smith-Hurd 1954); N.Y. Bus. Corp. Law §504 (McKinney 1963); ABA Model Bus. Corp. Act Ann. §18 (1969 rev.).

desire to accomplish corporate combinations without giving shareholders voting or appraisal rights, or at least holding such rights to a minimum, has probably been a major impetus behind the rise of the stock modes.[11]

§13.2. The Two Theories

The cases have formulated two conflicting theories to deal with this problem. The first, popularly known as the de facto merger theory, is usually identified with *Farris v. Glen Alden Cor-*

11. Cf. Sealy, The 1963 Acquisition and Merger Amendments, 5 Corp. Pract. Commentator 366, 367-368 (1964). It has been said that the newer modes (or at least the stock modes) were created "to avoid the impact of adverse, and to obtain the benefits of favorable, government regulations, particularly federal tax laws. . . ." Farris v. Glen Alden Corp., 393 Pa. 427, 432, 143 A.2d 25, 28 (1958). However, while in a given case any one non-cash mode may have distinct tax advantages, in the general run of cases the Internal Revenue Code treats the three non-cash modes substantially alike. See Int. Rev. Code of 1954, § §368(a)(1)(A)(classical mergers), 368(a)(1)(B)(stock-for-stock), 368(a)(1)(C)(stock-for-assets); Kaufman & Loeb, Corporate Reorganizations – Selected Securities, Corporate and Tax Law Considerations in Choice of Form, 16 S. Cal. Tax Inst. 199, 202-204 (1964). If anything, the Code favors the classical merger, since, for example, this mode gives the most leeway for issuing consideration other than voting stock to the transferor's shareholders without disqualifying the combination as a tax-free reorganization. See Kaufman & Loeb, supra, at 204-205; Sealy, supra, at 367 & n. 4.

Again, while in a given case one mode may be advantageous because of a non-income tax factor other than avoidance of voting and appraisal provisions, see A. Choka, Buying, Selling, and Merging Businesses 1-7 (1965); Darrell, The Use of Reorganization Techniques in Corporate Acquisitions, 70 Harv. L. Rev. 1183, 1186-1206 (1957); Kaufman & Loeb, supra, at 205-241, 253-254, 276-280; Stark, Non-Income Tax Aspects of Corporate Reorganizations: A Check List of the Issues and Problems Involved, N.Y.U. 24th Inst. on Fed. Tax. 1085 (1966), most such factors undoubtedly tend to cancel out in the general run of cases. It is often said that an important reason for using the newer modes is that the survivor wants to be free of some or all of the transferor's liabilities, particularly unknown, undisclosed, or contingent liabilities. However, in a stock-for-assets combination the survivor frequently agrees to assume the transferor's liabilities, and even if it does not it may become responsible for the transferor's liabilities under common law principles of transferee liability, see A. Choka, supra, at 105-110; Darrell, supra, at 1202-1204. In a stock-for-stock combination followed by a merger the same result will obtain under the merger statute itself. Then too, an assets transaction will generally produce the highest incidence of state and local taxes, see Darrell, supra, at 1200; Kaufman & Loeb, supra, at 253; Stark, supra, at 1087-1088. See generally Sato, The Sales Tax and Capital Transactions, 45 Calif. L. Rev. 450 (1957). Compliance with bulk sales laws may also be required, see Stark, supra, at 1101-1102, while a stock-for-stock combination will create the greatest SEC and Blue Sky complications, see A. Choka, supra, at 15-19; Darrell, supra, at 1192; Stark, supra, at 1104-1105, 1109-1111, 1119-1120. (But the difference in this last respect is less than it used to be. In a

poration, decided by the Pennsylvania Supreme Court in 1958.[12] The second, known as the equal-dignity theory, is usually identified with *Hariton v. Arco Electronics,* decided by the Delaware Supreme Court in 1963.[13] The gist of the de facto theory is that if a combination has the characteristics and consequences of a merger it will be treated like a merger, even though it purports to take the form of a purchase and sale. The gist of the equal dignity theory is that a transaction accomplished under one provision of the corporate statute cannot be tested by the demands of another.

Farris concerned a stock-for-assets transaction in which List Industries was the nominal transferor and Glen Alden the nominal survivor. (Actually, Glen Alden was issuing so many shares that List's shareholders would end up with 76.5 percent of the reconstituted corporation while Glen Alden's shareholders would end up with only 23.5 percent, and List directors were to comprise a majority of the board.) Under the Pennsylvania statute, in a merger the shareholders of both constituents had appraisal and voting rights, but in a sale of substantially all assets only the transferor's shareholders had such rights. Glen Alden submitted the transaction to its shareholders, but not on the theory that it was a merger, and the notice of meeting did not meet the statutory requirements applicable to mergers. Shareholders of Glen Alden then sought to enjoin the transaction on the ground that the notice was defective. Defendants argued that the notice was proper because the transaction was a purchase and sale of assets. They relied heavily on 1957 amendments to the Pennsylvania statute which provided that "the right of dissenting shareholders . . . shall not apply to the purchase by a corporation of assets whether or not the consideration therefore be . . . shares . . . of such corporation." The lower court, however, held that the transaction was a "*de facto* merger," and the Pennsylvania supreme court affirmed, principally on the theory that the legislature had granted

stock-for-stock combination in which the transferor is owned by more than a few shareholders, the survivor must deliver a prospectus to the transferor's shareholders in compliance with the 1933 Securities Act. However, if a merger or stock-for-assets combination requires approval by the shareholders of a corporation which is subject to the proxy rules promulgated by the SEC under the 1934 Securities Exchange Act, the proxy statement must contain information similar to that which must be given in a prospectus. See Stark, supra, at 1104-1105.)

12. 393 Pa. 427,143 A.2d 25 (1958).

13. 41 Del. Ch. 74, 188 A.2d 123 (1963).

the appraisal right to protect shareholders against an involuntary conversion of their stock in just such a situation as was involved in *Farris:*

> The amendments of 1957 do not provide that a transaction between two corporations which has the *effect* of a merger but which *includes* a transfer of assets for consideration is to be exempt from the protective provisions of [the merger section . . . but] only that the shareholders of a corporation which acquires the property or purchases the assets of another corporation, *without more,* are not entitled to the right to dissent from the transaction. So, as in the present case, when as part of a transaction between two corporations, one corporation dissolves, its liabilities are assumed by the survivor, its executives and directors take over the management and control of the survivor, and, as consideration for the transfer, its stockholders acquire a majority of the shares of stock of the survivor, then the transaction is no longer *simply* a purchase of assets . . . but a merger. . . .[14]

Two years later the New Jersey court applied the de facto merger theory to a stock-for-stock combination, in *Applestein v. United Board & Carton Corporation.*[15] United Board & Carton had entered into an agreement with Epstein, the sole owner of Interstate Container, which provided that United would acquire all of Epstein's Interstate shares in exchange for United stock, that Interstate would be "dissolved" by United, apparently through a short-form merger, and that United's board would be enlarged and reconstituted. As a result of the transaction Epstein would own 40 percent of United and would effectively control it. The New Jersey merger provisions gave shareholders of both constituents to a merger voting and appraisal rights.[16] In contrast, the provision empowering a New Jersey corporation to purchase stock was silent on the subject of voting and appraisal rights, while the short-form merger provisions specifically denied such rights to the survivor's

14. 393 Pa. at 437, 143 A.2d at 31 (emphasis added); see Marks v. Autocar Co., 153 F. Supp. 768 (E.D. Pa. 1957); Marks v. Autocar Co., 152 F. Supp. 408 (E.D. Pa. 1955); McCarthy v. Autocar Co., 152 F. Supp. 409 (E.D. Pa. 1954); Gilbert v. Burnside, 197 N.Y.S.2d 623, 183 N.E.2d 325 (Sup. Ct. 1959), revd. on other grounds, 13 App. Div. 2d 982, 216 N.Y.S.2d 430 (1961), affd. mem., 11 N.Y.2d 960, 229 N.Y.S.2d 10 (1962); Block v. Baldwin Locomotive Works, 75 Pa. D. & C. 24 (Dist. Ct. 1950). But cf. Troupiansky v. Henry Disston & Sons, 151 F. Supp. 609, 611-612 n. 4 (E.D. Pa. 1957).

15. 60 N.J. Super. 33, 159 A.2d 146 (1960), affd. per curiam, 33 N.J. 72, 161 A.2d 474 (1961).

16. 60 N.J. Super. at 343, 159 A.2d at 151-152.

shareholders. United nevertheless submitted the transaction to its shareholders, but not on the theory that it was a merger, and United shareholders brought suit, arguing that the notice of meeting did not meet the statutory requirements applicable to mergers. The court granted relief, on the theory that the purchase-of-assets and short-form merger provisions could not be used to accomplish a de facto merger and thereby subvert the general merger provisions:

> . . . [W]hen an authorized device, such as that provided for in a sale or purchase of assets, or a dissolution, is used to bring about a virtual consolidation or merger, minority shareholders may object on the ground that a direct method has been authorized for such a purpose. . . . It would be strange if the powers conferred by our Legislature upon corporations . . . for a purchase of the property and shares of another corporation and . . . for the merger of a parent corporation with a wholly-owned corporation can effect a corporate merger *de facto,* with all the characteristics and consequences of a merger, without any of the legislative safeguards and rights afforded to a dissenting shareholder in a *de jure* merger. . . . If that were so, we obtain the anomalous result of one part of the corporation law rendering nugatory another part of the same law in accomplishing the same result.[17]

Squarely in conflict with the de facto merger theory reflected in these cases is the equal-dignity theory applied by the Delaware court in a pair of 1963 decisions, *Hariton v. Arco Electronics*[18] and *Orzeck v. Englehard.*[19] *Hariton* involved, like *Farris,* a stock-for-assets combination: the transferor was Arco; the survivor, Loral. The Delaware statute gave appraisal rights to the shareholders of both constituents to a merger, but did not give such rights to the shareholders of either party to a sale of substantially all assets. An Arco shareholder sued to enjoin consummation of the transaction on the ground that it was a merger and he had unlawfully been denied his appraisal rights. The court denied relief. Whereas *Farris* and *Applestein* had focused on the fact that the combinations at issue had the *effect* of a merger, and therefore had to meet the requirements of the merger provisions, lest "we

17. 60 N.J. Super. at 344-345, 159 A.2d at 152-153.

18. 41 Del. Ch. 74, 188 A.2d 123 (1963), affg. 40 Del. Ch. 326, 182 A.2d 22 (Ch. 1962).

19. 41 Del. Ch. 361, 195 A.2d 375 (1963).

obtain the anomalous effect of one part of the corporation law rendering nugatory another part of the same law in accomplishing the same result," the Delaware court in *Hariton* concluded that all corporate statutory provisions were of equal dignity, and that if a transaction was accomplished under one provision it could not be tested by the demands of another:

> Plaintiff's contention that this sale has achieved the same result as a merger is correct. . . . [T]his result is made possible by the overlapping scope of the merger provision [and the sale-of-substantially-all-assets provision]. . . . The reorganization here . . . is legal. This is so because the sale-of-assets statute and the merger statute are independent of each other. They are, so to speak, of equal dignity, and the framers of a reorganization may resort to either type of corporate mechanics to achieve the desired end.[20]

Orzeck v. Englehard involved, like *Applestein,* a stock-for-stock combination. Bellanca Corporation agreed with C.D. and H.G. Olson that the Olsons would transfer to Bellanca all their stock in seven corporations in exchange for Bellanca stock, stock options, cash, and property. The transaction gave the Olsons control of Bellanca, and after the transfer Bellanca merged its seven new subsidiaries into itself through short-form mergers. A Bellanca shareholder challenged the transaction on the ground that it constituted a de facto merger and that the merger provisions had not been complied with. The Delaware court rejected this challenge, vigorously reiterating and elaborating the equal-dignity theory developed in *Hariton*:

> While the argument made may have a surface plausibility, it nevertheless is contrary to the uniform interpretation given the Delaware Corporation Law over the years to the effect that action taken in accordance with different sections of that law are acts of independent legal significance even though the end result may be the same under different sections. . . .
>
> The effect of the [Delaware] cases is to make it plain that the general theory of the Delaware Corporation Law is that action taken under one section of that law is legally independent, and its validity is not dependent upon, nor to be tested by the requirements of other unrelated sections under which the same final result might be attained by different means.[21]

20. 41 Del. Ch. at 76, 188 A.2d at 125.
21. Id. at 365-367, 195 A.2d at 377-378; see Heilbrunn v. Sun Chemical Corp.,

Two years later this theory was in turn squarely rejected by the Iowa Supreme Court in *Rath v. Rath Packing Company.*[22] That case concerned a stock-for-assets transaction along the lines of *Farris,* with Rath Packing nominally acquiring the assets of Needham Packing in exchange for its own stock. Under Iowa law a merger required two-thirds shareholder approval. The transaction was submitted to Rath's shareholders, but only because it required a certificate amendment, not on the ground that it was a merger. At the meeting the transaction was approved by shareholders holding only 60.1 percent of Rath's outstanding stock. Rath shareholders brought suit to enjoin consummation of the transaction, arguing that it was a merger and accordingly had not been properly approved. Rath argued that as to it the transaction was a certificate amendment and an issuance of stock, and therefore did not need to meet the requirements of the merger provisions by virtue of the equal-dignity theory. The court concluded that the transaction was a merger "under any definition of merger we know," and rejected the equal-dignity theory, under the *Applestein* principle that " 'one part of the corporation law [should not be permitted to render nugatory] another part of the same law in accomplishing the same result,' "[23] and also under the rule of statutory construction that the specific controls the general – so that a transaction which fell within the (specific) merger provision was therefore governed by that provision even if it also fell within the (more general) provisions involving issuance of stock.[24]

---

38 Del. Ch. 321, 150 A.2d 755 (1959); Fidanque v. American Maracaibo Co., 33 Del. Ch. 262, 92 A.2d 311 (Ch. 1952); cf. Stauffer v. Standard Brands Inc., 40 Del. Ch. 202, 178 A.2d 311 (Ch. 1952), affd., 41 Del. Ch. 7, 187 A.2d 78 (1962); Comment, Jurisdiction of the California Corporations Commissioner over Delaware Short Form Mergers, 52 Calif. L. Rev. 1016 (1964).

22. 257 Iowa 1277, 136 N.W.2d 410 (1965).

23. 257 Iowa at 1289, 136 N.W.2d at 417. But see Pomierski v. W.R. Grace & Co., 282 F. Supp. 385 (N.D. Ill. 1967) (purporting to apply Iowa law).

24. Cf. Knapp v. North American Rockwell Corp., 506 F.2d 361 (3d Cir. 1974); In re Penn Central Securities Litigation, 367 F. Supp. 1158, 1168-1170 (E.D. Pa. 1973); Frankford-Quaker Grocery Co. v. United States, 353 F. Supp. 93, 99-100 (E.D. Pa. 1972); Pratt v. Ballman-Cummings Furniture Co., 254 Ark. 570, 495 S.W.2d 509 (1973); Morris v. Investment Life Ins. Co., 27 Ohio St. 2d 26, 272 N.E.2d 105 (1971); 15 W. Fletcher, Cyclopedia of Corporations §7127 (rev. vol. 1961). But cf. Lamb v. Leroy Corp., 86 Nev. 276, 454 P.2d 24 (1969).

14

Stock-For-Assets Combinations

§14.1. Stock-For-Assets Combinations Under the Traditional Corporate Statutes — A Problem in Statutory Ambiguity

The Delaware position, although a minority view, has generally received the commentators' approbation.[1] Thus, the *Farris* result has been described as a "blaze of Platonism," because it is based upon finding "a 'true and real merger' that exists beyond, and is merely reflected in, the merger statutes,"[2] whereas the Delaware cases are praised for "requiring only adherence to form," thereby affording an objective test and avoiding "the inherent complexities of a judicial test which seeks a 'real' merger beyond the form of the transaction."[3] Is this analysis just?

Let us begin with the typical stock-for-assets combination, in which the survivor assumes all of the transferor's rights and obligations, and the transferor dissolves pursuant to the underlying agreement. The first question to be determined in such a case, obviously, is whether the transaction constitutes a "merger" or a "sale" within the meaning of the statute. The Delaware court has

1. See, e.g., Folk, De Facto Mergers in Delaware: Hariton v. Arco Electronics, Inc., 49 Va. L. Rev. 1261 (1963); Manning, The Shareholder's Appraisal Remedy: An Essay for Frank Coker, 72 Yale L.J. 223, 257 (1959); cf. Note, 47 Calif. L. Rev. 180 (1959); Note, 59 Colum. L. Rev. 366 (1959); Note, 51 Iowa L. Rev. 1096 (1966). But cf. 107 U. Pa. L. Rev. 420 (1959).

2. Manning, The Shareholder's Appraisal Remedy, supra note 1, at 257. See also Folk, De Facto Mergers in Delaware, supra note 1, at 1277.

3. Folk, De Facto Mergers in Delaware, supra note 1, at 1277.

dealt with this question by invoking its equal-dignity theory – that the validity of "action taken under one section of [the Delaware corporation] law . . . is not dependent upon, nor to be tested by the requirements of other unrelated sections." Applied to combination cases, this theory apparently means that the validity of action taken under sale-of-substantially-all-assets provisions is not to be tested by the requirements of the merger provisions. But such an answer is virtually irrelevant to the question it purports to address. The question in these cases is whether a given combination *is* a sale. It is in no way responsive to that question for the court to say, as Delaware says, that *if* a combination is a sale, it need not meet the requirements laid down for mergers. In applying its so-called equal-dignity theory to cases like *Hariton*, all the Delaware court has done is assume its own conclusion.

What led Delaware into this logical dead end? Pretty clearly, two implicit assumptions: (1) that the terms "merger" and "sale," as used in the corporate statutes, are unambiguous; and (2) that the combinations before the court were sales, and not mergers, within the meaning of those unambiguous terms. The first assumption, at least, is also reflected in the work of those commentators who have criticized cases like *Farris* for platonically finding "a 'true and real merger' that exists beyond, and is merely reflected in, the merger statutes." To a certain extent this assumption is implicit even in *Farris*, *Applestein*, and *Rath*, since the combinations in those cases were held to be mergers de facto rather than mergers within the meaning of the statutes.

A close examination of the statutes, however, reveals that the terms "merger" and "sale," rather than being unambiguous, are marked by nothing so much as by ambiguity. Take for example the New York statute, which is typical in this regard. Mergers between domestic corporations (other than short-form, parent-subsidiary mergers) are governed by Sections 901-904, 906, and 910.[4] Section 901(a)(1) provides that "[t]wo or more domestic corporations . . . may [m]erge into a single corporation which shall be one of the constituent corporations." Section 901(b)(1) provides that "[w]henever used in this article . . . '[m]erger' means a procedure of the character described in subparagraph (a)(1)." Section 902 provides that to consummate a merger, the

4. N.Y. Bus. Corp. Law §§901-904, 906, 910 (McKinney 1963 & Supp. 1974).

board of each constituent shall first adopt a plan of merger setting forth the name of each constituent, its capitalization, and the terms of the proposed merger, including the manner of converting the shares of each constituent into shares or other securities of the survivor, or the cash or other consideration to be paid, a statement of any amendments to the survivor's certificate, and such other provisions as the board considers necessary or desirable. Section 903 provides that the plan shall then be submitted to the shareholders of the constituents for their approval. Section 904 provides for the filing of a certificate of merger. Section 906 provides that upon the filing of such a certificate, the surviving corporation shall succeed to the assets, rights, and liabilities of each constituent. Section 910 provides for appraisal rights.

And that is all. The statute (and to repeat, the New York statute is typical in this regard) lays down the procedures to *effect* a merger, and it lays down the operative *results* of a merger, but it nowhere defines a merger. We know that if a merger is effected, two corporations become one. We know little more – at least from the statute. Why not? Probably because the legislature thought that a merger was a well-understood business transaction, no more in need of definition than a mare. In other words, a merger is *precisely* something that "exists beyond, and is merely reflected in, the merger statutes." A merger is a real-live-flesh-and-blood thing that businessmen do and legislators regulate.[5] The platonist is one who thinks that mergers are created by Caesar rather than Crassus.

But then what is the business transaction which the legislature contemplated? In common usage, as evidenced by *Webster's*, "merger" means the "absorption by a corporation of one or more others. . . ."[6] Similarly, *Black's Law Dictionary* defines a corporate merger as "the union of two or more corporations by the transfer of property of all to one of them, which continues in existence, the others being swallowed up or merged therein."[7]

5. Cf. In re South African Supply and Cold Storage Co., [1904] 2 Ch. 268, 281-282 (Buckley, J.); P. Anisman, Takeover Bid Legislation in Canada: A Comparative Analysis 189 (1974).

6. Webster's New International Dictionary of the English Language 1414 (3d ed. 1961).

7. Black's Law Dictionary 1140 (4th rev. ed. 1968); see, e.g., Rath v. Rath Packing Co., 257 Iowa 1277, 1285-1286, 136 N.W.2d 410, 415 (1965); Hellerstein, Mergers, Taxes and Realism, 71 Harv. L. Rev. 254 (1957).

Economic and financial usage tends to subsume under the term "merger" any business combination involving the issuance of stock.[8]

All this, and the statutory scheme itself, points in one direction: the prototypical transaction contemplated by the legislature when it used the term "merger" is a combination of two corporations, effected through the issuance of consideration – normally stock – by one in exchange for shares of the other, and resulting in a fusion of the constituents and the consequent disappearance of the transferor as a going enterprise. In fact, once it is understood that the statutes do not define a merger, it is difficult to see how the term can be construed so as not to include such combinations. The only alternative would be to construe the statutes to cover only combinations which the board *labels* a merger. But such a construction seems impermissible, First, it would render almost meaningless the legislative prescription that a merger requires shareholder approval and gives rise to appraisal rights. This prescription is intended to protect shareholders. Unless the legislature clearly so indicates, therefore, it cannot be presumed to intend that management could nullify these rights through the mere expedient of labeling. Indeed, the Delaware courts themselves have recognized that labels are of no consequence in determining whether a transaction is a merger or a sale. Thus in *Findanque v. American Maracaibo Company* (which held that a stock-for-stock combination was not a merger) the Vice-Chancellor stated that "there is no magic in the words applied to the transaction. Calling it a merger does not necessarily make it so and giving it another name does not prevent it from being a merger."[9] Similarly, in *Heilbrunn v. Sun Chemical Corporation* (which held that a stock-for-assets transaction was not a merger) the transaction was not labeled a purchase and sale, but the Delaware supreme court brushed this aside on the ground that "[t]he contract was in legal effect one of purchase and sale."[10]

Thus at least some stock-for-assets combinations seem to constitute mergers within the meaning of the corporate statutes – not

8. See, e.g., American General Agrees to Acquire Stock of Insurer, Wall St. J., July 10, 1968, at 4, col. 2.

9. 33 Del. Ch. 262, 269, 92 A.2d 311, 316 (Ch. 1952).

10. 38 Del. Ch. 321, 328, 150 A.2d 755, 759 (1959). In *Hariton, Rath,* and *Farris,* the transaction was labeled a "reorganization," not a "sale."

"de facto," but de jure. But this still leaves a second question: Are such transactions also sales? Based on common usage, a strong argument can be made that they are not. For example, suppose *A* and *B* organize a partnership, *AB*, and each contributes to the partnership a going business. Generally speaking, neither lawyers nor laymen would say that *A* has "sold" his business (or that *AB* has "purchased" it). The reason *A*'s transfer would not normally be called a "sale" is that the term "sale" usually refers to a transaction in which a transferor *disposes* of his interest in the thing transferred, whereas in the hypothetical *A* retains an interest in the transferred business. Now suppose that *AB* is not a partnership, but a corporation? Again, generally speaking neither lawyers nor laymen would call *A*'s transfer of his business to *AB* in exchange for *AB* stock a "sale" by *A* (or a "purchase" by *AB*), and for the same reason. So, for example, in *Paterson v. Shattuck Arizona Copper Company*, Shattuck Arizona and Denn Arizona agreed to transfer their assets to Shattuck Denn (a new corporation which they had caused to be organized) in exchange for Shattuck Denn Stock. The issue was whether this transaction constituted a sale by Shattuck Arizona. The court said it did not:

> In no proper view were the two Minnesota copper companies *selling* the Arizona copper mines. Their intention was to keep them and develop the Shattuck Denn. In effect the property of the Shattuck Arizona was to furnish the means of financing. No money passed or was intended to pass. . . . [The Corporation] might have sold . . . because it was a business-like thing to do. It did not.[11]

But then suppose *A* transfers his business to *AB* in exchange for *AB* stock when *AB* is an existing corporation, wholly owned by *B*? Here too the transaction would not normally be described as a "sale" of his business by *A* (or a "purchase" by *AB*), again for the same reason: *A*'s continuity of interest in the transferred business. But this last transaction is, of course, a stock-for-assets combination.[12]

11. 186 Minn. 611, 629-630, 244 N.W. 281, 288-289 (1932) (emphasis added); see Whicher v. Delaware Mines Corp., 52 Idaho 304, 15 P.2d 610 (1932); William B. Riker & Son Co. v. United Drug Co., 79 N.J. Eq. 580, 82 A. 930 (Ct. Err. & App. 1912). But see Hill v. Page & Hill Co., 198 Minn. 30, 268 N.W. 705 (1936), rehearing denied, 198 Minn. 34, 268 N.W. 927 (1936).

12. Cf. Rule 16b-7(b) under the Securities Exchange Act of 1934 ("A merger

On the other hand, usage does not point in one direction only. "Sale" is a very broad term, and at least some of its meanings can encompass stock-for-assets transactions. For example, section 2(3) of the 1933 Act provides that "[t]he term 'sale' or 'sell' shall include every . . . disposition of . . . a security . . . for value,"[13] and it is clear that even a statutory merger may constitute a "sale" within the meaning of the securities acts.[14] Furthermore, most sale-of-substantially-all-assets provisions explicitly contemplate transfers of assets in exchange solely for stock of the survivor. Thus the Illinois statute provides that "[a] sale . . . of all, or substantially all, the property and assets . . . of a corporation . . . may be made . . . [for consideration] which may consist, in whole or in part, of money or property . . . including shares of any other corporation."[15] Under such a statute it might seem impermissible to say that a stock-for-assets transaction is not a

---

within the meaning of this rule shall *include* the sale or purchase of substantially all the assets of one company by another in exchange for stock which is then distributed to the security holders of the company which sold its assets"), 17 C.F.R. §240.16b-7(b) (1974), and the definitions of "reorganization" in the 1921, '24, '26, '28, and '32 Revenue Acts, as quoted in R. Paul, Studies in Federal Taxation, Exhibit A (facing 164) (3d Series 1940) (the 1921 Act, for example, read: "[R]eorganization means . . . (A) a merger or consolidation (*including* the acquisition by one corporation of . . . substantially all the properties of another corporation")). (Emphasis added in both quotations.)

13. Securities Act of 1933, §2(3), 15 U.S.C. §77b(3) (1970).

14. See SEC v. National Securities, Inc., 393 U.S. 453 (1959); Vine v. Beneficial Fin. Co., 374 F.2d 627 (2d Cir.), cert. denied, 389 U.S. 970 (1967); cf. SEC Rule 133, 17 C.F.R. §230.133 (1974).

For a discussion of similar problems in the context of the sales tax, see Sato, The Sales Tax and Capital Transactions, 45 Calif. L. Rev. 450, at 469-476, 483-485 (1967).

15. Ill. Ann. Stat. ch. 32, §157.72 (Smith-Hurd 1954). See also, e.g., Cal. Corp. Code §§3901, 3903 (West 1955); Del. Code Ann. tit. 8, §271 (1974); N.Y. Bus. Corp. Law §909 (McKinney Supp. 1974); ABA Model Bus. Corp. Act §79 (1969 rev.).

Although the text focuses on the term "sale," the statutes typically use a string of terms, such as "sale, lease or exchange," see Del. Code Ann. tit. 8, §271 (1974); "sale, lease, exchange, or other disposition," see N.Y. Bus. Corp. Law §909 (McKinney Supp. 1974); ABA Model Bus. Corp. Act §79 (1969 rev.); cf. Ill. Ann. Stat. ch. 32, §157.72 (Smith-Hurd 1954), or "lease, sale, exchange, transfer, or other disposition," see Ohio Rev. Code Ann. tit. 17, §1701.76 (Page 1964); cf. Cal. Corp. Code §3901 (West 1955). In context, however, the terms "exchange" and "transfer" seem to be variants of the term "sale," in the sense that they contemplate a disposal of the corporation's assets for consideration. The apparent purpose of the added terms is to pick up dispositions for consideration other than cash, that is, barter-type transactions. Cf. Treas. Reg. §1.1001-1(a) ("Except as otherwise provided . . . the gain or loss realized from the conversion of property into cash, *or* from the *exchange* of property for other property differing materially either in kind or in extent, is treated as income or loss sustained" [emphasis added]).

sale just because there is some degree of continuity of interest on the part of the transferor or its shareholders.

It therefore appears that many stock-for-assets transactions could be deemed *either* mergers or sales under the corporate statutes. Which characterization should be applied must then depend on which would best reconcile the overlapping merger and sale provisions, and best effectuate the apparent statutory purpose. For reasons already reviewed, the label given the transaction cannot be dispositive. However, there are several other techniques, consistent with the statutory schemes, which may be employed to segregate sales and mergers. Thus, a distinction could be drawn between those stock-for-assets transactions which do not involve any other indicia of a merger – "without more," to use the language of *Farris* – and those which are accompanied by some such indicia; for example, a requirement that the transferor dissolve and an assumption by the survivor of the transferor's liabilities.[16] Alternatively, those transactions in which the survivor issues principally common or other voting stock could be distinguished from those in which it issues principally nonvoting securities – treating the former as a merger and the latter as a sale. There is ample analogy for such a distinction. In the tax area a stock-for-assets combination will qualify for treatment as a nontaxable reorganization, rather than constituting a taxable sale, if at least 80 percent of the transferor's property is acquired by the survivor in exchange for voting stock, but not otherwise.[17] Similarly, in the accounting area a transaction will qualify for pooling-of-interest treatment (in which the assets of the transferor are carried by the survivor at their book value in the transferor's hands) rather than a purchase (in which the assets must be written up to market value), if the survivor issues solely voting stock, but not otherwise.[18]

16. Such an approach has been criticized on the ground that an assumption of the transferor's liabilities merely constitutes additional consideration for the assets received, while dissolution of the transferor is "frequently, if not usually" an incident of a stock-for-assets transaction. 59 Colum. L. Rev. 366, 370 (1959). But if such requirements are "frequently, if not usually" an incident of stock-for-assets transactions, that may simply indicate that such transactions are "frequently, if not usually" mergers within the meaning of the statutes.

17. Internal Revenue Code §368(a)(1)(C), (2)(B).

18. American Institute of Certified Public Accountants, Accounting Principles Board Opinion No. 16, at 294-295, 298-302 (1970).

Still a third possibility would be to draw a distinction on the basis of the relative size of the two constituents.[19] Reverting to the hypothetical transfer of a business by *A* to the existing corporation *AB*, if *AB*'s business is so much larger than *A*'s that *A* receives only a negligible interest in *AB* – for example, if *A*'s business consists of several small supermarkets and *AB* is a national chain of supermarkets – both laymen and lawyers probably would say that *A* had "sold" his business.[20] This is so because while *A* retains a continuity of interest in his former assets, his stake in those assets and in *AB* as a whole is so small that for all practical purposes *A* has parted with substantially all of that interest. What constitutes a substantial stake? Although the corporate cases have not addressed themselves to this question, the courts are nevertheless not without guidelines; as will be shown below, several statutes and the rules of the American and New York stock exchanges have recognized 15-20 percent as a cutoff for closely related purposes.[21] Under this line of analysis, if the transferor's shareholders receive less than a 15-20 percent stake in the reconstituted enterprise the transaction would be deemed a sale within the meaning of the statute; if more, a merger.

§14.2. A Modern Statutory Treatment of Stock-For-Assets Combinations (Including Classical Mergers)

If we put aside the problems raised by the traditional statutes, and consider instead the optimal legislative treatment of stock-for-assets combinations and classical mergers, three things seem clear: (1) A classical merger (that is, a merger so denominated) is simply a special case of a stock-for-assets transaction; (2) Shareholder rights in such transactions should depend on the real impact of the transaction (which may of course include significant changes in legal rights), not on how the transaction is labeled;[22] and (3) The impact of such a transaction on share-

19. Cf. 59 Colum. L. Rev. 366, 372 (1959).

20. See B. Bittker & J. Eustice, Federal Income Taxation of Corporations and Shareholders ¶14.01 (3d ed. 1971).

21. See §§14.3, 15.2(B), infra.

22. Cf. Ballantine & Sterling, Upsetting Mergers and Consolidations: Alternative Remedies of Dissenting Shareholders in California, 27 Calif. L. Rev. 644, 672-673

holders of a transferor may differ from the impact on shareholders of a survivor, so that the rights of each body of shareholders must be considered separately.

A. The Transferor's Shareholders

On the transferor's side, the issues are relatively straightforward. If one corporation transfers substantially all of its assets to a second in exchange for stock in the latter (or indeed for any consideration other than cash), from the perspective of the transferor's shareholders the result is a radical reconstitution of the enterprise[23] – so radical that it should not only require approval by the transferor's shareholders, but give rise to appraisal rights for those of the transferor's shareholders who do not choose to participate; and this is true whether the transaction is denominated a merger, or not.[24]

B. The Survivor's Shareholders

On the survivor's side, the picture is somewhat more complex. If a stock-for-assets combination has a significant economic or legal impact on the survivor's shareholders it should certainly require approval by those shareholders, and give rise to appraisal rights on their part, for much the same reasons that apply to shareholders of the transferor. But if the amount of stock issued by the survivor is not significant in terms of its previously outstanding stock, and no significant change is made in the control structure of the legal entity in which the survivor's corporate enterprise is enveloped, the combination is unlikely to have a

(1939); Hills, Consolidation of Corporations by Sale of Assets and Distribution of Shares, 19 Calif. L. Rev. 349, 366 (1931); Lattin, Minority and Dissenting Shareholders' Rights in Fundamental Changes, 23 Law & Contemp. Prob. 307, 315-316 (1953); Skoler, Some Observations on the Scope of Appraisal Statutes, 13 Bus. Law. 240, 243 (1958).

23. This assumes the transaction is not an "upside-down" one, involving a camel transferor and a gnat transferee. Such transactions can be handled by treating them as if the gnat were the transferor.

24. This has been the long-term statutory trend, a number of states having added appraisal rights to their sale-of-substantially-all assets provisions within the last 30 years. See Manning, The Shareholder's Appraisal Remedy, supra note 1, at 256; Skoler, supra note 22, at 243; Note, Sale of Assets: Dissenting Shareholders' Appraisal Right in Absence of Appraisal Statute, 46 Calif. L. Rev. 283, at 283 n. 6 (1958).

significant economic impact on the survivor's shareholders. Such a transaction, therefore, should neither require approval of the survivor's shareholders nor give such shareholders appraisal rights; and this is true even if the combination is denominated a merger.

A pathbreaking statute, taking just this approach, was adopted by Ohio in 1963. As applied to the survivor in stock-for-assets combinations (including classical mergers), the Ohio statute has two elements: (1) If the transaction is not a classical merger (that is, not a merger so denominated) it nevertheless requires approval by the survivor's shareholders, and gives those shareholders appraisal rights, if the survivor issues shares which carry "one-sixth or more of the voting power . . . in the election of directors immediately after the consummation of such transaction."[25] (2) Correspondingly, if in a classical merger the shares issued by the survivor do *not* carry one-sixth of the voting power, the merger does not require approval by the survivor's shareholders, nor give those shareholders appraisal rights, unless the merger agreement makes a change in the survivor's certificate, or by-laws, or authorizes an action or makes a change in the board which would require shareholder approval independently of the merger.[26] The rationale of the statute was explained by the draftsmen as follows:

> Although there are legal and tax distinctions between an acquisition of assets and a merger . . . the business and financial world treat them as

25. Ohio Rev. Code Ann. tit. 17, § §1701.01(Q), (S), 1701.83(A), 1701.84(D) (Page Supp. 1974). The legislative technique involves a statutory definition of a "combination" as "a transaction . . . wherein . . . voting shares . . . are issued . . . in consideration in whole or in part for the transfer . . . of all or substantially all the assets of one or more corporations." §1701.01(Q), supra.

Shareholders of the *transferor* have voting and appraisal rights regardless of the number of shares issued, under the sale-of-substantially-all-assets section. Ohio Rev. Code Ann. tit. 17, §1701.76 (Page 1964).

26. Ohio Rev. Code Ann. § §1701.78(D), 1701.84(B) (Page Supp. 1974). Again, the transferor's shareholders are entitled to voting and appraisal rights in any event. Id. § §1701.78(D), 1701.84(A).

In 1959 Pennsylvania enacted an extremely limited forerunner provision, which (as it now reads) conferred appraisal rights on the shareholders of the survivor in a stock-for-assets combination if the stock issued to the transferor carries more than 50 percent of the voting power in the reconstituted corporation, so that, in effect, the nominal survivor is actually the transferor. Pa. Stat. Ann. tit. 15, §1311(F) (1974 Supp.). For an extended discussion of this provision, see Eisenberg, The Legal Roles of Shareholders and Management in Modern Corporate Decisionmaking, 57 Calif. L. Rev. 1, 122-126 (1969).

> the same in substance. Moreover, the courts in other states have held that the merger statute may apply to an acquisition of assets on the theory of de facto merger where the relatively large size or different nature of the business of the acquired corporation is such that the shareholder's investment in the acquiring corporation becomes a new investment in a different enterprise. . . . In the absence of a statutory definition of where the line falls, it is difficult, under the doctrine of these cases, to apply to many factual situations such distinctions of [as?] relative size of the corporations, relationship of their business and control.
>
> It is the intent of the new section . . . to avoid in Ohio any such problems of interpretation and any such possibility of de facto merger, by adopting . . . specific statutory quantitative test[s] . . . .[27]

While the Ohio statute marked a considerable advance over the traditional corporate statutes governing combinations, it is deficient in two respects. First, the statutory test is based on voting power "immediately after" consummation of the transaction. Assuming that "immediately after" means what it says,[28] this test fails to deal adequately with securities which are nonvoting when issued, but are convertible into voting stock.[29] Since convertible securities are commonly used to effect corporate combinations, a statute which employs a voting-power test should take such securities into account, preferably by assuming full conversion. (In the *Rath* case, which involved convertible stock, the Iowa court analyzed the transaction on just such a basis.)

Second, it is open to question whether a voting-power test should be used at all. Suppose the authorized stock of *S* Corporation consists of 200,000 shares of Class A voting common and

27. Ohio Rev. Code Ann. tit. 17, at 100 (Page 1964).

28. See Ohio Rev. Code Ann. tit. 17, §1701.01(T); McDonough, The Appraisal Remedy for Dissenting Shareholders in Iowa and the De Facto Merger Doctrine: Rath v. Rath Packing Co., 16 Drake L. Rev. 22, 26-27 n. 41 (1966).

29. Suppose, for example, that the authorized stock of *S* Corporation consists of 200,000 shares of voting common and 100,000 shares of nonvoting preferred convertible into common on a one-to-one basis, of which only 100,000 common shares are issued and outstanding. Under the Ohio statute, if *S* acquires substantially all of the assets of Corporation *T* by issuing 20,500 shares of common, *S*'s shareholders will have voting and appraisal rights, since the issued stock will carry one-sixth of the voting power "immediately after the transaction." But if *S* instead issues 19,500 shares of common and 80,500 shares of preferred, *S*'s shareholders presumably will not have voting or appraisal rights, since the preferred is nonvoting and the 19,500 shares of common will not carry one-sixth of the voting power, despite the fact that if all the preferred is converted the shares issued to *T* will account for 50 percent of total voting power.

200,000 shares of Class B nonvoting common, which shares equally with the Class A in dividends. At a time when *S*'s outstanding stock consists of 100,000 A shares, *S* issues 100,000 B shares in exchange for substantially all of *T*'s assets. Under the Ohio statute, *S*'s shareholders would not have voting or appraisal rights, because the B stock is nonvoting – despite the fact that it carries a claim to 50 percent of *S*'s earnings. This seems unsound if the basic criterion is economic impact, and it would therefore be preferable to adopt a test which turns on the amount of common stock, whether voting or nonvoting, which is issued or issuable as a result of the transaction.[30] This approach was taken by New Jersey when it adopted a provision similar to Ohio's in 1972.[31] Perhaps more important, it is also taken by the New York and American Stock Exchanges, which require shareholder approval as a condition to listing new stock issued by listed companies to effect business combinations, "[w]here the present or potential issuance [to the transferor] of common stock or securities con-

30. Cf. Folk, Corporation Statutes: 1959-1966, 1966 Duke L.J. 875, 944-945 (1966). See also Schulman, Shareholder Rights in Acquisition Transactions: A Dissent, 18 Wayne L. Rev. 1041, 1049-1051 & n. 36 (1972), suggesting that both voting-power and common-stock tests should be employed, principally to pick up voting nonconvertible preferred and debt securities.

31. N.J. Stat. Ann. 14A:10-12 (Supp. 1974). This section adopts an unduly high 40-percent-of-the-common-stock-outstanding-immediately-prior-to-the-transaction test (although §14A:10-3 adopts a 20-percent test in the case of a classical merger). The New Jersey Corporation Law Revision Commission's comments on §14A:10-12 are as follows:

"This section . . . codifies the de facto merger doctrine articulated in Applestein v. United Board & Carton Corp. . . . The Commission is of the opinion that shareholders should be granted the right to vote and to dissent to the same extent as in a merger in any corporate acquisition, however structured, involving the issuance of such a substantial number of shares. At the same time, the Commission believes that this codification will minimize the substantial uncertainties which Applestein created." N.J. Stat. Ann. §14A:10-12, Commissioners' Comment – 1972 Amendments (Supp. 1974). See also ch. 682, §§181(b), 1200, 1201, 1300, [1975-76 Reg. Sess.] Calif. Leg. Serv.; R.I. Gen. Laws Ann. §§7-1.1-67, 7-1.1-70.1, 7-1.1-73(b) (1969 & Supp. 1973). The revised California statute uses a one-sixth-of-voting-power-immediately-after-the-transaction test, measured by voting shares and securities convertible into voting shares. The Rhode Island statute uses a one-third-of-voting-power-immediately-after-the-transaction test, measured by voting shares and securities convertible into voting shares within one year.

Several states have adopted a relative-size test comparable to Ohio's to cut down the rights of the survivor's shareholders in a classical merger, without adopting any counterpart provision to insure shareholder rights in a stock-for-assets combination. See Del. Code Ann. tit. 8, §251(f) (Supp. 1975); Mich. Comp. Laws Ann. §450.1704 (1973).

vertible into common stock could result in an increase in outstanding common shares approximating 20% or more. . . ."[32] The sweep and longstanding nature of these rules, together with the Ohio experience, indicate that such a requirement is entirely feasible.[33] Indeed, it is ironic that almost all of the country's largest publicly held corporations are subject to such a rule by virtue of the fact that their stock is listed on either the New York or American exchanges, while no comparable rule is applicable to the great bulk of small and medium-sized publicly held corporations, where it may be most needed.

§14.3. A Modern Statutory Treatment of Stock-For-Assets Acquisitions Other Than Corporate Combinations

So far, the discussion has been limited to stock-for-assets *corporate* combinations — the exchange of one corporation's stock for substantially all of another corporation's assets. However, once it is recognized that the rights of a survivor's shareholders need not parallel those of a transferor's, the inquiry on the survivor's side can be enlarged to encompass *all* types of stock-for-assets combinations. That is, if Corporation *S* acquires a business in exchange for its stock, the impact on *S*'s shareholders does not fundamentally depend on whether the business comprises substantially all of the transferor's assets, or, for that matter, on whether the transferor is a corporation, a partnership, or a sole entrepreneur. Rather, the impact on *S*'s shareholders will depend on whether the amount of common stock issued or issuable by *S* is significant in

32. New York Stock Exchange, Company Manual, at A-284; CCH, American Stock Exchange Manual ¶10,032.

33. Moreover, in many cases a stock-for-assets combination is submitted to the survivor's shareholders even though the survivor's stock is not registered on the New York or American stock exchanges and the corporation takes the position that the transaction is not a merger. For example, the transaction may be submitted to shareholders because it was not negotiated at arm's length, see Heilbrunn v. Sun Chemical Corp., 38 Del. Ch. 321, 150 A.2d 755 (Sup. Ct. 1959), or because shareholder approval is required for a particular aspect of the combination, such as a reconstitution of the survivor's board or an amendment of the survivor's certificate to authorize a new class of stock, see Rath v. Rath Packing Co., 257 Iowa 1277, 136 N.W.2d 410 (1965); Farris v. Glen Alden Corp., 393 Pa. 427, 143 A.2d 25 (1958).

relation to its stock then oustanding. If it is, the transaction will usually involve a reconstitution of *S*'s ownership and enterprise which should require shareholder approval and (perhaps) appraisal rights, whatever the transferor's form. Thus the New Jersey statute provides that "[s]hareholders of a corporation which proposes to acquire . . . in exchange for its shares, obligations or other securities, some or all of . . . the assets of a corporation, a business trust, a business proprietorship or a business partnership," shall have voting and appraisal rights if a 40 percent test is met.[34] Similarly, the New York Stock Exchange requires shareholder approval as "a prerequisite to listing securities to be issued [by a listed company] for or in connection with . . . [t]he acquisition, direct or indirect, of a business, a company, tangible or intangible assets or property or securities representing any such interests" if a 20 percent test is met.[35] (The Exchange does not, of course, provide for appraisal rights; and it may be that in the case of a simple acquisition, at least, such rights should be less easily triggered than voting rights. Thus the New Jersey statute's 40 percent test may perhaps be appropriate for appraisal rights in simple acquisitions, although it is certainly much too high for voting rights in corporate combinations.)

34. N.J. Rev. Stat. Ann. §14A:10-12 (Supp. 1974).
35. New York Stock Exchange, Company Manual, at A-284.

15

Stock-for-Stock Combinations

A stock-for-stock combination is effected through the issuance by one corporation (the "survivor") of shares of its own stock directly to shareholders of another corporation (the "transferor"), in exchange for an amount of stock in the transferor – normally at least a majority – sufficient to carry control. The immediate result of such a combination, therefore, is that the transferor becomes the survivor's subsidiary. In terms of both the traditional statutes and optimal legislative solutions, such combinations pose much harder questions than stock-for-assets combinations.

§15.1. The Transferor's Shareholders

A. Under the Traditional Statutes

From the perspective of the transferor the most obvious and dramatic difference between a stock-for-stock and a stock-for-assets combination is that the former does not require corporate action on the transferor's part, since it is effected through the transfer of stock by individual shareholders. If *all* of the transferor's shareholders transfer their stock to the survivor, no problem of voting or appraisal rights is raised. Suppose, however, that less than all of the stock is transferred, and that the transferor continues in existence as the survivor's subsidiary. Since the two enterprises are not fused, the transaction does not seem to be either a merger or a sale of substantially all assets from the transferor's perspective.[1] Under the traditional statutes, therefore, the nontransferring shareholders would have neither voting nor appraisal rights. Nor would voting rights seem desirable in such cases. For one thing, by its very mechanics the transaction requires shareholder approval of sorts, because the combination cannot take place unless a sufficient number of the transferor's shareholders agree to exchange their shares for stock in the survivor. More important, it would seem unwise to give the shareholders as a body a right to vote on whether some shareholders can sell their stock, and it would seem virtually impossible to develop a mechanism pitched to that objective without placing an inordinate restriction on the normally free alienability of shares.

B. A Modern Statutory Treatment

In contrast, there are two strong grounds for giving nontransferring shareholders the equivalent of an appraisal right — a right to exit at a fair price.

The first ground which supports such a right is that of mutuality. Most important corporate statutes now include so-called short-form merger provisions, under which certain parent-subsidiary mergers can typically be effected simply by vote of the parent's board — that is, without a vote of the parent's shareholders, the subsidiary's shareholders, or the subsidiary's board, and without appraisal rights in the parent's shareholders.[2] Orig-

1. See Mitchell Investment Co. v. Republic Steel Corp., 63 F. Supp. 323 (N.D. Ohio 1944), affd. mem., 152 F.2d 105 (6th Cir. 1945); State ex rel. Carriger v. Campbell Food Markets, Inc., 60 Wash. 2d 478, 374 P.2d 435 (1962); Folk, De Facto Mergers in Delaware: Hariton v. Arco Electronics, Inc., 49 Va. L. Rev. 1261, 1283-1284 (1963); cf. Orzeck v. Englehart, 41 Del. Ch. 361, 195 A.2d 375 (1963); Fidanque v. American Maracaibo Co., 33 Del. Ch. 262, 92 A.2d 311 (Ch. 1952); Cummings v. United Artists Theatre Circuit, Inc., 237 Md. 1, 204 A.2d 795 (1964). Compare Architectural Building Products, Inc. v. Cupples Products Corp., 221 F. Supp. 154 (E.D. Wis. 1963), with Hoche Productions, S.A. v. Jayark Films Corp., 256 F. Supp. 291, 295-296 (S.D.N.Y. 1966).

2. See Cal. Corp. Code §4124 (West Supp. 1974); Del. Code Ann. tit. 8, §253 (1974); Ill. Ann. Stat. ch. 32, §§157.66a, 157.70 (Smith-Hurd Supp. 1974); N.J. Stat. Ann. §§14A:10-5, 14A:11-1(1)(a)(ii) (Supp. 1974); N.Y. Bus. Corp. Law §§905, 910 (McKinney 1963 & 1974 Supp); Ohio Rev. Code Ann. §§1701.80, 1701.84 (Page Supp. 1974); Pa. Stat. Ann. tit. 15, §§1515(L), 1902.1 (Supp. 1974); ABA Model Business Corp. Act §§70, 80 (1969 rev.).

The Ohio statute only dispenses with the requirement of approval by the shareholders of the two constituents, and the Pennsylvania statute apparently only dispenses with the requirement of approval by the parent's shareholders.

inally these provisions were probably conceived of as procedural in nature, primarily designed to simplify the mechanics of mergers between a parent and its wholly owned subsidiary.[3] Today, however, the reach of short-form merger provisions has been substantively extended in two important ways. First, many such provisions are now applicable to mergers between parents and less-than-100-percent-owned subsidiaries – typically, although not invariably, the floor is set at 90 percent.[4] Second, it has been held that when (as is often the case) the statute contemplates the issuance of cash by the parent, the latter can, if it chooses, issue cash alone, thus squeezing out the subsidiary's minority shareholders entirely, subject only to judicial review of the fairness of the price through appraisal proceedings.[5] As presently drafted and construed, therefore, these provisions are principally *cash-out* rather than *merger* statutes; but they are cash-out provisions which run in one direction only: the parent can make use of them, but not the subsidiary's shareholders. Thus the statutes are unacceptably tilted in favor of the parent, and in the interests of mutuality the short-form merger provisions should be balanced by reciprocal provisions which enable the minority shareholders to compel the parent to cash out their interest at a fair price.

The English experience in one sector of this area illustrates both the problem and the feasibility of the suggested correction. In 1929 there was introduced into the Companies Act what is now section 209(1),[6] which generally provides that where as a result of a tender offer one corporation holds at least 90 percent of the stock of another, the acquiring corporation can compel the re-

3. Cf. Comment, Jurisdiction of the California Corporations Commissioner Over Delaware Short Form Mergers, 52 Calif. L. Rev. 1016, 1018 (1964). Compare Note, Elimination of Minority Share Interest by Merger: A Dissent, 54 Nw. U.L. Rev. 629, 632 n. 18 (1959), with Comment, The Short Merger Statute, 32 U. Chi. L. Rev. 596, at 596 n. 2 (1965), and the statutes cited in note 2, supra.

4. See the Delaware, New Jersey, Ohio, Pennsylvania, and Model Act provisions cited in note 2, supra.

5. See Stauffer v. Standard Brands Inc., 41 Del. Ch. 7, 187 A.2d 78 (1962); Coyne v. Park & Tilford Distillers Corp., 38 Del. Ch. 514, 154 A.2d 893 (1959); Willcox v. Stern, 18 N.Y.2d 195, 219 N.E.2d 401 (1966); Beloff v. Consolidated Edison Co., 300 N.Y. 11, 87 N.E.2d 561 (1949); cf. Teschner v. Chicago Title & Trust Co., 322 N.E.2d 54 (Ill. 1975).

6. The Companies Act of 1948, 11 & 12 Geo. 6, c. 38, §209(1); cf. N.J. Stat. Ann. §14A:10-9 (Supp. 1974).

maining shareholders in the target-transferor to sell their shares at the tender-offer price.[7] The Cohen Committee, appointed by the British Government in 1943 to review the Companies Act of 1929, pointed out in its Report that:

> [w]hile a company, if it obtains 90 percent of the shares [for which a tender offer was made] can compel the dissentient minority to sell their shares, the dissentient minority have no power to compel the company to acquire the shares held by them although their position as a small minority in a subsidiary company may be anything but satisfactory.[8]

Accordingly, in 1948 section 209(2) was added to the Companies Act, providing that where the acquiring corporation has the right to compel minority shareholders to sell their shares under section 209(1), the minority has a reciprocal right to compel the acquiring corporation to purchase their shares at either the tender-offer price or a price fixed by the court.[9]

It might be objected that mutuality, taken alone, is an inadequate ground for providing minority shareholders in dominantly owned subsidiaries with a right to be cashed out at a fair price, in the absence of a substantive need. This leads to the second ground supporting such a right; the position of such shareholders is likely to be a very unhappy one. As Gower puts it:

7. See M. A. Weinberg, Take-Overs and Amalgamations 143-152 (2d ed. 1967). On application, the court has power to relieve minority shareholders of their obligation to sell, but "except in special circumstances, the onus upon the [minority] shareholder is a heavy one." Id. at 155.

8. Committee on Company Law Amendment, Report 89 (CMD No. 6659, 1945); cf. Law of Sept. 6, 1965, [1965] BGB1. I 1089, § § 291-292, 305 translated in CCH, German Stock Corporation Act (F. Juenger & L. Schmidt transl. 1967); Haskell, The New West German Law of "Related Business Units," 24 Bus. Law. 421, 430-431 (1969); Hetherington, Special Characteristics, Problems and Needs of the Close Corporation, 1969 U. Ill. L.F. 1, 22.

9. M.A. Weinberg, supra note 7, at 158-162.

Moreover, Rule 35 of the City [of London] Code on Take-overs and Mergers (1972 rev.) provides that "Any person who acquires, whether by a series of transactions over a period of time or not, shares which (together with shares acquired by other persons acting in concert with such person) carry 40% of the voting rights . . . attributable to the share capital of a company must, except in a case specifically approved by the Panel [on Take-overs and Mergers], extend within a reasonable period of time an unconditional offer to the holders of the remaining equity share capital of the offeree company . . . [to purchase their shares] at not less than the highest price . . . paid by such persons for shares of that class within the preceding 12 months."

> The [acquired] company's existence is not affected, nor need its constitution be altered; all that occurs is that its shareholders change. From the legal viewpoint this methodological distinction is formidable, but commercially the two things may be almost identical. If . . . a controlling interest is acquired, the [acquired] company . . . will become a subsidiary of the acquiring company . . . and cease, in fact though not in law, to be an independent entity. . . .
>
> This may produce the situation in which a small number of dissentient members are left as a minority in a company intended to be operated as a member of a group. As such, their position is likely to be unhappy, for the parent company will wish to operate the subsidiary for the benefit of the group as a whole and not necessarily for the benefit of that particular subsidiary.[10]

The closer the survivor's proportionate interest in the transferor approaches 100 percent the more likely this is to be true. Furthermore, as the survivor's proportionate interest approaches 100 percent, the market for the transferor's stock may be thinned almost out of existence.[11] Indeed, if the transferor is a listed corporation the transaction may result in delisting if the amount of stock which remains outstanding in the public's hands is insufficient to satisfy minimum Exchange requirements.[12] At the same time the survivor may, for its own business reasons, cut or even eliminate dividends by the transferor, reinforcing a possible diminution in market price caused by the thinness of the market.[13] Under such conditions the market price of the stock retained by nontransferring shareholders may fall well below its fair value. The need of such shareholders for a right to compel the parent to cash out their shares at a fair price is therefore not only at least as great as the parent's need for a right to cash them out, but sustainable on independent grounds. Furthermore, as long as the triggering percentage is that set in the short-form merger statute, the parent will already own so much of the subsidiary's stock that any burden

10. L. Gower, The Principles of Modern Company Law 561 (2d ed. 1957). See also R. Moon, Business Mergers and Take-Over Bids 138-143 (3d ed. 1968). For an example of such a situation, see Mitchell Investment Co. v. Republic Steel Co., 63 F. Supp. 323 (N.D. Ohio 1944), affd. mem., 152 F.2d 105 (6th Cir. 1945).

11. R. Moon, supra note 10, at 140.

12. See Note, 72 Harv. L. Rev. 1132, 1142 n. 66 (1959). This was apparently the case in Mitchell Investment Co. v. Republic Steel Co., 63 F. Supp. 323 (N.D. Ohio 1944), affd. mem., 152 F.2d 105 (6th Cir. 1945).

13. See R. Moon, supra note 10, at 140-142.

imposed by its contingent obligation to purchase the remaining shares would usually be well overweighed by the minority's interest in being able to compel such a purchase.

One possible objection to a provision of this type is that it could entail unduly high expense if each minority shareholder brought a separate action to compel the acquisition of his shares. It is not clear whether this would in fact be a serious problem, since the expense to the shareholders would be equally high, so that both parties would be under pressure to negotiate a fair price without resort to litigation. In any event, this problem could be easily met by providing that when a parent achieves the requisite percentage of ownership in a subsidiary it must give notice of that fact to all remaining shareholders; that minority shareholders who desire to be cashed out must so elect within a short period of time after such notice is given — say, six months; and that actions brought by shareholders to enforce this right must be brought in the corporation's domicile state.

§15.2. The Survivor's Shareholders

A. Under the Traditional Statutes

From the survivor's perspective, unlike the transferor's, stock-for-stock combinations do involve corporate action, since the survivor must issue stock. In this, they are comparable to stock-for-assets transactions. Like stock-for-assets combinations too, stock-for-stock combinations may be viewed as either a merger, on the one hand, or a purchase effected through the issuance of stock, on the other. Here, however, the resemblance ends, since the immediate result of a stock-for-assets transaction is a complete fusion at the corporate level, while the immediate result of a stock-for-stock transaction is not, and this difference may raise a number of complications.

1. Stock-for-stock combinations which include a preintended fusion of the constituents; application of the step-transaction theory. In many stock-for-stock combinations, the exchange of stock is followed by either a classical merger between the survivor and the transferor, a stock-for-assets combination, a short-form merger, or a liquidation of the transferor into the survivor.[14] If the exchange of stock in a stock-for-stock combination is followed by a classical merger, even under the traditional statutes the survivor's shareholders will normally have voting and appraisal rights by virtue of the merger provisions. If the *Farris-Applestein-Rath* line of cases is followed, the same result will obtain where the stock-for-stock is followed by a stock-for-assets combination. In contrast, a liquidation of the transferor into the survivor, or a short-form merger between the two constituents, will not in itself give voting or appraisal rights to the survivor's shareholders. Suppose, however, that the liquidation or short-form merger was a preintended (although chronologically separate) step of the combination? In that case, the two steps (stock-for-stock exchange and short-form merger or liquidation) should be viewed as an integrated whole under the step-transaction theory of statutory interpretation.[15] That is, since the transaction, as planned, involves a fusion of the transferor into the survivor effected through issuance of stock by the survivor, from the perspective of the survivor's shareholders it should be treated as a merger within the meaning of the traditional corporate statutes. In cases raising comparable problems under the tax laws the courts have reached just such a result under just this theory,[16] and this was also the result reached by the New Jersey court in *Applestein*, although the step-transaction theory was not there employed.

14. Cf. Hill, The Sale of Controlling Shares, 70 Harv. L. Rev. 986, 1028-1029 (1957); Comment, Jurisdiction of the California Corporations Commissioner Over Delaware Short Form Mergers, 52 Calif. L. Rev. 1016 (1964); Note, The Right of Shareholders Dissenting from Corporate Combinations to Demand Cash Payment for Their Shares, 72 Harv. L. Rev. 1132, 1141 (1959).

15. Cf. Commissioner v. Ashland Oil & Refining Co., 99 F.2d 588 (6th Cir. 1938), cert. denied, 306 U.S. 661 (1939); Walter S. Heller, 2 T.C. 371 (1943), affd., 147 F.2d 376 (9th Cir. 1945), cert. denied, 325 U.S. 868 (1945). See generally B. Bittker & J. Eustice, Federal Income Taxation of Corporations and Shareholders 1-19 – 1-20, 3-8 – 3-9, 3-33 – 3-37, 3-54, 14-30 – 14-31, 14-48, 14-101 – 14-106 (3d ed. 1971); Mintz & Plumb, Step Transactions in Corporate Reorganizations, N.Y.U. 12th Inst. on Fed. Tax. 247 (1954). But cf. Reliance Electric Co. v. Emerson Electric Co., 404 U.S. 79 (1972).

16. See King Enterprises, Inc. v. Commissioner, 418 F.2d 511 (Ct. Cl. 1969); South Bay Corp. v. Commissioner, 345 F.2d 698, 700-705 (2d Cir. 1965); Commissioner v. Ashland Refining Co., 99 F.2d 588 (6th Cir. 1938); Kimbell-Diamond Milling Co., 14 T.C. 74, affd. per curiam, 187 F.2d 718 (5th Cir. 1951), cert. denied, 342 U.S. 827 (1951); Sapienza, Tax Considerations in Corporate Reorganizations and Mergers, 60 Nw. U.L. Rev. 765, 783-784 (1966); Vesely, "A" Reorganizations – Statutory Mergers and Consolidations, 19 W. Res. L. Rev. 975, 981-984 (1968); cf. D. Herwitz, Business Planning 721 n. 6 (1966); Hill, The Sale of Controlling Shares, 70 Harv. L. Rev. 986,

2. Stock-for-stock combinations which do not include a pre-intended fusion of the two constituents.

a. Direct application of the merger provisions. Suppose now that the stock-for-stock combination is not followed by a preintended merger or liquidation? Although even in this case the two shareholder groups will have been largely or wholly fused, and the transferor's assets will come within the survivor's control, there will not be a complete fusion at the corporate level. The transferor's assets will be segregated from the survivor's assets by a corporate shell, and indeed where the survivor has acquired less than 100 percent of the transferor's stock, the transferor's separateness may be economic as well as legal. If, therefore, the term "merger" as used in the traditional corporate statutes involves a fusion, a stock-for-stock combination not followed by a pre-planned merger or liquidation may not seem to constitute a merger from the survivor's perspective within the meaning of the statutes.[17]

But that is not the end of the inquiry. Two complementary lines of analysis suggest that a stock-for-stock combination may require shareholder approval, and perhaps give rise to appraisal rights, even if it does not constitute a merger within the meaning of the traditional statutes.

1028-1035 (1957); Jennings, Trading in Corporate Control, 44 Calif. L. Rev. 1, 22-29 (1956). But cf. Orzeck v. Englehart, 41 Del. Ch. 361, 366-367, 195 A.2d 375, 378 (1963) (dictum).

The step-transaction theory normally need not be applied in favor of the transferor's shareholders in a stock-for-stock transaction because: (1) If a stock-for-stock exchange is followed by a classical merger between the survivor and the transferor, the transferor's minority shareholders will have both voting and appraisal rights under the merger provisions; (2) If a stock-for-stock exchange is followed by a stock-for-assets combination, the same result should obtain; (3) If a stock-for-stock exchange is followed by a short-form merger, the transferor's minority shareholders, unlike the survivor's shareholders, will have appraisal rights under the short-form merger provisions. (They will normally not have voting rights under that statute, but even if they had such rights, and voted against the transaction, if would nevertheless be adopted by virtue of the survivor's dominant stock ownership in the transferor.); (4) If a stock-for-stock exchange is followed by liquidation of the transferor, the transferor's minority shareholders will have voting rights under the dissolution provisions. (They will not have appraisal rights, but since the liquidation takes them out of the enterprise, the lack of such rights would normally not be a problem.)

17. See Cummings v. United Artists Theatre Circuit, Inc., 237 Md. 1, 204 A.2d 795 (1964). But cf. P. Anisman, Takeover Bid Legislation in Canada: A Comparative Analysis 189 (1974); English, Corporate Acquisitions — General Considerations, in Studies in Canadian Company Law 603, 604 (J. Ziegel ed. 1967).

b. Extending the ambit of the merger provisions; de facto doctrine revisited. The first line of analysis is based on the principle that in appropriate cases a statute, or the concept it embodies, will be deliberately extended to cover cases which do not lie within its literal scope. This principle has found frequent reflection in two basic types of situation in corporate law. One of these is the situation in which actors have made a good faith and colorable attempt to bring themselves within a provision of a corporate statute, but have failed to meet all of the statute's technical requirements. In such cases it is frequently held that the statute is nevertheless applicable. Probably the most common example is the doctrine of de facto incorporation, under which a business organization may be treated as a corporation for various purposes even though it has failed to comply with all of the requirements set down by the statute for the achievement of corporateness.[18] More to the point is the application of this principle to technically defective mergers. Thus in *Provident Security Life Insurance Company v. Gorsuch,*[19] United Security Life had purported to merge into Provident under Arizona law. The Arizona statute provided that a merger became effective upon the filing and recording of certified copies of the merger agreement in the appropriate state offices. Plaintiff, a United shareholder, attacked the validity of the merger on the ground, inter alia, that this requirement had not been met. Although defendant admitted that to be so, the court nevertheless upheld the merger's validity:

> Defendant concedes that a certified copy of the merger agreement was not recorded in the office of the county recorder prior to the commencement of this action. However, defendant argues in effect, the merger is in all other respects valid and, this being the case, tardy compliance with the statute in question left at least a de facto merger, and such a merger is not subject to attack by a nonconsenting shareholder. . . .
>
> There seems to be no Arizona court decision dealing with de facto mergers. But Arizona recognizes the doctrine of de facto corporations in general, and the rules pertaining thereto also apply to de facto consolidations and mergers.[20]

18. See generally H. Ballantine, Corporations 68-100 (rev. ed. 1946); N. Lattin, The Law of Corporations 181-189 (2d ed. 1971).

19. 323 F.2d 839 (9th Cir. 1963), cert. denied, 376 U.S. 950 (1964).

20. Id. at 844-854; cf. Terrell v. Industrial Commn., 19 Ariz. App. 468, 508 P.2d 355 (1973). See generally 15 Fletcher, Cyclopedia of The Law of Private Corporations § § 7152-7156 (1961 rev. vol.).

The second type of corporate-law situation in which the ambit of a statute may be deliberately broadened is the converse of the first; that is, the case in which rather than attempting compliance with a statute, the actors appear technically to have avoided it by running parallel to rather than within its coverage. It has frequently been recognized in such cases that legislative like judicial rules may be extended, by elaboration of the underlying principle and by analogy, to situations not precisely covered by the rule as originally formulated – and should be so extended if necessary to prevent subversion of the legislative policy.[21]

Anderson v. Abbott[22] is a good illustration. While a shareholder's risk is normally limited to the amount of his investment,[23] a shareholder in a national bank corporation was at one time subject to so-called "double liability," under a statutory provision which made him liable for the debts of the bank "to the amount of his stock therein, at the par value thereof in addition to the amount invested in such stock."[24] The question in *Anderson v. Abbott* was how to apply this statute when a national bank was a subsidiary corporation. The Supreme Court held that in such cases the parent's shareholders, rather than the parent, would be deemed shareholders of the bank subsidiary for purposes of the statutory double-liability provisions, on the ground that to hold otherwise would permit the purpose of those provisions to be undercut:

> It has often been held that the interposition of a corporation will not be allowed to defeat a legislative policy, whether that was the aim or only the result of the arrangement. . . .
>
> To allow this holding company device to succeed would be to put the policy of double liability at the mercy of corporation finance.[25]

21. Cf. Gellhorn, Contracts and Public Policy, 35 Colum. L. Rev. 679, 690-691 (1935); Landis, Statutes and the Sources of Law, in Harvard Legal Essays 213 (R. Pound ed. 1934); Pound, Sources and Forms of Law (pt. 3), 22 Notre Dame Law. 1, 36-45 (1946).

22. 321 U.S. 349 (1944).

23. See, e.g., Del. Code Ann. tit. 8, §102(b)(6) (1974).

24. Federal Reserve Act §23, ch. 6, §23, 38 Stat. 273 (1913). This provision paralleled National Bank Act §12, ch. 106, §12, 13 Stat. 102-103 (1864). The liability imposed by these provisions was severely qualified, and then effectively eliminated, by Act of June 16, 1933, ch. 89, §22, 48 Stat. 189, as amended, Act of Aug. 23, 1935, ch. 614, §304, 49 Stat. 708, as amended, Act of May 18, 1953, ch. 59, §2, 67 Stat. 27. Both provisions were finally repealed by Act of Sept. 8, 1959, Pub. L. 86-230, §7, 73 Stat. 457.

25. 321 U.S. at 362-363.

The Court stressed that its conclusion was not based on a finding of intent to evade the statute.[26]

A more sophisticated application of the principle was exhibited in *Aiple v. Twin City Barge & Towing Co.*[27] There, it will be recalled,[28] Twin City's management had sought to amend its certificate of incorporation to authorize additional shares of common stock for the purpose of increasing its equity capital, and Aiple, whose votes were needed to adopt the proposed amendment, had blocked it. Management then adopted an alternative plan, under which Twin City organized a new subsidiary to which it transferred the assets of a Twin City division and cash in exchange for 4000 of the subsidiary's 50,000 authorized shares. It was apparently contemplated that the subsidiary would thereafter sell a portion of its remaining 46,000 shares, thereby indirectly increasing Twin City's capital. Before these shares could be sold, however, Aiple moved to set the transaction aside. The court granted relief, on the ground that:

> If this can be done, the [statutory provisions governing certificate amendment] may be circumvented to the point where a corporation might fragment itself into any number of divisions, thus leaving minority stockholders without the protection that the statute was designed to give them.[29]

This line of analysis is also supported, of course, by *Farris, Applestein,* and *Rath.*

c. Application of common-law principles. The second line of analysis supporting a requirement that stock-for-stock combinations be approved by the survivor's shareholders, even under the traditional statutes, is based on the common-law principles, elaborated in chapter 8, that in the absense of express statutory provision, structural changes are shareholder rather than board matters. Application of these principles indicates that a

26. 321 U.S. at 357-358. See also Casanova Guns v. Connally, 454 F.2d 1320 (7th Cir.), cert. denied, 409 U.S. 845 (1972); Kavanaugh v. Ford Motor Co., 353 F.2d 710, 716-717 (7th Cir. 1965); Note, Efficacy of the Corporate Entity in Evasion of Statutes, 26 Iowa L. Rev. 350, 353-356 (1941).

27. 274 Minn. 38, 143 N.W.2d 374 (1966).

28. See chapter 8, text at notes 17-19, supra.

29. 274 Minn. at 45, 143 N.W.2d at 379; cf. O'Connor v. International Silver Co., 68 N.J. Eq. 67, 59 A. 321 (Ch. 1904), affd. on other grounds, 68 N.J. Eq. 680, 62 A. 408 (Ct. Err. & App. 1905); Small v. Sullivan, 245 N.Y. 343, 157 N.E. 261 (1927).

stock-for-stock combination should require approval by the survivor's shareholders when the amount of common stock issued or issuable by the survivor is material – say, 20 percent or more of the stock outstanding prior to the transaction. Such transactions normally effect both a significant restructuring of the enterprise and a significant reallocation of the underlying ownership interests, and normally involve investment rather than management kinds of considerations. (Furthermore, they usually take considerable time to consummate because of the necessity of registering the survivor's stock, so that a requirement of shareholder approval would be unlikely to cause untoward delay.) At least where the statute provides only that "the business and affairs of the corporation shall be managed by" the board, such transactions should therefore be for the body of shareholders.

B. A Modern Statutory Treatment

Turning now to the question of optimal statutory treatment, it seems clear that from the perspective of the survivor's shareholders, the statutory treatment accorded stock-for-stock combinations should parallel that accorded classical mergers and stock-for-assets combinations. Thus the Ohio statute provides for shareholder approval and appraisal rights in connection with the acquisition by the survivor of shares carrying a majority of the transferor's voting power, in exchange for shares in the survivor carrying one-sixth or more of its voting power immediately after the transaction.[30] Similarly, the New Jersey statute confers voting and appraisal rights on shareholders of the survivor, if the survivor acquires *any* amount of stock in exchange for common stock or other securities equivalent to 40 percent of its common stock outstanding after the transaction on a fully converted basis.[31] And both the New York and American stock exchanges require shareholder approval as a condition to the listing of stock which is issued in connection with the acquisition of securities, where the

30. Ohio Rev. Code Ann. tit. 17, §§1701.01(R), (S), (T), 1701.83(A), 1701.84 (D) (Page Supp. 1974). Voting power is measured by voting power in the election of directors.

31. N.J. Stat. Ann. §14A:10-12 (Supp. 1974). See also ch. 682, §§181(c), 1200, 1201, 1300, [1975-76 Reg. Sess.] Calif. Leg. Serv. 1808, 1852-1853; R.I. Gen. Laws Ann. §7-1.1-70.1 (1970).

present or potential issuance of common or convertible securities could result in an increase of 20 percent in the survivor's outstanding common.[32]

§15.3. The Cash Modes

As noted at the outset of Part IV, the two stock modes of combination are complemented by two cash modes: cash-for-assets and cash-for-stock. As in the case of the stock modes, the impact of cash combinations on shareholders turns in part on the perspective from which the transaction is viewed and whether the transaction involves assets or stock.

A. Cash-For-Assets Combinations

1. The transferor's shareholders. Under the traditional statutes, a sale of substantially all assets for cash requires the approval of the transferor's shareholders. This is as it should be: such a transaction constitutes a radical reconstruction of the enterprise from the transferor's perspective. There is, however, an important difference between a stock-for-assets and a cash-for-assets transaction. Where the transfer is for stock, the result is not only a radically restructured but a continuing enterprise; but where the transfer is for cash and the transferor is immediately liquidated (as is typically the case), the transferor's shareholders are not being brought along in a continuing enterprise, and appraisal rights may therefore be unnecessary, except perhaps as a check on the fairness of price in a self-dealing situation.[33]

2. The survivor's shareholders. A cash-for-assets transaction looks much different from the perspective of the survivor's shareholders. An initial question from this perspective is whether such transactions are mergers within the meaning of the traditional statutes. At one time it would have been fairly clear they were not, since a classical merger involved the issuance of stock by the

32. New York Stock Exchange, Company Manual, at A-284; CCH, American Stock Exchange Guide ¶10,032.

33. Cf. N.J. Stat. Ann. §14A:11-1(b)(ii) (Supp. 1974); N.Y. Bus. Corp. Law §910(B) (McKinney Supp. 1974); Model Bus. Corp. Act §80(b) (1969 rev.); Folk, Corporation Statutes 1959-1966, 1966 Duke L.J. 875, 945-946 (1966).

survivor. Today, however, it is common for merger provisions to contemplate the issuance of cash,[34] and it seems likely that, properly or improperly, these provisions will be interpreted to permit the issuance solely of cash.[35] Under such an interpretation, a cash-for-assets transaction could be viewed as a merger within the meaning of the traditional statutes. On the other hand, such transactions could also be viewed as purchases, and which view should be taken may properly depend on underlying policy considerations. Unlike stock-for-assets combinations, an acquisition of substantially all of a transferor's assets by a survivor for cash may involve neither an increase in the size of the survivor's assets (but instead only a reshuffling of liquid into fixed assets), nor a reallocation of ownership interests. From the survivor's perspective cash-for-assets combinations will therefore frequently be difficult to distinguish from internal expansion; that is, they will frequently not rise to the level of a structural change. Therefore, such transactions should not normally require approval by the survivor's shareholders nor give rise to appraisal rights for such shareholders.

B. Cash-For-Stock Combinations

1. The transferor's shareholders. It has already been shown that a stock-for-stock combination should not require *approval* by the transferor's shareholders, but that if the acquiring corporation achieves a dominant position, nontransferring shareholders should have a right to compel the survivor to cash them out. The reasons behind these conclusions, and therefore the conclusions themselves, are equally applicable to cash-for-stock combinations.

2. The survivor's shareholders. From the perspective of the survivor's shareholders a cash-for-stock combination is virtually identical to a cash-for-assets combination, and the same conclusions again follow: neither approval nor appraisal rights would normally be appropriate.

34. Del. Code Ann. tit. 8, §251(b) (1974); N.J. Stat. Ann. §14A:10-1 (2)(c)(Supp. 1974); N.Y. Bus. Corp. Law §902(a)(3) (McKinney 1963); Ohio Rev. Code Ann. §1701.78(B)(8) (Page Supp. 1974); Pa. Stat. Ann. tit. 15, §1902(A)(4) (Supp. 1974); ABA Model Bus. Corp. Act §71(c) (1969 rev.).

35. Cf. Kipp & Wallum, Acquisitions and Attendant Shareholder Rights, 23 Rutgers L. Rev. 723, 728-729, and the authorities cited in note 5, supra. But cf. Outwater v. Public Service Corporation, 103 N.J. Eq. 461, 143 A. 729 (Ch. 1928), affd., 104 N.J. Eq. 528, 158 A. 402 (Ct. Err. & App. 1929).

V
Structural Changes

CONTRACTIONS AND DIVISIONS

16

Corporate Contractions

SELL-OFFS AND PARTIAL LIQUIDATIONS

Part IV was concerned with corporate combinations, many of which center on the transfer by a corporation of substantially all of its assets. Another major set of modern corporate transactions, contractions and divisions, center on the transfer of a business which comprises a significant portion, but less than substantially all, of a corporation's total assets. Contractions will be considered in this chapter; divisions, in chapter 17.

§16.1. Sell-Offs

A. Treatment Under the Traditional Corporate Statutes

The simplest type of corporate contraction — frequently referred to as a sell-off[1] — is one in which the corporation disposes of a significant business (meaning a business comprising a significant portion but less than substantially all of its total assets) to a third party, in exchange for consideration which it retains, rather than distributes.[2] Such transactions are not explicitly covered by the traditional corporate statutes, unless they fall within the provi-

1. See, e.g., Corporate Sell-Off, Mergers & Acquisitions, Spring 1975, at 34.

2. Typically the consideration in such cases is cash, but not infrequently it consists of stock or notes of the transferee, or some combination of stock, notes, and cash. See, e.g., Dolly Madison to Sell Ice Cream Operations, Furniture Factories, Wall St. J., Apr. 1, 1970, at 14, col. 2; Fedders Acquires Borg-Warner's Norge Division, Wall St. J., July 3, 1968, at 2, col. 2.

sions governing a "sale . . . of all or substantially all of the assets of a corporation." One ambiguous term in these provisions – "sale" – has already been discussed.[3] A second ambiguous term must now be explored – "substantially all . . . assets."

1. Where the transferor does not retain significant operating assets. By hypothesis the transferor in a sell-off has not disposed of substantially all of its total assets. Assume first that while the transferor retains a significant amount of liquid assets (such as cash, accounts receivable, marketable securities held for investment, or the like), it does not retain significant operating assets; in short, assume the transfer involves less than substantially all of the transferor's *total* assets but substantially all of its *operating* assets. Whether the sale-of-substantially-all-assets provisions are applicable to such a case raises the question whether the measurement of "substantially all . . . assets" is strictly quantitative, that is, based solely on the proportion between the value of the assets conveyed and the value of the assets retained, or also has a qualitative aspect, that is, takes into account the nature of the assets conveyed and retained. To put this in statutory terms, does the term "assets" as used in these provisions mean "total assets" or "operating assets"?

This question has been but seldom confronted by the corporate-law cases. Of the relatively small number of cases in which the issue of what constitutes "substantially all" assets has been squarely raised, many have either been relatively simple – involving, for example, the disposition of more than 95 percent[4] or less than 10 percent[5] of the transferor's total assets – or have not made explicit the nature or amount of assets involved.[6] However, the background of the provisions sheds some light on the problem. It is generally accepted that at common law a sale of substantially all assets required unanimous shareholder approval, on the theory that it breached an implied contract among the shareholders to further the corporate enterprise, and that the purpose of the sale-of-substantially-all-assets provisions was to modify the rigor of this

3. See chapter 14, supra.

4. See Prince George's Country Club, Inc. v. Edward R. Carr, Inc., 235 Md. 591, 202 A.2d 354 (1964).

5. See Klopot v. Northrup, 131 Conn. 14, 37 A.2d 700 (1944).

6. See Keck Enterprises, Inc. v. Braunschweiger, 108 F. Supp. 925 (S.D. Cal. 1952); Frankel v. Tremont Norman Motors Corp., 21 Misc. 2d 20, 193 N.Y.S.2d 722 (Sup. Ct. 1959), affd., 10 App. Div. 2d 680, 197 N.Y.S.2d 576 (1960), affd., 8 N.Y.2d 901, 168 N.E.2d 823, 204 N.Y.S.2d 146 (1960).

rule by reducing the required shareholder approval from unanimity to two-thirds or a majority.[7] In other words, these provisions were aimed at dispositions which would have required unanimous approval at common law because they effectively put the corporation out of the business in which it was engaged. In light of this background, the provisions should be applicable if substantially all operating assets are disposed of, notwithstanding the retention of a large amount of liquid assets, unless perhaps the operating assets were themselves not significant.

The few cases that have explicitly considered transactions in the grey area tend to support this conclusion. Thus in *Stiles v. Aluminum Products Co.*, the corporation sold all of its operating assets but retained liquid (and a small amount of nonliquid) assets amounting to 35 percent of total assets. The court held that the transaction constituted a sale of "substantially all" of the corporation's assets within the meaning of the Illinois statute.[8]

Similarly, in *Campbell v. Vose*[9] Southwestern Cotton Oil Company transferred all of its tangible operating assets to a subsidiary, retaining cash, promissory notes, and an investment portfolio; the book value of the transferred assets was 495,000 dollars, against a book value of 981,000 dollars for those retained. A shareholder then brought an action for appraisal under the Oklahoma statute, on the ground that the transfer constituted a sale of substantially all assets. The court agreed:

> The statute is in purely quantitative terms, but the [plaintiff] urges that other considerations exist because the assets transferred were all the "operating assets," and only money or investments remained. The record shows that the Cotton Oil Company had engaged in dual activities for several years, the plant operations (storage and machine shops) on one hand, and investments of the accumulated earnings on the other hand.
>
> In the corporate resolution relating to the transfer, the recitation is made that the desire was to separate the "operating business activities from its investment activites." . . . Thus the corporate changes sur-

7. See, e.g., Note, Interplay of Rights of Shareholders Dissenting from Sale of Corporate Assets, 58 Colum. L. Rev. 251, 252-253 (1958); Note, Dispositions of Corporate Assets, 43 N.C.L. Rev. 957, 958-959 (1965).

8. 338 Ill. App. 48, 86 N.E.2d 887 (1949); cf. Philadelphia Natl. Bank v. B.S.F. Co., 41 Del. Ch. 509, 199 A.2d 557 (Ch. 1964), revd. on other grounds, 42 Del. Ch. 106, 204 A.2d 746 (Sup. Ct. 1964); Stephenson v. Plastics Corp., 276 Minn. 400, 414-415, 150 N.W.2d 668, 678-679 (1967).

9. 515 F.2d 256 (10th Cir. 1975).

> rounding the creation of the subsidiary, the separation of the business activities with the result that the parent corporation has only investments, makes the transfer of assets have much different implications than it would ordinarily have. . . . [F]or all practical purposes, "substantially" all of the assets were sold. All the effective operating assets were sold. The investment segment remaining was large in dollars but was the last and a large step in the change in the nature of corporate activity. In these circumstances, more than dollar values must be considered.[10]

Several other cases have also indicated in dicta that the applicability of substantially-all-assets provisions turns on such tests as whether the transaction "tends to interfere with the integrity of the corporation and to impair its capacity to perform its functions as a going concern,"[11] or involves "a part [of the assets] essential to the continuance of the corporate enterprise."[12]

10. Id. at 260. In Ostlind v. Ostlind Valve, Inc., 178 Ore. 161, 165 P.2d 779 (1946), the corporation's assets consisted of approximately 55,000 dollars in cash and a 27 percent interest in certain patents held by a trust. The corporation wished to have the patents sold by the trust for 100,000 dollars plus royalties. Plaintiff, a minority shareholder, brought an action in which he objected, among other things, to the use of corporate funds (rather than a broker working on a commission) to promote this sale. The court rejected this position, but noted that "The powers of directors are not unlimited but extend only to the ordinary or regular business of the corporation. . . . The sale of the corporation's last remaining asset, other than its cash, would not be, of course, the transaction of its ordinary business. . . . It need hardly be added that the sale . . . will not be valid unless made with the consent of two-thirds of the issued capital stock [under the relevant sale-of-substantially-all-assets provision]." 178 Ore. at 191-192, 165 P.2d at 791. In Krell v. Krell Piano Co., 23 Ohio N.P. (n.s.) 193 (Sup. Ct. 1920), affd. on other grounds, 14 Ohio App. 74, motion to certify record denied, 14 Ohio App. xxxviii (1921), a lower court held that a transfer of a corporation's entire operating assets for $155,000 worth of preferred stock was not a sale of the "entire property and assets" of the corporation within the meaning of the statute because non-operating assets (in excess of $200,000) were retained. An appellate court assumed, without deciding, that the transaction did constitute the sale of the corporation's entire property and assets, but upheld the lower court's decision on other grounds. In Gimbel v. Signal Cos., 316 A.2d 599, 605-608 (Del. Ch.), affd. per curiam, 316 A.2d 619 (Del. 1974), which held that a sale of operations accounting for 26 percent of total assets, 41 percent of total net worth, and 15 percent of revenues and earnings did not constitute a sale of substantially all assets, the Chancellor seemed to suggest, in a murky opinion, that the test under the Delaware statute was qualitative as well as quantitative, and distinguished the Philadelphia Natl. Bank case, supra note 8, on the ground that the corporation in that case had sold its "only substantial income producing asset."

11. Santa Fe Hills Golf & Country Club v. Safehi Realty Co., 349 S.W.2d 27, 36 (Mo. 1961).

12. Fontaine v. Brown County Motors Co., 251 Wis. 433, 438, 29 N.W.2d 744, 747 (1947). For comparable formulations of the common law rule, see In re De Camp Glass Casket Co., 272 F. 558, 564 (6th Cir.), cert. denied, 256 U.S. 703 (1921); Rollins

Similar results have been reached, in a different context, under the reorganization provisions of the Internal Revenue Code. Thus under section 368(a)(1)(C) of the Code, a stock-for-assets transaction may qualify as a reorganization if it involves "substantially all of the properties" of the transferor. In *Revenue Ruling* 57-518, the Commissioner ruled that in applying this provision, "what constitutes 'substantially all of the properties' . . . will depend upon the facts and circumstances in each case rather than upon any particular percentage. Among the elements of importance that are to be considered in arriving at the conclusion are the nature of the properties retained by the transferor, the purpose of the retention, and the amount thereof."[13] In *James Armour, Incorporated,* the tax court held that a comparable requirement in section 354(b)(1) was satisfied where "as a result of the transactions [the transferee] either acquired title to, or the use of, all the assets essential to the conduct of [the transferor's] business enterprise," although only 51 percent of the transferor's total assets had been conveyed.[14]

In short, shareholder approval should normally be required under the sale-of-substantially-all-assets provisions when a corporation sells substantially all of its operating assets, even though it does not sell substantially all of its total assets.

2. Where the transferor does retain significant operating assets. Now suppose that the transferor has two or more significant businesses, and disposes of only one. Should the sale-of-substantially-all-assets provisions still be applicable? Such a result would be hard to fit within the statutory language, even granted that the term "assets" refers primarily to operating assets.[15] But

---

v. Clay, 33 Me. 132, 139 (1851); In re Timmis, 200 N.Y. 177, 181, 93 N.E. 522, 523 (1910); Abbot v. American Hard Rubber Co., 33 Barb. 578 (N.Y. Sup. Ct. 1861); cf. Siegel, When Corporations Divide: A Statutory and Financial Analysis, 79 Harv. L. Rev. 534, 541 (1966).

13. 1957-2 Cum. Bull. 253, 254; cf. Rev. Proc. 66-34, 1966-2 Cum. Bull. 1232, 1233. See also Moffatt v. Commissioner, 363 F.2d 262 (9th Cir. 1966). See generally B. Bittker & J. Eustice, Federal Income Taxation of Corporations and Shareholders 14-41 to 14-44 (3d ed. 1971).

14. 43 T.C. 295, 309 (1964). See also American Mfg. Co., 55 T.C. 204, 221-222 (1970).

15. See Gimbel v. Signal Cos., 316 A.2d 599, 605-608 (Del. Ch.) affd. per curiam, 316 A.2d 619 (Del. 1974).

Again, this may be a result of corporate practice outrunning the statutes. When the sale-of-substantially-all-assets provisions statutes were enacted, single-purpose corthe fact that the transaction does not constitute a sale of substantially all assets does not necessarily mean that it is a board matter. For example, assume that a corporation has two businesses, *A* and *B*, which comprise 60 and 40 percent, respectively, of its operating and total assets. Presumably, 60 percent does not constitute "substantially all," yet it seems clear that a sale of business *A* would transcend "manage[ment of] the corporation's business"; and this would be equally true of any disposition of a significant corporate business, other than in the ordinary course. At least under those statutes which provide only that the board shall manage the corporation's business and affairs, therefore, such dispositions should be shareholder matters: they work a significant change in the structure of the enterprise; they involve investment rather than purely business skills – an evaluation of whether the business in question is worth the offering price; they occur relatively infrequently in the life of a corporation; and they are likely to take a relatively long time to consummate in any event.[16]

Against this view it might be argued that the effects of the sale-of-substantially-all-assets provisions is to render shareholder approval of a sale of less than substantially all assets unnecessary by negative implication. The historical context of these provisions, however, shows that such an argument would be unsound. There are two very different legal reasons for requiring shareholder approval for any given transaction: (1) because the transaction is impermissible under the certificate of incorporation, or (2) because the certificate or the relevant statute makes the transaction permissible only if shareholder approval is obtained. A transaction which falls into the first category normally requires *unanimous* shareholder approval, on the theory that a certificate is a contract between the shareholders, and absent a reserved-power

porations were dominant. E. Latty & G. Frampton, Basic Business Associations – Cases, Text and Problems 312 (1963); A. A. Berle, Economic Power in A Free Society, in The Corporation Take-Over 86, 88 (A. Hacker ed. 1965). In today's world, however, multibusiness corporations are common. For example, an analysis of the 500 largest industrial corporations showed that only 102 were operating in a single business category, while 235 were operating in four or more categories and 46 were operating in eight or more. O'Hanlon, The Odd News about Conglomerates, Fortune, June 1967, at 175. (This analysis employed 54 categories, derived from those employed in the U.S. Budget Bureau's Standard Industrial Classification Manual.)

16. But see Gimbel v. Signal Cos., 316 A.2d 599, 606 (Del. Ch.), affd. per curiam, 316 A.2d 619 (Del. 1974).

clause can therefore be amended only by unanimous consent. A transaction which falls into the second category, however, normally requires only *majority* approval (unless the law or certificate requires a stated high majority), on the theory that corporate bodies normally act by majority vote when acting within their powers. As has been shown, at common law a sale of substantially all assets required unanimous shareholder approval because it was regarded as a breach of an implied term of the certificate. A major purpose of the sale-of-substantially-all-assets provisions was to alleviate this rule;[17] there is nothing to indicate that these provisions were also intended to dispense with requirements of shareholder approval *otherwise* imposed by law.[18] Thus in *Fontaine v. Brown County Motors Corporation,* the court stated:

> The purpose of [the Wisconsin sale-of-substantially-all-assets provision] was to change the common law rule. . . . The subsection applies only to those conveyances for which unanimous consent was required at the common law. To the extent that corporate conveyances at the common law did not require unanimous consent, the statute is inapplicable and the common law remains in effect.[19]

B. A Modern Statutory Treatment

For reasons just examined, a modern corporate statute should require shareholder approval for the sale of a significant portion of a corporation's operating assets, not made in the ordinary course of business. Appraisal rights are a different matter;

17. See text accompanying note 7, supra. Thus many cases have held that where a sale of substantially all assets is in the ordinary course of business it does not require shareholder approval, despite the fact that the relevant sale-of-substantially-all-assets provision is literally applicable, on the theory that these provisions were not intended to affect such sales because at common law they did not require unanimous shareholder approval. See Note, Dispositions of Corporate Assets, supra note 7, at 960.

18. SEC, Report on the Study and Investigation of the Work, Activities, Personnel, and Functions of Protective and Reorganization Committees, pt. VII, at 576 (1938).

The silence of most statutes on the treatment of sales of less than substantially all assets is brought into sharp focus by the Connecticut statute, which explicitly deals with such transactions, albeit unwisely: "[A]ny sale of less than substantially all assets . . . may be made upon such terms and conditions and for such consideration as may be authorized by [the] board of directors." Conn. Gen. Stat. Ann. tit. 33, § 33-372(c) (Supp. 1975).

19. 251 Wis. 433, 437, 29 N.W.2d 744, 747 (1947); cf. Aiple v. Twin City Barge & Towing Co., 274 Minn. 38, 143 N.W.2d 374 (1966).

most such transactions do not work so radical a restructuring of the enterprise that dissenting shareholders should be given a right to exit. To facilitate planning, the statute should lay down a quantitative test of significance for voting-rights purposes — say, 20 percent of the net book value of a corporation's assets other than cash, accounts receivable, and interest-bearing obligations. The feasibility of such a measurement is indicated by the fact that a closely comparable measurement is already called for under the SEC's Form 8-K, which requires the reporting of dispositions involving "a significant amount of assets," defined to include those in which "the registrant's . . . equity in the net book value of such assets . . . exceeded 10 percent of the [registrant's] total assets. . . ."[20]

§16.2. Partial Liquidations

Where the proceeds of a sell-off are retained by the transferor, the immediate effect of the transaction is a contraction of its operating enterprise. In some cases, however, a sell-off is followed by a distribution of the proceeds to the transferor's shareholders; or, perhaps more rarely, the assets of a significant business may be distributed to the shareholders directly, while one or more other businesses are retained. Such transactions constitute not merely a contraction but a partial liquidation of the enterprise.

The tax laws have an important effect in motivating this type of transaction. A corporate distribution is normally taxed as a dividend at ordinary income rates, provided it is covered by earnings and profits accumulated in prior years or generated in the current year.[21] This tax treatment produces shareholder pressure to find methods of making distributions that will be taxed either not at all, or at capital gains rates. A distribution in complete liquidation normally qualifies for capital gains treatment,[22] but as long as the goose is laying golden eggs the shareholders may wish a

20. Form 8-K, Item 2, Instruction 4.

21. Int. Rev. Code §§301(a), 301(c)(1), 316(a). If the distribution is made out of accumulated earnings it will be taxed as a dividend only if the earnings were accumulated after February 28, 1913, but this limitation seldom comes into play. See B. Bittker & J. Eustice, supra note 13, at 7-2.

22. Int. Rev. Code §331(a)(1).

more palatable alternative. One such alternative is offered by sections 331 and 346 of the Internal Revenue Code, which provide, speaking very generally, that a distribution in connection with the termination of a corporate business may qualify as a distribution in partial liquidation, taxable at only capital gains rates, if one or more other businesses are retained.[23] Such a distribution leaves the shareholder in the best of all possible economic worlds, retaining stock in a going corporation, and receiving capital gains cash (or assets which are presumably convertible into cash). Thus the tax laws powerfully reinforce, if in fact they do not shape, the motives generating partial liquidations.

Such transactions are not explicitly covered by the traditional corporate statutes.[24] If they are nevertheless to be squeezed within the mold of those statutes, they must therefore be divided

23. Section 346(a)(2) provides that a distribution shall be treated as in partial liquidation if it "is not essentially equivalent to a dividend, is in redemption of a part of the stock of the corporation pursuant to a plan, and occurs within the taxable year . . . , including (but not limited to) a distribution which meets the requirements of subsection (b)." Section 346(b) provides that a distribution "shall be treated as a distribution described in subsection (a)(2) if . . . [it] is attributable to the corporation's ceasing to conduct, or consists of the assets of, a trade or business which has been actively conducted throughout the 5-year period immediately before the distribution" by the corporation – or, in certain cases, by a predecessor in interest – and the corporation retains at least one other such business. The businesses involved may not have to be separate prior to the distribution or exchange. See Treas. Reg. §1.346-1(c)(ii); Rev. Rul. 75-160, Int. Rev. Bull. No. 1975-18. Although §346(a)(2) does not specify what kinds of distributions it covers, other than those which qualify under §346(b), it is generally understood to contemplate distributions attributable to non-346(b) corporate contractions. See B. Bittker & J. Eustice, supra note 13, at 9-49. However, because of the uncertain contours of this concept, and the fact that a distribution which does not qualify under §346 would ordinarily be taxed at ordinary-income rates, taxpayers who are not sure they qualify under §346(b) may be reluctant to go forward under §346(a)(2). See id. at 9-56 to 9-57.

24. Illinois and Pennsylvania both have provisions requiring shareholder approval for distributions "in partial liquidation." Ill. Ann. Stat. ch. 32, §157.41a (Smith-Hurd 1954); Pa. Stat. Ann. tit. 15, §1703 (1967). However, as used in these provisions the term seems to refer to distributions out of reduction surplus (however created), rather than distributions out of the proceeds of a contraction at the business level. See Eisenberg, The Legal Roles of Shareholders and Management in Modern Corporate Decisionmaking, 57 Calif. L. Rev. 1, 163-169 (1969); Hackney, The Pennsylvania Business Corporation Law Amendments, 19 U. Pitt. L. Rev. 51, 73 (1957); Mulford, Corporate Distributions to Shareholders and other Amendments to the Pennsylvania Business Corporation Law, 106 U. Pa. L. Rev. 536, 548-549 (1958). See also Wis. Stat. Ann. §180.39 (1957 & Supp. 1974); Bugge, Unrealized Appreciation as a Source of Shareholder Distributions Under the Wisconsin Business Corporations Law, 1964 Wis. L. Rev. 292, 309-310.

into their component parts: the disposition of the business (assuming that the assets are not distributed directly), and the distribution of the proceeds. Whether a *disposition* requires shareholder approval under the traditional statutes would depend on whether it falls within the sale-of-substantially-all-assets provisions. As has been seen, these provisions are probably inapplicable to the sale of a significant business where, as in a partial liquidation, another is retained.[25] Whether the *distribution* requires shareholder approval would depend on the amount of surplus available for distribution to shareholders. If such surplus equals or exceeds the amount of the proposed distribution, board action would normally suffice. If not, then capital would have to be reduced to create reduction surplus sufficient to cover the distribution.[26] Under some[27] but not all[28] statutes, shareholder action would usually be required to effect such a reduction, although once the necessary reduction surplus was created, most statutes permit the board to make a distribution from that source without any further shareholder approval.[29]

In short, the traditional statutes explicitly require shareholder approval of a partial liquidation only where the amount to be distributed exceeds the surplus available to the board for dividends. However, the lack of an explicit requirement does not necessarily mean that board action suffices. It has already been shown that even a simple sell-off should be a shareholder matter if it involves a significant amount of the corporation's operating

25. See text at note 15, supra.

26. Cf. Siegel, supra note 12, at 547. But cf. Stephenson v. Plastics Corp., 276 Minn. 400, 409-411, 150 N.W.2d 668, 676-677 (1967); Hoberg v. John Hoberg Co., 170 Wis. 50, 173 N.W. 634, modified, 170 Wis. 57, 173 N.W. 952 (1919).

27. See Ill. Ann. Stat. ch. 32, §157.59 (Smith-Hurd 1954); Ohio Rev. Stat. Ann. §§1701.31(D), (E), 1701.69(B)(8) (Page 1964); Pa. Stat. Ann. tit. 15, §1706 (1967); ABA Model Bus. Corp. Act §69 (1969 rev.).

28. See Del. Code Ann. tit. 8, §244(a) (1974); N.J. Stat. Ann. §14A:7-19 (Supp. 1974); N.Y. Bus. Corp. Law §516 (McKinney 1963).

29. See Del. Code Ann. tit. 8, §170 (1974); N.J. Stat. Ann. §14A:7-14 (1974); N.Y. Bus. Corp. Law §510 (McKinney 1963 & Supp. 1974). But see Ill. Ann. Stat. ch. 32, §157.41a (Smith-Hurd 1954); Pa. Stat. Ann. tit. 15, §1703 (1967); ABA Model Bus. Corp. Act §46 (rev. 1969).

Where shareholder approval is not required such distributions may be subject to other safeguards, such as a requirement that the shareholders be notified of the source of the distribution. See Cal. Corp. Code §1500(c) (West Supp. 1974); N.J. Stat. Ann. §14A:7-17(1) (1974); N.Y. Bus. Corp. Law §510(c) (McKinney 1963).

assets. The case for requiring shareholder approval of a partial liquidation is even stronger, since its effect on the structure of the enterprise is more drastic. The feasibility of such a requirement is indicated by the fact that such approval must usually be obtained in any event, although for adventitious reasons. Since a distribution in partial liquidation is typically very large, shareholder approval is often needed to create reduction surplus to support it.[30] In addition, such approval is usually required as a practical matter if the shareholders want to enjoy the benefits of section 346. To qualify under that section, a distribution must be "in redemption of a part of the stock of the corporation pursuant to a plan. . . ."[31] This provision is normally satisfied through a voluntary pro rata surrender of shares, a reverse stock split effecting an involuntary contraction of the number of outstanding shares, or a reduction in the per-share par value of outstanding shares.[32] The first method implies informal but unanimous shareholder agreement; the latter two require amendment of the corporation's certificate, and therefore require formal shareholder approval.[33]

30. See Siegel, supra note 12, at 547.

31. Int. Rev. Code §346(a)(2).

32. Cf. Fowler Hosiery Co. v. Commissioner, 301 F.2d 394, 397 (7th Cir. 1962); B. Bittker & J. Eustice, supra note 13, at 9-52; Notice of Annual Meeting of Stockholders and Proxy Statement of The Murray Corporation of America, November 14, 1963, at 3-4, 6.

33. In theory, at least, the redemption might be accomplished without shareholder approval through a purchase by the corporation of the necessary amount of stock. However, state law may impose restrictions on the power of a corporation to purchase its own stock, see Ohio Rev. Code Ann. tit. 17, §1701.35 (Page Supp. 1966), and such purchases may also give rise to complications under Rule 10b-5. Furthermore, if such purchases are consummated through private agreements with less than all of the shareholders they may be subject to attack by nonparticipating shareholders on the ground of discriminatory treatment, cf. Iback v. Elevator Supplies Co., 118 N.J. Eq. 90, 93, 177 A. 458, 459 (Ch. 1935); General Inv. Co. v. American Hide & Leather Co., 98 N.J. Eq. 326, 331, 129 A. 244, 246 (Ct. Err. & App. 1925); Theis v. Durr, 125 Wis. 651, 104 N.W. 985 (1905); Herwitz, Stock Redemptions and the Accumulated Income Tax, 74 Harv. L. Rev. 886, 894 (1961); Israels, Are Corporate Powers Still Held in Trust?, 64 Colum. L. Rev. 1446, 1452-1453 (1964); but cf. Martin v. American Potash & Chem. Corp., 33 Del. Ch. 234, 92 A.2d 295 (Sup. Ct. 1952); if they are consummated on the market they may artificially drive up the price of the stock and subject management to a charge of waste; and if they are consummated through a tender offer the amount of the resulting distribution will be uncertain, and if it is significantly less than the proceeds "attributable to" the disposition within the meaning of §346(b), may not qualify for §346 treatment.

On the other hand, it is questionable whether a partial liquidation should give rise to appraisal rights. Although it may result in a drastically restructured enterprise, an integral part of the restructuring is the release to the shareholder of a significant portion of his capital. The appraisal right may therefore not be as important in this case as it is in transactions involving a rededication of the shareholder's investment.

17

Corporate Divisions

SPIN-OFFS, SPLIT-OFFS, AND SPLIT-UPS

The transactions considered in this chapter involve the division of a corporation into at least two parts, through the distribution or exchange of stock in one or more subsidiaries, each of which holds a significant business constituting less than substantially all of the parent's assets. In a *spin-off,* the parent distributes the subsidiary's stock to its shareholders on a pro rata basis. In a *split-off,* the parent exchanges with shareholders, pro rata or disproportionately, stock in the subsidiary for stock in itself. In a *split-up,* the parent distributes or exchanges, pro rata or disproportionately, the stock of two or more subsidiaries which constitute all of its assets.[1]

As in the case of partial liquidations, such transactions may be motivated by business or tax reasons. The most common business reason is a need to separate the ownership of the corporation's businesses, in response to such external pressures as antitrust or regulatory law, or such internal pressures as shareholder dissension.[2] As to tax reasons, it has already been seen that the income tax laws result in pressure to generate distributions which will not be taxed at ordinary income rates, and that section 346 of the Internal Revenue Code provides one outlet for this pressure. A similar outlet is provided by section 355, which, broadly speaking, provides that spin-offs, split-offs, and split-ups will be tax-free if

1. See Bales, The Business Purpose of Corporate Separations, 56 Va. L. Rev. 1242, 1243 n. 10 (1970); Siegel, When Corporations Divide: A Statutory and Financial Analysis, 79 Harv. L. Rev. 534, 535 (1966).

2. See generally Bales, supra note 1.

(1) the parent distributes stock representing at least 80 percent of the subsidiary's stock,[3] (2) immediately after the distribution the parent and the subsidiary (or in a split-up all of the subsidiaries) are engaged in the active conduct of a trade or business which has been actively conducted by parent or subsidiary during the preceding five years,[4] and (3) the transaction is not used "principally as a device for the distribution of earnings and profits."[5]

Business and tax reasons therefore combine to make these transactions fairly common.[6] Despite this fact, they are not explicitly dealt with by the traditional corporate statutes. If such transactions are nevertheless to be squeezed within the mold of those statutes, they must therefore be divided into their component parts – the transfer of a business to the subsidiary, and the distribution or exchange of the subsidiary's stock.

§17.1. The Transfer of a Business to a Subsidiary

Is shareholder approval required for a transfer to a subsidiary of a portion of the parent's assets in exchange for its stock? At common law, "the power of a corporation . . . [to] hold stock in other corporations . . . [was] involved in doubt."[7] Toward the

3. Int. Rev. Code § §355(a)(1)(A), (D), 368(c). In the case of voting stock, the measurement is by voting power; in the case of other shares, by number. If the parent owns more than 80 percent of the subsidiary's stock it may retain the excess if it can satisfy the Internal Revenue Service that retention is "not in pursuance of a plan having as one of its principal purposes the avoidance of Federal income tax." Id. at §355(a)(1)(D)(ii).

4. Id. at § §355(a)(1)(C), 355(b). In certain cases the five-year period may be satisfied by tacking on ownership by a corporate predecessor. The businesses involved do not necessarily have to be separate prior to the distribution or exchange. See Rev. Rul. 75-160, Int. Rev. Bull. No. 1975-18; Rafferty v. Commissioner, 452 F.2d 767 (1st Cir. 1971), cert. denied, 408 U.S. 922 (1972); United States v. Marett, 325 F.2d 28 (5th Cir. 1963); Edmund P. Coady, 33 T.C. 771 (1960), affd., 289 F.2d 490 (6th Cir. 1961).

5. Int. Rev. Code §355(a)(1)(B).

6. See Spinning Faster?, Forbes, March 15, 1968, at 46.

7. Robotham v. Prudential Ins. Co., 64 N.J. Eq. 673, 695, 53 A. 842, 851 (Ch. 1903). See J. Bonbright & G. Means, The Holding Company 55-57 (1932); 2 A. Dewing, The Financial Policy of Corporations 861-862 (5th ed. 1953); Note, Power of a Corporation to Acquire Stock of Another Corporation, 31 Colum. L. Rev. 281 (1931). See generally W. Noyes, A Treatise on the Law of Intercorporate Relations 472-509 (2d ed. 1909). This is not to say that the practice was unknown; a number of corporations had special charters empowering them to acquire and hold stock. See J. Bonbright & G. Means, supra, at 58-64; Compton, Early History of Stock Ownership by Corporations, 9 Geo. Wash. L. Rev. 125 (1940).

end of the nineteenth century, New Jersey enacted a provision in her general corporation law expressly conferring such a power,[8] and the other states soon followed suit.[9] However, since the legislative purpose was simply to confer a power upon the corporation, these provisions normally do not specify the body within the corporation which is to exercise the power. Two other provisions of the traditional statutes, though, may bear on the matter.

First, where the transfer involves substantially all of the parent's operating assets it might be deemed to fall within the sale-of-substantially-all-assets provision. In a spin-off or split-off, the transfer normally involves less than substantially all of the parent's operating assets. In a split-up, however, all of the parent's assets are held by subsidiaries, and at some point the parent therefore must transfer to one or more subsidiaries substantially all of the assets it then owns directly. But even that transfer may not fall within the traditional sale-of-substantially-all-assets provisions. For one thing, a transfer of assets to a subsidiary may not be deemed a "sale" within the meaning of these provisions, because of the transferor's continuity of interest in the transferred assets.[10] For

8. H. Ballantine, Corporations 236-237 (rev. ed. 1946).

9. See, e.g., Del. Code Ann. tit. 8, §123 (1974); Ill. Ann. Stat. ch. 32, §157.5(g) (Smith-Hurd Supp. 1974); N.J. Stat. Ann. §14A:3-1(f) (Supp. 1974); N.Y. Bus. Corp. Law §202(a)(6) (McKinney 1963).

10. See §14.1, supra. However, such a transaction was held to be a sale in Campbell v. Vose, 515 F.2d 256 (10th Cir. 1975):

> [Defendants] state in their brief that since the transferee was a wholly-owned subsidiary, the parent corporation still had enough "control" over the assets to prevent the transaction from being a sale. . . . [I]f the parent company has the usual relationship with the subsidiary . . . then the parent divested itself of possession and title to the assets, and placed them in the possession and control of the subsidiary. Thus it looks more like a sale or "other disposition" under the statute than anything else. An exchange for stock and for evidence of indebtedness was made, and the indicia of ownership were held by the subsidiary. We must hold that the transaction did bring into play the statutory rights of dissenting shareholders. . . .

Id. at 259-260.

The Pennsylvania statute explicitly requires shareholder approval for "[a] sale, lease, or exchange of all, or substantially all, the property and assets . . . of a corporation, whether to a subsidiary corporation or not. . . ." Pa. Stat. Ann. tit. 15, §1311(B) (1967). However, a sale, lease, or exchange to a wholly-owned subsidiary does not give rise to appraisal rights under the Pennsylvania statute unless "the preferences, qualifications, limitations, restrictions or special or relative rights, granted to or imposed upon the shares of any class of the parent corporation are . . . altered by such sale, lease, or exchange." Pa. Stat. Ann. tit. 15, §1311(D) (Supp. 1974).

another, if the transfers to the various subsidiaries take place over time, when the last transfer occurs, the parent, although it may not own any operating assets directly, will own a significant amount of such assets indirectly through its ownership of previously created subsidiaries. Even if the transfer constitutes a "sale," therefore, it may not constitute a sale of " substantially all" the parent's operating assets.

Second, where the subsidiary's certificate differs materially from the parent's, or the subsidiary retains authorized but unissued stock, the transfer might be deemed to fall within the traditional statutory provisions requiring shareholder approval for certificate amendments. For example, if the subsidiary's purpose clause differs from the parent's, the transferred assets may be dedicated to a purpose impermissible to the parent. If the subsidiary retains authorized but unissued stock, it may be possible for the board to create ownership rights in the transferred assets differing from the rights that could otherwise have been created without shareholder approval. In such cases, shareholder approval should be required to prevent subversion of the certificate-amendment provision. Thus in *Aiple v. Twin City Barge and Towing Company,*[11] the Minnesota court struck down a transfer of a division to a newly created subsidiary where only 10 percent of the subsidiary's authorized stock was to be issued to the parent and part or all of the rest would be sold to others:

> . . . Under the circumstances in this case the defendant corporation has attempted to split itself into two corporations for the obvious purpose of increasing the capital stock of the parent company without complying with the provisions of the statute governing that subject. The parent corporation has divided its assets with its own creature, capitalized a portion at a fixed valuation, and received back all of the shares of the stock issued by the subsidiary. If this can be done, the provisions [governing amendment of certificates] may be circumvented to the point where a corporation might fragment itself into any number of divisions, thus leaving minority stockholders without the protection that the statute was designed to give them.[12]

(The court further held that the statutory provisions empowering

11. 274 Minn. 38, 143 N.W.2d 374 (1966). This case is also discussed (and the facts are more fully stated) in chapter 8, text at notes 17-19, supra, and chapter 15, text at notes 27-29, supra.

12. 274 Minn. at 45, 143 N.W.2d at 378-379.

a corporation to acquire and hold stock "refer to the ordinary business transactions of the corporation and do not extend to a reconstruction of the corporate body itself."[13]) Similarly, in *Klopot v. Northrup,*[14] Newman Company proposed to transfer the assets of a division and cash to Miles Company, a corporation which it had organized, in exchange for Miles preferred and common stock. Under the plan Newman would retain the preferred, but would spin off the common to its shareholders. Miles's certificate contained two material provisions not present in Newman's: that its shareholders would have no preemptive rights, and that a contract approved by majority vote of the shareholders present at a meeting called for that purpose would be as valid as if all shareholders had approved, whether or not the contract would be otherwise open to legal attack "because of directors' interest or for any other reason." A shareholder in Newman attacked the plan as illegal. The court agreed, on the ground that the Miles certificate would work a significant change in the plaintiff's rights vis-à-vis the transferred assets:

> The reason why a stockholder . . . has . . . a pre-emptive . . . right . . . is that his ownership of a certain number of shares entitles him to a certain part in the assets and management of the corporation, and he is entitled of right to the opportunity to preserve his proportionate voice and interest. . . . As regards the business of manufacturing and selling the Miles garment, the plaintiff would have that share in it so long as it continued to be carried on by the Newman Company. Under the proposed plan, whether . . . he will continue to have the same proportionate interest will depend upon the will of directors of [Newman] company. When to this fact is added the further consideration that three of the defendants are a majority of the directors of the Miles Company and own a majority of the common stock, which alone has voting power, and that any act they may do as such directors in their private interests may, despite objection by the plaintiff, be validated by

13. 274 Minn. at 44, 143 N.W.2d at 378.

A dissenting judge argued that "The majority opinion in effect holds that the transfer of a part of the assets of defendant corporation to a subsidiary for the purpose of obtaining needed financing to attain corporate objectives cannot be regarded as within the ordinary course of the corporation's business. . . . In my judgment the conduct of corporate business through corporate subsidiaries . . . cannot be regarded as other than a common or ordinary manner of doing business." 274 Minn. at 45, 143 N.W.2d at 381. This argument misconceives the problem, which arose not from the transfer of assets to the subsidiary, but from the fact that it was contemplated that the subsidiary would issue stock to third parties.

14. 131 Conn. 14, 37 A.2d 700 (1944).

their votes as stockholders in a stockholders' meeting, the extent to which the interest of the plaintiff in the portion of business to be transferred to the Miles Company will be subject to the control of the defendant directors is apparent.[15]

§17.2. The Distribution or Exchange of the Subsidiary's Stock

The distribution or exchange in a split-up constitutes a complete liquidation, and accordingly requires shareholder approval under the provisions of the traditional statutes governing voluntary dissolution.[16] The distribution or exchange in a split-off or spin-off, however, does not involve a complete liquidation. The only provisions of the traditional statutes which might be applicable, therefore, are those requiring shareholder approval for the creation or utilization of reduction surplus where the amount of surplus required to cover the distribution or the acquisition of own shares would otherwise be lacking.[17]

15. 131 Conn. at 30, 37 A.2d at 707. See also Schwab v. E. G. Potter Co., 194 N.Y. 409, 87 N.E. 670 (1909); Moore v. Los Lugos Gold Mines, 172 Wash. 570, 21 P.2d 253 (1933). Although the principles enunciated in *Klopot* are sound the result may be questioned, because the proposed transaction had been approved by 78 percent of Newman's outstanding common and 54.3 percent of its outstanding preferred, apparently a sufficient number of votes to have amended the certificate. The court said that "even if . . . the certificate of [Newman] might be amended to include such provisions . . . the very directors who were instrumental in causing the provisions to be inserted in the certificate of incorporation of the Miles Company might not agree to their insertion in that of the parent company. . . ." 131 Conn. at 30, 37 A.2d at 707. However, it would seem preferable to permit the shareholders to approve the creation of a subsidiary with certificate provisions differing from those of the parent, provided the margin of approval is sufficient to have amended the parent's certificate.

16. Cal. Corp. Code §4600 (West 1955); Del. Code Ann. tit. 8, §275 (1974); Ill. Ann. Stat. ch. 32, §§157.75, 157.76 (Smith-Hurd 1954); N.J. Stat. Ann. §§14A:12-3, 14A:12-4 (1969); N.Y. Bus. Corp. Law §1001 (McKinney 1963); Ohio Rev. Code Ann. §1701.86 (Page 1964); Pa. Stat. Ann. tit. 15, §2102 (1967); ABA Model Bus. Corp. Act §§83, 94 (1969 rev.).

While in best usage "dissolution" probably should be restricted to termination of the legal entity, and "liquidation" to termination of the underlying enterprise, cf. 2 G. Hornstein, Corporation Law and Practice §§771-776 (1959), in requiring shareholder approval for "dissolution" the legislatures probably intended to cover termination of either entity or enterprise. Cf. Doe Run Lead Co. v. Maynard, 283 Mo. 646, 223 S.W. 600 (1920). In any event, as a practical matter liquidation of the enterprise is almost invariably accompanied by dissolution of the entity. Cf. 2 G. Hornstein, supra, at §775; Federal Crude Oil Co. v. State, 169 S.W.2d 283 (Tex. Civ. App.), cert. denied, 320 U.S. 758 (1943).

17. See chapter 16, text at notes 26-29; Siegel, supra note 1, at 547-548.

§17.3. An Integrated Approach

The fact that in many cases the traditional statutes do not explicitly require shareholder approval for dividing a corporation does not mean that such transactions are board matters. It has already been shown that shareholder approval should be required for a corporate contraction, if a significant business is involved, and a corporate division involving a significant business presents an even stronger case in this regard. "What was once an integrated business becomes legally separated immediately after the corporate division and, in time, economically separated. For this reason alone, stockholder vote would seem appropriate."[18] The feasibility of such a requirement is indicated by the fact that shareholder approval is often required as a practical matter in any event, because of the mechanics of the transactions. A split-up requires shareholder approval because it involves a complete liquidation. A split-off may be consummated by an exchange or a distribution. If it is consummated by an exchange, and the exchange is pro rata, either all the shareholders must informally agree, or there must be a reverse stock split, which requires formal shareholder approval. If the exchange is not pro rata it usually results from a unanimous shareholder agreement (and if it does not, shareholder approval would normally be sought to help forestall charges of discriminatory or unfair treatment). Finally, if a split-off is consummated by a distribution, shareholder approval is often required because the value of the distribution exceeds the surplus available to the board for dividends,[19] and the same is true of a spin-off.

To facilitate planning, a modern corporate statute should explicitly cover these transactions, and define significance for voting-rights purposes. A test which draws the line at 20 percent of operating assets on a consolidated basis would seem appropri-

18. Siegel, supra note 1, at 569; cf. Imperial Financial Services, Inc., [1964-1966 Transfer Binder] CCH Fed. Sec. L. Rep. ¶ 77,287, at 82,763-64 (S.E.C. 1965); Law No. 66-537 of July 24, 1966, on Commercial Companies, Articles 382-383, [1966] J.O. 6402, [1966] B.L.D. 353, translated in CCH, French Law on Commercial Companies (1971).

19. See Siegel, supra note 1, at 547.

ate. However, the immediate effect of these transactions on the shareholders' economic and control position may not be sufficiently drastic to require appraisal rights.

VI

Voting and Appraisal Rights in Parent-Subsidiary Complexes

18

Wholly Owned Subsidiaries

Under the corporate system which prevails in this country, ultimate ownership of business assets is typically once removed from the assets themselves.[1] Within the last two decades, however, the process has gone a step further: a significant portion of our business assets is now held, not by corporations whose stock is principally owned by investors, but by massive subsidiaries – megasubsidiaries – whose stock is principally owned by parent corporations.

These megasubsidiaries are to be found in all economic sectors, and in some sectors they have become the dominant form of business organization. For example, 24 of the country's 25 largest commercial-banking institutions,[2] including all 10 of the very largest – Bank of America, First National City, Chase Manhattan, J. P. Morgan, Manufacturers Hanover, Chemical, Bankers Trust, Western Bancorporation, Continental Illinois, and First Chicago – are either megasubsidiaries or holding companies whose banking business is done through one or more megasubsidiaries.[3] All told, institutions in holding-company form account for 62 percent of commercial-bank deposits and 63 percent of commercial-banking assets.[4] A comparable pattern also prevails or is

1. See, e.g., A. A. Berle & G. Means, The Modern Corporation and Private Property viii-ix, 13-16 (rev. ed. 1968).

2. Ranking is by assets. The Fifty Largest Commercial Banking Companies, Fortune, July 1974, at 114.

3. See Moody's Bank & Finance Manual (1974) under the corporation names in text.

4. American Bankers Assn., State Banking and Financial Data 115 (1974). For

emerging in other major regulated sectors – particularly investor-owned savings banks and insurance companies, transportation, and message-communications. The three largest savings-and-loan associations[5] – Home Savings, Great Western, and American Savings & Loan – are all megasubsidiaries,[6] and more than half the assets of federally insured investor-owned savings-and-loan associations are under holding-company control.[7] As of 1970, 39 of the 63 largest investor-owned life-insurance companies, all of the insurers listed on the New York Stock Exchange, and 60 of the approximately 140 stock insurance companies carried in *Barron's* stock listings, were members of a holding-company complex.[8] The eight largest investor-owned life insurance companies[9] – Aetna Life, Connecticut General, Travelers, Lincoln National, National Life & Accident, Occidental of California, Continental Assurance, and American National – and the seven largest investor-owned property-liability insurers[10] – Allstate, Travelers, Hartford Fire, Aetna Life & Casualty, Continental, INA, and Fireman's Fund – are either megasubsidiaries or holding companies which do their insurance business through such subsidiaries.[11]

---

details on the growth of the one-bank holding company, see Eisenberg, Megasubsidiaries: The Effect of Corporate Structure on Corporate Control, 84 Harv. L. Rev. 1577, 1580-1583 (1971). See also Holding-Firm Law Designed to Limit Banks Instead Opens New Finance-Service Vistas, Wall St. J., Jan. 7, 1972, at 20, col. 1.

5. Ranking is by assets. Moody's Bank & Finance Manual a57 (1974).

6. See id. under H. F. Ahmanson & Co., Great Western Financial Corp., and First Charter Financial Corp.

7. See Brigham & Pettit, Effects of Structure on Performance in the Savings and Loan Industry, in 3 U.S. Federal Home Loan Bank Board, Study of the Savings and Loan Industry 971, 1102-1103 (1969). Almost 80 percent of the assets of savings-and-loan associations are accounted for by mutual associations, but stock associations, including holding companies, are growing faster than mutuals. Id. at 981, 1102-1105, 1167.

8. See Dirks & Dirks, More Aggressive Policy, Barrons, Jan. 12, 1970, at 5; Diversification Survey, Best's Rev. (Life/Health ed.), Jan. 1970, at 12. See generally 2 SEC, Institutional Investor Study Report, H.R. Doc. No. 92-64, 93d Cong. 2d Sess. 511-520, 796-798 (1971); Brigham & Pettit, supra note 7, at 1120; Main, Why Nobody Likes the Insurers, Fortune, Dec. 1970, at 83, 87, 119; Rose, "The Future Largest Landlords in America," Fortune, July 1970, at 90, 133-134; Note, The Insurance Holding Company Phenomenon and the Search for Regulatory Controls, 56 Va. L. Rev. 636 (1970).

9. Ranking is by assets. The Fifty Largest Life-Insurance Companies, Fortune, July 1974, at 116.

10. Ranking is by property-liability premiums. Moody's Bank & Finance Manual a58 (1973).

11. See Moody's Bank & Finance Manual (1974) under the corporation names in

Many of the country's largest railroads are held by megasubsidiaries, including the Southern Pacific, Seaboard Coast Line, Union Pacific, Atchison, Topeka & Santa Fe, and Chessie, and so are several important airlines, including United and Braniff.[12] The five largest domestic-message and communications companies, comprising almost the entire sector[13] – AT&T, General Telephone, United Telecommunications, Continental Telephone, and Western Union – are all in holding-company form.[14] The trend has also spread to the securities industry: 35 stockbrokerage and investment-banking houses, including Merrill Lynch, E. F. Hutton, and Morgan Stanley, have either formed parent holding companies or transferred their operations to newly formed subsidiaries.[15]

This dominance of many business sectors by megasubsidiaries and holding companies is a recent development.[16] All but a hand-

---

text. As in the case of savings-and-loan associations, many insurance companies are mutuals, rather than investor-owned. See The Fifty Largest Life-Insurance Companies, supra note 9, at 206.

12. See Moody's Transportation Manual (1974) under the names in text. For relative size, see The Fifty Largest Transportation Companies, Fortune, July 1974, at 122.

Penn Central also is – or was – a megasubsidiary.

13. See The Fifty Largest Utilities, Fortune, July 1974, at 124.

14. See Moody's Public Utility Manual (1974) under the corporation names in text.

15. See Morgan Stanley Holdings Formed, N.Y. Times, July 2, 1975; Merrill Lynch, 2 Other Big Brokerage Firms Forming Holding Companies to Diversify, Wall St. J., March 15, 1973, at 7, col. 1. See also Diversification Trend of Securities Firms May Get SEC Study; Limits Are Possible, Wall St. J., Aug. 21, 1972, at 4, col. 2.

16. A similar but more limited phenomenon occurred during the Twenties and early Thirties when holding companies dominated the public-utility sector and were common, although not dominant, among the industrials. Beginning in the mid-Thirties, however, this pattern was reversed. Many of the industrials dropped the holding-company form in favor of a simplified corporate structure, compare J. Bonbright & G. Means, The Holding Company 76-79, 90-95 (1932), with 2 A. Dewing, The Financial Policy of Corporations 985-987, 999-1006 (5th ed. 1953), and public utility holding companies fell under the "death-sentence" clause of the Public Utility Holding Company Act of 1935, §11(b), 15 U.S.C. §79k(b) (1964). See 1 L. Loss, Securities Regulation 131-141 (2d ed. 1961); 4 id. at 2276 (Supp. 1969). (For recent developments in the public-utility sector, see SEC Staff Plans to Take a Harder Look at Utility Holding Firms That Diversify, Wall St. J., July 19, 1971, at 4, col. 3; 'Exempt' Utility Holding Companies' Right To Diversify Is Subject of SEC Inquest, Wall St. J., Nov. 22, 1971, at 8, col. 3.)

There were also some important bank and railroad holding companies in the Twenties, but the form was not widespread in those areas, and many of the companies which did adopt it later dropped it in favor of corporate simplification. See J. Bonbright & G. Means, supra at 223-224, 323-324; 2 A. Dewing, supra at 958-963, 986-987.

ful of the sector-dominating megasubsidiaries were independent corporations as late as the mid-1950s, and many or most were independent as late as the mid-1960s.[17] Even more striking than the rapidity of this development, however, is the way in which it has occurred. In most cases, a theretofore independent corporation has turned itself into a subsidiary by reversing normal corporate biology and creating its own parent – the so-called upstream holding company. The reasons for such a seemingly unusual procedure, and indeed for the megasubsidiary phenomenon as a whole, are grounded in part on legal and economic considerations unique to each business sector. At least in the regulated sectors, however, some motives are recurrent. These include a desire to diversify into nonregulated businesses; to lessen the grip of the applicable regulatory agency and the applicable body of regulatory law (particularly limitations on capital structure), and to share in the higher stock multiples often associated with the nonregulated area.[18]

That these are not the only motives for the formation of upstream holding companies, however, is evidenced by the spread of the upstream-holding-company device into the nonregulated area. For example, among corporations listed on the New York Stock Exchange, Walter E. Heller,[19] Marsh & McClennen,[20] Gen-

17. See, e.g., Heinemann, Bank Holding Battles Are Only Begun, N.Y. Times, Jan. 10, 1971, §3, at 1, col. 8. Compare Staff of House Comm. on Banking and Currency, 91st Cong., 1st Sess., The Growth of Unregistered Bank Holding Companies – Problems and Prospects 7 (Table 2) (Comm. Print. 1969), with Hearings on S. 1052, S. 1211, S. 1664, S. 3823, and H.R. 6778 [to amend the Bank Holding Company Act] before the Senate Comm. on Banking and Currency, 91st Cong., 2d Sess. 12 (1970).

18. See C. Clawson, F. Barsalou, et al., The Savings and Loan Industry in California VI-5 to -7, VI-10 to -13 (Stanford Research Institute Project No. I-3065, 1960); 2 SEC, Institutional Investor Study Report, supra note 8, at 511-520, 796-798 (1971); U.S. Federal Home Loan Bank Board, Report on Savings and Loan Holding Companies 4-5, 16 (1960); Brigham & Pettit, supra note 7, at 979, 1105-19; Main, supra note 8; Nadler, The One-Bank Holding Company, Banking, December 1968, at 34-35; Rose, supra note 8; Shapiro, The One-Bank Holding Company Movement: An Overview, 86 Banking L.J. 291, 297-299 (1969); Whitsel, Economics of the One-Bank Holding Company, The Banker's Magazine, Winter 1969, at 28, 30-31; Note, supra note 8, at 639-642; Notice of Annual Meeting of Stockholders and Proxy Statement of United Air Lines, Inc., Mar. 12, 1969, at 4; Notice of Special Meeting of Shareholders and Proxy Statement of Aetna Life Insurance Co., Oct. 2, 1967, at 3-4.

19. See Moody's Bank & Finance Manual 1589-1590 (1970).

20. (Now Marlennan.) See id. at 2355-2356.

eral Acceptance Corporation,[21] and R. J. Reynolds[22] have created parents for themselves within recent years. And, of course, some corporations, such as Exxon, have traditionally operated in holding-company form.[23]

Perhaps a more significant phenomenon in the nonregulated area, however, is the increasing number of parent-subsidiary complexes in which members of the public hold a noncontrolling stock interest in the subsidiary. This type of structure is frequently a product of two techniques which are relatively new in either conception or extent of application. One of these techniques is the partial takeover. If (i) the target of a takeover bid is publicly held, (ii) the bidder is a corporation, and (iii) the bid is for an amount of shares which carries effective control but constitutes less than 100 percent of the target's stock, the effect of a successful bid is to convert an independent corporation into a subsidiary with outside ownership. This sequence has occurred with increasing frequency during recent years.[24] The second technique is the partial spinoff. Here the parent of a wholly owned subsidiary distributes a minority interest in the subsidiary to the parent's shareholders, or sells (or causes the subsidiary to sell) a minority interest in the subsidiary to the public at large. The purposes for such transactions include raising cash for the parent or the subsidiary, conserving the parent's cash through a distribution of stock in a subsidiary in lieu of an ordinary dividend, enabling the subsidiary to issue securities

21. See id. at 1614, 1617.

22. See Moody's Industrial Manual 3321 (1970).

In their proxy statements, both General Acceptance and R. J. Reynolds stated as a major reason for adopting the holding-company form that it would permit some activities of the restructured corporate complex to be free from restrictions arising under debt instruments or preferred stock. R. J. Reynolds also stated that the restructuring would permit "more appropriate reflection of managerial responsibilities in respect of [the] diversified activities" of the corporate complex, would substantially increase "flexibility in the assignment and deployment of personnel," and would "provide a more advantageous vehicle for future acquisitions and further diversification." Notice of Annual Meeting and Proxy Statement of R. J. Reynolds Tobacco Co., March 16, 1970, at 6. See Notice of Annual Meeting and Proxy Statement of General Acceptance Corp., April 2, 1968, at 1-2; Notice of Annual Meeting and Proxy Statement of R. J. Reynolds Tobacco Co., March 16, 1970, at 6.

23. See Moody's Industrial Manual 514, 515 (1974).

24. See Brudney & Chirelstein, Fair Shares in Corporate Mergers and Takeovers, 88 Harv. L. Rev. 297, at 297 (1974); Fleischer & Mundheim, Corporate Acquisition by Tender Offer, 115 U. Pa. L. Rev. 317, at 317-318, 328 (1967).

which will not represent an interest in all of the parent's assets, and establishing a market price for the subsidiary's shares so as to raise the value or increase the bankability of the stock the parent retains.[25] The technique was brought into prominence by L-T-V in 1964,[26] and a number of other major corporations – including Brunswick, Studebaker-Worthington, Howmet, Walter Kidde, Armour, Gulf & Western, and Standex International – subsequently followed L-T-V's lead.[27]

Part VI will consider the corporate-law consequences of these various phenomena, and more particularly, the manner in which the rules governing the allocation of powers between shareholders and management are affected by the fact that the total corporate enterprise is allocated among various entities in a parent-subsidiary or holding-company complex. The relevant questions are these: suppose that a subsidiary proposes to take an action which comes within the statutory province of shareholders. Who are then "the shareholders" whose approval is statutorily required – the parent, or the parent's shareholders? If the parent, which of its corporate organs has power to determine whether the approval will be forthcoming – its board, or the body of its shareholders? It appears to have been commonly assumed that the power to vote a subsidiary's stock inheres in the parent's board.[28] This assumption may be adequate in the case of the typical subsidiary – one which is

25. See Brown, Jimmy Ling's Wonderful Growth Machine, Fortune, January 1967, at 137, 172-173; McDonald, Some Candid Answers from James J. Ling, Fortune, Aug. 1, 1969, at 92, 95, 162-163; Merjos, Straw Into Gold?, Barron's, Nov. 25, 1968, at 5; LTV Keeps Expanding on Borrowed Money, Stock Price Increases, Wall St. J., Aug. 18, 1967, at 1, col. 6.

26. See materials cited in note 25, supra.

27. See Moody's Industrial Manual 2676-2677, 2681, 2684 (1970); More Companies Shed Partners They Bought During Merger Binge, Wall St. J., April 13, 1971, at 1, col. 6. For other examples, see Merjos, supra note 25. See also View of Less Successful ITT Acquisition Is Provided by Canteen Corp. Registration, Wall St. J., June 26, 1972, at 5, col. 1.

In some cases a partial spinoff has eventually been followed by a further spin-off which reduced or eliminated the parent's interest in the subsidiary, or a tender offer or merger which eliminated the outside interest. See LTV Proposes Corporate Restructuring, Plans Full Ownership of Aerospace Unit, Wall St. J., March 2, 1972, at 26, col. 2; LTV, Wilson Boards Set Definite Terms on Proposed Merger, Wall St. J., July 7, 1972, at 11, col. 1; LTV Plans Offer For Rest of Stock of Its J & L Unit, Wall St. J., Aug. 28, 1974, at 4, col. 2; Gulf & Western Declares Payout of Athena Stock, Wall St. J., March 10, 1972, at 21, col. 6.

28. See, e.g., Murphy, Corporate Divisions vs. Subsidiaries, 34 Harv. Bus. Rev., Nov.-Dec. 1956, at 83, 90.

wholly owned by its parent, and which itself holds only an insubstantial share of the total assets within the parent's control. In such cases, a rule that the parent's board votes the parent's stock in the subsidiary would usually be unobjectionable. Since by hypothesis the subsidiary is wholly owned by the parent, no one except the parent's shareholders would normally have a recognizable interest in the identity of the persons who vote the subsidiary's stock; and since by hypothesis the subsidiary does not account for a significant portion of the assets within control of the corporate complex, the parent's shareholders would usually be indifferent even to major changes in the subsidiary's structure.

However, where a subsidiary accounts for a significant amount of the assets within the complex's control, or is less than wholly owned by its parent, a rule that the parent's board has power to vote the parent's stock in the subsidiary would have a real bite. If the subsidiary plays a significant economic role in the corporate complex, the parent's shareholders might have a substantial interest in certain types of action which the subsidiary might undertake; while if stock in the subsidiary is publicly held, the outside shareholders may have a substantial interest in the manner in which the parent exercises its control. It will be shown in Part VI that in some such cases, at least, the right to vote the subsidiary's stock either inheres in the parent and is exercisable by the body of the parent's shareholders, or passes through the parent directly to the parent's shareholders. Chapter 18 will consider wholly owned subsidiaries; chapter 19, subsidiaries in which members of the public own a significant interest. The material will be organized on the premise that the allocation of corporate powers is most profitably discussed in the context of particular transactions. In particular, the focus will be on those transactions that normally require shareholder vote under the corporate statutes — sale of substantially all assets, merger, election of directors, certificate amendment, and dissolution.

§18.1. Subsidiaries Which Hold Substantially All of the Assets Owned by the Corporate Complex

In many parent-subsidiary complexes, substantially all of the assets under the complex's control are held by one subsidiary. This pattern is particularly common where the complex has been created through the formation of an upstream holding company, whose major asset is typically its stock in the subsidiary which caused its formation. Since such complexes have accounted for a very substantial portion of the recent flurry in holding-company activity, the problems raised are of considerable practical importance.

A. Sale of Substantially All Assets and Merger

Under the corporate statutes, a sale of substantially all assets normally must be approved by the holders of a majority or two-thirds of the selling corporation's outstanding shares, and a merger normally must be approved by the holders of a majority or two-thirds of the outstanding shares of both corporate parties.[29] Assume now that a wholly owned subsidiary which holds substantially all of the assets owned by a corporate complex proposes to sell those assets for cash, or to exchange its assets for the stock of a merger partner. Who has the right to vote the subsidiary's stock to approve or refuse to approve the transaction?

1. Solution One. – The parent is entitled to vote the subsidiary's stock, and the parent's shareholders as a body determine how the parent will vote. Since in form, at least, the parent is the subsidiary's shareholder, one approach to the problem would be to accept this form as governing, and deem the parent entitled to vote the subsidiary's stock. Even under this approach, however, a question remains: which of the parent's corporate organs determines how the parent's shares will be voted? At common law, "the power of a corporation . . . [to] hold stock in other corporations . . . [was] involved in doubt."[30] Toward the end of the nineteenth century, New Jersey enacted a provision in its general corporation law expressly conferring such power.[31] Other states soon followed

29. See the statutes cited in chapter 1, notes 8 and 9, supra.

30. Robotham v. Prudential Ins. Co., 64 N.J. Eq. 673, 695, 53 A. 842, 851 (Ch. 1903). See J. Bonbright & G. Means, supra note 16, at 55-57; 2 A. Dewing, supra note 16, at 861-862; Note, Power of a Corporation to Acquire Stock of Another Corporation, 31 Colum. L. Rev. 281 (1931). See generally W. Noyes, A Treatise on the Law of Intercorporate Relations 472-509 (2d ed. 1909). This is not to say that the practice was unknown; a number of corporations had special charters empowering them to acquire and hold stock. See J. Bonbright & G. Means, supra note 16, at 58-64; Compton, Early History of Stock Ownership by Corporations, 9 Geo. Wash. L. Rev. 125 (1940).

31. H. Ballantine, Corporations 236-237 (rev. ed. 1946).

suit, so that today most corporate statutes specifically empower corporations to hold stock in other corporations and to vote that stock.[32] Normally, however, the statutes do not designate which corporate organ can exercise that power,[33] and the issue therefore arises whether the parent's board can vote the subsidiary's stock in favor of a proposal to sell substantially all of the subsidiary's assets, or to effect a merger between the subsidiary and another corporation, when the subsidiary itself holds substantially all of the assets of the parent-subsidiary complex.

The answer to this question seems clear. Such a transaction would transcend the power of the parent's board to "manage the business" of the parent; so much is indicated not only by the economic nature of the transaction, but also by the statutes themselves, which provide that such transactions must normally be approved by the shareholders. Furthermore, a major purpose of the statutory requirement of shareholder approval for merger or sale of substantially all assets is to prevent consummation of such transactions by management action alone, without approval by those who own the equity underlying the corporate enterprise. That purpose would be completely subverted if a parent-subsidiary complex, substantially all of whose assets were held by a wholly owned subsidiary, could sell those assets, or merge the entity in which they are enveloped, merely by the concurrent action of the parent's and subsidiary's boards — two bodies which may, indeed, have an identical composition.

Thus the first possible solution to the problem at hand is that while the parent is entitled to vote the subsidiary's stock on such transactions, the body of the parent's shareholders is the corporate organ which determines how that stock will be voted.

2. Solution Two. — For purposes of the relevant statutory provisions, the parent's shareholders are entitled to vote the sub-

32. See, e.g., Del. Code Ann. tit. 8, § 123 (1974); Ill. Rev. Stat. ch. 32, § 157.5(g) (Smith-Hurd Supp. 1974); N.J. Stat. Ann. § 14A:3-1(f) (Supp. 1974); N.Y. Bus. Corp. Law § 202(a)(6) (McKinney 1963). Some statutes specifically empower a corporation to own shares of other corporations, but do not explicitly empower a corporation to vote such shares. See, e.g., Ohio Rev. Code Ann. § 1701.13(F)(3), (G) (Page Supp. 1974). However, the effect is the same as if the power to vote were explicitly conferred, since the power to own shares carries with it an implied power to vote them. Toledo Traction, Light & Power Co. v. Smith, 205 F. 643, 653 (N.D. Ohio 1913); Bouree v. Trust Francais des Actions de la Franco-Wyoming Oil Co., 14 Del. Ch. 332, 127 A. 56, 62 (Ch. 1924).

33. See statutes cited in note 32 supra. But see note 38 infra.

sidiary's stock directly. The first solution, while undoubtedly preferable to permitting the parent's board to vote the subsidiary's stock on such transactions, still has several significant drawbacks.

To begin with, most statutes provide that a merger or a sale of substantially all assets requires approval by the holders of a majority or two-thirds of the corporation's total outstanding shares. That requirement would be negated under the first solution. Absent special provision, the body of shareholders acts by a simple majority of the votes cast or present at a duly constituted meeting – not by a percentage of total outstanding shares.[34] In most publicly held corporations, a quorum consists of a majority of outstanding shares, and often less.[35] Under the first solution, therefore, a sale of substantially all of the assets held by the corporate complex, or a merger of the entity in which those assets are enveloped, could be approved by just over twenty-five percent of the parent's total outstanding shares, and by even less than twenty-five percent where the parent's bylaws provided for a less-than-majority quorum.

Furthermore, the first solution is predicated at least in part on the assumption that the relevant statute confers upon the board only the power to manage the corporation's business, or its business and affairs, and that there is no relevant certificate or bylaw provision. Some statutes, however, confer upon the board all powers not specifically reserved to the shareholders.[36] Even

34. See 5 W. Fletcher, Cyclopedia of the Law of Corporations §2020 (rev. vol. M. Wolf ed. 1967).

35. See, e.g., By-Laws of AMF, Inc., as amended through March 2, 1971, §5 (majority); By-Laws of American Express Co., art. II, §2.4 (majority); By-Laws of Avco Corp., as amended through Oct. 25, 1974, art. II, §3 (majority); By-Laws of Eastman Kodak Co., as amended through Aug. 19, 1971, art. I, §5 (majority); By-Laws of General Motors Corp. §11 (30 percent); By-Laws of Mobil Oil Corp., as amended to Jan. 25, 1974, art. II, §4 (one-third).

36. See, e.g., Cal. Corp. Code §800 (West Supp. 1974); Ohio Rev. Code Ann. tit. 17, §1701.59(A) (Page Supp. 1974); Pa. Stat. Ann. tit. 15, §1302 (Supp. 1974).

A strong argument could be made that such provisions should not be read to authorize a parent's board to vote the stock of an economically dominant subsidiary in favor of a sale of substantially all assets or a merger. A statutory, certificate, or by-law provision conferring upon the board all corporate powers not reserved to the shareholders should be read, in light of the common law background of the corporate statutes, to refer to those powers necessary to manage the business of the corporation – not to the power to make fundamental or structural changes in the corporation. See 2 W. Fletcher, supra note 34, at §540 (rev. vol. M. Wolf & E. Comiskey eds. 1969); H. Ballantine, supra note 31, at 520; cf. Automatic Steel Products, Inc. v. Johnston, 31 Del.

where this is not so, the certificate may contain such a provision.[37] And statutes[38] or bylaws[39] sometimes contain a boilerplate provision specifically conferring upon the board the power to vote shares of stock which the corporation owns.

Finally, both a sale of substantially all assets and a merger normally give rise to appraisal rights. Under the first solution, however, appraisal rights would be cut off: since the body of shareholders would vote the parent's stock as a unit, there would be no dissenting shareholders.

All of these drawbacks stem from the fact that under the first approach the parent is deemed to be the subsidiary's shareholder. Accordingly, they would be eliminated by treating the parent's shareholders as entitled to vote the subsidiary's stock on an individual basis – that is, by passing the right to vote the subsidiary's stock on such transactions *through* the parent to the parent's shareholders. Each shareholder in the parent corporation would thus be entitled to vote that proportion of the subsidiary's stock which equaled his proportionate holding of the parent's stock. Since the subsidiary's stock would be voted by the parent's individual shareholders in parcels, rather than by the body of the parent's shareholders as a unit, the integrity of statutory require-

Ch. 469, 64 A.2d 416 (Sup. Ct. 1949); Bruch v. National Guar. Credit Corp., 13 Del. Ch. 180, 185-190, 116 A. 738, 740-743 (Ch. 1922).

37. See, e.g., the Delaware certificate-of-incorporation forms in G. Seward, Basic Corporate Practice 131 (1966).

38. Statutory provisions to this effect are not uncommon. See, e.g., Cal. Corp. Code §§2218-2224 (West 1955); Ill. Ann. Stat. ch. 32, §157.30 (Supp. 1974); N.J. Stat. Ann. §§14A:5-14 through 17 (1969); Ohio Rev. Code Ann. §§1701.46-47 (Page 1964). However, in corporate as in noncorporate law, language – including grants of power to corporate organs – is not always to be taken literally, but must be given a purposive interpretation. See, e.g., Hayes v. Canada, Atl. & Plant S.S. Co., 181 F. 289, 292-293 (1st Cir. 1910) (interpretation of bylaw); Bruch v. National Guar. Credit Corp., 13 Del. Ch. 180, 188-190, 116 A. 738, 742-743 (interpretation of statute); Maryland Trust Co. v. National Mechanics' Bank, 102 Md. 608, 634-635, 63 A. 70, 79-80 (1906) (interpretation of bylaw); Fensterer v. Pressure Lighting Co., 85 Misc. 621, 625-626, 149 N.Y.S. 49, 52-53 (City Ct. 1914), appeal denied, 167 App. Div. 904, 151 N.Y.S. 1115 (1915) (same). The major purpose of these provisions is to eliminate doubt concerning the validity of proxies executed in a corporate name. Cf. N.J. Stat. Ann. §14A:5-14, Commissioners' Comment (1969). See text and notes at notes 59-65, infra. Similar considerations apply to comparable certificate and bylaw provisions.

39. See, e.g., W. Cary, Cases and Materials on Corporations, app. C, at A-100 (4th ed. 1970); G. Seward, Basic Corporate Practice 131 (Supp. 1969); By-Laws of General Motors Corp. §70; cf. By-Laws of American Express Co., art. VII, §7.2.

ments that a merger or sale of substantially all assets be approved by a majority or two-thirds of outstanding shares would be preserved, as would be the integrity of the appraisal provisions. And since the right to vote the subsidiary's stock would inhere directly in the parent's shareholders, rather than in the parent, boilerplate provisions in the parent's certificate or bylaws concerning the voting of stock which it holds would be irrelevant, as would generalized provisions (statutory or otherwise) conferring on the board the right to exercise corporate powers.

While a pass-through of rights adhering to a subsidiary's stock might appear at first glance to be a novel conception, in fact the pass-through technique is no stranger to the corporate institution. For example, it has long been settled that in certain situations a shareholder may bring a derivative action asserting a claim on behalf of his corporation. But it is now also established that in an appropriate case a shareholder in a parent corporation can bring a derivative action on behalf of a *subsidiary,* despite the fact that technically he is not a shareholder in the subsidiary.[40] Although there is some discord as to the precise theory justifying this result, the commentators are agreed that such an action may be brought even where the subsidiary's corporate entity would be respected

40. See, e.g., Goldstein v. Groesbeck, 142 F.2d 422, 425 (2d Cir.), cert. denied, 323 U.S. 737 (1944); United States Lines, Inc. v. United States Lines Co., 96 F.2d 148 (2d Cir. 1938); Birch v. McColgan, 39 F. Supp. 358, 366 (S.D. Cal. 1941); Holmes v. Camp, 180 App. Div. 409, 167 N.Y.S. 840 (1917); Note, Suits by a Shareholder in a Parent Corporation to Redress Injuries to the Subsidiary, 64 Harv. L. Rev. 1313, 1313-1316 (1951).

There are also a number of cases in which the shareholder's right to inspect books and records has been extended to cover the books and records of a subsidiary. See Woodworth v. Old Second Natl. Bank, 154 Mich. 459, 117 N.W. 893 (1908); State ex. rel. United Brick & Tile Co. v. Wright, 339 Mo. 160, 95 S.W.2d 804 (1936); Siravo v. Sirian Lamp Co., 124 N.J.L. 433, 12 A.2d 682 (Ct. Err. & App. 1940); Bailey v. Boxboard Prod. Co., 314 Pa. 45, 170 A. 127 (1934); Williams v. Freeport Sulphur Co., 40 S.W.2d 817 (Tex. Civ. App. 1930); cf. Martin v. D. B. Martin Co., 10 Del. Ch. 211, 88 A. 612 (Ch. 1913). But cf. Lisle v. Shipp, 96 Cal. App. 264, 273 P. 1103 (1929); State ex rel. Rogers v. Sherman Oil Co., 31 Del. 570, 117 A. 122 (Super. Ct. 1922).

As another example, in appropriate cases the right to recover damages awarded in a simple derivative action brought on a corporation's behalf may be passed through the corporation directly to its shareholders, so that those shareholders who are not barred on personal grounds can recover individually, on a pro rata basis according to their holdings. See Perlman v. Feldmann, 219 F.2d (2d Cir.) cert. denied, 349 U.S. 952 (1955); Grenier, Prorata Recovery by Shareholders on Corporate Causes of Action as a Means of Achieving Corporate Justice, 19 Wash. & Lee L. Rev. 165 (1962).

for other purposes.[41] Thus in permitting such actions, the law in effect permits the parent's right to bring an action on the subsidiary's behalf to be passed through the parent to the parent's shareholders. At least one reason for permitting pass-through of the right to bring suit is similar to the reason for permitting a pass-through of voting rights. Absent such a pass-through, a vital shareholder right (the right to a loyal and careful management) could be subverted merely by the insertion of an extra layer of entity between ownership and management: "The free use of holding companies . . . would prevent the righting of many wrongs, if an action [on a subsidiary's behalf] might not be maintained by a stockholder of a holding company."[42]

Other existing pass-throughs involve the voting right itself. Many large corporations have created employee pension trust funds whose investment policies are under the sole or joint control of the corporation's management, acting through the pension fund's trustees. Often such funds invest in stock of the employer corporation. To prevent management from voting such stock to perpetuate itself in office, many pension funds provide that the right to vote such stock is passed through the trustees to the employee beneficiaries.[43] One commentator listed 101 corporations which had adopted such pass-throughs, including many of the country's largest corporations, such as Chrysler, Ford, du Pont, Mobil, U.S. Steel, Alcoa, A & P, Standard Oil of New Jersey (now Exxon), and Sears, Roebuck.[44] Some pension-fund pass-throughs have been adopted voluntarily. Many others have been

41. See Painter, Double Derivative Suits and Other Remedies With Regard to Damaged Subsidiaries, 36 Ind. L.J. 143, 147-149 (1961); Note, supra note 40, at 1313; Note, Corporations — An Examination of the Multiple Derivative Suit and Some Problems Involved Therein in Light of the Theory of the Single Derivative Suit, 31 N.Y.U.L. Rev. 932, 937-938 (1956).

In contrast, the cases permitting inspection of books and records of subsidiaries, note 40 supra, have a piercing-the-veil flavor.

42. Holmes v. Camp, 180 App. Div. 409, 412, 167 N.Y.S. 840, 842 (1917). See also Kaufman v. Wolfson, 1 App. Div. 2d 555, 151 N.Y.S.2d 530 (1956); Note, supra note 41, at 940; 2 How. L.J. 263, 265 (1956).

43. Hone, Pass Through Voting: An Analysis, 17 Profit Sharing, October 1969, at 22. See, e.g., Prospectus of DeSoto Employees Savings and Profit Sharing Pension Fund, May 27, 1970, at 6, 8; Prospectus of The Savings and Profit Sharing Pension Fund of Sears, Roebuck and Co. Employees, May 25, 1970, at 5-6, 8.

44. Hone, supra note 43, at 26-27 n. 1.

adopted to comply with the practices of the New York Stock Exchange: if a corporation which seeks an original or supplementary listing has a pension fund holding a material amount (approximately one percent or more) of its own voting stock, the Exchange requires, as a condition to listing, assurance that the corporation will provide for a pass-through of the voting rights on that stock.[45] Perhaps more in point for present purposes is another, somewhat less formalized, Exchange policy. If more than ten percent of the stock of a corporation which applies for listing is controlled by a closely held corporation, the Exchange normally requires, as a condition to listing, that the right to vote the listed stock be passed through the closely held corporation to its shareholders.[46] Indeed, where a significant part of the closely held corporation's stock is held in trust, the Exchange normally requires a second pass-through to the ultimate beneficiaries of the trust.[47]

A pass-through is also explicitly required by at least two corporate statutes. The New Jersey statute provides that a sale of substantially all assets by a subsidiary shall be treated as a sale by the parent, if the subsidiary constitutes substantially all of the parent's assets. The Pennsylvania statute provides, more simply, that a sale of assets by a subsidiary shall be deemed a sale by the parent for voting and appraisal-rights purposes.[48]

45. Id. at 22. The same applies to retirement, stock-purchase, and other employee plans.

46. Letter to the author from Merle S. Wick, Vice President, New York Stock Exchange, January 23, 1970.

47. Id. In a similar vein, after the Supreme Court ruled that du Pont's holding of 23 percent of General Motors' stock was an antitrust violation, United States v. E. I. du Pont de Nemours & Co., 353 U.S. 586 (1957), du Pont proposed a decree allowing it to retain the GM stock but requiring a multiple pass-through of voting rights in the stock. United States v. E. I. du Pont de Nemours & Co., 177 F. Supp. 1, 8 (N.D. Ill. 1959). The district court adopted a modified version of the company's proposal. Id. at 39-46. On appeal, however, the Supreme Court held that complete divestiture was required. United States v. E. I. du Pont de Nemours & Co., 366 U.S. 316 (1961).

48. N.J. Stat. Ann. §14A:10-11(3) (Supp. 1974); Pa. Stat. Ann. tit. 15, §1311(B) (1967). The New Jersey statute provides that one corporation is a subsidiary of another if the latter controls sufficient shares to elect a majority of the former's board. N.J. Stat. Ann. §14A:1-2(r) (1969). The relevant Pennsylvania provision is pitched in terms of control by one corporation of the other. Pa. Stat. Ann. tit. 15, §1311(B) (1967).

Pass-throughs have also been advocated for situations in which a subsidiary holds stock in its parent. The normal rule is that the subsidiary cannot vote such stock. See

The relatively widespread use of voting pass-throughs in a number of different contexts testifies, among other things, to the feasibility of the device. Indeed, as used in the pension-fund area, a pass-through results in the extension of the voting right to hundreds or thousands of otherwise nonenfranchised employees, while as applied to shareholders of a corporate complex whose principal assets are held by a subsidiary, pass-through only results in a vote which would have been required in any event had a parent-subsidiary structure not been employed.

3. Legal principles supporting pass-through. — Two related legal principles, which have already been discussed, provide support for the concept that a pass-through is required when a subsidiary which holds substantially all of a corporate complex's assets proposes to sell those assets or merge with another corporation.

The first principle recognizes that statutes not only regulate activities within their literal scope, but often serve as an expression of legislative policies of wider application. That being so, legislative rules, like judicial rules, may be extended, by elaboration of the underlying principle and by analogy, to situations not precisely covered by the rule as originally formulated — and should be so extended if necessary to prevent subversion of the legislative policy.[49]

This principle has found frequent reflection in corporate law, often in situations very similar to that under consideration. For example, in *Aiple v. Twin City Barge & Towing Co.*,[50] the court held that management could not negate the shareholders' right to determine the amount of authorized stock by creating, without shareholder approval, a subsidiary with authorized but unissued stock:

---

text at notes 56-58, infra. It has been argued, however, that the right to vote that portion of the subsidiary's shares in the parent which is attributable to the outside shareholders of the subsidiary should be passed through to them. Note, The Voting of Stock Held in Cross Ownership, 76 Harv. L. Rev. 1642, 1651-1655 (1963); Comment, 28 U. Chi. L. Rev. 151, 152 (1960); see Yoran, Advance Defensive Tactics Against Takeover Bids, 21 A.J.C.L. 531, 546-555 (1973); cf. O'Connor v. International Silver Co., 68 N.J. Eq. 67, 70, 59 A. 321, 323 (Ch. 1904), affd. on other grounds, 68 N.J. Eq. 680, 62 A. 408 (Ct. Err. & App. 1905); Ex parte Holmes, 5 Cow. 426 (N.Y. Sup. Ct. 1826). But see Dal-Tran Serv. Co. v. Fifth Ave. Coach Lines, Inc., 14 App. Div. 2d 349, 220 N.Y.S.2d 549 (1961).

49. See chapter 15, text at notes 21-29, supra.

50. 274 Minn. 38, 143 N.W.2d 374 (1966).

> If this can be done, the [statutory provisions governing certificate amendment] may be circumvented to the point where a corporation might fragment itself into any number of divisions, thus leaving minority stockholders without the protection that the statute was designed to give them.[51]

If a wholly owned subsidiary which holds substantially all of the assets owned by a corporate complex could sell those assets, or merge with another corporation, without the approval of the parent's shareholders, or with the approval of only twenty-five percent or less of those shareholders, the sale-of-substantially-all-assets and merger provisions would be similarly "circumvented . . . , thus leaving . . . stockholders without the protection that the statute was designed to give them."

The second principle supporting a pass-through – perhaps more accurately, a special case of the first principle – is that in applying statutory rules a corporate entity will be disregarded if regard for the entity would frustrate a statutory purpose. "[A] corporation will be looked upon as a legal entity as a general rule, and until sufficient reason to the contrary appears; but, when the notion of legal entity is used to defeat public convenience . . . the law will regard the corporation as an association of persons."[52]

Several of the cases applying this principle are particularly instructive for present purposes. One such case is *Anderson v. Abbott,*[53] which concerned a statutory provision imposing double liability on shareholders of a national bank. The Supreme Court held that where a national bank was a subsidiary of another corporation, the parent's shareholders, rather than the parent, would be deemed shareholders of the bank subsidiary, on the ground that to hold otherwise would permit the purpose of the statutory provisions to be undercut:

51. 274 Minn. at 45, 143 N.W.2d at 379. (The facts in this case are set forth in greater detail in chapter 8, text at notes 17-19, supra.) Cf. Applestein v. United Board & Carton Corp., 60 N.J. Super. 333, 159 A.2d 146 (Ch. 1960), affd. per curiam, 33 N.J. 72, 161 A.2d 474 (1960); Small v. Sullivan, 245 N.Y. 343, 157 N.E. 261 (1927). See also Klopot v. Northrup, 131 Conn. 14, 37 A.2d 700 (1944); Schwab v. E. G. Potter Co., 194 N.Y. 409, 87 N.E. 670 (1909); Moore v. Los Lugos Gold Mines, 172 Wash. 570, 21 P.2d 253 (1933).

52. United States v. Milwaukee Refrigerator Transit Co., 142 F. 247, 255 (E.D. Wis. 1905); accord, W. Cary, supra note 39, at 148. See also E. Latty, Subsidiaries and Affiliated Corporations 41-42, 54-57, 67-68, 74-76 (1936); Note, Efficacy of the Corporate Entity in Evasion of Statutes, 26 Iowa L. Rev. 350 (1941).

53. 321 U.S. 349 (1944).

> It has often been held that the interposition of a corporation will not be allowed to defeat a legislative policy, whether that was the aim or only the result of the arrangement. . . .
>
> To allow this holding company device to succeed would be to put the policy of double liability at the mercy of corporation finance.[54]

The Court stressed that its conclusion was not based on a finding of intent to evade the statute.[55]

Even more in point are several cases dealing directly with the effect of subsidiaries on the allocation of control over a corporate complex. It is well established that treasury stock — stock of a corporation owned by the corporation itself — cannot be voted.[56] This rule is reflected in many corporate statutes by provisions such as, "Shares of its own stock belonging to a corporation shall not be voted, directly or indirectly. . . ."[57] Suppose, however, that a subsidiary holds shares of stock in its parent. In that case the statute would not be literally applicable, since, at least in form, neither the parent nor the subsidiary would hold "shares of its own stock." Nevertheless, the cases hold that the voting of such shares by the subsidiary falls within the ambit of such a statute:

> That the shares of corporation A owned by it through its ownership of all the shares in corporation B are within the equity of this statute as well as within the mischief which it was intended to prevent, is too plain for argument.[58]

54. 321 U.S. at 362-363. (The facts in this case are set forth in greater detail in chapter 15 text at notes 22-26, supra.)

55. 321 U.S. at 357-358. See also Capital Telephone Co. v. FTC, 498 F.2d 734 (D.C. Cir. 1974); Casanova Guns v. Connally, 454 F.2d 1320 (7th Cir.), cert. denied, 409 U.S. 845 (1972); Kavanaugh v. Ford Motor Co., 353 F.2d 710, 717 (7th Cir. 1965); Note, Efficacy of the Corporate Entity in Evasion of Statutes, supra note 52, at 353-356.

56. See H. Ballantine, supra note 31, at 402-403.

57. Ill. Ann. Stat. ch. 32, §157.28 (Smith-Hurd 1954). See also Note, The Corporate Fiduciary's Power to Vote its Own Stock, 68 Colum. L. Rev. 116, 117-119 (1968).

58. O'Connor v. International Silver Co., 68 N.J. Eq. 67, 71, 59 A. 321, 323 (Ch. 1904), affd. on other grounds, 68 N.J. Eq. 680, 62 A. 408 (Ct. Err. & App. 1905); accord, Italo Petroleum Corp. v. Producers Oil Corp., 20 Del. Ch. 283, 290-291, 174 A. 276, 279 (Ch. 1934). See Continental-Midwest Corp. v. Hotel Sherman, Inc., 13 Ill. App. 2d 188, 141 N.E.2d 400 (1957); Thomas v. International Silver Co., 72 N.J. Eq. 224, 73 A. 833 (Ch. 1907); H. Ballantine, supra note 31, at 403; 5 W. Fletcher, supra note 34, at §2040; cf. Lawrence v. I. N. Parlier Estate Co., 15 Cal. 2d 220, 100 P.2d 765 (1940); American Ry.-Frog Co. v. Haven, 101 Mass. 398 (1869); Ex Parte Holmes, 5 Cow. 426 (N.Y. Sup. Ct. 1826). But cf. Vanderlip v. Los Molinos Land Co., 56 Cal. App. 2d 747,

Applying the principle reflected in these cases to the problem at hand, the fact that there are two layers of corporate entity between shareholders and enterprise, rather than one, should not be allowed to defeat important shareholder rights established by statute. To preserve the integrity of the sale-of-substantially-all-assets and merger provisions, where substantially all of the assets owned by a corporate complex are held by a wholly owned subsidiary, for purposes of those provisions shareholders of the parent should be treated as shareholders of the subsidiary; that is, the right to vote the subsidiary's stock should be passed through the parent to the parent's shareholders.

4. The Cross Properties case. – Although the general principles of corporate law support pass-through where a wholly owned subsidiary, which holds substantially all of a complex's assets, sells those assets or engages in a merger, the case most directly in point – *Cross Properties, Inc. v. Brook Realty Co.*[59] – looks the other way. This case concerned a complex consisting of four companies: Dollar England, an English holding company whose principal asset was 90 percent of the stock of Dollar Canada; Dollar Canada, an Ontario corporation which owned thirteen pieces of real estate and all the stock of County Dollar; County Dollar, a New York corporation which owned the Cross County Shopping Center in Yonkers and all the stock of Dollar U.S.; and Dollar U.S., a New York corporation which owned a shopping center in Texas, an office building in Florida, and a fractional interest in a parcel of real estate in Alabama.

In mid-1968, major shareholders of Dollar England were engaged in a dispute with its board concerning the complex's American properties. The board wanted to sell all of these properties, while the shareholders wanted to retain the Cross County Shopping Center, which was by far the most important. In the midst of

---

133 P.2d 467 (1943). See generally Yoran, supra note 48, at 546-555; Note, supra note 48.

The statutes of some states now explicitly provide that a subsidiary cannot vote shares of its parent if the parent owns a majority or plurality of the shares entitled to vote in the election of the subsidiary's directors. See, e.g., Del. Code Ann. tit. 8, §160(c) (1974); N.J. Stat. Ann. §14A:5-13 (1969); N.Y. Bus. Corp. Law §612(b) (McKinney 1963); Wis. Stat. Ann. §180.25(6) (Supp. 1974); ABA Model Bus. Corp. Act §33 (1969 rev.).

59. 37 App. Div. 2d 193, 322 N.Y.S.2d 773 (1971), affd. on opinion below, 31 N.Y.2d 938, 293 N.E.2d 95 (1972).

this controversy a shareholder filed a requisition to hold a special shareholders' meeting for the purpose of removing one of the board's four members, French, and amending the articles of Dollar England to require directors to hold at least one percent of its qualifying shares, which would disqualify the three others. Prior to the meeting French resigned. At the meeting, which was held on July 25, a majority of the shareholders voted in favor of the proposed amendment, but it failed of passage because a greater-than-majority vote was required. With the handwriting on the wall, a requisition was then filed for a second special shareholders' meeting to remove the three remaining directors. The incumbent board rejected this requisition; the English High Court of Justice held the rejection wrongful; and on October 23 the second meeting was held and the remaining directors were ousted. However, in the interim between July 25 and October 23, the then-incumbents caused County Dollar and Dollar U.S. to agree to sell the shopping centers and the office building – constituting 70 percent of the assets under the complex's control – to Brook Realty, a New York corporation. This agreement was approved by the boards of the three subsidiaries, but not by the shareholders of Dollar England.[60]

Objecting Dollar England shareholders immediately brought a derivative action in New York to enjoin and cancel the sale on the ground that it constituted a sale of substantially all of Dollar England's assets and therefore required approval by Dollar England's shareholders. Sections 909(a)(1)-(3) of the New York Business Corporation Law provide that after the board has approved a sale of substantially all assets: (1) it must submit the transaction "to a vote of shareholders," (2) notice of the meeting must be given "to each shareholder of record, whether or not entitled to vote," and (3) the transaction must be approved by "vote at a meeting of shareholders of the holders of two-thirds of all outstanding shares entitled to vote thereon." The court denied relief on the ground that at least as concerned the third party, Brook, New York law was applicable[61] and approval by the record share-

60. Most of the facts are drawn from the Appellate Division's opinion; the remainder, none of which appeared to be in dispute, are drawn from the briefs on appeal. The corporate names used in the text are those used by the court for convenience, rather than the legal names.

61. The court also assumed that under English law approval by Dollar England's

holders (Dollar Canada and County Dollar) sufficed to satisfy the requirements of section 909.

Even as applied to third parties, *Cross Properties* can be distinguished from the problem at hand, since the court took the position that if the various corporate veils had been pierced the properties involved would not have comprised substantially all of Dollar England's assets.[62] However, the court's reasoning was broad enough to cover cases in which substantially all of a complex's assets were involved:

> The appellants argue that section 909 was intended by the Legislature to protect the ultimate beneficial owners against the sale of all or substantially all the assets of the corporation by management without prior approval by two thirds of the shareholders. They urge, and not without substance, that when the assets of a corporation are held by a wholly owned subsidiary, management of the subsidiary could deprive the parent shareholders of this protection unless section 909 is read to require approval by the ultimate beneficial owners. We cannot accept this construction of section 909.
>
> This court is not unmindful of the trend in recent years toward the development of conglomerate corporate enterprises and so-called megasubsidiaries. . . . We recognize that utilization of pyramiding corporations often results in the dilution or denial of many shareholder prerogatives. However, this fact was before the Legislature in 1962 when substantial amendments were made to the Business Corporation Law. . . . Section 909 was amended at that time. . . . If the Legislature had intended such a departure from the plain language of subdivision (a) of section 909, it would have so indicated. It is clear that the "shareholders" referred to in paragraph (3) are the "shareholder[s] of

---

shareholders would have been required for a sale of substantially all of its assets. This assumption is perhaps open to question, see M. A. Weinberg, Takeover Bids and Amalgamations 46-47 (2d ed. 1967), as is the applicability of New York rather than English law to determine whether the approval of Dollar England's shareholders was required, but I shall follow these assumptions in the text in order to deal with the court's opinion on its own terms.

62. The court stated: "Furthermore, by urging that we pierce the corporate veil, the [plaintiffs] place themselves in an awkward position. Dollar Canada owns 13 properties in addition to its stock in County Dollar. Thus, the sale here would not be of all or substantially all *its* (Dollar Canada's) assets and clearly could not be viewed as such by Dollar England, which owns about 90 percent of Dollar Canada." 37 App. Div. 2d at 201, 322 N.Y.S.2d at 780 (emphasis in original).

For purposes of the analysis in §18.1, Cross Properties can also be distinguished on the ground that Dollar Canada, the second-tier subsidiary, was 90-percent rather than wholly owned by Dollar England. However, for reasons that will be discussed in §18.2, infra, that distinction should not be critical.

record" who must receive notice by the terms of paragraph (2). Furthermore, section 909 must be read together with subdivisions (a) and (i) of section 612 of the Business Corporation Law. These two sections make clear that "shareholder" refers to a shareholder of record.[63]

Section 612, which is entitled "Qualification of Voters," concerns the voting of stock which is not held by an individual, or in which more than one person has rights — for example, stock which has been pledged, or is held by a fiduciary or a corporation. Subdivision (a) provides that shareholders of record shall be entitled to one vote per share unless the certificate states otherwise. Subdivision (i) provides notwithstanding any other subdivision a corporation shall be protected in treating the record holder of stock as the owner for all purposes. The general thrust of section 612, and particularly subdivisions (a) and (i), is to facilitate intracorporate administration, not to override otherwise applicable rules governing the rights, as between themselves, of persons with conflicting or overlapping interests in shares of stock.[64] Indeed, the court itself apparently recognized that the relevance of section 612 was marginal at best, since it utilized that section only to bolster its interpretation of section 909.[65]

Bolstered or unbolstered, however, that interpretation is difficult to accept. Although the court states that the "dilution or

63. 37 App. Div. 2d at 199-200, 322 N.Y.S.2d at 779-780; cf. Baum v. Baum Holding Co., 158 Neb. 197, 62 N.W.2d 864 (1954); Southmoor, Inc. v. Baptist Mem. Hosp., 60 Tenn. App. 148, 444 S.W.2d 716 (Tenn. Ct. App.), cert. denied (Tenn. Sup. Ct. 1969). The court also rejected an argument based on the proposition that County Dollar and Dollar U.S. "were mere instruments or departments" of Dollar England and Dollar Canada. 37 App. Div. 2d at 200-201, 322 N.Y.S.2d at 780.

64. See Note, Shareholder Approval of Substantial Asset Sales in the Multi-subsidiary Context, 45 U. Colo. L. Rev. 339, 348-349 (1974): "Section 612 and . . . [related] provisions were designed as rules of administrative convenience for the corporation in its preparation of voting lists prior to shareholder meetings or in distribution of dividends to owners as of the record date — a practical necessity in an age when thousands of a corporation's shares change hands each day. Such provisions were not enacted to answer the fundamental question of whether the parent's officers, the parent's directors or the parent's shareholders should be called upon to approve the sale of substantial subsidiary assets." Cf. In re Bacon, 287 N.Y. 1, 38 N.E.2d 105 (1941); Flagg-Utica Corp. v. Baselice, 14 Misc. 2d 476, 178 N.Y.S.2d 860 (1958).

65. Section 612(g) of the New York Business Corporation Law provides that shares standing the name of another corporation may be voted "by such officer . . . as the by-laws of such corporation may provide, or, in the absence of such provision, as the board of such corporation may determine." It is striking that the court did not rely on this provision even indirectly. See note 38 supra.

denial of many shareholder prerogatives" made possible by pyramiding "was before the Legislature in 1962" when it reenacted section 909, nothing is cited in support of this proposition, and it is extremely unlikely that any support could have been adduced. The megasubsidiary problem did not begin to take on major dimensions until the mid-1960s, prior to that time the pyramiding phenomenon of the Twenties and Thirties seemed to have all but disappeared, and even in the mid-1960s the corporate-law problems raised by megasubsidiaries had not really been identified. And although the court states that it is "clear" that the "shareholders" whose approval is required under subdivision (a)(3) must be the shareholders of record to whom notice must be sent under subdivision (a)(2), if one thing is clear it is that the groups identified in these subdivisions need not be identical, since subdivision (a)(3) speaks to voting, while subdivision (a)(2) requires that notice be sent "to each shareholder of record, *whether or not entitled to vote.*" Thus neither the legislative history nor the language of section 909 compelled the court's result; and in terms of legislative purpose, it is difficult to conceive how the court could conclude that a statute requiring the approval of two-thirds of the shareholders for a sale of substantially all assets is satisfied where substantially all of the assets under a corporation's control are sold not only without the approval of its shareholders, but against their evident wishes. Accordingly, one commentator found the court's reasoning "puzzling,"[66] and another observed that

> If the . . . purpose of Section 909(a) . . . is to protect the shareholder's control over his investment, then clearly that purpose is effectuated only if the equitable owners of subsidiary assets – the parent's shareholders – approve their disposition in cases when substantially all of the parent-subsidiary assets are to be sold. Titular ownership of the assets by a separate, subsidiary entity should not bar the beneficial owners' rights.[67]

Although the reasoning and probably the result in *Cross Properties* were defective,[68] the opinion actually does not hold

66. Weiss, Business Associations and Securities Regulation, 23 Syr. L. Rev. 331, 347 (1972).

67. Note, supra note 64, at 352, 354-355.

68. Whether a corporation should be able to avoid a sale of assets on the ground that the requisite shareholder approval has not been obtained is perhaps debatable, but if

that the sale by a subsidiary of substantially all the assets of a parent-subsidiary complex can be decided solely by the corporations' boards. On the contrary, for the court strongly indicated that a different result might well have followed if the duties of Dollar England's directors, rather than the rights of an innocent third party, had been in question:

> In essence, the [plaintiffs], in advancing the "piercing" argument, are claiming a breach of fiduciary obligation of directions to their shareholders. Ordinarily, knowledge by the directors of Dollar England that all their shareholders opposed the sale proposed here would be irrelevant because no approval is required by the Board of Dollar England to consummate a sale of the assets of County Dollar or Dollar U.S. However, where the directors of Dollar England are really making the decisions and controlling the votes of each of the subsidiaries, their knowledge may be imputed to the directors of the subsidiaries. A sale thus known to be opposed by the majority of the shareholders of the parent (although approved by the directors of the subsidiaries) might constitute a breach of fiduciary obligation.
>
> We do not decide that question, however, because we find that even if a breach of fiduciary obligation by the directors of the Dollar companies could be established, the September 13 contract is valid and enforceable because Brook was a *bona fide* purchaser without notice of any fraud or misuse of power by the directors. A distinction must be drawn between the absence of power in a corporation to act *(ultra vires)* and the misuse of corporate power by the directors.[69]

B. Election of Directors

Who has the power to elect the board of a wholly owned subsidiary which holds substantially all of the assets owned by a corporate complex? In such a complex, the parent's board will have only the most limited functions to perform. Since the operat-

---

such avoidance is generally permitted, there appears to be no need to distinguish the case in which approval of a *parent's* shareholder should be required, at least where the buyer has reason to know such approval was not given. The court expressed concern that a requirement of approval by a parent's shareholders "would jeopardize the definiteness required for the orderly transaction of corporate affairs and would substantially impair the marketability of real estate held by corporate subsidiaries by making the necessity for approval a complex question of fact." 37 App. Div. 2d at 200-201, 322 N.Y.S.2d at 780. However, since the question whether a sale involves substantially all of the assets under a parent's control involves pretty much the same kind of inquiry as the question whether a sale involves substantially all of a corporation's assets, it is difficult to see why these conclusions follow.

69. 37 App. Div. 2d at 201, 322 N.Y.S.2d at 781.

ing assets are located in the subsidiary, it is the subsidiary's board, rather than the parent's, which will have the legal power to appoint the enterprise's operating officers, determine what portion of enterprise earnings will be retained for use in the enterprise and what portion paid out as dividends, and give or withhold approval of structural changes in both the enterprise and the corporate entity in which it is enveloped. That being so, effectuation of the statutory provisions vesting in shareholders the right to elect the persons who legally exercise these crucial corporate powers requires that the right to elect the board of such a subsidiary be passed through the parent to the parent's shareholders.

It might be argued that such a pass-through is unnecessary, on the ground that the right to elect those who elect the subsidiary's board is tantamount to the right to elect the subsidiary's board itself. This argument, however, would fly in the face of experience; in few situations is the right to elect those who elect others the functional equivalent of the right to elect those others directly.[70] Alternatively, it might be argued that election of the subsidiary's board by the parent's shareholders would serve no real purpose, since the subsidiary's board will necessarily be under the control of the parent's board. This argument, however, seems circular, since it assumes that the parent's board has the right to elect the board of the subsidiary. If that right is vested in the parent's shareholders, the subsidiary's board would have a power base of its own, through its access to the subsidiary's proxy machinery.

Furthermore, both arguments ignore the fact that the statutes do not simply require that the board be elected by the shareholders; they also limit a director's permissible term of office.[71] If the parent's directors had the right to elect the subsidiary's board, they could elect themselves as directors of the subsidiary for terms ending after the expiration of their terms as directors of the parent. The parent's directors could thereby perpetuate their con-

70. See, e.g., Gray v. Sanders, 372 U.S. 368, 378 (1963). Compare U.S. Const. art. I, §3, with U.S. Const. amend. XVII.

71. See, e.g., Cal. Corp. Code §§805, 2200-2201 (West 1955) (one year); Del. Code Ann. tit. 8, §141(d) (Supp. 1975) (three); N.J. Stat. Ann. §14A:6-4 (1969) (five); N.Y. Bus. Corp. Law §704 (McKinney 1963) (four); Ohio Rev. Code Ann. §1701.57 (Page 1964) (three); Pa. Stat. Ann. tit. 15, §1403 (Supp. 1970) (four); ABA Model Bus. Corp. Act §37 (1969 rev.) (three).

trol over the complex's enterprise beyond the statutorily permissible term and beyond the term for which they were elected by the complex's ownership.[72] A comparable problem would be presented in cases where cumulative voting is mandatory.[73] This technique is designed to enable a sufficiently large block of minority shareholders to acquire board representation. If the parent's shares in the subsidiary were voted by the parent, however, they would be voted as a unit, and a bare majority of the parent's board (or, under solution one, of the parent's shareholders) could elect all the members of the subsidiary's board. The minority shareholders of the parent could thus be frozen out of representation on the only board with power to control the corporation's enterprise, and mandatory cumulative voting would be completely undercut. Pass-through solves this problem, since it enables the parent's shareholders to vote their pro rata share of the subsidiary's stock individually, and therefore to cumulate their votes.

C. Certificate Amendment

Unlike a merger or a sale of substantially all assets, an amendment of a corporation's certificate of incorporation does not in itself materially change the structure of the corporation's enterprise. An amendment may, however, significantly change the relative position of management and shareholders in the control structure enveloping that enterprise. For example, an amendment may increase the amount of authorized stock, which can then be issued by the board without further shareholder approval, or may authorize a new type of business, which can then be entered without further shareholder approval. Accordingly, to preserve the rights of the owners of the corporate enterprise the corporate statutes

72. Cf. Sherman & Ellis, Inc. v. Indiana Mut. Cas. Co., 41 F.2d 588 (7th Cir. 1930); Kennerson v. Burbank Amusement Co., 120 Cal. App. 2d 157, 260 P.2d 823 (1953); Long Park, Inc. v. Trenton-New Brunswick Theatres Co., 297 N.Y. 174, 77 N.E.2d 633 (1948).

Not incidentally, such a technique might discourage outsiders from launching a bid to take over the parent, since the fruits of a victory could be long delayed. Cf. Gower, Corporate Control: The Battle for the Berkeley, 68 Harv. L. Rev. 1176 (1955).

73. See, e.g., National Bank Act §11, as amended, 48 Stat. 186 (1933), 12 U.S.C. §61 (1970); Cal. Corp. Code §2235 (West 1955); Ill. Ann. Stat. ch. 32, §157.28 (Smith-Hurd 1969); Ohio Rev. Code Ann. §1701.55(C)-(D) (Page 1964).

normally require that amendments of the corporation's certificate be approved by the holders of a majority or two-thirds of the corporation's outstanding shares.[74]

If an amendment of the certificate of a wholly owned subsidiary which holds substantially all of a complex's assets would significantly augment the powers of the complex's management vis-à-vis its owners, the right to vote on the amendment should be passed through to the parent's shareholders, lest a primary purpose of the statutory provisions governing certificate amendment be undercut. So, for example, an amendment increasing the authorized stock of such a subsidiary should require the approval of the parent's shareholders, since otherwise management could confer upon itself the power to restructure ultimate ownership of the complex's enterprise without any approval by the complex's owners. Indeed, *Aiple v. Twin City Barge & Towing Co.*[75] is directly in point, since it held that in light of the statutory provisions requiring shareholder approval for certificate amendment, the board could not create a subsidiary with authorized but unissued stock. There is no meaningful distinction in this regard between creation of a subsidiary with authorized but unissued stock, and amendment of a subsidiary's certificate to increase authorized but unissued stock. Similarly, an amendment creating staggered terms for the subsidiary's board should require shareholder approval, particularly if the parent's board is not staggered, since it would work a material change in the control structure enveloping the enterprise.

But not every amendment of the subsidiary's certificate should require approval by the parent's shareholders. For example, an amendment authorizing the subsidiary to engage in a type of business already authorized for the parent should not normally require such approval, since it would not significantly augment management's powers over the complex's enterprise.

74. See, e.g., Cal. Corp. Code §3632 (West Supp. 1974); Del. Code Ann. tit. 8, §242(c) (1974); Ill. Rev. Stat. ch. 32, §157.53(c) (Smith-Hurd Supp. 1974); N.Y. Bus. Corp. Law §803(a) (McKinney Supp. 1974); Ohio Rev. Code Ann. §1701.71 (Page 1964); Pa. Stat. Ann. tit. 15, §1805(A) (Supp. 1974); ABA Model Bus. Corp. Act §59(c) (1969 rev.). But see N.J. Stat. Ann. §14A:9-2(4) (Supp. 1974) (majority of votes cast).

75. 274 Minn. 38, 143 N.W.2d 374 (1966). See text at notes 50-51, supra, and chapter 8, text at notes 17-19, supra.

D. Dissolution

Dissolution of a subsidiary neither alters the complex's enterprise nor brings it out of corporate solution. Indeed, the effect is to extract a layer of corporate entity lying between the complex's enterprise and the complex's owners, thereby bringing the enterprise one step closer to the owner's control. Therefore, dissolution of a subsidiary should normally not require approval by the parent's shareholders, even if the subsidiary holds substantially all of the corporate complex's assets.

§18.2. Subsidiaries Which Hold Less Than Substantially All of the Assets Owned by the Corporate Complex

To what extent are the principles formulated in §18.1 applicable to wholly owned subsidiaries which hold less than substantially all of a complex's assets? For intracorporate purposes, there may be little practical difference between such a subsidiary and a corporate division:

> [A] "true" division might be defined as an organizational unit that acts in all respects like a subsidiary whose stock is held by the parent or holding company, differing primarily in the fact that it has no legal existence apart from the parent company.
>
> Such a quasi-subsidiary division has a full complement of officers and sales, production, and other functional departments. Also, it often has some form of supervisory or advisory board, which corresponds roughly to the board of directors of a subsidiary company. . . . In extreme cases the division may even be permitted to use "divisional seals" and to go through the motions of declaring dividends.[76]

That being so, important rights of the parent's shareholders should not be made to turn on whether a corporate enterprise is held through a division or through a wholly owned subsidiary. This suggests the following working rule: in the case of a wholly owned subsidiary, the right to vote should normally be passed through to the parent's shareholders if, but only if, the transaction

76. Murphy, supra note 28, at 84-85.

in question would have required the approval of the parent's shareholders had the subsidiary's assets been held by the parent through a division. The balance of this section will examine the application of this working rule to the transactions discussed in §18.1.

A. Sale of Substantially All Assets and Mergers

Assume that a wholly owned subsidiary which holds less than substantially all of the assets owned by the corporate complex proposes to sell its assets. The traditional sale-of-substantially-all-assets provision should be inapplicable to such a sale, since it would not have been applied if the subsidiary's assets had been held by the parent through a division and no reason is apparent why the presence of a subsidiary should give the parent's shareholders greater rights than they would otherwise have had. The same result should obtain in a merger in which such a subsidiary is the transferor. This type of transaction is functionally equivalent to a disposition by the parent of the assets held by the subsidiary in exchange for stock in the survivor. If a division rather than a subsidiary were concerned, the sale-of-substantially-all-assets provision would be inapplicable since the transaction would involve less than substantially all of the parent's assets, and the traditional merger provision would be inapplicable since it would not involve a fusion of the transferor and the survivor. These provisions should be equally inapplicable where a subsidiary rather than a division is involved, although shareholder approval should be required under common law principles where a significant amount of assets is involved.[77]

Suppose the subsidiary is the survivor rather than the transferor in a merger? In that case the transaction would be comparable (although not equivalent) to an acquisition by the parent of the assets of another corporation in exchange for shares of the parent's stock. If a division rather than a subsidiary were concerned, the transaction would involve a fusion of the parent and the transferor through the issuance of parent stock in exchange for the transferor's assets. Such a transaction should be deemed a merger if the amount of stock issued by the parent is significant.[78]

77. See §16.1, supra.
78. See chapter 14, supra.

On that basis, it is arguable that a comparable transaction by a subsidiary should require approval by the parent's shareholders, if the merger provisions are not to be subverted. This is even clearer when, as is often the case, the parent is directly involved. Many statutes now provide that shares of a constituent to a merger can be converted into shares of a parent or other nonconstituent corporation rather than into shares of the survivor.[79] Under such provisions it has become common to stage triangular mergers, in which a third-party corporation is merged into a subsidiary in exchange for stock of the parent, and reverse triangular mergers, in which a subsidiary is merged into a third-party corporation – nominally the survivor but substantively the transferor – whose shareholders end up with stock in the parent.[80] If the parent issues a significant amount of its own stock to effect such a merger, pass-through is explicitly mandated under several statutes[81] and all-but-explicitly mandated for any corporation whose stock is listed on the New York or American stock exchanges.[82] The same result should be reached even without explicit provision, if the

79. See, e.g., Cal. Corp. Code §4103 (West Supp. 1974); Del. Code Ann. tit. 8, §251(b)(4) (1974); Ill. Ann. Stat. ch. 32, §157.61 (c) (Smith-Hurd Supp. 1974); N.J. Stat. Ann. §14A:10-1(2)(c) (Supp. 1974); Pa. Stat. Ann. tit. 15, §1902(A)(4) (Supp. 1974); ABA Model Bus. Corp. Act §71(c) (1969 rev.). See also ABA Model Bus. Corp. Act §72-A, 30 Bus. Law. 992 (1975).

80. See generally, Dell & Hackney, A New Pennsylvania Statute: Tax-Free Reorganization by Merger Without Shareholder Vote, 47 Taxes 491 (1969); Scriggens, Business Combinations – Developments in Combining Techniques and Constraints in Accounting Rules, 27 Bus. Law. 1245, at 1245-1250 (1972); Note, Three-Party Mergers: The Fourth Form of Corporate Acquisition, 57 Va. L. Rev. 1242 (1971).

Such a transaction provides the simplicity of a conventional merger (which avoids both the conveyances required in stock-for-assets transactions and the potential complications of fractional shares, stock options, and warrants which may be involved in stock-for-stock transactions), and the tax advantages of a conventional merger (which provides more leeway than stock-for-assets or stock-for-stock transactions in the use of consideration other than voting stock), without necessarily involving the explicit assumption of liabilities and the disappearance of the transferor's entity which are consequences of a conventional merger.

81. Both the New Jersey and Ohio statute specifically address combinations effected through the issuance of a parent corporation's stock, as does the proposed new California statute. Ch. 682, §§181, 1200-1201, [1975-76 Reg. Sess.] Calif. Leg. Serv. 1808, 1852-1853; N.J. Stat. Ann. §14A:10-12 (Supp. 1974); Ohio Rev. Code Ann. tit. 17, §§1701.01(Q)-(S), 1701.83 (Page Supp. 1974).

82. See New York Stock Exchange, Company Manual at A-284 (covering "the acquisition, direct or indirect, of a business"); 2 CCH, American Stock Exchange Manual ¶10,032 (same); Schulman, Shareholder Rights in Acquisition Transactions: A Dissent, 18 Wayne L. Rev. 1041, 1057 (1972); §14.3, supra.

protections of the merger provisions are not to be subject to complete nullification.

B. Election of Directors

Under the traditional statutes, the persons holding those legal powers over an enterprise which are vested in the board must be elected by the shareholders. At least where a subsidiary is significant, to permit its board to be elected by the parent's board rather than the parent's shareholders would be to subvert those statutory provisions, and also, in some cases, statutory limits on the length of a director's term of office and mandatory provisions for cumulative voting.[83] On the other hand, where the subsidiary is not significant, by hypothesis its board would not have a significant role to play in the corporate complex, and it is at least arguable that in such cases direct election of the subsidiary's board by that of the parent would not be objectionable. What constitutes economic significance in this context is, of course, a question of judgment. The SEC's Regulation S-X defines a "significant subsidiary" to mean one which accounts for 10 percent of the assets or revenues of the corporate complex of which it is a member.[84] For regulatory as opposed to disclosure purposes, a 20 percent test might be more appropriate.[85]

C. Certificate Amendment

If an enterprise is owned directly through a division, management cannot alter its own powers or duties in relation to the enterprise in a manner requiring certificate amendment without obtaining approval of the corporation's shareholders. No reason is apparent why management should be able to accomplish the same

83. Cf. Sherman & Ellis, Inc. v. Indiana Mut. Cas. Co., 41 F.2d 588 (7th Cir. 1930); Kennerson v. Burbank Amusement Co., 120 Cal. App. 2d 157, 260 P.2d 823 (1953).

84. Reg. S-X, Rule 1.02(t), 17 C.F.R. §210.1-02(t) (1974).

85. One situation in which a pass-through of the right to elect the board should perhaps be required, even in the case of a subsidiary which is not significant, is where a substantial amount of the parent's assets are held through such subsidiaries, since the parent's shareholders would otherwise have no direct voice in the election of those directors who have effective control over a substantial amount of the parent's assets.

result simply because the enterprise is segregated into a wholly owned subsidiary rather than a division.[86]

D. Dissolution

It has already been seen that dissolution of a subsidiary which holds substantially all of a complex's assets should not require approval by the parent's shareholders, since its effect is to bring those shareholders one step closer to the underlying assets.[87] It follows that dissolution of a subsidiary which holds less than substantially all of a complex's assets should also not require approval by the parent's shareholders.

86. See Klopot v. Northrup, 131 Conn. 14, 37 A.2d 700 (1944), discussed in chapter 17, text at notes 14-15, supra.

87. See §18.1(D), supra.

19
Subsidiaries with Public Ownership

§19.1. Under the Traditional Statutes

If a parent's stock in a subsidiary constitutes substantially all of its assets, the interests of the parent's shareholders in voting that stock will by and large not be affected by the fact that outside shareholders also own stock in the subsidiary.[1] However, the outside shareholders often themselves face serious problems as a result of their corporation's subsidiary status, including the risk of unfair intercorporate dealings, permanent loss of the control-value element which normally adheres to corporate stock, and pyramiding. A major virtue of pass-through is that it may ameliorate these problems as well as those of the parent's shareholders.

A. Unfair Intercorporate Dealings

Unfair dealings between a corporation and its controlling shareholders can of course occur whether a corporation is controlled by individuals or by another corporation. However, while controlling individuals may not be engaged in business themselves,

1. Cf. Goldstein v. Groesbeck, 142 F.2d 422, 425 (2d Cir.), cert. denied, 323 U.S. 737 (1944); Saltzman v. Birrell, 78 F. Supp. 778, 783 (S.D.N.Y. 1948); Craftsman Fin. & Mortgage Co. v. Brown, 64 F. Supp. 168, 176 (S.D.N.Y. 1945); Continental-Midwest Corp. v. Hotel Sherman, Inc., 13 Ill. App. 2d 188, 141 N.E.2d 400 (1957); Robotham v. Prudential Ins. Co., 64 N.J. Eq. 673, 53 A. 842 (Ch. 1903). But see Baum v. Baum Holding Co., 158 Neb. 197, 62 N.W.2d 864 (1954); cf. Adams v. Clearance Corp., 35 Del. Ch. 459, 121 A.2d 302 (1956); Dal-Tran Serv. Co. v. Fifth Ave. Coach Lines, Inc., 14 App. Div. 2d 349, 220 N.Y.S.2d 549 (1961).

a parent corporation almost invariably is. Therefore, at the least a parent is likely to supply its subsidiary with various headquarters services (managerial, accounting, legal, and the like) on a fee basis; and if the parent's business is related to the subsidiary's, there will probably be substantive business transactions between the two corporations, and allocation of business opportunities, as well.[2] In *Jones v. H. F. Ahmanson & Co.,* Chief Justice Traynor pointed out the dangers in this kind of situation:

> If . . . a controlling interest [in one corporation is acquired by another] the [acquired] company . . . will become a subsidiary of the acquiring company . . . and cease, in fact though not in law, to be an independent entity. . . .
>
> [T]he parent company will wish to operate the subsidiary for the benefit of the group as a whole and not necessarily for the benefit of that particular subsidiary.[3]

The checks on unfair dealing by the parent are few. In theory, of course, the fairness of the parent's behavior is subject to the check of judicial review; but in practice such review is difficult even where the courts have the will to engage in it,[4] and they often lack the will.[5]

A different kind of check may exist where the parent's controlling interest is significantly less than a majority. In such cases, gross exploitation of the subsidiary might be eschewed simply because it could goad the outsiders into a proxy fight, or alternatively, drive down the price of the subsidiary's stock and make it worthwhile for an outsider to acquire an overmatching control

2. See, e.g., Ewen v. Peoria & E. Ry., 78 F. Supp. 312, 315-317 (S.D.N.Y. 1948) (L. Hand, J.), cert. denied, 336 U.S. 919 (1949); Alliegro v. Pan Am. Bank, 136 So. 2d 656 (Fla. Dist. Ct. App. 1962), cert. denied, 149 So. 2d 45 (Fla. 1963); Ripley v. International Rys., 8 N.Y.2d 430, 171 N.E.2d 443, 209 N.Y.S.2d 289 (1960).

3. Jones v. H. F. Ahmanson & Co., 1 Cal. 3d 93, 112, 460 P.2d 464, 474, 81 Cal. Rptr. 592, 602 (1969) (Traynor, C.J.) (quoting from Gower, The Principles of Modern Company Law 561 (2d ed. 1957)).

4. See Ewen v. Peoria & E. Ry., 78 F. Supp. 312, 315-317 (S.D.N.Y. 1948) (L. Hand, J.), cert. denied, 336 U.S. 919 (1949).

5. See, e.g., Western Pac. R.R. v. Western Pac. R.R., 206 F.2d 495 (9th Cir.), cert. denied, 346 U.S. 910 (1953); Sinclair Oil Corp. v. Levien, 280 A.2d 717 (Del. 1971); Meyerson v. El Paso Natural Gas Co., 246 A.2d 789 (Del. Ch. 1967); Case v. New York Cent. R.R., 15 N.Y.2d 150, 204 N.E.2d 643, 256 N.Y.S.2d 607 (1965); cf. Everett v. Phillips, 288 N.Y. 227, 43 N.E.2d 18 (1942). But see Alliegro v. Pan Am. Bank, 136 So. 2d 656 (Fla. Dist. Ct. App. 1962), cert. denied, 149 So. 2d 45 (Fla. 1963); Ripley v. International Rys., 8 N.Y.2d 430, 171 N.E.2d 443, 209 N.Y.S.2d 289 (1960).

block. Suppose, however, that the parent owns a majority of the subsidiary's stock. In that case, even this possible check would fail if the parent's shares in the subsidiary were voted as a unit. But if the right to vote the stock was passed through to the parent's shareholders, the efficacy of this check on unfair dealing might be reinstated: in some cases, at least, the subsidiary's minority shareholders could gain control of the subsidiary by purchasing shares of the parent and adding the pass-through votes adhering to those shares to the votes on their stock in the subsidiary. Furthermore, even if the minority shareholders do not actually buy shares in the parent, the fact that they could do so may keep the parent honest.

B. Loss of the Element of Control Value

If the parent's shareholding constitutes a majority of the subsidiary's stock, and the shareholding is voted as a unit, the outside shareholders will face still another problem: except for transactions which require approval by two-thirds of outstanding shares, voting by the minority shareholders becomes an all-but-meaningless gesture. This problem is likely to be reflected in the value of the minority's shares. Where a corporation is controlled by individuals, an element of control value normally attaches even to those voting shares which are not presently members of the control block. Since such a block faces dismemberment by death and taxes, voting shares which are not members of today's control block may become members of tomorrow's, and that fact should be reflected in their price.[6] A parent corporation, on the other hand, has perpetual life. If, therefore, a parent's majority block can be voted as a unit, the minority stock would be permanently condemned to de facto nonvoting status, and the element of control value that normally attaches to the voting right would be lost.

In some cases, at least, pass-through could restore this control-value element to the minority shares. On any given issue, including election of directors, a combination of the subsidiary's minority shareholders and some fraction of the parent's shareholders could prevail. Persons seeking control of the subsidiary

6. See Honigman v. Green Giant Co., 208 F. Supp 754 (D. Minn. 1961), affd., 309 F.2d 667 (8th Cir. 1962), cert. denied, 372 U.S. 941 (1963); Jones v. H. F. Ahmanson & Co., 1 Cal. 3d 93, 460 P.2d 464, 81 Cal. Reptr. 592 (1969); Allen v. Chase Natl. Bank, 180 Misc. 259, 40 N.Y.S.2d 245 (Sup. Ct. 1943); §6.2, supra.

might therefore be willing to buy minority shares, since control of the subsidiary could be obtained by combining those shares with shares of the parent.

C. Pyramiding

The two problems already described may be compounded by pyramiding.

> This involves the owning of a majority of the stock of one corporation which in turn holds a majority of the stock of another — a process which can be repeated a number of times. An interest equal to slightly more than a quarter or an eighth or a sixteenth or an even smaller proportion of the ultimate property to be controlled is by this method legally entrenched. By issuing bonds and nonvoting preferred stock of the intermediate companies the process can be accelerated. . . . The owner of a majority of the stock of the company at the apex of a pyramid can have almost as complete control of the entire property as a sole owner even though his ownership interest is less than one percent of the whole.[7]

In the 1920s, fantastic corporate pyramids were constructed, particularly, although not exclusively, in the public-utility sector.[8] Pyramiding in that sector came under legal control by virtue of the Public Utility Holding Company Act of 1935.[9] However, there is little direct legal control over pyramiding in other sectors,[10] and while pyramiding has apparently subsided, it has by no means disappeared.[11]

7. A. A. Berle & G. Means, The Modern Corporation and Private Property 69 (rev. ed. 1968). See also J. Bonbright & G. Means, The Holding Company 18-20 (1932).

8. See A. A. Berle & G. Means, supra note 7, at 69; J. Bonbright & G. Means, supra note 7 at 18-20, 108-123, 253-262; Brigham & Pettit, Effects of Structure on Performance in the Savings and Loan Industry, in 3 U.S. Federal Home Loan Bank Board, Study of the Savings and Loan Industry 971, 1131 (1969).

9. 15 U.S.C. §79k(b)(1964). See chapter 18, note 16, supra.

10. There is at least one indirect control. The New York Stock Exchange generally refuses to list common stock of a corporation in which 30 percent or more of the common stock is held by another publicly held corporation, or which is otherwise controlled through a voting pyramid, principally on the ground that listed stock should carry voting rights, and that voting rights should be related to investment. Letter from Merle S. Wick, Vice-President, New York Stock Exchange, Jan. 23, 1970.

11. See, e.g., Adams v. Clearance Corp., 35 Del. Ch. 459, 121 A.2d 302 (Sup. Ct. 1956); Baum v. Baum Holding Co., 158 Neb. 197, 62 N.W.2d 864 (1954); cf. Jones v. H. F. Ahmanson & Co., 1 Cal. 3d 93, 460 P.2d 464, 81 Cal. Rptr. 592 (1969).

A major vice of pyramiding is that it tends to magnify the problems of a subsidiary's outside shareholders. The risk of unfair intercorporate transactions is increased, because ultimate voting power is so enormously disproportionate to ultimate investment stake. And because pyramiding is usually associated with high-ratio debt leverage, corporations closer to the apex may draw excessive funds out of corporations closer to the base in order to service their own debt obligations.[12] For the same reason, corporate pyramids tend to be financially unstable, since failure at any one level may resonate throughout the entire system.[13]

The problems faced by outside shareholders in corporations which are members of a pyramid would be significantly ameliorated by pass-through. A major foundation of pyramiding is the supposed legal rule that the parent's stock in a subsidiary is voted as a unit. If the right to vote the subsidiary's stock is passed through the parent to its shareholders, however, pyramiding loses much of its appeal to the promoter. To illustrate, suppose that Corporation *A* owns 51 percent of the stock of Corporation *B*. If *A* can vote its stock in *B* as a unit, then a 51 percent interest in *A* can be pyramided into absolute control of *B*, although it represents only a 26 percent equity interest in *B*. If, however, the right to vote the *B* stock is passed through *A* to *A*'s shareholders, it becomes possible for an outsider to acquire control of *B* by combining an *A* and a *B* shareholding, and firm pyramids could not be constructed on the basis of razor-thin majorities.[14]

12. See 2 A. Dewing, The Financial Policy of Corporations 1011-1014 (5th ed. 1953).

13. See J. Bonbright & G. Means, supra note 7, at 19-20, 46-47; 2 A. Dewing, supra note 12, at 1013-1014.

14. Cf. Robotham v. Prudential Ins. Co., 64 N.J. Eq. 673, 704-705, 53 A. 842, 854-855 (Ch. 1903), where the court said, in dicta:

"In an ingenious and able brief, presented on behalf of these defendants, the following statement is made of a situation claimed now to be legally possible and unassailable under the laws of New Jersey:

'One man controls a company of $10,000,000 capital. He may form a new company with a capital of $5,100,000 to hold a majority of the stock. He may then sell all but $2,600,000 of the stock to company No. 2 and transfer his remaining stock to a new company with a capital of $2,600,000. He may then sell to company No. 3 all but $1,400,000 and transfer that to a new company. This process may go on until the power of the whole chain of corporations is vested in the holder of a few thousand dollars of stock in the ultimate company, and the same chain can be used for an unlimited number of companies.'

In light of the benefits of pass-through to a subsidiary's outside owners, it might be argued that the parent's shareholders might prefer foregoing pass-through to preserve the benefits to the parent that result from voting its shares as a unit. However, the principal concern of the parent's shareholders would normally be their own rights in the subsidiary, which pass-through effectuates, and the subsidiary's earnings, which pass-through does not affect. Moreover, the parent's noncontrolling shareholders may welcome any legal technique that reduces their own vulnerability to pyramiding. Of course, dollars which the subsidiary saves because of constraints on unfair intercorporate dealings are dollars that would otherwise have gone into the parent's treasury; but any interest of the parent's noncontrolling shareholders in facilitating unfair dealings would not be worthy of legal cognizance. And though pass-through might entail some diminution in the market value of the parent's shares in the subsidiary due to dilution of the de jure control rights which would otherwise be carried by those shares, this problem is likely to be negligible, because the parent's shares would normally continue to carry de facto control rights and in any event would normally not be held for sale.

What of the case in which the parent's equity in a subsidiary constitutes less than substantially all of its assets? There, the working rule developed in §18.2 – that pass-through is appropriate if, but only if, approval by the parent's shareholders would have been required had the subsidiary's assets been held through a division – should continue to be applied, even where pass-through would serve the interests of the subsidiary's outside shareholders. Pass-through under present law must be based on the statutory rights of the parent's shareholders. The interests of a subsidiary's outside shareholders may be taken into account when they reinforce those rights, but it is doubtful whether they would independently justify pass-through under the traditional corporate statutes. Solutions to the problems of outside shareholders in that

"The brief concludes that 'the check on the process is not in the law, but in the difficulty of unloading the minority shares of each company.'

". . . This startling proposition suggests a variety of interesting questions . . . such as . . . [w]hether the actual, beneficial owners of the $5,100,000 of stock could not break through the chain of corporate fictions which separated them from their property and dictate how its voting power should be exercised."

context must therefore await statutory reform; specifically, provision for pass-through in all cases where a subsidiary has outside shareholders.

Needless to say, pass-through, whether effected under present law or under new provisions, is not a panacea for the problems of a subsidiary's outside shareholders. Among other problems, its usefulness to such shareholders decreases as the parent's holding in the subsidiary approaches 100 percent. On the other hand, as the parent's holding in the subsidiary approaches 100 percent, the temptation to unduly favor the parent in intercorporate transactions is proportionately diminished, and the problem of pyramiding avoided. Furthermore, other statutory remedies, such as a mandatory buy-out of minority shareholders, may then become possible.[15]

§19.2. A Revised Statutory Treatment of Pass-Through

Because of the importance of planning in corporate affairs — and also because of the uncertainty of judicial behavior, as indicated by *Cross Properties* — a modern statute should not leave pass-through to statutory interpretation, but should codify the doctrine and define its parameters. To begin with, the statute should provide that for purposes of voting and appraisal rights, a sale, merger, or issuance of stock by a subsidiary should be deemed to be a sale, merger, or issuance by the parent. Whether the transaction requires approval by the parent's shareholders or gives them appraisal rights would then depend on the statute's substantive provisions; if the subsidiary is not wholly owned, all relevant calculations under these provisions should be based on the parent's proportionate interest in the subsidiary's assets.[16] In the case of certificate amendment the statute should make pass-through turn on the significance of the subsidiary and the subject matter of the amendment (for example, whether it changes authorized stock or the powers and duties of corporate organs). Finally,

15. See §15.1(B), supra; cf. Hetherington, Special Characteristics, Problems, and Needs of the Close Corporation, 1969 Ill. L.F. 1, 22.

16. A corporation should be deemed a subsidiary if it is under the effective control of another corporation.

in the election of directors a distinction should be drawn between wholly-owned and less-than-wholly-owned subsidiaries. In the former case, the statutory applicability of pass-through should turn on the subsidiary's significance to the parent in terms of its assets or contribution to earnings. In the latter case, however, pass-through should always be in force to protect the interests of the subsidiary's outside shareholders.

20

Conclusion

NORMATIVE MODELS OF THE CORPORATION

Under the received legal model of the corporation, the board manages the corporation's business and makes business policy; the officers act as agents of the board and execute its decisions; and the shareholders elect the board and decide on "major corporate actions," or "fundamental," "extraordinary," or "organic" changes. The defects of this model are by now apparent. It makes no distinction between closely and publicly held corporations. It entirely omits several critical elements of corporate structure, such as the place of the appraisal right and the role of the accountant. In allocating power between shareholders and management, it is appropriate in its thrust but insufficiently articulated to provide useful guidance on the really difficult issues. In allocating power between officers and directors, it is both insufficiently articulated and inappropriate.

A major purpose of this book has been to develop new normative models which would overcome these shortcomings. Although the elements of these models have been developed separately, they must of course fit together architecturally if the models are to stand. It is therefore appropriate at this point to summarize the major elements of the models, and say a few further words about implementation.

A normative model of the closely held corporation. The underlying rule which should govern the internal affairs of closely held corporations is that the shareholders, acting unanimously, should be able to shape the corporate structure as they choose. In the absence of such a choice, suppletory rules, based principally on the protection of fair expectations, should govern: business decisions in the ordinary course should be solely for the board; business decisions out of the ordinary course should be for the board, but subject to intervention by the body of shareholders; and structural decisions should be solely for the shareholders, acting by two-thirds majority. The structural category should include both decisions which would make substantial changes in the structure of the business enterprise, and decisions which relate to the control apparatus of the entity in which the enterprise is enveloped. More specifically, it should include the classic fundamental changes (merger, sale of substantially all assets, certificate amendment, and dissolution) and the modern fundamental changes (business combinations other than mergers, corporate contractions, and corporate divisions) – provided that the transaction in question is economically significant. Where a structural change is sufficiently radical, dissenting shareholders should have the right to exit from the reconstituted enterprise at a fair price. If the corporation becomes a subsidiary, a comparable right should be granted to minority shareholders, at least if the percentage of stock held by the parent corporation reaches a requisite level. If the corporation becomes a parent, the right to vote its subsidiary's stock should be passed through to its own shareholders where necessary to preserve the integrity of voting and appraisal rights.[1]

A normative model of the publicly held corporation. All the elements of the close-corporation model are also applicable to publicly held corporations, with two exceptions and several additions. The exceptions are that the rules governing the structure of such corporations should be mandatory rather than suppletory, that is, should not be subject to variation by the corporation's certificate or by-laws; and that all business decisions,

1. Under some statutes, minority shareholders in closely held corporations can sue for dissolution as a remedy for oppression or persistent unfairness – in a few cases, with a corresponding right in the majority to purchase the plaintiff's shares at fair value. (In theory, but not in practice, several such provisions can also be availed of by shareholders in publicly held corporations.) See, e.g., Cal. Corp. Code § §4650, 4651 (West 1955 & Supp. 1974); N.J. Stat. Ann. § 14A:12-7(1)(c), (8) (Supp. 1974); ABA Model Bus. Corp. Act §97 (1969 rev.); cf. Folk, Corporation Statutes 1959-1966, 1966 Duke L.J. 875, 954-957. This extremely useful technique may be viewed as a variant of the appraisal right, and carried far enough, cf. Hetherington, Special Characteristics and Needs of the Close Corporation, 1969 Ill. L. Forum 1, 20-25, could be regarded as a structural rather than simply a remedial element.

including those which are out of the ordinary course, should be solely for the board. The additions fall into two broad groups:

(1) Because the proxy-solicitation process replaces the shareholder's meeting in publicly held corporations, a normative model of such corporations must provide rules to govern access to that machinery. Under those rules, the incumbent board should be entitled to make nominations through the corporate proxy materials, as should shareholders – or at least, shareholders owning a requisite percentage of the corporation's stock. Incumbents should also be entitled to reimbursement for their expenses in matching an insurgent campaign. Insurgents' expenses should be reimbursable as a matter of discretion by the body of shareholders, and perhaps as a matter of right in proportion to the votes they gather. Shareholders as well as the board should be entitled to use the corporate proxy machinery to make proposals for shareholder action. Management – that is, the executives – should have no access to the corporate proxy machinery except through the board.

(2) Because the body of shareholders in a publicly held corporation cannot provide a first-line check on executive performance, other corporate organs must be structured to assure effective monitoring. Two objectives must be met in this regard. First, the board must be independent of the executives. To this end, at least 60 percent of the directors should be persons who are not officers of, suppliers to, or professionals retained by the corporation; and a nominating committee consisting solely of independent directors should have exclusive access to the corporate proxy machinery on the board's behalf. Second, the body of shareholders and the board must have a capacity for acquiring reliable information on the executives' performance. To this end, the exclusive power to select and dismiss the corporation's accountant should be vested in the body of shareholders; an audit committee, consisting solely of independent directors, should have exclusive power to nominate and recommend dismissal of the accountant on the board's behalf, to direct the accountant's activities, and to set the terms of his engagement; and the accountant rather than management should be responsible for selecting the accounting principles employed in the preparation of corporate financial statements.

Overall, this model of the publicly held corporation recognizes that in most such corporations business decisions and even business policy must be made by the executives. Accordingly, it looks to other corporate organs not as a primary source of business decisions or business policy, but as institutions of control and as the source of power over changes in corporate structure. The organs of control in this model are the board – and more specifically the independent directors as a subset within the board – with power to elect and dismiss the executives; the accountant, who reports the results achieved by the executives to the board and the shareholders; and the body of shareholders, with power to select and dismiss the board and the accountant. Legal power over structural change is located in the shareholders: conceptually, because that body holds ultimate ownership of the enterprise; pragmatically, because power over structural changes must be split off from management if irreconcilable conflicts of interest are to be avoided, and the body of shareholders is the most appropriate alternative organ in which to lodge that power. The intent of the model is both to protect the legitimate interests of shareholders and to insure, as far as structural elements may insure, that the resources allocated to the corporation will be managed as efficiently as possible, subject to other applicable constraints of social policy.

Implementation of the models. Throughout the text I have tried to indicate both the extent to which the elements of these models could be judicially implemented under the traditional statutes, and the direction legislative revision should take. Historically, corporate legislation has been a matter for the states. By and large, however, the states have defaulted on their responsibilities in this area, by focusing on considerations of franchise-tax revenue rather than fairness and efficiency, and by delegating the modernization of corporate law to committees dominated by management lawyers,[2] which have in most cases been unable to transcend their narrow base. As a result, most state statutes fail even to address the distinctively modern corporate problems, such

2. See Eisenberg, The Model Business Corporation Act and the Model Business Corporation Act Annotated, 29 Bus. Law. 1407 (1974); Folk, Some Reflections of a Corporate Law Draftsman, 42 Conn. B.J. 409 (1968); Comment, Law For Sale: A Study of the Delaware Corporation Law of 1967, 117 U. Pa. L. Rev. 861 (1969).

as access to the proxy machinery, the role of the accountant, and power over the modern fundamental changes. While many elements of the normative models can be implemented by the courts even under the traditional statutes, in some cases such implementation would require a degree of judicial sophistication which has not always been forthcoming, in some cases it would leave an area of uncertainty which might be deemed undesirably large, and in some cases unaided judicial implementation is simply not possible. If full implementation of the normative models is to be achieved, therefore, significant statutory revision will be required.

Perhaps it is still not too late to hope for action by the states in this regard. If, however, such action is not forthcoming, a response must be sought at the national level; we are, after all, talking about the national economic system. Some problems, such as access to the corporate proxy machinery and independence of the accountant, can be dealt with at that level by the Securities Exchange Commission, at least in part. Other problems may require congressional solutions, at least by way of minimum standards for state law.[3] Whether state or federal action is sought, the first step toward thorough-going revision should be the creation, by private or public means, of a national body which can dispassionately study the problems of corporate law and recommend objective solutions to serve as a staging-ground for reform.

3. See Cary, Federalism and Corporate Law: Reflections Upon Delaware, 83 Yale L.J. 663 (1974).

Table of Cases

Index

*As used in this index, a "dominant" subsidiary is a subsidiary that holds substantially all of the assets held by a parent-subsidiary complex; a "nondominant" subsidiary is one that holds less than substantially all of the assets held by such a complex.

www.ingramcontent.com/pod-product-compliance
Ingram Content Group UK Ltd.
Pitfield, Milton Keynes, MK11 3LW, UK
UKHW041830200726
13854UKWH00002BA/976

9 781587 982880